Training in Organizations:
Needs Assessment, Development,
and Evaluation
SECOND EDITION

Training in Organizations: Needs Assessment, Development, and Evaluation

S E C O N D   E D I T I O N

Irwin L. Goldstein
University of Maryland

Brooks/Cole Publishing Company
Pacific Grove, California

Brooks/Cole Publishing Company
A Division of Wadsworth, Inc.

Printed in the United States of America

10   9   8   7   6

Library of Congress Cataloging-in-Publication Data

Goldstein, Irwin L., [date]
   Training in organizations.

   Rev. ed. of: Training. 1974.
   Bibliography: p.
   Includes index.
   1. Employees, Training of.   2. Employees, Training
of—Evaluation.   3. Assessment center (Personnel
management procedure)   I. Goldstein, Irwin L.,
1937-   . Training. II. Title.
HF5549.5.T7G543 1985   658.3'12404   85-21348
ISBN 0-534-05604-0

Sponsoring Editor: C. Deborah Laughton   Production Editors: C. Diane Brown,
S. M. Bailey   Manuscript Editor: Shirley Mills   Permissions Editor: Carline Haga
Interior and Cover Design: Victoria Van Deventer   Art Coordinator: Judith Macdonald
Interior Illustration: John Foster   Typesetting: Linda Andrews, Ashland, OR
Printing and Binding: Malloy Lithographing, Inc., Ann Arbor, MI

*To the beautiful memories
of my father, Benjamin Goldstein,
and my dear friend, C. J. Bartlett*

Preface

This book is a complete revision of a text originally published in 1974. It is written for undergraduate and graduate students as well as practitioners who are concerned with needs assessment, systematic development, and thoughtful evaluation of training programs in a variety of organizational settings. It is hoped that the book provides a framework for examining present efforts and establishing new, viable training programs in education, business, and government environments. It is my goal to capture the excitement of the many research and systems issues that abound both when training is introduced and considered and when new trainees enter the world of the work organization through training programs.

Part One of this book emphasizes the needs assessment and learning processes that form the foundation for training programs. The first chapter of this section presents background information about the scope of training efforts that presently exists in our society and provides some perspective on the status of the training enterprise. Following this introductory material, Chapter 2 presents a training systems model which gives the reader an overview of all the interacting components of needs assessment, design, development, and evaluation of training programs. In that sense, this chapter provides a summary of many of the topics that follow. Chapter 3 describes the needs assessment process including the organizational, task, and person analyses, which in turn provide inputs for the consideration and design of training programs. This chapter has been almost entirely rewritten for this edition since many techniques of needs assessment, including the analysis of the ways in which training as a system fits into an organization, have been developed since the first edition of this book. Chapter 4 describes the learning environment, including material related to the preconditions of learning, the conditions of learning, the variables that support transfer, and factors that determine a quality training environment. Again, most of this material is either new or rewritten because it is now possible to begin asking about factors that support learning environments for adult learners.

Part Two focuses on the evaluations process. For me evaluation is the systematic collection of descriptive and judgmental information necessary to make effective training decisions related to the selection, adoption, value, and modification of various instructional activities. The objectives of instructional programs reflect numerous goals ranging from trainee progress to organizational goals. From this perspective, evaluation is an information-gathering technique that cannot possibly result in decisions that categorize programs as good or bad. Rather, evaluation should capture the dynamic flavor of the training program. The necessary information will then be available to revise training programs to achieve multiple instructional objectives. Chapter 5 discusses the establishment of criteria that are used to measure the multiple objectives of many of these programs. Chapter 6 presents materials about the various evaluation models that are available to provide information for intelligent revisions of training programs. Both of these chapters contain information that has developed since 1974. This includes material on different models of the evaluation process, including considerations about utility, content validity, and individual difference models. The general flavor of many of the designs that have developed reflects a positive attitude about the use of models that best fit the constraints of the environment. There is also more recognition that our values and attitudes can have a dramatic effect on what an evaluator is likely to find.

Part Three provides information about training approaches. Chapter 7 presents a variety of approaches including programed instruction, audiovisual techniques, machine simulators, behavior modification, and on-the-job training. Most of these topics have been updated since the first version of this book. Also, for a number of the techniques, such as computer-assisted instruction, there have been major developments resulting from advances in technology. Chapter 8 covers techniques that pertain to managerial and interpersonal skills, including behavioral role-modeling, McClelland's achievement motivation training, Fiedler's Leader Match, and rater training. This chapter is almost entirely new. A few of these techniques, such as business games, case studies, and role-playing, were included in the previous edition, but even in these cases there have been major developments (for example, the Looking Glass simulation). Many topics, such as behavioral role-modeling training and rater training, simply didn't exist as topics when the first edition of this volume appeared. In both chapters 7 and 8 material that elaborates on the needs assessment, evaluation, and learning materials presented earlier in the book is presented. Special approaches to training issues are discussed in Chapter 9, the final chapter. Here the emphasis is on topics relating training to larger systems issues, and updates on materials relating training programs to the problems of the hard-core unemployed and persons seeking second careers or trying to avoid obsolescence. There are also new sections relating training to issues of discrimination and fair employment practices. The chapter closes with a section on the ways in which training affects persons who enter organizations and how training might be related to the ways in which trainees become socialized into organizations.

In the preface to the first edition I noted that there was little to be gained by putting an enormous amount of effort into the development of instructional programs unless there were data to tell the implementers where to revise and where to proceed. Although I retain this viewpoint, I am more confident now that there are models both to provide that information and to provide input into the design of programs, thereby increasing the likelihood that they will achieve intended goals. My book is written with the hope that it will contribute information and ideas to those who wish to partake in this process and who wish to understand some of the dynamics involved when an organization says "training is the answer."

This volume is a result of the efforts of many generous people. I am indebted to all the authors and researchers who took time from their busy schedules to graciously share their articles, data, ideas, and manuscripts. Those of you who are fortunate enough to be involved in the Society for Industrial and Organizational Psychology know what I mean when I say that our members' generosity in sharing ideas and helping each other is overwhelming. In this regard I am indebted to the work of many colleagues and friends, including John Campbell, Gary Latham, Robert Pajer, Ken Wexley, and others too numerous to mention. I am especially indebted to the faculty and graduate students of the industrial-organizational psychology group at Maryland. The excitement of hall talk as well as classroom conversations has contributed to most of the ideas in this book. I am saddened that my close friend, Jack Bartlett, will not see this volume, but I know that the reader will see many places that were influenced by his thoughts. I consider myself lucky to be influenced by my good friend and colleague Benjamin Schneider. His specific thoughts on the book were important, but his warm personal style and way of thinking about issues is critical for my own career development. I am thankful to Erich Prien for all of his insights and for his willingness to be a continual sounding board for professional and personal issues. I must especially thank Paul Thayer for being a sounding board on nearly all of the ideas in this book. For the past twenty years he has continually contributed insights to discussions about training issues. Paul's friends will appreciate the fact that he gave up a day of golf in North Carolina on January 1, in 90-degree weather, in order to read the pre-publication version of this book. I am indebted to my editor, C. Deborah Laughton, of Brooks/Cole Publishing Company. She has provided smiles and reminders such that this book is now completed. Her friendship will always be meaningful. I cannot express enough gratitude to the staff at the University of Maryland, including Carol Fox, Ellie Lehan, Nancy Gehman,

Betty Padgett, and Terri Proctor. They not only typed the manuscript but managed also to allay my anxieties. This book is most of all the result of a loving and caring environment designed by my wife, Micki, and my children, Beth and Harold. They understand what support is, and they specialize in love. Finally, the saddest moment for me will be when this book is published and I am unable to share it with my father.

Irwin L. Goldstein

Contents

P A R T   2
Evaluation 109

P A R T   3

Instructional Approaches   181

Needs Assessment and Learning Environment

Introduction

Throughout our lives learning experiences are a potent source of stimulation. This text emphasizes the systematic modes of instruction designed to produce environments that shape behavior to satisfy stated objectives. From this point of view, *training* is defined as the systematic acquisition of skills, rules, concepts, or attitudes that result in improved performance in another environment. Therefore, training programs are planned to produce a more considerate foreman or a more competent technician in working environments. Similarly, the school environment is designed to enable primary-school children to read books, newspapers, and magazines in their homes or the dental student to repair cavities in an office. In some cases, such as on-the-job training, the instructional environment is almost identical to the actual job environment. In other instances, such as a classroom lecture on electronics theory for technicians, the learning environment is far removed from the job situation. However, in both circumstances effective training stems from a learning atmosphere systematically designed to produce changes in the working environment.

As stated in the preface, the purpose of this book is to present the interacting components of training systems, including materials related to the ways in which training needs are assessed and the training effort is evaluated. Information is also presented about different types of training programs and the issues involving needs assessment and evaluation of these programs. In addition, the book explores issues which intersect between training and societal concerns, such as training and the hard-core unemployed or training and fair employment practices. This chapter presents background information about the scope of training in our society and focuses on the status of the training enterprise.

SCOPE OF THE INSTRUCTIONAL PROCESS

Training programs are big business in terms of both the amount of effort expended and the money spent. For example, consider the following illustrations gleaned from a variety of time periods and instructional approaches:

1. A report by the Carnegie Foundation (Eurich, 1985) indicated that education and training has become a booming business, with industrial corporations spending more than $40 billion a year on programs that include training in basic skills such as reading as well as programs for the development of managers and executives.

2. In 1981 over 21 million persons participated in adult education programs. This was an increase of almost 17% from 1978 (U.S. Department of Education, 1982).

3. The FAA has decided that flight simulators have become so sophisticated that business jet pilots can use the simulator to meet many of their training requirements without requiring actual flying time in the plane (Caro, 1984).

4. Most surveys indicate that over 90% of private corporations have some type of systematic training program. Reilly and Manese (1979) note that it costs $25,000 per trainee for a 6-month electronic switching system program designed for Bell System employees.

5. A General Accounting Office study of federal government training programs indicates that the government spends $500 million each year to train approximately one in three employees (General Accounting Office, 1979).

None of these activities suggests the startling innovations that may soon be upon us. Humorist Art Buchwald discusses a continuing educational plan developed by Irwin Feifer (reprinted in the *Training and Development Journal,* Feifer, 1970, p. 43).

Mass transportation is definitely one of the major problems of the next decade. The ideal solution would be faster, cleaner and safer transportation for everyone. But since this is impossible, other solutions must be found to make commuting worthwhile.

Irwin Feifer, who specializes in manpower problems, has come up with an idea which certainly deserves consideration.

Mr. Feifer says that as a commuter of the Long Island Railroad, he has been able to give hours of time to studying the transportation nightmare of the '70s.

Each month a true-or-false test would be given by the conductor. Those who received 90 or over would be granted a $5.50 reduction on their commuter ticket for the following months. Those scoring 80 or above would get a $3.25 reduction and those who passed with a 65 would not be given a money reduction, but would be assured a seat on the train for the next four weeks.

The Feifer Plan is not necessarily aimed just at people who take railroads (a subway educational plan where people can study while being delayed in tunnels is now being worked out), but could also be applied to people driving to work in the morning.

Those signing up for credits would listen to lectures on the radio in the morning and evening rush hours, and do their book studying at traffic bottlenecks and red lights.

The driver–students would hand in their tests and toll collectors would grade them as they make change.

Most people would not mind traffic delays as it would give them more time to get their homework done.

The Feifer Plan would provide for graduation exercises every six months. In the case of the railroads, the ceremonies would be held at the railroad stations with the Secretary of Transportation handing out the diplomas.

Automobile college graduates would receive their diplomas from the license bureau, and each license plate would indicate how many degrees the driver possessed.

The plan, if put into effect, would make Americans the most educated people in the world. It would also turn train delays and traffic jams into a profit. But more important, with everyone going to school, the generation gap could become a thing of the past.[1]

In a recent speech, I presented the Buchwald editorial as an introduction to material on training systems. Much to my surprise, a participant noted that such a program was already in existence. Adelphi University offers a program called "Classroom-on-Wheels" that takes place in special commuter cars equipped with frosted windows, microphones, and blackboards. During a five year period, the program awarded both B.B.A. and M.B.A. degrees. This example should serve as an illustration of the ingenuity that is possible in the design of instructional systems.

Further insights are provided into the ever-increasing emphasis on instructional systems by examining the scope of activities for professionals involved in training and development activities. The extent of growth in this area is evidenced by the number of persons belonging to only one of the professional societies involved in these activities. The American Society for Training and Development had 15 members in 1943, 5000 members in 1967, 9500 members in 1972, and 20,000 members in 1980. This does not include many persons involved in training activities who may be members of other societies, like the American Psychological Association, the American Educational Research Association, or the American Academy of Management. Pinto and Walker (1977) surveyed American Society for Training and Development members to determine which activities were a significant part of their work. Based upon almost 3000 responses, these authors performed a factor analysis, which is a technique used to determine the common dimensions among the job activities. Table 1.1 presents the activities identified in the survey. The authors note that the activities which occupied the most significant part of the training practi-

---

[1] From Buchwald, A. Training on the Train. Copyright 1970 by the Washington Post Company. Reprinted by permission.

tioners' work were program design and development, in order to meet needs for specific learning and behavior changes.

TABLE 1.1   Training and development practitioner roles

a. *Needs Analysis and Diagnosis*
   —Construct questionnaires and conduct interviews for needs analysis, evaluate feedback, etc.

b. *Determine Appropriate Training Approach*
   —Evaluate the alternatives of "ready-made" courses or materials, use of programmed instruction, videotape, computer managed and other structured techniques versus a more process-oriented organization development/team-building approach.

c. *Program Design and Development*
   —Design program content and structure, apply learning theory, establish objectives, evaluate and select instructional methods.

d. *Develop Material Resources (Make)*
   —Prepare scripts, slides, manuals, artwork, copy, programmed learning, and other instructional materials.

e. *Manage Internal Resources (Borrow)*
   —Obtain and evaluate internal instructors/program resource persons, train others how to train, supervise their work.

f. *Manager External Resources (Buy)*
   —Hire, supervise, and evaluate external instructors/program resource persons; obtain and evaluate outside consultants and vendors.

g. *Individual Development Planning and Counseling*
   —Counsel with individuals regarding career development needs and plans; arrange for and maintain records of participation in programs, administer tuition reimbursement, maintain training resource library, keep abreast of EEO.

h. *Job/Performance-Related Training*
   —Assist managers and others in on-the-job training and development; analyze job skill and knowledge requirements, determine performance problems.

i. *Conduct Classroom Training*
   —Conduct programs, operate audio-visual equipment, lecture, lead discussion, revise materials based on feedback, arrange program logistics.

j. *Group and Organization Development*
   —Apply techniques such as team-building, intergroup meetings, behavior modeling, role-playing simulation, laboratory education, discussions, cases, issues.

k. *Training Research*
   —Present and interpret statistics and data relating to training; communicate through reports, proposals, speeches, and articles; design data collection.

l. *Manage Working Relationships with Managers and Clients*
   —Establish and maintain good relations with managers as clients, counsel with them and explain recommendations for training and development.

m. *Manage the Training and Development Function*
   —Prepare budgets, organize, staff, make formal presentations of plans, maintain information on costs, supervise the work of others, project future needs, etc.

n. *Professional Self Development*
   —Attend seminars/conferences, and keep abreast of training and development concepts, theories, and techniques; keep abreast of activities in other organizations.

From "What Do Training and Development Professionals Really Do?" by P. R. Pinto and J. W. Walker. In *Training and Development Journal,* July 1978, *28*, pp. 58–64. Copyright 1978 by the American Society for Training and Development, Inc. Reprinted by permission.

In another analysis of survey results (Clement, Walker, & Pinto, 1979), data were reported about the most important skill or knowledge requirement for the training practitioner. In this instance, members of the American Society for Training and Development were asked, "What is the most important skill or knowledge requirement for success as a training and development professional?" Table 1.2 shows the results for this question. The largest number of responses were for human relations skills, which include developing mutual trust and interpersonal relationships. These responses were especially focused on relationships to managers with whom trainees must work in designing training programs. The next largest group of responses was related to communications skills needed as part of the training process. The next set of responses emphasized knowledge of the training field, including recent developments, understanding new training technology, and how adults learn. The fourth item, analytical skill, was related to abilities to analyze performance deficiencies, assess training needs, and so on. *Management skill* refers mainly to items related to managing the training department. *Knowledge about the organization* refers to the kind of knowledge that makes it possible to anticipate training needs and understand organizational goals. The activities presented in Table 1.1 and the knowledge and skill titles in Table 1.2 present good illustrations of the complex role of the training practitioner.

TABLE 1.2   Most important skill or knowledge requirements

Response Category	Responses	Percentage
Human relations skill	698	35.1%
Communications skill	506	25.4%
Knowledge of training and development field	277	13.9%
Analytical skill	203	10.2%
Management skill	136	6.8%
Knowledge of the organization	95	4.8%
Other	74	3.7%
Total	1989	100.0%

From "Changing Demands on the Training Professional," by R. W. Clement, J. W. Walker, and P. R. Pinto. In *Training and Development Journal,* March 1979, *29,* pp. 3-7. Copyright 1979 by the American Society for Training and Development, Inc. Reprinted by permission.

THE TRAINING STRUGGLE

The increased emphasis on professional activities presented in Table 1.1 has resulted in programs that meet instructional objectives based upon clearly specified needs. The types of instructional goals have varied from those of a school district that desires to raise the test scores of its students above the national average to an industrial organization that expects quality goods to be produced in a shorter time period, a reduction in accidents with a corresponding decrease in insurance premiums, and a more satisfied work force, which in turn could help reduce turn-over, absenteeism, sabotage, and grievances. The potential number of goals is unlimited. While training is not a panacea for all the ills of society, well-conceived training programs have achieved beneficial results. This text will present many examples of training programs that work. However, it would be unrealistic to pretend that most programs are either based upon appropriate needs assessment or that these pro-grams are examined to determine the degree to which they achieve their objectives. Unfortunately, most organizations do not have information available to determine the utility of their own instructional programs. Their techniques remain unevaluated, except for the high esteem with which they are regarded by training personnel. For example, the *Catalog of Basic Education Systems* (U.S. Civil Service Commission, 1971a) lists 55 basic reading programs for educationally disadvantaged employ-ees. For these programs, four publishers list some type of validation program, two publishers offer case studies, and the other 49 indicate that validation data are not available. Yet, when evaluation studies are completed, it is often found that the techniques are not achieving the desired results, and in many cases the evaluation could provide clues to the modifications necessary to enable the program to work. Kozoll (1971) described a personnel training program in an article with the un-usually descriptive title "The Air Left the 'Bag'—A Training Program That Failed." His analysis indicated that the program failed to develop jobs for the hard-core unemployed trainees in the supermarket industry because the interest and involvement of the potential employers were ignored. Thus, Kozoll's analysis has provided valuable insights into one of the factors that helps establish successful training programs.

Too many training analysts appear to have adopted a "fads" ap-proach to instructional design. This approach emphasizes the use of the newest training technique. Indeed, I continually receive calls in-quiring about the newest training techniques. Campbell (1971) dis-cerned the following pattern to the fads approach.

1. A new technique appears with a group of followers who announce its success.
2. Another group develops modifications of the technique.
3. A few empirical studies appear supporting the technique.
4. There is a backlash. Critics question the usefulness of the new technique but rarely produce any data.
5. The technique survives until a new technique appears. Then, the whole procedure is repeated.

When there are no empirical data to evaluate techniques, the cycle of fads continues. Evaluation must be sold as a tool to provide informa-tion rather than as a technique to determine passing and failing. Then, we may be able to shift from the cycles of fads to the more mature question of which technique works for which individuals, behaviors, or organizational settings. There is no supertechnique that will work for all given situations. It is not even certain which learning variables support performance or which instructional media are best for learning particular types of behavior. The level of analysis rarely reaches the point at which different techniques are actually compared.

The difficulties that must be confronted in order to produce sound, effective training programs and research are described in "The Riddle of Training in Business and Industry" (DePhillips, Berliner, & Cribbin, 1960, pp. 5-6).

> Few organizations would admit that they can survive without it—yet some act as though they could.
> Everyone knows what it is—yet management, unions, and workers often interpret it in light of their own job conditions.
> It is going on all the time—yet much of it is done haphazardly.
> It is futile to attempt it without the needed time and facilities—yet often those responsible for it lack either or both.
> It costs money—yet at times there is not adequate budgetary appropriation for it.
> It should take place at all levels—yet sometimes it is limited to the lowest operating levels.
> It can help everyone do a better job—yet those selected for it often fear it.
> It is foolish to start it without clearly defined objectives—yet this is occasionally done.
> It cannot be ignored without costing the company money—yet some managers seem blind to this reality.
> It should permeate the entire organization and be derived from the firm's theory and practice of management—yet sometimes it is shunted off to one department that operates more or less in isolation from the rest of the business.[2]

Observers of instructional programs would agree that the riddle is equally applicable to educational and industrial programs. They might also concur that the riddle would be more complete by adding: "It is accepted as working but too often there is little evidence to support this viewpoint." One of the goals of this book is to present information that will convince the reader that the conditions described by the riddle are worth changing. It is hoped that the text will also serve as a source for information and techniques necessary to design and evaluate training programs.

THE FUTURE OF INSTRUCTIONAL PROGRAMS

A significant portion of our lives is spent in educational and training programs. It is predicted that instructional technology will have an even greater influence upon our future lives. The reasons for this include the advent of high technology, the needs of minorities, and the demand for accountability.

[2] From *Management of Training Programs*, by F. A. DePhillips, W. N. Berliner, and J. J. Cribbin. Copyright © 1960 by Richard D. Irwin. Reprinted by permission.

The Effects of High Technology

Technological developments during the past 40 years include nuclear energy, jet aircraft, computers, and laser technology. These developments have created a demand for highly skilled individuals who typically require many hours of training. An illustration of the effects of increased training demands can be found in the development of the General Electric Company's new multimillion dollar training facility, which will be used to train 3000 craftsmen annually in the most recent technological innovations (*Training and Development Journal,* 1980). Some of the training will include instruction in safe handling of radioactive materials, maintenance of solid-state data communications equipment, use of sensors to detect hot spots in equipment and buildings, and computerized failure analysis of construction equipment. The dire consequences of failing to provide adequate training were demonstrated in the nuclear power plant accident at Three Mile Island. A major finding (United States President's Commission, 1979) of that investigation was that key maintenance personnel did not have adequate training for their jobs. Microelectronic circuits, which provide the foundation for thousands of applications ranging from television games to pocket calculators to digital watches to space probes, promise extraordinary changes in the workplace. The use of electronic mail systems, personal computer networks, and word processing machinery promises to revolutionize the typical work office and corresponding training requirements.

Advances in computer technology and work techniques have already led to changes in training requirements for many jobs in industrial enterprises. Each new advance has the potential to change job requirements as well as to create or abolish entire job categories. Automation generally requires higher levels of skill from the operators who desire to continue in their present job, but more jobs are created with requirements related to systems control, monitoring, and electronics maintenance. The effects on organizations are not always predictable. In almost all cases, however, the need for training and retraining increases. Usually, the training is limited to those concerned with immediate work requirements, but it is likely that the increasing complexity of the organization will necessitate retraining at all levels within the organization.

Training Technology Development

The changes in high technology that are likely to affect the work environment are also likely to change training technology. Some individuals are predicting a revolution in the development of instructional systems. These predictions are based upon the development of electronic systems, such as computers, cable television, and video cassettes, for full-time college students. There is increasing recognition that the use of techniques like television and computer-assisted instruction for the off-campus instruction of adults and in industrial training programs will modify many traditional views of training programs. The declining population of college-bound students has resulted in universities and other interested parties turning their attention and resources to even more adult education and industrial training programs. While some persons believe that the decline will reverse sometime in the 1990s, it is likely that future groups of students, young and old, are likely to use the same technology that is changing the workplace and revolutionizing instructional systems.

Special Groups

Minority groups and hard-core unemployment. Instructional programs have been offered as a possible solution to the problem of equal opportunities. All segments of our society, from the federal government to the local school system, have begun to offer programs that give previously unemployed individuals an opportunity to obtain the skills necessary for future employment. These programs include basic language skills, job skills, consumer information, and counseling. The design and implementation of these programs require a special sensitivity to the needs of the applicant population and to job requirements. As difficult as the initiation of these programs may be, there is little dispute that the need for such efforts will greatly increase in the next decade. In many cases, hard-core unemployed groups include large numbers of non-White trainees. These particular minority groups have faced problems of substantial unemployment as well as job discrimination related to promotional opportunities. Previously, the Equal Employment Opportunities Commission (EEOC) focused on those firms that unfairly discriminated against minority employees in their selection practices. Increasingly, however, the EEOC has had to deal with firms that fail to provide opportunities to move up the corporate ladder or organizations that deny persons jobs in occupations that were previously the province of one select group. Thus, women are finding opportunities to enter managerial jobs or craft jobs. With this focus, the question of training programs and their fairness to minority groups (particularly those related to sex, race, and age) has become a serious issue. Training techniques that have not been validated and that are discriminatory in promotional and job opportunities are being struck down by the courts. Indeed, the lack of opportunity to participate in a valid training program is a serious discrimination issue which is being scrutinized by the courts. Examples of the importance of these issues can be found in court cases being tried everywhere in the country. It is not unusual in these suits to hear charges that little or no training is being offered to employees seeking technical or professional jobs and that announcements of vacancies are not posted. Settlements often involve millions of dollars in back pay to current employees and training to enable the employees to qualify for better jobs. Many of these issues involve complex questions about needs assessment and evaluation that will be presented and discussed later in the text.

Legislation has also recognized the large numbers of individuals who are over 45 years of age and cannot find work. Some of these individuals are victims of changing job requirements that render their skills obsolete. Employers have hired younger workers who have more recently developed skills and who cost the employer less in terms of health insurance premiums and pension plans. It is likely that as the courts turn their attention to this issue there will be more empirical efforts to develop effective training programs that utilize older people's years of experience and skills.

Accountability

The amount of rhetoric concerning evaluation methodology, including information about criterion development, evaluation designs, values and ethics, and problems of performance evaluations in organizations, has exploded. While some of the literature appears to be prompted by accountability concerns in the area of criminal and civil justice, social welfare, fertility control, mental health, and medical treatment, it is clear that many of the same issues are directly relevant to individuals concerned with the evaluation of training programs in organizational environments. The tremendous costs of instructional programs have naturally resulted in questions about their effectiveness. It is not unusual for companies to accept contracts with school systems where their payment is directly related to the degree of improvement made by students on nationally standardized achievement tests. In management circles, it is becoming more conventional to question the effects of expensive training and development programs. This is a healthy trend that will test the ingenuity of training analysts to determine the effectiveness of their program in terms of performance improvements, costs, and other subsidiary benefits through the establishment of systematic evaluation programs.

TRAINING AS A SUBSYSTEM

A text which only considers the technical aspects of needs assessment and evaluation design misses out on most of the dynamics concerning training systems. Training programs exist within organizations. It is unrealistic to think of training systems as if they were in a vacuum. Many investigators have been disappointed with the results of their training programs because they assumed that success would always follow the implementation of a well-conceived program. In some instances, supervisors do not permit the employee to use the skills that were acquired in the training program. In other cases, training is not the answer. For example, Sheridan (1975) describes, with pointed clarity, the AT&T attempt to comply with a government order to place 19% females in outside craft jobs. Despite rigorous recruiting and training efforts, the women they did manage to recruit dropped from training at an average rate of 50%. The individuals who completed training usually did not last a full year. Their analysis determined that physical differences between men and women made the job extremely difficult to perform. Some of the most serious problems concerned the use of a ladder which is both long and heavy. Utilizing basic principles of human factors, the job was redesigned so that it could be performed by both men and women.

In other instances, training analysts have thoughtfully considered the organizational environment to decide what type of program might work. For example, Thayer and McGehee (1977) describe an instance where the motivation to attend a formal training program was so low that any such program was doomed to failure. Instead of developing such a program, they developed a very difficult open-book test which, in this case, was on the topic of the terms of the union contract. As an incentive to do well on the test, they offered a steak dinner for the foreman who submitted the most correct answers. McGehee encouraged plant managers to wager with each other as to whose foreman would do best on the test. As a result, managers began to encourage their foremen to organize group study sessions. The test designer was besieged by phone calls for the entire week following distribution of the very difficult exam; callers argued that there were two or more correct answers to almost every question. By the end of the week, all exams were in and were perfect or near-perfect. Faced with such performance, the company president decided to host a steak dinner for all the foremen and their managers. Interestingly, the exam was the most popular topic during the dinner. Certainly, most "training programs" would have been delighted about the degree of involvement for this "non-training" approach. The point is that organizations are very complex systems and training programs are but one subsystem. Thus, changes in the selection system which can result in persons with higher or lower job-relevant skills and abilities will have a dramatic effect on the level of training required. Changes in jobs as new technologies develop can have similar effects. Also, of course, more effective training programs can affect all the other systems in the work organization.

The dynamics of training systems must include the realization that one of the first places to which many new employees in an organization are sent is a training program. Similarly, when individuals change positions as a result of a career change or promotion, many enter a training program. It is as important to understand the effects of training experiences as part of the socialization process in entering organizations as it is to evaluate specific training outcomes. The purpose of this text is to provide some understanding of the dynamics of training systems as well as information related to systematic development and evaluation of training programs.

The next chapter presents an instructional model that outlines the various factors to be considered in the design of systematic programs. The description of these interacting components should clearly indicate that there is no easy technique or gadget that can be used in the development of well-conceived programs. Instructional materials will have a profound effect on everyone's life. Present knowledge should be utilized in the development of new programs; it can only be hoped that such efforts will contribute more information to our existing state of knowledge.

A Systematic Approach to Training

INSTRUCTIONAL TECHNOLOGY

While the term *technology* commonly refers to the development of hardware, *instructional technology* refers to the systematic development of programs in training and education. The systems approach to instruction emphasizes the specification of instructional objectives, precisely controlled learning experiences to achieve these objectives, criteria for performance, and evaluative information. Other characteristics of instructional technology include the following:

1. The systems approach uses feedback to continually modify instructional processes. From this perspective, training programs are never finished products; they are continually adaptive to information that indicates whether the program is meeting its stated objectives.

2. The instructional-systems approach recognizes the complex interaction among the components of the system. For example, one particular medium, like television, might be effective in achieving one set of objectives, while another medium might be preferable for a second set of objectives. Similar interactions could involve learning variables and specific individual characteristics of the learner. The systems view stresses a concern with the total system rather than with the objectives of any single component.

3. Systematic analysis provides a frame of reference for planning and for remaining on target. In this framework, a research approach is necessary to determine which programs are meeting their objectives.

4. The instructional systems view is just one of a whole set of interacting systems. Training programs interact with and are directly affected by a larger system involving corporate policies (for example, selection and management philosophy). Similarly, educational programs are affected by the social values of society.

The various components of the instructional-systems approach are not new. Evaluation was a byword years before systems approaches were in vogue. Thus, the systems approach cannot be considered a magic wand for all the problems that were unsolved before its inception. If the training designer were convinced that his program worked, a systems approach would be unlikely to convince him that his program required examination. However, the systems approach does provide a model that emphasizes important components and their interactions, and there is good evidence that this model is an important impetus for the establishment of objectives and evaluation procedures. As such, it is a useful tool that enables designers of instructional programs (as well as authors of books like this one) to examine the total training process.

Figure 2.1 presents one model of an instructional system. Most of the components of this model (for example, derive objectives and develop criteria) are considered important to any instructional system, although the degree of emphasis changes for different programs. The chapters that follow discuss material related to each of these model components. This chapter provides an overview of the complete system and the relationships among the components.

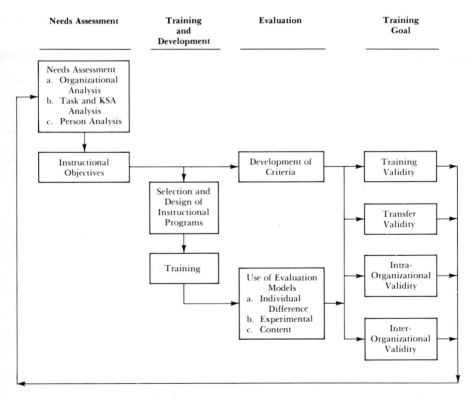

FIGURE 2.1 An instructional system. There are many other instructional-system models for military, business, and educational systems.

ASSESSMENT PHASE

Assessment of Instructional Need

This phase of the instructional process provides the information necessary to design the entire program. An examination of the model indicates that the training and evaluation phases are dependent upon input from the development phase. Unfortunately, many programs are doomed to failure because trainers are more interested in conducting the training program than in assessing the needs of their organizations. Educators have been seduced by programed instruction and industrial trainers by sensitivity training before they have determined the needs of their organization and the way the techniques will meet those needs. The needs assessment phase consists of organization analysis, task analysis, and person analysis.

Organizational analysis. Organizational analysis begins with an examination of the short- and long-term goals of the organization, as well as of the trends that are likely to affect these goals. Often, this analysis requires that upper-level management examine their own expectations concerning their training programs. Training designed to produce proficient sales personnel must be structured differently from programs to train sales personnel who are capable of moving up the corporate ladder to managerial positions. As school systems examine their goals, they recognize that their programs are designed for academically oriented students, and it becomes clearer why vocationally oriented students feel like second-class citizens. When organizational analysis is ignored, planning difficulties abound. Many corporations have spent considerable sums of money retraining personnel because the original training programs and decisions on performance capabilities were based on a system that soon became obsolete. Another aspect of the organizational analysis focuses on training programs and supporting systems—for example, selection, human-factors engineering, and work procedures. Particular operating problems might best be resolved by changes in selection standards or redesign of the work environment.

Task and knowledge, skill, and ability analysis. The second part of the needs assessment program is a careful analysis of the job to be performed by the trainees upon completion of the training program. The analysis is usually divided into several separate procedures. The first step is a *job description* in behavioral terms. It is not a description of the worker. The narrative specifies the individual's duties and the special conditions under which the job is performed. The second procedure, most commonly referred to as *task specification,* further denotes all the tasks required on the job so that eventually the particular skills, knowledge, and attitudes required to perform the job will become clear. Thus, a brief description of the job of an airline reservation clerk might indicate that the clerk makes and confirms reservations, determines seat availability, and so on. The task specification would consist of a complete list of tasks providing information about *what* the worker does, *how* the worker does it, to *whom* or *what,* and *why.* Thus, a task for the airline reservation clerk might be "Inspects availability board to determine seats available for passengers on stand-by status." In addition to developing tasks which describe the job, choices are also made about the collection of information about those tasks. Thus, depending on how the analysis will be used, data might be collected about how important each task is or how frequently it is performed, etc.

The organizational analysis and task analysis provide a picture of the task and the organizational setting in which the task occurs. One critical consideration is missing—that is, the knowledge, skills, and abilities (KSAs) required of the individual who will be in the training program. Task requirements must be translated into the knowledge, skills, and abilities necessary to perform those tasks. This is a difficult but necessary job based on inferences from the tasks. Essentially, we are asking for judgments concerning which KSAs make a difference in the performance of those tasks. The determination of the learning environment and instructional media is directly dependent on the particular knowledge, skills, and abilities necessary to perform the tasks. Another facet of the KSA analysis is the examination of characteristics of the KSAs in terms of the information necessary to make training decisions. For example, it is possible to determine which KSAs are critical to job performance, which you should expect to have before being selected, and which should be learned in training as opposed to on the job.

Person analysis.   This analysis is concerned with how well a specific employee is carrying out the tasks which make up the job (McGehee & Thayer, 1961). As such, this component of the needs assessment is very much related to the determination of the knowledge, skills, and abilities necessary to perform the tasks. However, here the emphasis is not on determining which KSAs are necessary but rather on assessing how well the employees actually demonstrate the KSAs required by the job. In order to actually perform the person analysis, it becomes necessary to derive measures of job performance known as *criteria.* This will be discussed further in the evaluation section. It also shows the important interaction between needs assessment and other aspects of training systems, such as the evaluation component. It is important to determine which necessary KSAs have already been learned by the prospective trainees. Too many training programs are exercises in boredom because they focus on skills already acquired. The determination of the target population is also necessary. Some training programs are designed for individuals who are already in the system, while others are for trainees who are not yet part of the organization. In any case, it is senseless to design the training environment without acknowledging the characteristics of the groups to be trained.

Instructional Objectives

From information obtained in the assessment of instructional needs, a blueprint emerges that describes the objectives to be achieved by the trainee upon completion of the training program. These objectives provide the input for the design of the training program as well as for the measures of success (criteria) that will be used to judge the program's adequacy. One approach to the establishment of instructional objectives is known as *specification of the behavioral objectives* (Mager, 1962). The following is an example of one behavioral objective for a gas-station attendant.

> By reading the gasoline pump, the employee can determine the cost of the product and provide correct change to the customer without resorting to paper and pencil for computations. Performance will be judged adequate if the employee
> 1. always provides correct change for single items (for example, gas) up to a total of $30;
> 2. always provides correct change when the customer pays cash up to $100;
> 3. successfully completes 20 trials by providing the correct change.

Similar statements could be designed for instructional systems in a variety of settings. For example, the following behavioral objective is appropriate to the solution of a particular servicing aspect of a Xerox machine (Cicero, 1973).

> Given a tool kit and a service manual, the technical representative will be able to adjust the registration (black line along paper edges) on a Xerox 2400 duplicator within 20 minutes according to the specifications stated in the manual. (p. 15)

Another way of looking at instructional objectives is to ask what, given a particular task and the specification of the KSAs necessary to perform the task, are the effective behaviors that will tell you that the task is being performed correctly? It is also possible to ask what ineffective behaviors will tell you that the task is not being performed correctly. Using this approach, Latham and Wexley (1981) have identified various procedures for identifying effective and ineffective behaviors. Some examples of these behaviors for the job of a mechanic in a bowling alley are:

> Clean air conditioning system once a week, for example, vacuums filters.
> Informs others when a machine is not working properly.

> Can make most repairs within 5 minutes because major repairs are minimized through preventive maintenance checks. (pp. 215-218)

Well-written instructional objectives which are based on tasks and KSAs specify what the trainee will be able to accomplish when successfully completing the instructional program. They also indicate the conditions under which the performance must be maintained and the standards by which the trainee will be evaluated (Mager, 1962). Thus, objectives communicate the goals of the program to both the learner and the training designer. From these goals, the designers can determine the appropriate learning environment and the criteria for examining the achievement of the objectives.

Chapter 3 examines the assessment phase, which includes organizational, task, and person analyses as well as the development of behavioral objectives.

TRAINING-DEVELOPMENT PHASE

The Training Environment

Once the tasks, KSAs, and objectives have been specified, the next step is to design the environment to achieve the objectives. This is a delicate process that requires a blend of learning principles and media selection, based on the tasks that the trainee is eventually expected to perform. Gilbert (1960) described the temptations that often lead to a poor environment.

> If you don't have a gadget called a teaching machine, don't get one. Don't buy one; don't borrow one; don't steal one. If you have such a gadget, get rid of it. Don't give it away, for someone else might use it. This is a most practical rule, based on empirical facts from considerable observation. If you begin with a device of any kind, you will try to develop the teaching program to fit that device. (p. 478)

Gilbert's remarks are equally appropriate for any device or method, from airline flight simulators to educational television. It is important to consider the tasks that are performed and the knowledge, skills, and abilities necessary to perform those tasks and ask what type of training program will produce the best results. "The best available basis for the needed matching of media with objectives . . . is a rationale by which the kind of learning involved in each educational objective is stated in terms of the learning conditions required" (Briggs, Campeau, Gagné, & May, 1967, p. 3). This is the same process that gardeners use when they choose a certain tool for a certain job. In the same manner, trainers choose simulators that create the characteristics of flight in order to teach pilots; however, the simulator is not usually considered appropriate to teach an adult a foreign language. The analysis of job tasks and performance requirements, and the matching of these behaviors to those produced by the training environment, is at this point as much an art as a technology. Although the preceding examples of pilot training and language learning are misleading because they represent obvious differences between tasks, there could be significant improvements in the design of training environments if more emphasis were placed on this matching of training environments to required behaviors.

Learning Principles

In training environments, the instructional process involves the acquisition of skills, concepts, and attitudes that are transferred to a second setting (for example, on the job or in another classroom). The acquisition phase emphasizes learning a new task. Performance on the job and in the next environment focuses on transfer of learning to a second setting. Both theoretical and empirical sources of information are available to aid in the design of environments to improve worker performance. Unfortunately, a definitive list of principles from the learning environment that could be adapted to the training setting has not completely emerged. The learning literature is weak in describing the variables that affect human beings, especially those pertaining to various forms of skilled behavior. Basic research has centered on simpler behaviors for which there are available laboratory tasks. However, learning theorists have progressed to a stage of development at which it is clear that the choice of the proper learning variable or level of that variable cannot be based on random option. Learning variables interact with the training environment. Thus, it is not appropriate to ignore the information from the learning literature or to accept a particular variable (for example, feedback or knowledge of results) as useful for all tasks. An illustration of these interactions is provided in a review by Gagné (1962), which suggests that feedback—one of the most sacred variables—is not effective in improving performance on some types of motor-skill training. This does not mean that feedback is not a potent variable for some tasks. It does, however, imply that there are complex interactions that will require consistent research before definitive answers can be found.

Chapter 4 discusses the learning principles that underlie training processes. The chapter includes discussions about the acquisition and transfer process, as well as about the learning variables that interact with the training environment. Chapters 7 and 8 examine some major training techniques prevalent in education and industry. These chapters discuss the objectives of a particular environment, provide illustrations, note the learning principles involved, and discuss the evaluation techniques that are employed to determine the value of these training procedures. Chapter 9 discusses special issues which interrelate societal concerns and training programs, for example, training the hard-core unemployed and fair employment practices and training concerns. This chapter, then, reflects on many components of the instructional model.

EVALUATION PHASE

Since the development of a training program involves an assessment of needs and a careful design of the training environment, the trainee is expected to perform his job at acceptable criterion levels. Unfortunately, this statement of faith displays a sense of self-confidence that is far from justified. Careful examinations of the instructional process disclose numerous pitfalls resulting from mistakes or deficiencies in our present state of knowledge. The assessment of instructional need might have omitted important job components, or the job itself might have changed since the program was designed. In other instances, there are uncertainties about the most appropriate training technique to establish the required behaviors.

Unfortunately, few programs are evaluated. Indeed, the word *evaluation* raises all sorts of emotional defense reactions. In many cases, the difficulties seem related to a failure to understand that instructional programs are research efforts that must be massaged and treated until the required results are produced. An experience of mine may illuminate this problem.

A community agency was offering a program for previously unemployed individuals to help them obtain jobs. A colleague and I were invited to visit and offer suggestions about improvements to the program. Our questions about the success of the program were answered by reference to the excellent curricula and the high attendance rate of the participants. A frank discussion ensued related to the objectives of the program, with particular emphasis on the criteria being utilized to measure the adequacy of the program—that is, how successful the participants were in obtaining and holding jobs. This discussion led to the revelation that the success level simply was not known, because such data had never been collected. Of course, it was possible that the program was working successfully, but the information to make such a judgment was unavailable. Thus, there was no way to judge the effectiveness of the program or to provide information that could lead to improvements.

The evaluation process centers around two procedures—establishing measures of success (criteria) and using experimental and nonexperimental designs to determine what changes have occurred during the training and transfer process. The criteria are based on the behavioral objectives, which were determined by the assessment of instructional need. As standards of performance, these criteria should describe: the behavior required to demonstrate the trainee's skill, the conditions under which the trainee is to perform, and the lowest limit of acceptable performance (Mager, 1962).

Criteria must be established for both the evaluation of trainees at the conclusion of the training program and the evaluation of on-the-job performance (referred to as transfer validity in the model). In educational settings, the criteria must pertain to performance in later courses as well as to performance in the environment where the instructional program was instituted. One classification (Kirkpatrick, 1959, 1960) for this purpose suggests that several different measures are necessary, including reaction of participants, learning of participants in training, behavior changes on the job, and final results of the total program. Other serious issues pertain to the integration of the large number of criteria often needed to evaluate a program and to the difficulties (for example, biased estimates of performance) associated with the collection of criterion information. These issues are discussed in Chapter 5.

In addition to criterion development, the evaluation phase must also focus on the necessary design to assess the training program. As indicated in Figure 2.1, there are a number of different designs which can be used to evaluate training programs, and to some extent the choices are dependent on what you want to obtain information about and the constraints under which you operate. In the last column of the diagram a number of potential goals are listed. They are:

1. *Training validity.* The question here is whether the trainees learn during training.
2. *Transfer validity.* The issue is whether what has been learned in training transfers as enhanced performance in the work organization.
3. *Intra-organizational validity.* This concept refers to whether the performance for a new group of trainees in the same organization that developed the training program is consistent with the performance of the original training group.
4. *Inter-organizational validity.* In this instance, the analyst is attempting to determine whether a training program validated in one organization can be used successfully in another organization.

As discussed in Chapter 6, these different questions often result in different evaluation models, or, at the very least, different forms of the same evaluation model. For example, the experimental design model is based upon the use of pre- and posttests and also uses control groups as a way of accounting for extraneous effects. Some startled trainers have discovered that their control group performed as well as trainees enrolled in an elaborately designed training program. This often occurred because the control groups could not be permitted to do the job without training. Thus, they either had on-the-job training or were instructed through a program that existed before the implementation of the new instructional system. Clearly, if you are interested in transfer validity, the experimental design must include posttest measures not only at the end of training but also at an appropriate time in the work environment or transfer setting.

In addition to experimental designs, there are other approaches to evaluation which provide varying degrees of information. For example, individual differences designs relate individual performance in training to individual performance on the job. It asks whether persons who tend to perform better in training also perform better on the job. If that is the case, the training score can be used to select the better job performers. However, as discussed in Chapter 6, it will become clear that such a model does not tell you very much about the actual quality of the training program. Individuals who do well in training may also do well on the job, even when the training program does not teach as much as it should. Another model also represented in the diagram is content validity. This refers to whether the critical knowledge, skills, and abilities (KSAs) determined in the needs assessment are emphasized in the training program. That doesn't assure you that the material was learned, but then again, if the critical KSAs are not included in the training program there is not much hope for the effort.

Chapter 6 stresses that the rigor of the design affects the quality and quantity of information available for evaluation. There are situations in which it is not possible to use the most rigorous design because of cost or because of the particular setting. In these cases, it is important to use the best design available and to recognize those factors that affect the validity of the information.

A training program should be a closed-loop system in which the evaluation process provides for continual modification of the program. An open-loop system, in contrast, either does not have any feedback or is not responsive to such information. In order to develop training programs that achieve their purpose, it is necessary to obtain the evaluative information and to use this information for program modifications.

The information may become available at many different stages in the evaluation process. For example, an effective monitoring program might show that the training program has not been implemented as originally planned. In other instances, different conclusions might be supported by comparing data obtained from the training evaluation or transfer evaluation. If the participant performs well in training but poorly in the transfer setting, the adequacy of the entire program must be assessed. As indicated by the feedback loops in the model (refer again to Figure 2.1), the information derived from the evaluation process is utilized to reassess the instructional need, thus creating input for the next stage of development.

Even in those instances in which the training program achieves its stated objectives, there are continual developments that can affect the program, including the addition of new media techniques and changes in the characteristics of trainees. These changes often cause previous objectives to become obsolete. The development of training programs must be viewed as a continually evolving process.

One purpose of this overview of the instructional process is to provide the reader with a model that can be used to organize the material in the following chapters. We shall begin the more comprehensive discussion of the components of instructional programs in the next chapter by examining the first step—assessment of instructional need.

The Needs Assessment Phase

Training programs are designed to achieve goals that meet instructional needs. There is always the temptation to begin training without a thorough analysis of these needs; however, a reexamination of the instructional model introduced in Chapter 2 will emphasize the danger of beginning any program without a complete assessment of tasks, behaviors, and environment. The model shows that the objectives, criteria, and design of the program all stem from these analyses. Goals and objectives are the key steps in determining a training environment, and unless they are specified, there is no way to measure success. Machinists don't choose their tools before they examine their job; builders don't order their materials or plan their schedules until they have their blueprints (Mager, 1962). Why is it, then, that trainers and teachers argue over the merits of particular teaching aids without even specifying what the aid is to accomplish?

Perhaps the following example will illustrate the dangers of a "let's do it in our heads" approach. This outlandish memo was intercepted by a student as it made the rounds of the federal office buildings in Washington, D.C.

Memorandum for the Director of Personnel

Proposed: Allocation of a position titled:
Director of Personnel, Industrial and Agrarian Priorities
Description of duties and responsibilities.

1. Without direct or intermediate supervision, and with a broad latitude for independent judgment and discretion, the incumbent directs, controls, and regulates the movement of the wealth of the American economy.

2. The decisions of the incumbent are important since they affect with great finality the movement of agricultural products, forest products, minerals, manufacturer's goods, machine tools, construction equipment, military personnel, defense materials, raw materials and products, finished goods, semi-finished products, small business, large business, public utilities, and government agencies.

3. In the effective implementation of these responsibilities the incumbent must exercise initiative, ingenuity, imagination, intelligence, industry, and discerning versatility. The incumbent must be able to deal effectively with all types of personalities and all levels of education from college president to industrial tycoon to truck driver. Above all, the incumbent must possess decisiveness and the ability to implement motivation on the part of others consistent with the decision the incumbent had indicated. An erroneous judgment, or a failure to properly appraise the nuance of an unfolding development, could create a complete obfuscation of personnel and equipment generating an untold loss of mental equilibrium on the parts of innumerable personnel of American Industry who are responsible for the formulation of day-to-day policy and guidance implementation of the conveyance of transportation both intra-state and inter-state.

4. In short, on highway construction projects where only one-way traffic is possible, the incumbent waves a red flag and tells which car to go first.

Many analysts insist that job descriptions dictated by this "let's do it in our heads" approach or by a "we know it all already" approach can be just as far from practical application as our illustration. Certainly, it would be hard to design a training program based on the flowing descriptors in this document. Carefully described objectives that set forth required behavior are needed to plan effective training programs; moreover, there should be a direct relationship between these objectives and the type of instruction. A doctor diagnoses illness using X rays and laboratory tests before he attempts to prescribe a cure through medication, surgery, or other techniques. The training analyst also makes a diagnosis using organizational analysis, task analysis, and person analysis to determine if a cure is necessary and which cure is most likely to produce the desired result. While each of these analyses is discussed separately, they all interact with each other; for example, information for task analyses often results from organizational analyses.

ORGANIZATIONAL ANALYSIS

Persons concerned with training are required to face a serious problem. That is, the persons who participate in training programs are required to learn something in one environment (training) and then use their acquired knowledge, skills, and abilities in another environment (on-the-job in the organization). Thus, the trainee will enter a new environment subject to the effects of all the interaction components that represent organizations today. The nature of the environment called an *organization* can be appreciated from Schein's definition.

> An organization is the planned coordination of the activities of a number of people for the achievement of some common, explicit purpose or goal, through division of labor and function, and through a hierarchy of authority and responsibility. (1980, p. 15)

The problem is that often these goals are *not* explicit and many times there is conflict among individuals about both the activities to be performed and the goals to be achieved. When this occurs, the trainee is often left with a bag of knowledge, skills, and abilities that is not usable on the job.

Organizational analysis refers to an examination of the system-wide components of the organization that may affect a training program's factors beyond those ordinarily considered in task and person analysis. Task and person analysis are more specific, focusing on job tasks and the required person characteristics (knowledge, skills, and abilities) appropriate for training. Organizational analysis has a much broader scope. It is concerned with the system-wide components of an organization that may have impact on a training program. It includes an examination of organizational goals, resources of the organization, climate for training, and internal and external constraints present in the environment.

As implied above, many training programs are judged to be failures because of organizational system constraints. For example, the statements "start training at the top" and "I wish my boss had been exposed to this training program" indicate real differences between the approach or values of the training program and those of upper-level supervisors. However, it is too late to compare the goals of upper-level supervision with those of the training program after the instructional program has been instituted. Training programs that are in conflict with the goals of the organization are likely to produce confused and dissatisfied workers. A study by Fleishman, Harris, and Burtt (1955) illustrates the difficulties that arise when the training program and the working environment promote different values. These researchers designed a training program to increase the amount of consideration (friendship, mutual trust) in foremen. The initial results, collected at the end of the training program, indicated success (as shown by the training scores). However, a follow-up of the program showed that the consideration factor was not maintained on the job. The researchers discovered that the day-to-day social climate, influenced by the supervisors, was not sympathetic to the new values. This study illustrates the need to examine transfer behavior (from the training program on the job) and the importance of experimental designs that enable researchers to specify effects. Just as important, however, the study provides an example of a training program that did not achieve the expected result because its goals and those of the organization were not consistent.

A startling example of the seriousness of this type of problem was provided by an in-depth study of three federal agencies (Salinger, 1973). The results of this study described a series of disincentives to effective employee training and development. As shown in Table 3.1, Salinger notes that the benefits of training and development are not

TABLE 3.1   The training disincentives process

1. The benefits of training and development are not clear to top management.

2. Top management rarely evaluates and rewards managers and supervisors for carrying out effective training and development.

3. Top management rarely plans and budgets systematically for training and development.

4. Managers usually do not account for training and development in production planning.

5. Supervisors have difficulty meeting production norms with employees in training and development.

6. Therefore, supervisors and managers train and develop employees unsystematically and mostly for short-term objectives.

7. Behavioral objectives of training are often imprecise.

8. Training programs external to the agency sometimes teach techniques and methods contrary to practices of the participant's organization.

9. Timely information about external training programs is often difficult to obtain.

10. The employee development specialist provides limited counseling and consulting services to the rest of the organization.

From Salinger, R. D. *Disincentives to Effective Employee Training and Development.* Washington, D.C.: U.S. Civil Service Commission Bureau of Training, 1973.

clear to top management. This results in the failure of top management to appropriately budget and plan for training or to provide rewards or support for effective training. In turn, these disincentives affect the organization in various negative ways, which include supervisors having difficulty performing their jobs while employees are in training. Also, since there is little participation by top management or supervisors in the needs assessment and development process, training programs often teach techniques and methods contrary to the practices of the organization.

The process underlying appropriate analysis suggests an interactive system. First, the training organization needs the information from the working organization in order to design effective training systems. Just as important, it is necessary for the training program to gain the cooperation of the working organization in order to have appropriate support for the training system. This suggests an interactive give and take relationship to work out the necessary goals, relationships, and so on. It also means that it is necessary to work out organizational conflicts before the instructional program is designed and implemented. Glaser and Taylor (1973) reported on case studies which examined factors that determine the success of applied research. One of the interesting applicable findings of research on the design of training systems is that successful studies were characterized by highly motivated persons who developed, early in the program, a two-way communication network. The projects had early and active contacts with all pertinent parties. In many cases, this involved resolving many conflicts. One particular vignette from these case studies focused on this issue.

> When a group of people or a team are truly involved and participating
> . . . they look ahead and conceive of their role in time and space in such a
> manner that includes what they see themselves doing in relation to the
> project. They usually attempt to interject their own pet theories and
> questions. . . . At the very least there's usually a rather heated discussion
> to work out the details, whether they be of an administrative nature or
> concern the ideas embodied in the design. . . . (p. 142)

A critical parameter in these case studies was the behavior of the person heading the team. Successful investigators negotiated differences, cleared up misunderstandings and strongly discouraged members of their group from adopting a "we versus they" attitude. The less successful studies were more insular and were characterized as having "tunnel vision." One suspects in training effort that the persons who eventually suffer as a result of organizational tunnel vision are the trainees who eventually have to transfer from the training department to the on-the-job·work organization.

The actual components of an organizational analysis are dependent upon the type of program being instituted and the characteristics of the organization. To be perfectly candid, it is only recently that industrial–organizational psychologists have begun to realize how important these issues are in the implementation of their programs. Thus, the procedures and issues are not completely understood. Also, the scope of the organizational analysis is probably dependent on a number of variables, including who is to be trained, what type of training is contemplated, the size of the organization, and so on. However, it is possible to begin examining some of the concerns and to make suggestions about some of the procedures that can be used to collect the necessary information. The following broad categories should be considered.

The Specific Goals

When organizational goals are not considered in the implementation of training programs, objectives and criteria which ensue from the needs assessment process are not evaluated. Later, the organizations are not able to specify their achievements because they have not collected the necessary information. Clearly, if the goals are not specified, it is not very likely that they are included in the design of the instructional program. Lynton and Pareek (1967) describe a program that successfully trains foreign engineers but does not meet the goals of the organization.

> Perhaps the most striking example of the dangers of paying inadequate attention to this dimension is the cumulative residue in industrially advanced countries of newly trained managerial and technical personnel from overseas. In the last 20 years, 30,000 foreign engineers alone have remained in the United States after completing their training. That they are able to make a living in competition with native Americans confirms their individual competence. Even if many stayed on because of attractive living standards, others did so because they were trained "out" of their country in the same way that school in a less developed country such as India seems to educate young people "out of their village." The training qualified them for settings and conditions that do not (yet) exist at home. This may be good for the individual, i.e., good education. As training, that is, for achieving development in their home organizations, such overseas training has obviously been unrealistic and unsuitable. (p. 32)[1]

If the goals of the trainee's home country included the return of the trainee, the program was a failure. The program may have failed because there was no job commensurate with the skills developed, but the specification of the goals would have provided the first step toward a solution.

Similarly, organizations might expect training programs to provide trainees with expectations about the job or particular views toward performance requirements. It is not unusual, for example, to discover that police training programs are devoted to skill requirements (for example, operating a police vehicle or utilizing firearms) or information requirements (knowing the difference between a felony and misdemeanor). Yet, organizational analyses often discover that there are organizational expectations regarding interpersonal relationships with the public and concern for all citizens regardless of race, color, or creed. Obviously, if these organizational philosophies and emphases are not clearly defined and specified during the needs assessment phase, they will not be considered in the design of the training program and at best will receive only passing attention in the instructional sequence. In this case, the problem is further complicated by the fact that it is a lot easier to teach weapons procedure than to instruct in the topic of interpersonal relations. Thus, certain topics may be deemphasized and sometimes organizations only become aware that they have a problem when they are facing a series of complaints. At that point, everyone wonders why the organizational objectives were not translated into

---

[1] From Lynton, R. P., & Pareek, U. *Training for Development.* Copyright 1967 by Richard D. Irwin, Inc.

training and job requirements. In short, many training programs are based upon teaching skill requirements rather than the unspecified and unidentified organizational objectives. Yet, paradoxically, organizations often judge the value of a program on the basis of their own objectives which were never specified, never considered in the design of the program, and never utilized in designing the evaluation model. Thus, the financial cost of some instructional programs results in their early demise because the instructional system analysis did not identify that variable as an organizational objective.

The history of training programs for the hard-core unemployed (HCU) reflects similar problems. Many programs failed to specify organizational objectives that go beyond the components of work ordinarily stemming from job analysis. Miller and Zeller (1967) state the problem this way: "It might have been helpful to have included within the training experience itself practice in job hunting, assistance in contacting employers before the end of training, and following-up counseling and job-placement help" (p. 31). The themes of job placement, counseling, and attention to the needs of the trainee appear in most programs that have evidence of success. In some cases, the attention is manifested by health care for individuals who previously were not able to attend training because of illness. In other cases, the consideration is careful transportation directions because the trainees cannot find their way to the training or job site. It appears that training programs cannot just attend to job skills but must also consider the trainee as an individual within a social system. In many instances, the trainee not only lacks job skills but also is not knowledgeable about many aspects of being a worker, such as health care, transportation, child care, promptness, and so on. These factors make careful organizational analysis and needs assessment procedures imperative. It is a formidable task to require all relevant persons to express their goals related to the instructional program. Often, this involves extensive interviewing with the various customers of the training effort, such as top level management, direct supervisors, trainees, and union representatives. However, the effort often results in goals which the program should address. Also, as indicated in the next section, the interviews often uncover conflicts that, if left unresolved, could undermine the training effort.

The Determination of the Organizational Training Climate

As complex as the specification of systemwide organizational objectives appear to be, the determination of objectives alone will not do the job. Unfortunately, many situations are marked by organizational conflicts, which are very disruptive. For example, conflicts between government sponsors of the program, employers, and training institutions can completely disrupt HCU programs (Goodman, 1969). Many of these conflicts are based upon the different parties to the program having different sets of equally unspecified goals and expectations. Thus, the community training organizations might see their role as introducing people into the world of work, while the employer is concerned with obtaining and retraining people at a minimum cost. When these conflicts remain unidentified they remain unresolved, and the result is a climate with conflicting goals and objectives which eventually undermines the potential success of the HCU.

The importance of a supportive organizational training climate is documented by the Baumgartel and Jeanpierre (1972) study of 240 managers who attended programs in India designed to promote the introduction of advanced technology. They found that managers only utilized skills they had gained back in their home setting when the organizational climate was favorable. This was especially true for low status managers. In their study, the climate which facilitated the transfer of learning back home consisted of the organization stimulating and approving innovation and technology; management's willingness to spend money for training; free and open communication among the management group; and the expression by the organizations of their desire for managers to use the knowledge gained in management courses.

The study of Salinger (1973) discussed previously in this chapter characterizes the negative consequences of a poor climate. In her study, top management had a generally negative view of training and no direct knowledge of its benefits. This resulted in a system which failed to reward managers for effective training efforts and in failure to plan or budget for training. It is not difficult to guess that whatever training was provided did not serve much of a purpose for either the individual or the organization. Certainly, the reward structure would not tend to lead the managers to support the skills of the trainees. More likely, there are insidious conflicts that (with a magic wand) the training program is somehow supposed to resolve. Even assuming that the training program could be appropriately designed in such a situation, it is likely that it would succumb to the conflict.

A recent experience of mine concerning these issues was especially illuminating because everyone I told about the incident responded with similar types of experiences. I was invited by an organization's top management to design a needs assessment package which would be used to establish rating scales for performance appraisal. As part of that process, I requested that the first meeting be with a union-management committee which I had heard about from top management. The committee had representatives from all parts of the organization. The hostility in the atmosphere at the meeting was made quite apparent by questions like "What are you trying to sell us?," "Did you ever do this type of work before?," "Are you trying to stick us with a system you developed for someone else?" Finally, after several hours of "conversation," I learned that this committee had at the request of top management developed an earlier plan for the project. After countless hours of volunteer time, they submitted a report. On the same day their report was submitted, they were informed that an outside consultant had been asked to perform the same activity. Unfortunately for me, I was the chosen consultant. I decided not even to try to begin the project. Instead we arranged for meetings between top management, the committee, and our research team to work out everyone's feelings and to establish appropriate roles for each group. Eventually, we proceeded with the project with everyone's cooperation. Months later, members of the committee noted that if we had not met with them and if we had not resolved these difficulties no one in the organization would have cooperated during the needs assessment; they had intended to subvert the entire needs assessment process. I have no doubt that they would have accomplished their purpose.

The temptation for the training analyst in these types of situations is to ignore the conflict and hope it will go away. However, conflicts do not usually go away; they usually become more troublesome. Perhaps, more seriously, some intervention programs exacerbate the conflict and the program itself is blamed for the failure. The only solution is to perform the organizational analyses, determine the conflicts, and resolve the issues. Thus, part of the needs assessment process is the clarification of the objectives upon which the program will be developed and evaluated. In many cases, the solution to these types of problems is not training programs but conflict resolution procedures, which must first be used to resolve such difficulties.

The Identification of Relevant External System Factors

The preceding sections on organizational analysis have identified issues related to the failure to specify organizational goals and the problems of organizational conflicts. The issue examined in this section is the failure to recognize the importance of the interacting constraints acting on an organization and their effects upon training programs. These considerations could be treated as a failure to specify organizational goals or as organizational conflicts. However, external constraints are becoming a very serious problem in the design of training programs. Therefore, they are treated as a separate section.

The design of instructional programs is affected by legal, social, economic, and political factors. Interrelationships of these variables should be carefully specified during organizational analysis. An example of these factors is provided by Salinger's study (1973), which found instances of writing and typing styles having been taught to government clerical workers that were prohibited on the job. The discrimination suits arising from failure to provide training and promotional opportunities have important implications for the needs assessment process, the design of programs, the evaluation of programs, the selection of participants, and even the type of records that must be maintained. It should be noted that the constraints of fair employment legislation are only an illustration of the large number of factors that must be considered. In other cases, the constraint might be a technological change, which would result in new goals, new types of trainees, or new jobs. In yet other cases, it might be new federal or state safety or environmental requirements that affect the objectives of training programs. Again, it must be noted that the solution to some of these problems does not involve design of training programs. Instead, it might require organizational responses, such as the resolution of conflicts, job redesign, or any of a variety of different approaches. Thus, one critical aspect of the organizational analysis is to determine what problems actually exist and what interventions are necessary. It would not be unusual for an organization to believe it had a "simple training problem" when the difficulties were actually related to other issues within the organization, such as a poor selection system, management conflict, or poor job design.

Resource Analysis

It is difficult to establish working objectives without determining the human and physical resources that are available. This analysis should include a description of the layout of the establishment, the type of equipment available, and the financial resources. More important, human-resource needs must include personnel planning that projects future requirements. Too often, organizations respond to personnel needs only in a crisis situation—for example, when they realize they are losing 5% of their work force through retirement. Few organizations plan for change within the organization. Yet, people leave to take jobs in different organizations, or they retire, or they are promoted within the same organization. Typically, this results in a series of changes in order to fill the jobs that are suddenly available. There is often a frantic search to determine if anyone within the organization has performed similar tasks or if anyone has the knowledge, skills, and abilities necessary to perform the job. Often decisions are made to move outside the organization or to quickly design a training program to provide instruction for persons inside the organization to prepare them for the new job. Progression charts, which show who is available for promotion, the knowledge, skills, and abilities the person has acquired, and the training necessary for performance of the new job, are extremely valuable as planning documents. Table 3.2, designed by McGehee and Thayer (1961), presents some of the important resource questions that should be asked.

Some Organizational Analysis Questions

The issues discussed in this section indicate the importance of organizational analysis procedures as part of a needs assessment. As a result of this type of analysis, it may be possible both to identify organiza-

TABLE 3.2   Data required for person resource inventory

1. Number of employees in the job classification
2. Number of employees needed in the job classification
3. Age of each employee in the job classification
4. Level of skill required by the job of each employee
5. Level of knowledge required by the job of each employee
6. Attitude of each employee toward job and company
7. Level of job performance, quality and quantity, of each employee
8. Level of skills and knowledge of each employee for other jobs
9. Potential replacements for this job outside company
10. Potential replacements for this job within company
11. Training time required for potential replacements
12. Training time required for a novice
13. Rate of absenteeism from this job
14. Turnover in this job for specified period of time
15. Job specification for the job

From *Training in Business and Industry,* by W. McGehee and P. W. Thayer. ©1961 by John Wiley & Sons, Inc. Reproduced by permission.

tional goals and to resolve potential organizational conflicts. The instructional program is then more likely to be relevant and to produce transfer to the work organization. It is even possible to suggest that training analysts might take a self-diagnostic test to determine whether training is really ready to begin. Some of the questions that could be asked are listed below. To the extent that the analyst is left with a feeling of uncertainty in answering these questions, there is probably a lot of work to do before implementing a training program.

Are there unspecified organizational goals which should be translated into training objectives or criteria?

Are the various levels in organization committed to the training objectives?

Have the various levels and/or interacting units in the organization participated in the development of the program beginning at the end assessment?

Are key personnel ready both to accept the behavior of the trainees and to serve as models of the appropriate behavior?

Will trainees be rewarded on the job for the appropriate learned behavior?

Is training being utilized as a way of overcoming other organizational problems or organizational conflicts that require other types of solutions?

Is top management willing to commit the necessary resources to maintain work organizations while individuals are being trained?

TASK AND KNOWLEDGE, SKILL, AND ABILITY ANALYSIS

Just as an organizational analysis is necessary to determine the organizational objectives, a task analysis is used to determine the instructional objectives that will be related to the performances of particular activities or job operations. The task analysis results in a statement of the activities or work operations performed on the job and the conditions under which the job is performed. It is not a description of the worker but rather a description of the job.

As presented in Figure 3.1, Pearlman (1980) shows the various levels of analysis in looking at a job.

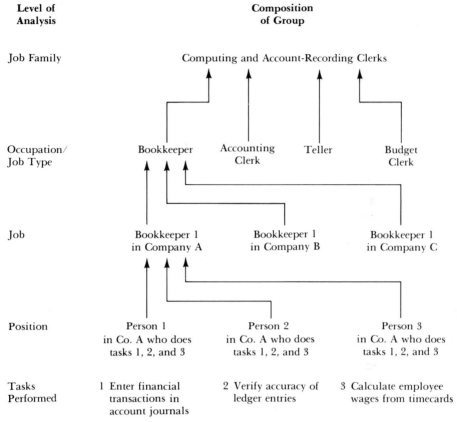

Level of Analysis	Composition of Group

FIGURE 3.1   Examples of different types of job groupings at different levels of analysis. (*From "Job Families: A Review and Discussion of Their Implications for Personnel Selection," by K. Pearlman. In* Psychological Bulletin, *1980, 87, pp. 1–18. Copyright 1980 by the American Psychological Association. Reprinted by permission.*)

In the example presented, the tasks performed are the fundamental units of analysis. They determine the groupings at each of the levels in the diagram. Pearlman thus identifies three of the many tasks performed by persons in the same position in Company A who hold the job of Bookkeeper 1. He also labels four of the occupation/job types (bookkeeper, accounting clerk, teller, and budget clerk) which constitute the job family computer and account-recording clerks.

Task analysis consists of several components, each of which further delineates the performance required to succeed at the task. Thus, the analysis begins with a task description, followed by a detailed specification of tasks and a scaling of tasks on various dimensions, such as criticality, frequency of occurrence, and so on.

Task Description

The task description serves as a job summary statement describing the major focus and duties of the job. The statement should completely describe all the essential activities of the job, including "worker's actions and the results accomplished; the machines, tools, equipment, and/or work aids used; materials, products, subject matter, or services involved; and the requirements made of the worker" (*Handbook for Analyzing Jobs,* 1972, p. 30). The statement includes the characteristics of the environment (for example, noise or extreme temperature variations) and any special features (for instance, stress) that further delineate the job. A short list of some of the environmental conditions that could potentially affect many jobs is presented in Table 3.3.

The description should contain material about each of the kinds of activities involved, either in order of their importance or in the chronological order in which they are performed. An interesting example of a job description, presented in the U.S. Department of Labor *Handbook for Analyzing Jobs* (1972), is for the job of manager of a

TABLE 3.3   Environmental conditions and physical demands

Environmental conditions	*Physical demands*

1. Environment
    Inside _____ %   Teamwork _____ %
    Outside _____ %   Proximity _____ %
                              Isolation _____ %
2. Extreme cold with or without temperature changes
3. Extreme heat with or without temperature changes
4. Wet and/or humid
5. Noise
    Estimated maximum number of decibels
6. Vibration
7. Hazards
    Mechanical
    Electrical
    Burns
    Explosives
    Radiant energy
    Other
8. Atmospheric conditions
    Fumes
    Odors
    Dusts
    Mists
    Gases
    Poor ventilation
    Other
	1. Strength (lifting, carrying,
	    pushing, and/or pulling)
	    Sedentary work
	    Light work
	    Medium work
	    Heavy work
	    Very heavy work
	2. Climbing and/or balancing
	3. Stooping, kneeling, crouching,
	    and/or crawling
	4. Reaching, handling, fingering,
	    and/or feeling
	5. Talking and/or hearing
	6. Seeing

From Manpower Administration, U.S. Department of Labor. *Handbook for Analyzing Jobs.* Washington, D.C.: U.S. Government Printing Office, 1972.

hunt club. The description states that this job consists of the following activities:

> Coordinates hunt activities of hunt club and supervises workers engaged in care and training of horses and hounds used in fox hunting. Purchases feed and supplies for animals. Supervises personnel engaged in training animals, in detection of early stages of animals' illness, and in repairing and repainting stables and kennels. Assists master of foxhounds in setting up obstacles on hunt course, in scenting hunt trail when live quarry is not used, and in staging horse shows. Rides with participants of hunt to control hounds and times horses, using stopwatch. (p. 186)

Another example is for a person who arranges for airline passenger reservations. This description states:

> Makes and confirms reservations for passengers' scheduled airline flights. Arranges reservations and routing for passengers at request of supervisor or customer, using timetables, airline manuals, reference guides and tariff book. Inspects availability board to determine seats available, and prepares reservation card. Telephones customer or supervisor to advise of changes in flight plan to cancel or confirm reservation. (p. 188)

The handbook suggests that the descriptions be terse, in the present tense, and started with an action verb. Each word should give necessary information, and words that have more than one meaning should be avoided.

Development of Task Statements

The next phase in the task analysis is to completely specify the tasks performed. The collection of this type of information involves a number of techniques, including interviewing job experts and observing the job being performed. These techniques are described in a later section in this chapter. The rules for the specification of tasks have been evolving for a number of years. The following summary is a synthesis of the work of a number of individuals (U.S. Department of Labor, 1972; Ammerman & Pratzner, 1977; Prien, Goldstein, & Macey, 1985).

1. Use a terse, direct style avoiding long involved sentences that can confuse the organization. The present tense should be used. Words that do not give necessary information should be avoided. Examples of task statements from a study of the job of police sergeant (Bartlett & Goldstein, 1977) are presented in Table 3.4.

TABLE 3.4   Examples of task statements for police sergeant

Counsel employees regarding their future with the organization.
Review performance appraisals completed by subordinate managers for accuracy and completeness.
Adjust work schedules to meet emergency conditions.
Brief police officers on recent court rulings which affect their work activities.
Inspect police vehicles to determine that they are properly serviced and maintained.

Adapted from *Job Analysis of Police Officers and Sergeants,* by C. J. Bartlett and I. L. Goldstein. Unpublished data, College Park, MD: University of Maryland, 1977.

2. Each sentence should begin with a functional verb which identifies the primary job operation. It is important for the word to specifically describe the work to be accomplished.

3. The statement should describe *what* the work does, *how* the worker does it and to *whom/what*, and *why*. The following illustration stems from the job of a secretary:

What?	To Whom/What?
Sorts	*correspondence forms and reports*

Why?	How?
in order to facilitate filing them	*alphabetically.*

The next example comes from the job of a supervisor:

What?	To Whom/What?	Why?
Inform	*next shift supervisor*	*of departmental status*

How?
through written or verbal reports.

Examination of the tasks illustrated above and in Table 3.4 reveals that the development of task statements is not limited by the particular type of job or task dimensions.

4. The tasks should be stated completely but they should not be so detailed that it becomes a time and motion study. For example, a task could be "slides fingertips over machine edges to detect ragged edges and burrs." However, it would not be useful for the identification of tasks to say that the worker raises his or her hand onto table, places fingers on part, presses fingers on part, moves fingers to the right six inches, and so on. Rather, each statement should refer to a whole task in a way that makes sense. Usually, the breaking down of tasks into a sequence of activities is useful when the task is being taught in the training program. However, that step doesn't occur until the total task domain is identified and it is determined which tasks should be taught in the training program. Similarly, mention of trivial tasks like unlocking the file cabinet or turning out the lights when leaving the office should usually be avoided.

Determination of Relevant Task Dimensions

Once the tasks are specified, it is necessary to collect judgments concerning their relevance for the design of training programs. These judgments of tasks are ordinarily collected from groups of subject matter experts such as experienced workers, supervisors, and personnel specialists. The determination of what questions to ask about a task is an important issue. For example, it would not ordinarily be useful to design a training program for tasks which are not important, not performed frequently, and which are easily learned on the job. Similarly, a task that is not very important, frequently performed, and easy to learn would not require the attention that should be given to an infrequently performed but critical task that is difficult to learn. Thus, after the tasks are identified, it is necessary to decide which questions should be asked about each task. Some examples of the dimensions which can be addressed are presented below (adapted from Ammerman & Pratzner, 1977).

1. Importance
   a. Importance in terms of criticality of task for the job.
   b. Importance in terms of consequences of error in performing task.
2. Time-Frequency
   a. Tasks actually performed last year.
   b. Frequency with which tasks were performed on the job.
   c. Most recent time the task was performed on the job.
   d. Time spent performing the task on the job.
3. Difficulty of Learning Task
   a. How difficult is it to learn task?
   b. How difficult is it to learn the task on the job?
   c. How much opportunity is given to learn task on the job?
4. Difficulty of Performing Task
   a. How difficult is it to perform task?
   b. Why is it difficult to perform task (complexity of task, lack of training, monotonous work task, and so on)?
5. Miscellaneous
   a. Where should task be learned (from training to on the job, etc.)?
   b. What level of worker proficiency on task is expected after training?

The particular questions that are asked depend on the purpose of the task analysis. If the purpose of the analysis is to determine which tasks should be learned on the job and which tasks should be learned in training, then answers to questions like "How difficult is it to learn this task on the job?" and "Where should the task be learned?" are very useful. Just as it is important to carefully select the questions to meet the purposes of the analysis, it is also critical to carefully design the response dimensions for each question. An example of a set of task importance dimensions and instructions which were used for the police sergeant tasks listed in Table 3.4 is presented in Table 3.5. Similar types of response scales can be built for each of the questions about the task. The data collected are analyzed to determine average responses, variability, degree of agreement between different judges, and so on. Sometimes, in these types of analyses, the researchers discover that different groups of judges, for example, supervisors and employees, don't agree on what tasks are required to perform the job. In those instances, it would be important to resolve the disagreement before training programs are designed. It should be noted that the type of information collected in task analyses is useful for decisions that extend beyond the training program. For example, it is also possible to develop questions related to what tasks individuals should be able to perform before being selected for the job.

TABLE 3.5   Instructions for scaling task importance items for the job of police sergeant

---

Task Importance Checklist

On the following pages there is a list of tasks performed by members of the police department. We need to know the importance of performing these tasks by persons at your rank and in your job category (i.e., patrol, investigation, administration and support, or community relations).

Please respond to each of these items according to the following scale:

A	OF NO IMPORTANCE	Errors in the performance of this task would not be likely to have any consequence to the unit or department and would require no corrective action. How one performs this task should not make any difference in evaluation of performance.
B	OF MINOR IMPORTANCE	Errors or poor performance on this task would have only minor consequences for the unit or department and could be easily corrected. How one performs this task should not make a great deal of difference in the evaluation of performance.
C	OF IMPORTANCE	Errors or poor performance on this task would create a problem for the unit or department and would require correction. Competence at this task should be expected of someone who is average or above.
D	OF HIGH IMPORTANCE	Continued errors or poor performance on this task would seriously hamper the effectiveness of the unit or department and corrective action would be mandatory. Consistent effectiveness at this task should be an indication of above average performance.
E	OF CRITICAL IMPORTANCE	Errors or poor performance at this task would probably result in a serious incident such as personal injury, a bad image for the unit or department, or a loss in morale. Correction or compensation for such an error would be difficult. Consistent effectiveness at this task should be an indication of outstanding performance.

If some of these tasks are totally irrelevant to your rank and job category, do not make a response for that phrase. Leave it blank.

Adapted from *Job Analysis of Police Officers and Sergeants,* by C. J. Bartlett and I. L. Goldstein. Unpublished data, College Park, MD: University of Maryland, 1977.

Development of Knowledge, Skill, and Ability Analysis

The organizational analysis and the task analysis provide a picture of the task and the environmental setting. However, the task analysis provides a specification of the required job operations regardless of the individual performing the task. There remains a very critical part of the total process—the human being. Two populations must be considered; the first consists of those persons who are already performing the job, while the second involves those persons who will be trained.

In some instances these are the same individuals, but other cases involve new trainees. Since these new individuals differ from those already performing the task, it is necessary to examine this second population. The key issue is what personal capabilities are necessary to effectively perform the job. After these capabilities are specified it becomes possible to analyze the performance of the target population to determine whether training is necessary.

Specification of Human Capabilities

There are several different systems for specifying human capabilities. One system advocated by Prien (for example, Prien, 1977; Goldstein, Macey, & Prien, 1981) emphasizes the knowledge, skills, and abilities (KSAs) necessary to effectively perform the tasks developed in the task analysis. Prien defines these categories as follows:

> Knowledge (K) is the foundation upon which abilities and skills are built. Knowledge refers to an organized body of knowledge usually of a factual or procedural nature, which, if applied makes adequate job performance possible. It should be noted that possession of knowledge does not insure that it will be used. Examples of knowledge, skill and ability characteristics are presented in Table 3.6.
>
> Skill (S) refers to the capability to perform job operations with ease and precision. Most often skills refer to psychomotor type activities. The specification of a skill usually implies a performance standard that is usually required for effective job operations.
>
> Ability (A) usually refers to cognitive capabilities necessary to perform a job function. Most often abilities require the application of some knowledge base.

Prien recommends the use of interview procedures with job supervisors, personnel specialists, or experienced successful incumbents to develop the KSA information. Often, the best procedure is to supply a panel of five to eight knowledgeable persons with a list of the tasks

TABLE 3.6   Examples of knowledge, skills, and ability characteristics

Knowledge Characteristics
Knowledge of standard accounting principles and procedures
Knowledge of the state and local regulations concerning fire inspection practices
Knowledge of points of wear on the labeling machine
Knowledge of needs assessment procedures for use in the design of training programs

Skills Characteristics
Skill in adjusting cutting blades on labeling machine
Skill in operating a motor vehicle during a high speed chase
Skill in simultaneously adjusting volume and temperature of water spray

Ability Characteristics
Ability to shift priorities in response to a change in supply conditions
Ability to evaluate the capabilities of subordinates for promotion
Ability to identify causes of employee discrimination complaints
Ability to recognize the usefulness of information supplied by others

Adapted from Prien, E., Goldstein, I. L., and Macey, W., 1985.

(developed from the task analysis) and ask the following types of questions.

> Describe the characteristics of good and poor employees on (*name of task*).
> Think of someone you know who is better than anyone else at (*name of task*). What is the reason they do it so well?
> What does a person need to know in order to (*name of task*)?
> Ask panel to recall concrete examples of effective or ineffective performance. Then lead a discussion to explain causes or reasons.
> If you are going to hire a person to perform (*name of task*), what kinds of KSAs would you want the person to have?
> What do you expect persons to learn in training that would make them effective at (*name of task*)?

On the basis of this input, the job analyst would obtain the information necessary to write KSA statements. Some of the guidelines for such statements include:

> 1. Maintains a reasonable balance between generality and specificity. Exactly how general or specific the KSA statement should be will depend on its intended use. When the information is being used to design a training program, it must be specific enough to suggest what must be learned in training.
>
> 2. Avoid simply restating a task or duty statement. Such an approach is redundant and usually provides very little new information about the job. It is necessary to ask what knowledge, skills, and abilities are necessary to perform the task. For example, a task might be to "analyze hiring patterns to determine whether company practices are consistent with fair employment practices guidelines." Clearly, one of the knowledge components for this task will involve "knowledge concerning federal, state and local guidelines on fair employment practices." Another component might involve "ability to use statistical procedures appropriate to perform these analyses." Both the knowledge and ability components would have implications in the design of any training program to teach individuals to perform the required task.
>
> 3. Avoid including trivial information when writing KSA statements. For example, for a supervisor's job "knowledge of how to order personal office supplies" might be trivial. Usually, it is possible to avoid many trivial items by emphasizing the development of KSAs only for those tasks that have been identified in the task analysis as important for the performance of job operations. However, because the omission of key KSAs is a serious error, borderline examples should be included. When the KSAs are judged according to their criticality (as described next), unimportant KSAs will be eliminated.

The final step in this procedure is similar to the phase in the analysis of task statements where the items are judged along relevant dimensions. Some of the dimensions which might be used for KSA statements are:

> Difficulty to learn—the item is judged on how difficult it is to gain competence with reference to the knowledge, skill, or ability for job performance.
> Importance—the item is judged on the criticality of the knowledge, skill, or ability for job performance.

Opportunity to acquire—judgments are collected pertaining to the opportunity to acquire the requisite knowledge, skill, or ability on the job.

As discussed in the task analysis section, the questions and response scales must be specifically designed for the purpose of the needs assessment. It is then possible to obtain ratings on the scales for each of the KSAs and use that information for program design. For example, it might be useful to design training content based upon a measure which identifies the important KSAs necessary for job performance, with the main emphasis being on KSAs for which there is a minimum opportunity to learn on the job.

A second type of analysis procedure, described in the *Handbook for Analyzing Jobs* (1972), emphasizes a trait approach. This type of analysis is an interpretation of the job in terms of human attributes necessary for success. This difficult specification is based on inferences drawn from the analyses of organization and task components. Thorndike (1949) notes that a sound set of categories is required to describe the qualities of behavior. He suggests that these categories should have the following characteristics:

1. They should be comprehensive and systematic in covering the complete range of traits or qualities.
2. Whenever possible, they should be independent.
3. They should be psychologically meaningful in terms of behavior.
4. They should suggest testing operations for their measurement.

The *Handbook for Analyzing Jobs* (1972) includes a general list of worker traits, with a series of behavioral descriptions related to different levels of performance for each of the traits. These traits include categories based on training time, aptitudes, temperaments, and interests. As an example of these groupings, the aptitude and temperament categories are presented in Table 3.7. To illustrate the details of each aptitude, Table 3.8 presents the levels of numerical aptitude. Note that the trait approach still requires the specification of characteristics. Simply stating that numerical ability is necessary for the job does not provide the kind of input necessary to design training programs.

PERSON ANALYSIS

As stated by McGehee and Thayer (1961), the final step in determining training needs focuses on whether the individual employees need training and exactly what training is required. At this stage, the needs assessment has already accomplished an organizational analysis which permits understanding of where the training systems fit in the work environment and what facilitators and inhibitors exist. Also, the task analysis has determined what important tasks are performed and the knowledge, skills, and abilities analysis has established which KSAs are important for task performance. The KSA analysis provides considerable information for the person analysis, including data indicating whether the KSA should be learned before entering the job, on the job, during training, etc. However, in the person analysis, the emphasis is not in determining which KSAs are necessary but rather in assessing how well the actual employees perform the KSAs required by the job. In order to actually perform a person analysis, it becomes necessary to develop measures of criteria which are indicators of performance. This will be discussed in Chapter 5. However, it should be clear that many of these criteria are important for a number of purposes in the design of training programs. We can use the criteria to assess performance before training, immediately after training, and on the job. The important

TABLE 3.7 Worker traits

Aptitudes are the specific capacities or abilities required of an individual in order to facilitate the learning of some task or job duty. The following are the aptitudes included in this component:

G	Intelligence
V	Verbal
N	Numerical
S	Spatial
P	Form Perception
Q	Clerical Perception
K	Motor Coordination
F	Finger Dexterity
M	Manual Dexterity
E	Eye–Hand–Foot Coordination
C	Color Discrimination

Temperaments, for the purpose of collecting occupational data, are defined as "personal traits" required of a worker by specific job–worker situations. This component consists of the following 10 factors:

D-DCP	Adaptability to accepting responsibility for the direction, control, or planning of an activity.
F-FIF	Adaptability to situations involving the interpretation of feelings, ideas, or facts in terms of personal viewpoint.
I-INFLU	Adaptability to influencing people in their opinions, attitudes, or judgments about ideas or things.
J-SJC	Adaptability to making generalizations, evaluations, or decisions based on sensory or judgmental criteria.
M-MVC	Adaptability to making generalizations, evaluations, or decisions based on measurable or verifiable criteria.
P-DEPL	Adaptability to dealing with people beyond giving and receiving instructions.
R-REPCON	Adaptability to performing repetitive work, or to performing continuously the same work, according to set procedures, sequence, or pace.
S-PUS	Adaptability to performing under stress when confronted with emergency, critical, unusual, or dangerous situations or situations in which working speed and sustained attention are make-or-break aspects of the job.
T-STS	Adaptability to situations requiring the precise attainment of set limits, tolerances, or standards.
V-VARCH	Adaptability to performing a variety of duties, often changing from one task to another of a different nature without loss of efficiency or composure.

Adapted from Manpower Administration, U.S. Department of Labor. *Handbook for Analyzing Jobs.* Washington, D.C.: U.S. Government Printing Office, 1972.

TABLE 3.8 Numerical aptitude—the ability to perform arithmetic operations quickly and accurately

Level 1
Conducts research in fundamental mathematics, in application of mathematics, and in application of mathematical techniques to science, management, and other fields; solves or directs solutions to problems in various fields by mathematical methods.
Tests hypotheses and alternative theories.

Level 2
Applies principle of accounting to install and maintain operation of general accounting system.
Applies numerical reasoning to design or modify systems to provide records of assets, liabilities, and financial transactions; applies arithmetic principles to prepare accounts, records, and reports based on them; audits contracts, orders, and vouchers; prepares tax returns and other reports to government agencies.

Level 3
Sets up and operates X-ray unit to obtain photographs of internal structure of body, using standard formulas based on principles of algebra and geometry to computer amperage and voltage settings, exposure time, and distances of film from object and X-ray tube.

Level 4
Makes women's garments such as dresses, coats, and suits according to customer specifications and measurements.
Measures customer to determine dimensions of garment; adds and subtracts to adjust pattern to customer's dimensions.

From Manpower Administration, U.S. Department of Labor. *Handbook for Analyzing Jobs.* Washington, D.C.: U.S. Government Printing Office, 1972.

point in this section on person analysis is that the criteria can also be used to determine the capabilities of the persons on the job so that training is designed for the particular KSAs that are required by that population of persons. The results of the person analysis provide important clues to the proper strategy for developing training programs. If the performance is substandard and the analyses indicate that the personnel do not have the capabilities to perform the tasks, the training personnel must decide whether training could provide a solution to the problem or whether new personnel are needed. These analyses and the decisions that come from them are complex, and they interact with the information obtained throughout the entire needs assessment program. Few, if any, organizations can afford instructional programs on every aspect of the job.

In summary, an instructional program must be based on the characteristics of the group that will be placed in the training environment. If the program is intended for those persons already on the job, the data from the performance, task, and person analysis provide the required information for an analysis of the target population. However, if the target population is a new job or a new group of employees, the analyses are incomplete. Observers have commented on the differences in values between those students entering school and work situations today and those of preceding generations. Such differences must be considered in program design. For example, particular errors may occur on a job due to difficulties related to computer analysis ability. However, entering trainees may have the prerequisite skills in computer techniques and need less emphasis in that particular area. Thus, the organization may need different training programs for persons presently employed and those coming to the job.

Unfortunately, it is sometimes difficult to analyze the incoming target population because they are not presently employed. Potential solutions might consist of examining employees who have recently been hired or consulting with similar organizations that have recently hired trainees. The latter procedure must be performed carefully, because small differences between firms can radically change the characteristics of the entering population. Thus, two corporations with the same characteristics but differing locales (for example, rural versus urban) may attract employees with significantly different characteristics. It is necessary to match the characteristics of the target population to the requirements for successful performance.

It should also be clear that while this chapter focuses on tasks and knowledge, skills, and abilities as input to the training process, there are other aspects to the training process that need consideration. Thus, trainees are socialized into the organization by what happens in training. In some cases, they receive realistic job previews not only about their tasks but also about their organization. These issues and their relationship to training design are treated in Chapter 9 in the section on organizational entry, training, and socialization.

Summary

In summary, the results of task, person, and performance analysis can provide critical input information concerning such items as present level of performance, criticality of tasks and KSAs, frequency of occurrence, opportunity to learn, difficulty in learning on the job, and so on. These responses can be organized into composite indices which reflect the different judgments provided for the task and KSA statements. For example, one index can be developed to reflect the logic that the tasks most important to consider in the development of training content are those given the highest priority in the job, and which are also those for which it is difficult to acquire proficiency. Similarly, the content to be included in the training curriculum can be identified with reference to a composite index identifying the knowledge, skills, and abilities important for full job performance, and for which there is a minimum opportunity to learn on the job. The composite indices are thus evaluated to determine the content and priorities of the training curriculum.

In addition to providing input for the design of new instructional programs, the thoughtful application of job analysis procedures can provide useful input relevant to a variety of training development and evaluation questions. Some of the other potential applications include the following:

1. Examination of previously designed training programs—It is possible to compare the emphasis of training programs presently being used with the needs assessment information. This type of comparison could determine whether the emphasis in training is being placed on tasks and KSAs which are important and which are not easily learned on the job.

2. Design of trainee assessment instruments—Needs assessment information provides valuable information on the capabilities of trainees to perform the job appropriately. As such, the needs assessment procedures can provide input to design performance appraisal instruments to assess the capabilities of trainees at the end of training and on the job. It is also possible to design performance appraisal instruments to determine which employees presently occupying jobs might need further training.

3. Input to the interaction between selection systems and training systems—The determination of the task and person elements domains can provide input into the selection system by specifying the KSAs required to perform the various job tasks. The degree to which the selection system is able to identify and hire persons with various KSAs affects the design of the training system. For example, training programs should not emphasize those KSAs already in the repertoire of the trainee. Often this results in a training program which is not only more interesting but also less time consuming.

It is important to emphasize that the choice of a particular methodology should be based on an analysis of the particular application requiring job information. Further, even the choice of questions within a particular methodology is dependent upon the application. Thus, in some cases, criticality of performance information is important while in other cases opportunity to learn or information related to where learning takes place is the key issue. In other instances, a whole variety of questions must be addressed. The critical point is that thoughtful planning which considers the variety of methods and applications must precede any needs assessment effort. It is a waste of valuable resources to conduct a needs assessment effort only to discover that the wrong questions have been asked or the wrong problem solved. It is, of course, an even more serious waste of valuable resources to design a training program without a careful needs assessment. Unfortunately, even when needs assessment is performed and the training program is well designed, there appear to be instances when training does not result in learning being transferred onto the job. As noted in the earlier section on organizational analysis, it is necessary to realize that analyses of training programs force consideration of the fact that something learned in one environment (training) will be performed in another (on the job). Thus, the trainee will enter a new environment to be affected by all the interacting components that represent organizations today. Certainly there are some aspects of the environment which help determine the success or failure of training programs beyond the attributes the trainee must gain as a result of attending the instructional program. The reader is invited to review the organizational section. When the types of issues described in the organizational analysis are ignored, the advantages gained from careful task and person analysis are lost.

GATHERING JOB INFORMATION

This section will describe both sources of job information and various methods used to collect job information. There are many different methods for collecting information about the task and the organization. The purpose of these methods is to provide valid and reliable information; therefore, it is important to make sure an individual method does not bias the quality of the information. Unfortunately, this is more easily said than done. Each method has unique characteristics that can affect both the kinds and the quality of information obtained. An interview is dependent on the interviewer's skills and biases, while a mail questionnaire is subject to the sampling biases that occur when a substantial number of participants do not return the survey. It is important to be aware of these difficulties and to carefully design methodology to avoid potential sources of biased information.

This involves several steps. First, it is important to be aware of the potential problems in each of the methods and design the needs assessment to avoid as many difficulties as possible. Thus, interviewers should be trained and questionnaire systems should be designed to achieve maximum rates of return. Also, it is necessary to use more than one type of methodology. Each method is likely to produce information sources with particular biases. One way to avoid this difficulty is to use, for example, both interviews, job observations, and questionnaire methods; or, when interviews are being used, there should be both individual and group interviews, and there should be more than one interviewer. Another important point is that the respondents should represent cross samples of the organization who have relevant information about the job. Thus, in the organizational analysis where the concerns are issues such as unspecified organizational goals or organizational conflict, it is critical to involve top level management as well as the direct supervisors of the trainees. Also, it is important to involve all relevant parts of the work organization, including union representatives, personnel representatives, training representatives, and the like. Similarly, the collection of tasks and KSAs and judgments about these components (such as task criticality) should be collected from experienced job incumbents as well as direct supervisors. If the information collected is not consistent, the best approach of the training analyst is first to determine why this is so, rather than simply to design a training program. O'Reilly (1973) reported a study where there was widespread disagreement between supervisors and subordinates as to which tasks were performed at all. In this study, the analysts concluded that in many instances the supervisors were misreporting what their subordinates were actually required to do in their jobs. Whether those tasks should have been part of the job was not determined in this study. However, it is clear that more information was needed before it would be possible to design an effective training program.

While there are no hard and fast rules about conducting needs assessment, Steadham (1980) suggests several guidelines.

> Energy Conservation: Do not use so much time and effort in the assessment process that there is no energy left for the actual educational activity.
>
> Methods Potpourri, or Never Use One When Two Will Do: Select two or more methods in such a way that the advantages of one offset the disadvantages of another. There is strength in a good blend; improved reliability of the needs data is the result.
>
> Freedom to Respond: Each assessment method exerts a degree of control on its subject (your client). Reduce the control and increase the method's flexibility, to allow the client to respond in the way he/she considers important.
>
> Having Something Happen: Needs assessment efforts that never lead to a relevant response are useless. Be clear with the client system's decision makers that you expect an appropriate response to the assessment data. Reach an understanding before you begin the data collection and then stick to it. (p. 60)

Source of Task Information

A number of available sources contain information that is potentially useful in needs assessment analyses. The material is organized into two major categories—previous analyses of tasks and documentary materials.

Previous analyses of tasks.   Information on any series of tasks is usually available from government sources. For industrial tasks, the Manpower Administration (U.S. Department of Labor) has extensive materials related to worker functions, task requirements, and worker traits, as well as information related to the proper procedures for performing task analyses. The *Dictionary of Occupational Titles* (1965) presents brief analyses of job tasks and worker requirements for a large number of different occupations. Similar information is available in military and educational technical reports through the National Technical Information Service (for military documents) and the ERIC Clearinghouse on Educational Media and Technology (for educational documents).

Documentary materials.   There is also a substantial literature describing training programs and other aspects of organizations. It includes catalogs and descriptions prepared by the organization itself; technical literature prepared by trade associations, labor unions, and professional societies; pamphlets and books prepared by federal, state, and municipal departments in the appropriate field (health, education, or labor); and books and pamphlets generally related to the subject.

Previous needs assessment and documentary materials provide useful introductions to tasks being investigated. However, they are not substitutes for the extensive analysis that must be performed each time a training program is designed. Although the analysis of previous tasks describes the tasks as they are generally found in any setting, the literature search is not likely to produce the particular task, conditions, and target population required by the training analyst. In many cases, careful examination shows that only the names of the task or the job are the same. Even if the tasks are similar, organizational characteristics may demand a completely different program. These problems are often compounded in the examination of documentary materials in which particular viewpoints may affect the report. Documents published by different organizations (for example, labor or management) may make the same job very different. Thus, these sources provide information that is useful in the initial examination of the task, but the final analysis must be performed on the organization and task of immediate concern.

Methods of Collecting Task Information

As indicated previously, there are many different methods of collecting task information, each with its own advantages and disadvantages. It is important to be aware of these limitations and to carefully design the needs assessment methodology to take advantage of the benefits of each method. Steadham has produced a table describing the various methods (see Table 3.9).

EXAMPLES OF NEEDS ASSESSMENT TECHNIQUES

Functional job analyses.   This system of job analysis is primarily based upon the work of Fine (Fine, 1978; Olson, Fine, Myers, & Jennings, 1981). He emphasizes the fact that the whole person is involved in job performance and the method of observation must clearly specify what to look for, record, and emphasize in order to have total coverage. This system focuses on tasks as the fundamental unit. Fine's format for task statements includes the following questions.

> Who?
> What action?
> To accomplish what immediate results?
> With what tools/equipment/work aids?
> Upon what instructions? (p. 7)

An example of a task statement using these criteria is presented in Table 3.10 for a person who operates a grader. Fine's system requires that the tasks be specified thoroughly enough to be able to classify the worker according to the degree of involvement with data, people, and things. The various levels of involvement for each of these are as follows:

Data	*People*	*Things*
6. Synthesizing	7. Mentoring	3. Precision Working
5. Coordinating	6. Negotiating	Setting Up
Innovating	5. Supervising	Operating–Controlling II
4. Analyzing	4. Consulting	2. Manipulating
3. Computing	Instructing	Operating–Controlling I
Compiling	Treating	Driving–Controlling
2. Copying	3. Coaching	Starting Up
1. Comparing	Persuading	1. Handling
	Diverting	Feeding–Offbearing
	2. Exchanging Information	Tending
	1. Taking Instructions–	
	Helping, Serving	

The scales are designed to capture all of the ways that persons function to accomplish their work. Also, each of the functions are designed to include the activities listed below that activity but exclude those listed above. Thus, on the people scale, a task requiring a person to operate at level 2 (exchanging information) means that the person also performs level 1 functions (taking instruction) but not those functions listed at 3 (coaching) and above.

To develop this system, the job analyst would both observe the job and work with subject matter experts familiar with the particular job. As a result of this analysis, task statements such as the one presented in Table 3.10 would be developed. Then, for that task, the data, people, and things items would be derived. For example, for the tasks listed in the table, the following types of sample functions were determined.

Data	*People*	*Things*
Determine best procedures for doing work	Take continuing instructions from supervision as necessary	Adjust front wheel to counteract side-thrust
Check direction of drainage requirements	Respond to signals from other operators and grade checkers	Manipulate controls to position blade to desired angle of economic operation

Based upon an analysis of all the data, people, and thing functions, the task is classified. For example, the task of grader (in Table 3.10) is classified as compiling (for data), taking instructions (for people), and for operating–controlling II (for things). Fine also indicates the degree of involvement with each of these functions by assigning 100 points to be spread out among the data, people, and thing functions. For this task, 25% is assigned to data, 10% to people, and 65% to things, indicating the high relative emphasis of the grader task to the kinds of functions found in the things category. On the basis of this type of information, Fine completes the information found in Table 3.10. Thus, he lists the performance standards at a descriptive level which indicates the

TABLE 3.9 Advantages and disadvantages of nine basic needs assessment techniques

	Advantages	Disadvantages
Observation	• can be as technical as time-motion studies or as functionally or behaviorally specific as observing a new board or staff member interacting during a meeting. • may be as unstructured as walking through an agency's offices on the lookout for evidence of communication barriers. • can be used normatively to distinguish between effective and ineffective behaviors, organizational structures, and/or process.	• minimizes interruption of routine work flow or group activity. • generates in situ data, highly relevant to the situation where response to identified training needs/interests will impact. • (when combined with a feedback step) provides for important comparison checks between inferences of the observer and the respondent.	• requires a highly skilled observer with both process and content knowledge (unlike an interviewer who needs, for the most part, only process skill). • carries limitations that derive from being able to collect data only within the work setting (the other side of the first advantage listed in the preceding column). • holds potential for respondents to perceive the observation activity as "spying."
Questionnaires	• may be in the form of surveys or polls of a random or stratified sample of respondents, or an enumeration of an entire "population." • can use a variety of question formats: open-ended, projective, forced-choice, priority-ranking. • can take alternative forms such as Q-sorts, or slip-sorts, rating scales, either pre-designed or self-generated by respondent(s). • may be self-administered (by mail) under controlled or uncontrolled conditions, or may require the presence of an interpreter or assistant.	• can reach a large number of people in a short time. • are relatively inexpensive. • give opportunity of expression without fear of embarrassment. • yield data easily summarized and reported.	• make little provision for free expression of un-anticipated responses. • require substantial time (and technical skills, especially in survey model) for development of effective instruments. • are of limited utility in getting at causes of problems or possible solutions. • suffer low return rates (mailed), grudging responses, or unintended and/or inappropriate respondents.

Key Consultation	• secures information from those persons who, by virtue of their formal or informal standing, are in a good position to know what the training needs of a particular group are:
	  a. board chairman
	  b. related service providers
	  c. members of professional associations
	  d. individuals from the service population
	• once identified, data can be gathered from these consultants by using techniques such as interviews, group discussions, questionnaires.
		• is relatively simple and inexpensive to conduct.
		• permits input and interaction of a number of individuals, each with his or her own perspectives of the needs of the area, discipline, group, etc.
		• establishes and strengthens lines of communication between participants in the process.
			• carries a built-in bias, since it is based on views of those who tend to see training needs from their own individual or organizational perspective.
			• may result in only a partial picture of training needs due to the typically non-representative nature (in a statistical sense) of a key informant group.

Print Media	• can include professional journals, legislative news/notes, industry "rags," trade magazines, in-house publications.	• is an excellent source of information for uncovering and clarifying normative needs. • provides information that is current, if not forward-looking. • is readily available and is apt to have already been reviewed by the client group.	• can be a problem when it comes to the data analysis and synthesis into a useable form (use of clipping service or key consultants can make this type of data more useable).

Method	Advantages	Disadvantages
Interviews • can be formal or casual, structured or unstructured, or somewhere in between. • may be used with a sample of a particular group (board, staff, committee) or conducted with everyone concerned. • can be done in person, by phone, at the work site, or away from it.	• are adept at revealing feelings, causes of and possible solutions to problems which the client is facing (or anticipates); provide maximum opportunity for the client to represent himself spontaneously on his own terms (especially when conducted in an open-ended, non-directive manner).	• are usually time consuming. • can be difficult to analyze and quantify results (especially from unstructured formats). • unless the interviewer is skilled, the client(s) can easily be made to feel self-conscious. • rely for success on a skillful interviewer who can generate data without making client(s) feel self-conscious, suspicious, etc.
Group Discussion • resembles face-to-face interview technique, e.g., structured or unstructured, formal or informal, or somewhere in between. • can be focused on job (role) analysis, group problem analysis, group goal setting, or any number of group tasks or themes, e.g., "leadership training needs of the board." • uses one or several of the familiar group facilitating techniques: brainstorming, nominal group process, force-fields, consensus rankings, organizational mirroring, simulation, and sculpting.	• permits on-the-spot synthesis of different viewpoints. • builds support for the particular service response that is ultimately decided on. • decreased client's "dependence response" toward the service provider since data analysis is (or can be) a shared function. • helps participants to become better problem analysts, better listeners, etc.	• is time consuming (therefore initially expensive) both for the consultant and the agency. • can produce data that are difficult to synthesize and quantify (more a problem with the less structured techniques).
Tests • are a hybridized form of questionnaire. • can be very functionally oriented (like observations) to test a board, staff, or committee member's proficiency. • may be used to sample learned ideas and facts. • can be administered with or without the presence of an assistant.	• can be especially helpful in determining whether the cause of a recognized problem is a deficiency in knowledge or skill or, by elimination, attitude. • results are easily quantifiable and comparable.	• the availability of a relatively small number of tests that are validated for a specific situation. • do not indicate if measured knowledge and skills are actually being used in the on-the-job or "back home group" situation.
Records, Reports • can consist of organizational charts, planning documents, policy manuals, audits and budget reports. • employee records (grievance, turnover, accidents, etc.) • includes minutes of meetings, weekly, monthly program reports, memoranda, agency service records, program evaluation studies.	• provide excellent clues to trouble spots. • provide objective evidence of the results of problems within the agency or group. • can be collected with a minimum of effort and interruption of work flow since it already exists at the work site.	• causes of problems or possible solutions often do not show up. • carries perspective that generally reflects the past situation rather than the current one (or recent changes). • need a skilled data analyst if clear patterns and trends are to emerge from such technical and diffuse raw data.
Work Samples • are similar to observation but in written form. • can be products generated in the course of the organization's work, e.g., ad layouts, program proposals, market analyses, letters, training designs. • Written responses to a hypothetical but relevant case study provided by the consultant.	• carry most of the advantages of records and reports data. • are the organization's data (its own output).	• case study method will take time away from actual work of the organization. • need specialized content analysts. • analyst's assessment of strengths/weaknesses disclosed by samples can be challenged as "too subjective."

TABLE 3.10   Functional job analysis system for person who operates a grader

Task:
Operates grader manipulating controls to travel forward/back, turn, raise/lower blade; position wheels and blade at correct angles; follows work order, drawing on knowledge and experience, monitoring the performance of the equipment and adapting to the changing situation, constantly alert to the presence and safety of other workers/equipment, in order to perform routine grader tasks such as backfilling, haul road maintenance, snow removal.

TO DO THIS TASK

Performance Standards	*Training Content*
Descriptive Operates equipment properly. Is alert and attentive. *Numerical* All work meets work order requirements. No accidents/damage due to improper operating technique.	*Functional* How to operate grader. How to do routine grader tasks such as back- filling, scarifying, windrowing, cutting fire- break, maintaining haul road, snow removal. *Specific* Knowledge of specific grader. Knowledge of work requirements. Knowledge of specific job site (that is, layout, soil condition, environment).
TO THESE STANDARDS	*THE WORKER NEEDS THIS TRAINING*

From Fine, S. A., Contribution of the job element and functional job analysis approaches to content validity. Presented at the International Personnel Management Assessment Council Annual Conference, Atlanta, Georgia, 1978.

wholeness of the performance and the numerical standards which are designed to cover very limited, measurable aspects of performance. From the performance standards, Fine derives the training content. As shown, the functional training content is designed to indicate the general training the person should bring to the job; the specific training content is designed to indicate the specific training necessary for the establishment in which the person is working. It should be noted that the items included in the table are examples and only represent a sample of the material which would appear in a full job analysis of the grader task.

Multimethod job analyses. Prien (see Prien, 1977; Goldstein, Macey, & Prien, 1981) has developed a system of job analysis that emphasizes tasks, elements, and performance domains. His concept of tasks is consistent with the task analysis described earlier in this chapter; elements refer to the characteristics of knowledge, skills, and abilities also previously described. The performance domain refers to incidents which describe the behavior of persons performing the job. These incidents can describe superior or poor performance of an individual using their knowledge, skills, or abilities to perform a task. These incidents often form the basis for rating scales which are used as criteria to measure the success of persons in performing their job. This type of criterion development is discussed in Chapter 5. Prien uses the term *multimethod job analysis* to stress the fact that emphases on task,

KSA, person, or performance characteristics, and the questions asked about each of these components will change depending on the purpose of the job analysis—for example, design of a selection program or training program or rating scale, or all of these programs.

Prien, Goldstein, and Macey (1985) described a case study where the job analysis purpose was the determination of what should be included in the training program. The setting for the study was a regional bank with a large central organization and many branch offices distributed throughout the region. Branch offices ranged in size from three employees to full service operations of several hundred employees. The focus of the study included a broad range of both jobs across the locations of bank operations. The management purpose for conducting the job analysis was to examine and evaluate job content both to identify the opportunities for on-the-job training through selective job assignment rotation and to differentiate the job components which required classroom training because there were few opportunities to learn on the job. These authors indicate that they went through the following phases to complete their study.

Phase 1. They developed a structure or framework for organizing and describing the content domain data acquired through the application of various data collection procedures. This was achieved in the present case through an examination of available training records and materials, and direct observation of the work setting and process by the researcher. The information acquired in this stage provided a general understanding of business operations, terminology, and so on. The outcome of this research phase was a broad framework within which information acquired in later phases of the project could be placed.

Phase 2. The second phase of the job analysis involved a series of interviews with individuals who could be qualified as subject matter experts, drawn from the entire organization. The purpose of these interviews was to collect information about the tasks employees perform, and the duty-based knowledge, skills, and abilities required to perform those tasks. These researchers often found that it was easiest to obtain KSAs by supplying the subject matter experts with tasks and asking them what KSAs were required to perform those tasks. The result of these interviews was a set of descriptors in the task and element domain. These task and job elements (knowledge, skills, and abilities) statements were then evaluated for ambiguity, clarity, and accuracy by the researchers and training representatives to ensure that all of the content domain was represented.

Phase 3. In this phase of the project, subject matter experts (including job incumbents, supervisors, and members of management) representing the organization provided further information about the job content domains. In order to meet the requirements of identifying training needs, subject matter experts completed structured questionnaires comprising the task and element statements by providing ratings representing a number of judgments. The two judgments relevant to this illustration are *importance* (ratings of the criticality of knowledge, skills, and abilities for full job performance), and *opportunity to learn on the job* (ratings of the opportunities to acquire knowledge, skills, and abilities on the job).

Phase 4. The fourth phase of the needs assessment strategy comprised the data analyses necessary to define the content of the job domain relevant for training purposes. The various components of the job were determined and importance and opportunity to learn indices were computed. For purposes of illustration, a few knowledge and ability items for the construct of customer relations are presented in Table 3.11. The two jobs identified are work done in branch operations

TABLE 3.11   Customer relations knowledge, skills, and abilities

	Group 1— Branch Operations		Group 2— Auditing/Staff Services	
	Importance[1]	*Opportunity to*[1] *Learn on Job*	*Importance*[1]	*Opportunity to*[1] *Learn on Job*
Knowledge of bank security investment policies	1.3	1.1	1.1	.6
Knowledge of standard accounting principles and procedures	2.5	1.9	4.1	2.7
Ability to identify key individuals in client organizations	4.1	3.4	.0	.0
Ability to identify areas of inquiry from bank customers which require specialized assistance from individuals outside the bank	3.3	3.1	.3	.1
Ability to explain bank policy and procedure to customers dissatisfied with bank performance	4.8	4.5	.3	.1
Ability to recognize necessity of change in audit procedure from that originally identified in audit program	1.4	1.5	3.4	3.0

[1] The higher the number, the greater the importance and the greater the opportunity to learn. From "Multi-Method Job Analysis: Methodology and Applications," by E. P Prien, I. L. Goldstein, and W. H. Macey. Unpublished paper. Memphis, TN: Performance Management Associates, 1985.

and auditing and staff services. Examination of the data in the table reveals that, in general, importance and opportunity to learn on the job operations judgments are quite different for the two job examples. It is possible to compare the data displays for all KSAs and tasks and for all job groups simultaneously on various judgments (for example, criticality). An analysis of all tasks provided the answers to issues related to training content, where training was to be obtained (on the job versus in the classroom), and, for on-the-job training, what assignment would be most appropriate.

DERIVATION OF OBJECTIVES

The organizational analyses, task analyses, and person analyses provide the information necessary for the assessment of instructional need. This assessment makes it possible to specify the objectives of the training program. The objectives provide direct input for the design of the training program and help specify the criterion measures that will be used to evaluate the performance of the trainee at the end of the training program and in the transfer setting (on the job, in the next program, and so on). The assessment of instructional need tells the trainer where to begin, and the specification of the objectives tells him the completion point of the program.

Mager and Beach (1967) describe the characteristics of objectives in the following manner:

1. An objective is a statement about a student; it is not a text or teacher.
2. The objective refers to the behavior of the student. It not only specifies what he is to know but also defines *knowing* by indicating how the student will demonstrate his knowledge.
3. An objective is stated in terms of terminal performance. Thus, it is a description of the end product, not the method for reaching the end product.
4. An objective describes the conditions under which the student will perform. Thus, if the student is expected to perform with the use of a training aid (for example, a calculator), the objective specifies its use.
5. An instructional objective indicates the level of performance necessary to achieve that objective. Thus, statements related to the number of errors permitted and the speed of performance are included as part of the objective.

Sound objectives communicate to the learner what he is expected to be able to do when he finishes the program. Some trainers have suggested (not without a note of sarcasm) that if the instructor communicated these objectives, the success of the program would be assured.

The difficulties that can result from not using a system like Mager's to specify behavioral objectives are apparent in expressions like *to appreciate safety*. A close examination of this objective indicates that it does not state what the learner is doing when he or she appreciates safety and does not indicate the desired terminal behavior or the conditions under which the behavior will be performed. As a matter of fact, the objective, as stated, would permit any of the following behaviors to be considered as meeting the goal, although it is doubtful that most trainers would consider their course successful if these events occurred.

1. The employee passed a safety knowledge test with a minimum score of 75%.
2. The employee bought a Red Cross handbook on safety.
3. The employee wears safety goggles when the foreman is present.
4. The employee indicates that safety is important on questionnaires handed out by top management. (Goldstein, Tuttle, Wood, & Grether, 1975, p. 48)

Certainly the design of the training program should be dependent on the definition of appreciation of safety. The following example comes from an analysis of safety problems stemming from persons being injured by grinding wheels. An analysis indicated that this problem occurred when the wheel was warming up, so it was important for individuals not to stand in front of the wheel during warm-up time. The example states:

> When the trainee turns on the grinding wheel, the trainee should always tend to stand to the left of the wheel and out of the path of any exploding particles for the 30 seconds necessary for the wheel to reach maximum velocity. (Goldstein et al., 1975, p. 49)

Note that the behaviorial objective specifies the educational intent, communicates to the learner what he will be doing, and describes the terminal behavior, conditions, and criteria of successful performance.

Similar objectives can be written for all the important aspects of a training program. In many cases, the trainer will discover that the objectives of the training program are not exactly the same as those for successful job performance. When the job is complex, the trainee cannot be expected to exhibit the same behavior as persons who have been performing the task for many years. Thus, one set of objectives and criteria is designed for the initial training analyses, and other objectives and criteria are designed to be used at a later time on the job. These issues are discussed further in Chapter 5. However, the specification of these different objectives will in itself clear up many misunderstandings about trainee requirements upon completion of the program.

Thus far, the objectives discussed have been related to specific aspects of trainee behavior. They represent only one level of analysis. There are also objectives that are concerned with the performance of a system as a whole, rather than behaviors of individual trainees. Some observers (Cogan, 1971) have suggested that two organizational objectives of educational systems should be to individualize instruction and to prevent "dropouts." These objectives must also be specified through behavioral outcomes, performance conditions, and criteria of successful performance. Although this is difficult, the determination of the achievement of policy and organizational objectives is dependent on these specifications.

One specification program, typically called "management by objectives" (MBO), has been recognized by industry for a number of years. Strauss (1972, p. 11) states that

> MBO (at least when it works as it should) requires management to define exactly what it wants to accomplish and to specify all important objectives, especially those commonly ignored. It reduces the emphasis on short-run profits, increases the number of managerial goals and forces the explicit consideration of exactly what steps must be taken if these goals are to be fulfilled. In this way, it helps subordinates learn what is required of them, thus reducing their need for guesswork. As a result, it makes decision-making more rational, for both boss and subordinate. In sum, MBO can become a coordinated process of planning which involves every management level in determining both the goals that it will meet and the means by which they are to be met.

There are several difficulties associated with the MBO process. One group of conflicts is related to the procedures used in implementing the system. There are complaints about the amount of paperwork required, as well as about the great flourish with which objectives and goals are announced—only to be forgotten six months later. These complaints appear to be related to the failure to properly implement the program. Another more serious criticism is related to who designs the objectives and how the objectives are used—procedures that often lead to conflict between personal and corporate goals. Often the information gathered is used simply to exercise a greater degree of control over the organization. These controversies pertain to participative action, in which all individuals have an opportunity to help in the determination of goals and objectives. Whether the system is participative or not, goals and objectives are ultimately designed by someone at the policy level. It is as important to determine the success of the policies as it is to determine the success of an individual worker performing his task. Certainly, the specification of goals provides information that can lead to changes in the objectives as well as measures of their achievement.

CONCLUDING STATEMENTS

The purpose of this chapter is to describe the various components of needs assessment, including organizational analysis, task and KSA analysis, and person analysis. The needs assessment provides all of the critical input for both the design of the training environment and the evaluation of the actual training program. The needs assessment may provide information indicating that training is not the intervention that is needed or that a number of other programs (for example, conflict resolution between different organization units) have to be accomplished before training can be considered. In any case, at the conclusion of the needs assessment, the objectives of the training should be apparent. "The best available basis for the needed matching of media with objectives is a rationale by which the kind of learning involved in each educational objective is stated in terms of the learning conditions required" (Briggs, Campeau, Gagné, & May, 1967, p. 3). The process of going from task analysis to systematic identification of the behaviors to be learned remains one of the most difficult phases in the design of training programs. Some of the techniques being used in this process will be discussed in the next chapter.

The other aspect of our training program that follows from the analyses discussed in this chapter is the evaluation process. The criteria and methods for evaluating programs cannot be conveniently added onto the end of the project without disrupting the training program. In addition, some of the data must be collected before and during the training program, as well as some time after the student has completed training. The evaluation design is an integral part of the entire program but is often a neglected function. This is discussed in Chapters 5 and 6.

The Learning Environment

The learning environment discussed in this chapter refers to the dynamics of the instructional setting with particular emphasis on those components which support learning in the training setting. The components of the learning environment which must be built are described in this chapter. First, there is consideration of trainee readiness which has to do with the learner characteristics which must be brought to the instructional setting. Another section describes the conditions of learning, including principles, such as knowledge of results, that contribute to learning. Finally, materials are presented on transfer of learning with a particular focus on what is necessary to ensure transfer from the learning environment to the on-the-job environment. The chapter concludes with material on the characteristics of an effective environment and effective trainer.

LEARNING AND INSTRUCTION

The basic foundation for instructional programs is learning. The establishment of instructional procedures is based on the belief that it is possible to design an environment in which learning can take place and later be transferred to another setting. The close relationship between learning and instruction is suggested by most learning definitions.

> Learning is the process by which an activity originates or is changed through reacting to an encountered situation, provided that the characteristics of the change cannot be explained on the basis of native response tendencies, maturation, or temporary states of the organism (e.g., fatigue, drugs, etc.). (Hilgard & Bower, 1966, p. 2)

This definition implies that the change is relatively permanent, but it does not assume that all changes lead to improvements in behavior. Although most learning does lead to improvements, there is clear evidence that people can acquire behavioral tendencies toward drugs or racial hatred that might be injurious. It is also important to note that learning is an inferred process that is not directly observable. In some cases, learning becomes immediately observable through performance, but in other cases a considerable period of time passes before learning becomes apparent. The care with which the inference must be established is demonstrated by the effects of alcohol and other drugs on behavior. In many instances, the use of drugs can cause poor performance. However, it should not be inferred that learned behavior has been forgotten. When the effects of the drugs have worn off, the performance level can return to normal, without any intervening training (Hilgard & Bower, 1966).

From the preceding discussion, it seems that traditional learning principles applied to modern training or instructional settings would be effective. Thus, the rest of this chapter should be devoted to a review of the learning principles that have been developed in the last 100 years. However, the assumption is invalid. There is a wide gulf separating learning theories and principles from what is actually needed to improve performance. The transition will not be accomplished easily or quickly, for many reasons.

> 1. The learning theorist has tended to focus on highly specific laboratory experimentation, which has made generalizations to field settings extremely difficult. Much research has focused on distinctions that are important in theoretical debates, with little attention to the broader interpretations of data necessary for the training specialist. Thus, the trainer is left with data that do not seem particularly relevant to his needs, and theoretical interpretations, which could provide the link, do not exist (Howell & Goldstein, 1971).
>
> 2. Until recently, the learning theorist has ignored the complex areas of human behavior. Thus, there is relatively little information available on problem solving, perceptual motor learning, concept learning, and other topics directly relevant to the needs of the training specialist.
>
> 3. The training specialist often demands quick answers and ready solutions to complicated problems (McGehee & Thayer, 1961). When easy solutions are not immediately apparent, the practitioner often assumes that the learning theorist's entire program is irrelevant to his needs. Thus, instead of adding to existing knowledge with what he can glean from the learning field, the practitioner ignores learning theory and contributes little information of his own.

The basic gulf between learning theory and its applications to instructional methodology has led many researchers to believe that an intervening link must be developed between the theorist in the laboratory and the practitioner in the applied setting. As Bruner (1963) states the problem:

> A theory of instruction must concern itself with the relationship between how things are presented and how they are learned. Though I myself have worked hard and long in the vineyard of learning theory, I can do no better than to start by warning the reader away from it. Learn-

ing theory is not a theory of instruction. It describes what happened. A theory of instruction is a guide to what to do in order to achieve certain objectives. Unfortunately, we shall have to start pretty nearly at the beginning, for there is very little literature to guide us in this subtle enterprise. (p. 524)

The views expressed by persons like Bruner were supported by empirical analyses. Thus, Gagné (1962) examined the utility of laboratory learning principles in the performance of a series of tasks. He found that the best-known principles, including feedback, distribution of practice, and meaningfulness, were "strikingly inadequate to handle the job of designing effective training situations" (p. 85). He reached this conclusion after examining data from a variety of different tasks, including tracking and problem solving. Gagné (1962) suggests that it is necessary to organize the total task into a set of distinct components that mediate final task performance. When these component tasks are present in the instructional program, there should be an effective transfer of learning from the instructional setting to the job setting. Thus, the principles of training design would consist of identifying the task components that make up final performance, placing these parts into the instructional program, and arranging the learning of these components in an optimal sequence. This approach suggests a concern with "task analysis, terminal behaviors, component task achievements, the fidelity of training-task components, and sequencing" (J. P. Campbell, 1971, p. 567).

During the 1970s, researchers began the task of developing instructional theories relying on both theoretical and experimental analysis in the laboratory and applied problems taken from instructional settings (Glaser, 1982). Thus, these researchers asked questions about the kinds of knowledge necessary to learn to read an instructional manual or to learn a new language (including computer language). Theories were developed about how the learner organized and integrated information and how information was stored. Thus, Glaser noted that a possible difference between persons with high and low learning aptitude is the ability of learners to organize and use information in ways that make it possible to transfer it from old to new problems.

The goals of instructional theory are made quite clear by the following quote from Glaser:

> The development that I anticipate is a macro-theory of teaching and instruction: "macro" in the sense that it is concerned with the large practical variables dealt with in schools such as the allocation and efficient use of time, the structure of classroom management, the nature of teacher feedback and reinforcement to the student, the organizational pattern of teacher–student interaction, the relationship between what is taught and what is tested, the degree of classroom flexibility required for adapting to learner background, and the details of curriculum materials as these

relate to student achievement. . . . As theory at this level develops, it will be undergirded by the more micro-studies of human thinking and problem solving. . . . (p. 299)

Instructional approaches for training should involve a series of steps. First, it is necessary to conduct a needs assessment (such as the type described in the preceding chapter). Based upon the training objective developed as part of the needs assessment, it is important to determine the type of learning necessary for acquiring the essential behaviors. One system (Gagné & Briggs, 1979) formulates five types of learning (intellectual skill, cognitive strategy, information, attitude, and motor skills). Another system (Harmon, 1968) divides the objectives into three groups, including verbal, physical, and attitudinal performance. In each of these systems, the researcher analyzes the objectives and determines the required behaviors and the type of learning necessary to acquire that behavior.

Next, the behavior is matched to the most appropriate learning environment and instructional media. *Learning environment* refers to the dynamics of the instructional setting, with particular emphasis on instructional variables—for example, knowledge of results or massed and spaced practice. The components of the learning environment that must be built are described in this chapter. First, there is consideration of trainee readiness which considers the ability and motivation that must be brought to the instructional setting. Another section describes the conditions of learning. In this section, various learning principles, such as knowledge of results that contribute to the learning environment, are discussed. The final component described is transfer of learning. In this section, material is presented about what is necessary in order to ensure transfer from the learning environment to the on-the-job environment. In addition to the learning environment, it is also necessary to choose instructional media appropriate for the behavior to be learned.

Instructional media refers to particular devices and techniques, like simulators, programed instruction, films, and lectures. In some cases, the instructional medium itself helps predetermine the learning variables. It is relatively easy to obtain individual feedback with a teaching machine, but it is difficult to do so with lecture material. In other cases, however, teaching machines can be used without individual feedback, and simulators may present the entire task (whole learning) or components of the task (part learning). In either case, it is important for the learning environment and instructional media to be determined by the objectives and the form of performance required.

Training sponsors understand, for instance, that simulators are not the best media available for learning a foreign language but that they may be excellent for learning driving skills. However, inappropriate techniques are often used because they are readily available. Unfortunately, the design of the learning environment and the selection of the appropriate instructional variables have not been treated with the same degree of awareness. Often a training designer insists that knowledge of results, or feedback, is necessary, without first determining what kinds of behavior are desired and whether feedback is appropriate for learning those particular behaviors. The approach emphasized in this test stresses the determination of objectives through needs assessment and the analysis of those objectives to determine the behaviors required. After that has been accomplished, the proper learning environment, with appropriate learning variables, media, and techniques can be selected. Later chapters in this text describe specific media and techniques available. The final step in this sequence relates to the assessment of training performance. This involves determining the initial state of the learner and the assessment of later performance after the acquisition of new knowledges and skills. The next chapter in this book describes the criteria used to assess performance and the following chapter presents materials on evaluation design.

Thus, the content of this chapter is the learning environment. The material begins with a section on trainee readiness, continues with materials on the conditions of learning, and follows with an analysis of transfer issues. There is also material on the positive qualities of training environments and trainers. The chapter should conclude by reaching the following goal (Goldstein, 1980):

> It should be possible on the basis of need assessment techniques to determine what tasks are performed, what behaviors are essential to the performance of those tasks, what type of learning is necessary to acquire those behaviors, and what type of instructional content is best suited to accomplish that type of learning. (p. 262)

The goal, while still elusive, has become the focus of instructional theory efforts. Thus, a final section of this chapter discusses such an approach developed by Gagné and Briggs (1979).

THE INSTRUCTIONAL ENVIRONMENT

Preconditions of Learning

Before trainees can benefit from any form of training, they must be ready to learn; that is, they must have the particular background experiences necessary for the training program, and they must be motivated. There is a tendency to believe that some individuals perform poorly in training because they either were ill-prepared to enter the program or did not want to learn. If these reasons are valid and the cause is not an ill-conceived program, the implementer must be certain that the preconditions for learning are satisfied. Gilbert (1982) describes the complex interaction between the training environment, the individual's prior knowledge and skill, and the incentives necessary to perform by referring to the facets of behavior involved in assembling a tricycle. These facets are presented in Figure 4.1.

FIGURE 4.1   Six facets of the behavior of assembling a tricycle. (*From "A Question of Performance—Part 1—The Probe Model," by T. F. Gilbert. In* Training and Development Journal, *1982, 36(9), pp. 20–30. Copyright 1982 by the American Society for Training and Development, Inc. Reprinted by permission.*)

Gilbert notes that his behavior can be changed (or trained) in the following ways:

The *data* that the manufacturer had provided me as the instructions for assembly, by making them clearer or more confusing. (All manufacturers whose products I have bought wrote confusing instructions.)

My *skill* in using that data. (My training in reading mechanical instructions was sadly inadequate.)

The *instruments* to do the job. (Last Christmas the manufacturer forgot to supply the small wrench that its packing list promised.)

My *capacity* to make the required responses. (My fingers, eyesight and temper are all too short.)

The *incentive* of a beautifully finished product. (Or sooner or later you'll give up.)

The *motives* to do the job. (1982, p. 27)

Trainee readiness.   Trainee readiness refers to both maturational and experiential factors in the background of the learner. Since trainee readiness is critical in the learning process, the instructor must be concerned with the ability of the trainee to perform certain tasks. Some psychologists (Gagné, 1970) believe that differences in developmental readiness are primarily due to the number and kind of previously learned intellectual skills. Supporters of this view would argue that many of the abstract rules of calculus could be taught to fourth-graders if they had first attained the skills (for example, algebra concepts) prerequisite to the form of learning. This point has particular significance for instructors responsible for designing instructional programs involving more mature individuals. Programs will fail if the prerequisite skills necessary to perform successfully are not considered. Particular emphasis should be placed on the determination of the incoming trainee characteristics. Previously, when needs assessment was discussed the point stressed was that the assessment provide the information necessary for the design of the instructional program. In the next chapter, it will be noted that the needs assessment also provides input on what is to be learned so that criteria can be developed to assess the progress of the instructional program. A related point is that this same information provides the training analyst with information on the characteristics of trainees. Measuring trainees on what they know before they begin training will provide information indicating which trainees may already know this material, which trainees may require remedial work, and which trainees are ready for training. Too often, training analysts think that the only purpose of a pretest before training is to compare the results to a posttest after training in order to evaluate the instructional program. Pretests also serve the purpose of providing information about trainee readiness.

Trainee Motivation

Motivation involves behavior that is active, purposive, and goal-directed (Bourne & Ekstrand, 1973). Most researchers agree that motivational level affects performance through an energizing function. Thus, the motivated individual is an active participant and will probably work harder as motivational level increases. Training analysts must recognize that there are a variety of factors that influence motivational levels in human beings and that they might not be the same factors for each individual. As will be indicated in the next section on conditions of learning, it is important to use as many motivational variables in the instructional setting as possible in order to enhance learning. On the other hand, it is also clear that individuals who are motivated upon entry into the training program have an advantage from the very beginning. Some interesting data concerning motivation of trainees upon entry was collected in a study of the Navy School for Divers (Ryman & Biersner, 1975). The investigators had trainees fill out a training confidence scale before training. Some of the motivational items on the scale were:

> If I have trouble during training, I will try harder.
> I will get more from this training than most people.
> I volunteered for this training as soon as I could.
> Even if I fail, this training will be a valuable experience.

The trainees rated these items on a five-point scale from "Disagree Strongly" to "Agree Strongly." The investigators discovered that scores on these items predicted eventual graduation from the program. Thus, the more the pre-trainees agreed with these statements, the more likely they were to graduate.

Sanders and Yanouzas (1983) have further developed these ideas in terms of the trainers' ability to socialize trainees to the learning environment. They note that trainees come to the learning environment with certain attitudes and expectations and these may or may not be helpful in the learning process. Table 4.1 describes a number of aspects of the role of a student in the class. Trainees who have expectations which are positive and supportive of these types of activities are more likely to be ready for training. If attitudes are generally negative, then it becomes necessary to determine the source of the difficulties and correct the problems before training begins. Without such intervention, learning is not likely to occur.

Motivation

As noted in the previous section on preconditions of learning, motivation involves behavior that is active, purposive, and goal-directed (Bourne & Ekstrand, 1973). Industrial psychologists examining the effects of motivational states on performance have directed their atten-

TABLE 4.1 Indicators of trainee readiness

	SD	D	N	A	SA
As a student in this class, my role is to . . .					
1. Accept personal responsibility for becoming involved in learning experiences.					
2. Be willing to participate actively in classroom analysis of learning activities.					
3. Be willing to engage in self-assessment.					
4. Be willing to learn from classmates.					
5. Believe that information learned will be useful in the future.					
6. Complete assignments and readings prior to class.					

SD Strongly disagree
D Disagree
N Neutral
A Agree
SA Strongly agree

Adapted from "Socialization to Learning," by P. Sanders and J. N. Yanouzas. In *Training and Development Journal*, 1983, *37*, pp. 14–21. Copyright 1983 by the American Society for Training and Development, Inc. Adapted by permission.

tion to two sets of theories. Process theories seek an explanation of how behavior is energized, directed, sustained, and stopped, and content theories consider what specific things motivate people (for a review of these theories and the empirical research, see Steers & Porter, 1983). Most of this research is related to performance on the job rather than to learning in the training environment. However, the role of motivation performance on the job can provide important insights into performance in training environments. Also, if the motivational level in the transfer setting is extremely poor, learning in the instructional setting becomes an academic exercise.

Reinforcement theory. The following sections discuss some of the factors that appear to be important in the establishment of motivational levels in learning settings. When the consequence of a response leads to the response being repeated, the consequence is called a *positive reinforcer*. B. F. Skinner, the father of programed-instruction techniques, is the individual most often associated with the development of reinforcement theory. In this form of learning, the person's response is instrumental in gaining a consequence that reinforces or rewards. The responses can vary in complexity from a person producing a product at work to a rat pressing a bar, and the rewarding stimuli can vary from praise for the person to a pellet of food for the rat. The list of stimuli that have served as reinforcers in various environments is endless but could include praise, gifts, money, and attention.

An example of the use of reinforcement principles is illustrated by the work of Pedalino and Gamboa (1974), who were concerned with the reduction of absenteeism and lateness in a manufacturing/distribution plant. These researchers used the following poker game incentive plan as a reinforcement device.

> Each day an employee comes to work and is on time, he is allowed to choose a card from a deck of playing cards. At the end of the five day week, he will have five cards or a normal poker hand. The highest hand wins $20. There will be eight winners, one for approximately each department. (p. 696)

Over a four-month period, the experimental group achieved an 18.27% reduction in absenteeism. Unfortunately, the study had to be stopped at this point because sensitive union negotiations were due to begin, which should serve as another reminder of the complexities of organizational factors that reflect life in work organizations. Other researchers, such as Yukl and Latham (1975), have demonstrated the effects of reinforcers on tasks like tree planting.

Some of the aspects that a trainer should consider when using reinforcers include the following.

Timing of reinforcement.   Reinforcement should be given immediately following the appropriate response. Any delay might lead to the reinforcement of extraneous, inappropriate behaviors that are emitted after the correct response is made. For example, a parent may reinforce a child's tantrum by ignoring appropriately made requests but immediately attending to the child's screams. Fortunately, human learners can be reinforced by many stimuli. Thus, a trainee may participate in a learning program in order to earn a new job or a higher pay rate. In these cases, the learners can be rewarded with feedback concerning their progress until they successfully complete the program and earn the new job. The feedback serves to reinforce correct responses and also helps to extinguish incorrect responses while the learner works toward a more ultimate reward.

Partial reinforcement.   Experiments in the learning laboratory have also produced results that indicate that it is not necessary to reinforce every correct response for learning to take place. This phenomenon is known as partial reinforcement. Skinner and his associates have examined many schedules on which the learner was not reinforced for every correct response, and they have discovered that learning proceeds in an orderly fashion even with intermittent reinforcement. Data indicate that if the learners are reinforced only after a certain number of correct responses, they will perform vigorously and quickly until the required number of responses is achieved. These data also show that responses learned under conditions of partial reinforcement are much more resistant to extinction than those learned under conditions of complete reinforcement. Behavior at slot machines provides a clear illustration of the effects of partial reinforcement. Even though each response is not rewarded with a payoff, the infrequent jackpots maintain the responses. Unscrupulous gamblers often provide one or two payoffs to card players early in the game to hook them and then depend on that partial reinforcement to keep the game going even though the payoffs become less and less frequent. In training settings, it is useful to provide continuous reinforcement until the correct response has been learned. At that point, partial reinforcement will maintain the behavior and make the responses more resistant to extinction. Unfortunately, the same principles apply to undesirable behavior, as illustrated by the difficulties that novices have in learning complex motor skills. For example, tennis beginners using inefficient responses every so often hit a good shot, thus being partially reinforced for poor responses. When the learner decides on formal instruction, it is difficult for the instructor to extinguish these partially reinforced responses.

Punishment.   Punishment can be conceptualized as stimuli that the learner would like to avoid. Workers might be penalized for unsafe behavior by losing some of their pay or by being criticized by their foreman—both aversive stimuli. The implications of punishment are not as well defined as those associated with positive reinforcement, but it is clear that punishment does not always reduce the likelihood of the same response occurring again. Some of the difficulties with aversive stimuli include the following:

1. Often the behavior of the respondent is positively reinforced before punishment occurs. The worker may have performed some unsafe behavior, like failing to wear uncomfortable safety equipment, but may be positively reinforced by being more comfortable. The positive reinforcement has a strong influence because it follows the inappropriate response more immediately than does the aversive stimulus.

2. Punishment tends to become associated with specific stimuli. The worker learns to wear his safety equipment when the foreman is present but quickly discards it when the foreman is not there.

3. There is a tendency to be inconsistent in the application of aversive stimuli. Thus, the parent does not punish the child each time the behavior is inappropriate, and some foremen look the other way to avoid noticing unsafe behavior, because most individuals do not like to administer punishment. There is also a tendency to feel guilty about the use of punishment, which leads the administrator to follow punishment with positive rewards.

4. Laboratory research suggests that the effects of punishment are largely emotional and only suppress, rather than extinguish, the inappropriate behavior. Once the emotional effects disappear, the behavior reasserts itself.

5. Punishment can lead to undesirable side effects. Anxiety associated with punishment can often create an unfavorable environment for learning and hostile attitudes toward the administrator of the punishment as well as the institutions they represent.

One interesting question is whether punishment is necessary. Bass and Vaughan (1966) suggest that it is needed when it is the only way to define the limits of behavior. Even in those situations, however, punishment should be used judiciously to avoid adverse effects.

Learning without reinforcement.   As discussed in the above section on reinforcement theory, early learning theorists argued that persons make a response to a stimulus and when that response is reinforced, a connection is formed between the stimulus and response. Eventually, reinforcements of the response strengthen the neutral connections so that the behavior will occur in the presence of the stimulus.

Many contemporary psychologists feel that this explanation for behavior ignores the mental activity going on inside the organism and is not as applicable to more complex human behavior, such as the cognitive processes involved in thinking (Smith, in press). Psychologists who espouse the cognitive viewpoint argue that the learner forms structures or schema in memory which preserve and organize information about what has been learned. An example of this process is what a person does when given a question on a test. In this situation, "the subject takes the stimuli (the questions) and scans them against memory to determine an appropriate action. What he or she does depends on the cognitive structure retrieved from memory and the context in which the text occurs" (Hilgard, Atkinson, & Atkinson, 1979, p. 208).

From this framework, Bandura (1969, 1977) helped develop social learning theory which argues that learning can occur without reinforcement being a necessary requirement. He argues that simply watching another person make a particular response permits the observer to learn the response. Bandura notes that observational learning occurs when an observer watches a model exhibit a set of responses. This set of learned behaviors becomes part of the individual's repertoire of potential behavior even though it may not be overtly performed for some time. Bandura believes that these responses, known as *modeling,* are acquired through symbolic mental processes which function as the observer watches the behavior of a model. Bandura and his colleagues are not saying that reinforcement is unimportant for learning social behavior. Rather, they are saying it is unimportant for the original learning. Reinforcement is much more important in getting persons to actually exhibit the behavior which has already been learned. Much of Bandura's original research studied children and how they observed and then imitated the behavior they had observed. As described later in this book, social learning theory has provided an important foundation for a training technique appropriately known as behavioral role modeling. In addition to this technique, the ideas of cognitive processes have had strong implications for the way theorists believe that we learn and think. Some of these ramifications will be discussed later in this chapter in the section on instructional psychology.

Instrumentality   theory   and   motivation.   Vroom (1964) has developed a process theory of motivation related to the question of how behavior is energized and sustained. The theory is based on cognitive expectancies concerning outcomes that are likely to occur as a result of the participant's behavior and on individual preferences among those outcomes. The expectancy can vary, as can the valence, or strength of an individual's preference for an outcome. Vroom states that outcomes have a particular valence value because they are *instrumental* in achieving other outcomes. For instance, money and promotion have potential valence value because they are instrumental in allowing an individual to achieve other outcomes, like an expensive home or a college education for his children. The motivational level is based on a combination of the individual's belief that he can achieve certain outcomes from his acts and the value of those outcomes to him.

Training programs have a valence value for individuals if they believe they will permit them to achieve other outcomes. Thus, training becomes a low-level outcome that permits the achievement of higher-level outcomes (such as a job, a promotion, or a raise), which in turn might lead to other outcomes. The instrumentality theory implies that it will be necessary to show the individual the value of the instructional program in order to properly motivate him. Programs that appear unrelated to future outcomes will probably not meet the desired objectives.

Need   theory   and   motivation. There are a number of content theories that emphasize learned needs as motivators of human behavior. These theories concentrate on the needs that are to be satisfied and do not attempt to specify the exact processes by which these needs motivate behavior. The theories suggest to the training researcher that his or her programs must meet particular needs in order to have a motivated learner.

One need theory that has been given considerable attention involves the need for achievement motivation (nAch), which is described by Atkinson and Feather (1966) as a behavioral tendency to strive for success. It is assumed to operate when the environment signals that certain acts on the part of the individual will lead to need achievement. An illustration of this approach can be found in the studies of McClelland and Winter (1969), which were designed to instill achievement motivation through training programs. In one study, they found that participants in their training program were successful in later economic ventures. A series of studies (Raynor, 1970; Raynor & Rubin, 1971) combining the approaches of the need and instrumentality theories indicated that persons capable of high achievement don't necessarily perform well unless their behavior is viewed as being instrumental for later success. Thus, students with high achievement motivation received superior grades when they regarded the grades as important for career success.

Maslow (1954) has developed a hierarchy of needs and suggested that needs at lower levels must be satisfied before the higher-level needs can serve as energizers of behavior. Maslow's needs include:

1. Physiological needs: These include the basic needs of the organism, including food, water, and oxygen.
2. Safety needs: These needs refer to an individual's desire for a safe environment, with minimum threats to his or her existence.
3. Social needs: These needs include friendship and love.
4. Esteem needs: These needs include an individual's desire for self-respect and self-esteem and are based on positive self-evaluations.
5. Self-actualization: Self-actualization involves the need for self-fulfillment, which is based on the achievement of one's life goals.

Maslow's theory is not based on empirical evidence, but it does have important implications for the training researcher. The theory suggests that it is necessary to consider the individual goals of the learner. An extension of this viewpoint indicates that the fulfillment of needs does not always involve positive consequences. The individual may be confronted with conflicting goals that have both positive and negative aspects or with two goals, both essentially negative. He or she may be faced with attending the training program or losing his job, while neither may be very satisfying.

Need theory emphasizes the importance of learning as much as possible about the various needs and viewpoints of trainees. An illustration of such an approach is a study that examines the work goals of engineers and scientists (Ritti, 1968). The author found that the goals of the scientists were largely related to academic achievement (like publication of data and professional autonomy), while the goals of the engineers were related to advancement and decision making. The organization's attempts to increase the professional aspects of the engineering positions were viewed as inconsistent with the goals of the engineer and as not effective motivationally.

Two-factor theory. Herzberg has postulated two sets of work motivators—extrinsic factors and intrinsic factors (Herzberg, Mausner, & Snyderman, 1959). Extrinsic factors (such as pay, job security, supervision, company policy, and working conditions) stem primarily from the organizational environment and are not directly influenced by the individual. Intrinsic factors are based on the individual's relationship to the job and include achievement, recognition, responsibility, and advancement. Herzberg maintains that extrinsic factors can only prevent the onset of job dissatisfaction or the removal of job dissatisfaction, while intrinsic factors do not have any influence on job dissatisfaction but will operate to increase job satisfaction.

Although the evidence regarding this theory is controversial, the hypothesis that the basic conditions surrounding work (extrinsic factors) cannot provide satisfaction has led to increased emphasis on the use of intrinsic factors as motivators of performance. Herzberg feels that individuals receive their rewards from their performance of the tasks. Thus, motivation to work is related to an individual's achievement and his or her recognition of that achievement.

Since trainers often design the environments that lead to achievement, the use of intrinsic factors may often be built directly into the instructional program. Other writers have reached similar conclusions about the importance of intrinsic interest in a task, without necessarily subscribing to Herzberg's two-factor view of motivation. Gagné and Bolles (1959) have stated that

> the idea that motivation should be intrinsic rests not so much upon the role motivation plays in learning or in performance during learning; rather, it reflects a concern with the transfer criterion (of efficient training). It seems reasonable to suppose that motives and goals intrinsic to the task are more likely to transfer to the job situation. (p. 10)

There can be little disagreement with a view that argues for the design of interesting and meaningful training programs. However, it is a long step from this view to an understanding of how to initially develop interest (McGehee & Thayer, 1961). Suggestions include stressing the future utility or value of the activity, providing feedback that shows the degree of accomplishment attained, relating the material to meaningful activity outside the instructional setting, finding tasks that are interesting because they are challenging, and enlarging the job to make it more interesting and to provide greater degrees of responsibility (which usually means enlarging the training program, too!)

Extrinsic factors such as pay scales and company policy are potentially useful; however, they are often not within the direct control of those persons concerned with instructional programs. In those cases in which there is some degree of control, extrinsic factors are potentially useful. Despite Herzberg's theories, there is considerable doubt that extrinsic factors are related only to job dissatisfaction. In addition, some learning tasks display very little potential for the application of intrinsic motivators. The extrinsic motivators with the most general applicability to training settings are those related to gaining rewards and avoiding punishments, usually in the form of praise or reproof but sometimes consisting of financial incentives. In these cases, the recommended technique is to use rewards instead of punishments, because of the many negative aspects associated with punishment.

Goal setting and motivation.   Locke, Latham, and their colleagues (see, for example, Latham & Locke, 1979; Locke, Shaw, Saari, & Latham, 1981) have conducted and reviewed an extensive set of studies describing the effects of setting goals on behavior. In their 1981 review, they found that in 90% of the laboratory and field studies specific and challenging goals lead to higher performance than easy goals, do-your-best goals, or no goals. These authors postulate that goals affect task performance by "directing energy and attention, mobilizing energy expenditure or effort, prolonging effort over time (persistence) and motivating the individual to develop relevant strategies for goal attainment" (1981, p. 145). These authors have also detailed a number of specific conditions that affect performance. They include the following points:

1. Individuals who are given specific, hard, or challenging goals perform better than persons given specific easy goals or do-best goals or no goals at all.
2. Goals appear to have more predictable effects when they are given in specific terms rather than as a vague set of intentions.
3. The goals must be matched to the ability of the individuals such that the person is likely to be able to achieve the goal.
4. Feedback concerning the degree to which the goal is being achieved is necessary in order for goal-setting to have an effect.
5. In order for goal-setting to be effective, the individual has to accept the goal that is assigned or set. Often the acceptance of the goal is related to the degree of support or commitment of the organization to the goal-setting program.

These points, based on extensive research studies, suggest a number of ways that training programs can be more effective. The setting of specific challenging goals which are matched to the ability of the individual followed by feedback on degree of goal achievement provide a solid foundation for the design of an instructional program.

Equity theory. Equity theory is based on the belief that people want to be treated fairly. Thus, individuals compare themselves to other people to see if their treatments are equitable. As stated by Adams (1965), "Inequity exists for a person when he perceives that the ratio of his outcomes to inputs and the ratio of others' outcomes to inputs are unequal" (p. 280). In this definition, outcomes include all factors viewed as having value—for example, pay, status, and fringe benefits. Inputs include all those factors that the persons bring with them (such as effort, education, seniority) and perceives as being important for obtaining some benefit (Pritchard, 1969). Inequity is said to create tension that has motivating qualities, requiring the person to reduce or eliminate the discrepancy. This tension is created whether the person compared is perceived as under- or over-rewarded.

While equity theory appears to be especially relevant to the subject of wage factors, it may also have important implications for training. As already noted (Pritchard, 1969), the a priori determination of a variable as input or outcome is not always possible. Training provides such an illustration; that is, instructional programs may be viewed as an input or an output. In the input case, individuals who have acquired the necessary training experiences may view as inequitable promotions and pay raises earned by individuals without equal educational experiences. In the output case, persons may perceive that they are not given the opportunity to attend advanced training courses. While there has not been any direct utilization of equity theory in such instances, some interview data (Dachler, 1974) suggest that female managers view their opportunities from an equity-theory framework. They feel that, given the same training background as men, they do not have equal opportunities for job advancement or for participation in advanced training. While the results of this situation are difficult to hypothesize, it is interesting to speculate on the behavior expended during the training effort when the trainee perceives that the outcomes are not available. In addition, there are interesting possibilities about job behavior when the employee perceives that future training and other opportunities are not available.

Task difficulty and motivational level.   While Locke has found that difficult goals produce better performance, the relationship of motivational level to task difficulty indicates that there are other factors that must be considered. The learning literature suggests that increases in motivation beyond some level lead to poorer performance. The colloquial expression used for this lower performance level is that the person is trying too hard. The Yerkes–Dodson law describes the performance curves related to motivational level but adds one more factor—task difficulty. Essentially, the principle states that if the task is an extremely easy one, high motivational levels are extremely desirable. As the task becomes more difficult, intermediate levels of motivation lead to the best performance, with both very high and very low motivational levels leading to correspondingly poorer performance. At the most difficult task levels, the best performance is achieved by those individuals who have lower motivational levels. Thus, the studies relating learning to motivational level and task difficulty indicate that high levels of motivation may not serve the instructional purpose well when the tasks are particularly difficult.

Motivation—A summary. While the theoretical and empirical developments concerning the motivational literature are complex, there are some generalizations that can be made regarding the best hypotheses about the use of motivational factors in instructional settings. The following implications are offered.

1. While some learning theories indicate that learning does occur without explicitly designated rewards, it would be foolhardy for most instructional programs to proceed without a plan of action for the institution of motivational variables.
2. There are a variety of motivational needs that may work in any given setting, but the same incentives are not necessarily rewards for everyone.

3. Empirical evidence exists to indicate that motivational variables are more effective if they are (a) viewed as instrumental for future activities; (b) intrinsic; (c) positive rather than aversive stimuli when extrinsic motivators are used; (d) set in terms of specific challenging goals matched to the ability of the individual followed by feedback on degree of achievement.
4. Learning data indicate that there is a relationship between motivational levels and task difficulty, with correspondingly lower motivational levels resulting in better task performance when the difficulty of the task increases.

CONDITIONS OF LEARNING

It is clear that the amount of original learning in the instructional setting is an important determinant of the amount of transfer that will eventually occur in the job situation. Learning theorists have developed information about a large number of variables that can be used to enhance the degree of original learning. In this section, information will be presented concerning those features of the learning environment that have been found to be most useful in contributing to learning. However, it is important to remember that the usefulness of any particular condition of learning is very much dependent upon the type of task and learning behavior being considered. Thus, knowledge of results is an important component of the conditions of learning, but some researchers (Gagné, 1962) have demonstrated that its use is not a guarantee of learning. As discussed in the concluding section of this chapter, instructional theorists have begun systematically to explore some of these relationships. In this section, some of the more important conditions of learning will be presented.

Whole versus Part Learning

This variable is related to the size of the units practiced during the training session. When whole procedures are employed, the learner practices the task as a single unit. The utilization of part procedures breaks the task into components that are practiced separately. The complexity of the task and the relationship among the components determine the usefulness of whole and part methods (Holding, 1965). Naylor (Naylor, 1962; Blum & Naylor, 1968) suggested that the difficulty of any particular subtask (complexity) and the extent to which the subtasks are interrelated (organization) determine total difficulty. He used the example of a person driving a car to illustrate both the complexity and the organization functions. Driving in rush-hour traffic usually places the greatest strain on forward-velocity control (assuming the driver stays in the same lane), because the operator must continually use the accelerator and brake pedal to maintain varying degrees of speed. When the driver operates the vehicle on a curved section of highway, the steering component becomes the most complex part of the task. Task organization can be illustrated by the interrelationship of forward-velocity control and steering. When the operator desires to make a turn, the two components must be interrelated in order to properly carry out the turning sequence. Naylor's examination of the part–whole literature since 1930 (see Table 4.2) supports the following basic training principles concerning part and whole methods: When a task has relatively high organization, an increase in task complexity leads to whole methods being more efficient than part methods, and when a task has low organization, an increase in task complexity leads to part methods being more efficient.

The use of part methods suggested by Naylor's analysis does raise some concerns related to the eventual performance of the entire task. Holding's (1965) review of the problem indicated that those tasks that are easily separated can be combined at a later time without difficulty for the learner. The job must be analyzed to discover the important components and to determine the correct sequence for learning the components. During this process, it is necessary to make sure that the student has developed the capabilities necessary to proceed to the next part of the task (Briggs, 1968). If the job is properly analyzed and ordered, a progression method may be used. Here, the learner practices one part at the first session. Then, at the next session, a second part is added, and both parts are practiced together. The addition of parts continues until the whole skill is learned.

Massed versus Spaced Practice

It is important to determine whether the learner benefits more from as little rest as possible until they have learned their task or from rest intervals within practice sessions. Although the data are not definitive, they suggest that spaced practice for motor skills is typically more effec-

TABLE 4.2 Percentages of post-1930 studies finding whole or part methods superior as a function of task complexity and organization

	Task complexity	*Task high*	*Organization low*
Whole	High	100	0
	Medium	50	50
	Low	25	50
Part	High	0	25
	Medium	19	50
	Low	63	50
Inconclusive	High	0	75
	Medium	31	0
	Low	12	0

From *Industrial Psychology: Its Theoretical and Social Foundations,* rev. ed., by Milton L. Blum and James C. Naylor. Copyright © 1968 by Harper & Row, Publishers, Inc. Reprinted by permission.

tive in acquisition and leads to better retention. DeCecco (1968) presented data obtained by Lorge (1930) that examined massed versus spaced practice on a motor-skill task. The subjects were required to draw a figure from a mirror image. One group, performing the task under massed-practice conditions, was given 20 trials without any rest periods. The other two groups performed the task under spaced conditions. One group was given one-minute rest periods between trials and the other group one-day rest periods between trials. As Figure 4.2 indicates, there were consistent differences between the spaced-practice groups and the massed-practice group, with the spaced-practice groups demonstrating better performance. Later research (Digman, 1959) indicated that spaced groups benefited from the opportunity to mentally rehearse the tasks, while massed groups suffered from a buildup of fatigue during the practice sessions. These data show that the massed group, after an evening's rest, often performed better on the first trial of the new session than on the last trial of the previous day's session. This has led some researchers (Holding, 1965) to conclude that massed conditions do not hamper learning; they only depress performance. These views are supported by data showing that massed groups perform as well as spaced groups when they are switched to spaced-group conditions or when both groups are given retention tests after a few days have passed (Reynolds & Bilodeau, 1952).

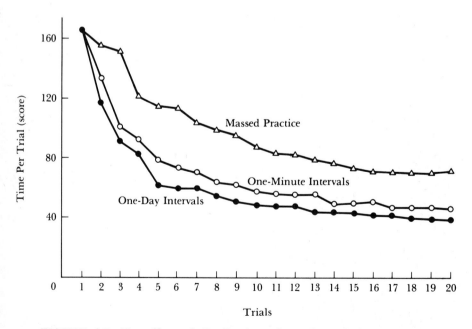

FIGURE 4.2 The effect of distribution of practice on mirror drawing. (*Adapted from Irving Lorge,* Influence of Regularly Interpolated Time Intervals upon Subsequent Learning. *Copyright © 1930 by Teachers College, Columbia University. Reproduced by permission.*)

Research exploring the acquisition and retention of verbal skills is not nearly as definitive, although it is still possible to conclude that practice will not be as efficient if the learner has to concentrate for long periods of time without some rest. As most students have discovered, cramming for examinations tends to produce high test scores but rapid forgetting. This example is supported by research (B. J. Underwood, 1964) showing that massed practice is better than spaced practice for acquisition but poorer for retention. Since the retention of learned material is important for the transfer process in training settings, spaced practice is the more useful technique.

Thus, the literature indicates that distributed practice utilizing reasonable rest periods is the favored technique. However, this generalization is not without penalties or exceptions. Massed practice does take less time than spaced practice, which requires learning time plus rest intervals. As DeCecco (1968) has noted, students have ignored warnings against using massed practice just because spaced practice takes more time. In situations in which the error tendency is high or the student is likely to forget critical responses, the time between practice periods must be either shortened or eliminated (DeCecco, 1968). This is often the case in problem-solving situations in which the learner must discover the correct answers from a variety of possible solutions. The learner goes through a large number of incorrect solutions before arriving at the correct answer. Here, forgetting the previous inappropriate responses would lead to an increase in learning time. In a more obvious case, it is often more efficient to mass, rather than space, trials when the material to be learned is relatively brief.

Overlearning

Another condition of practice that has implications for both acquisition and transfer is overlearning. Since the criterion of success during training is often arbitrarily set by instructors, the intent of the overlearning concept is to ensure thorough learning of the task (McGehee & Thayer, 1961). The importance of overlearning is based on several factors.

First, overlearning is especially important when the task is not likely to be practiced often in the transfer setting. Second, Fitts' (1965) review of the research in this area has led him to believe that overlearning is necessary in order to maintain performance during periods of emergency and stress. He has found that improvements in one criterion of the task may asymptote (for example, reduction of errors), but other measures (like response time) might show progressive improvement, implying that learning is still continuing.

A study by Schendel and Hagman (1982) examining psychomotor skills used, for example, in the disassembly and assembly of weapons demonstrated the positive benefits of overlearning. They trained soldiers to criterion and then gave 100% overtraining. Thus, if a particular performer took 10 trials to perform one errorless disassembly and assembly of the weapon, then he or she received ten additional trials as part of initial training. Another group of soldiers received overtraining but in this case each person received their particular extra trials midway through the eight-week retention period. This training was referred to as refresher training. At the end of the eight-week interval, both the overtrained and the refresher group performed significantly better than a control group which was given just initial training. The overtraining group was superior to both the refresher group and the control group in terms of the amount retained. Interestingly, the number of trials of overtraining to reach criterion for both the refresher and overtraining groups was about equal. However, the costs for the overtraining group were considerably less than for the refresher group. The authors strongly recommended overtraining as a potentially powerful method, especially in those situations where performance must be maintained over long periods without much practice.

Knowledge of Results

Holding (1965) traced the series of experiments that established the importance of this variable in the learning process. He noted that one of the earliest studies of knowledge of results was provided by E. L. Thorndike (1927), who had two groups of subjects (both blindfolded) draw hundreds of lines measuring 3, 4, 5, or 6 inches over a period of several days. The members of one group were given feedback that indicated whether their response was right or wrong within the established criterion of a quarter-inch of the target area. The members of the second group were not given any feedback. These data indicated that the group that received the knowledge of results improved considerably in its performance, while the other group continued making errors. A later study (Trowbridge & Cason, 1932) repeated this experiment but included a group that received feedback stating the degree of error. The subjects in this group gained even greater accuracy than the group that was just told that the answers were right or wrong. These two studies are examples of the many experiments that have demonstrated the importance of feedback. There is even evidence to indicate that learners often provide their own feedback when other external cues are not available. For example, an analysis of the original Thorndike data by Seashore and Bavelas (1941) showed that the group members who had not received any feedback became more consistent in their performance, even though they continued to make large errors. In this case, the subjects learned to match their previous attempts. Thus, as Holding suggested, learners who are not provided with external standards will often develop their own performance requirements.

Researchers suggest that the reason why knowledge of results improves performance can be attributed to motivational and informational functions. The feedback in Thorndike's experiment can be viewed as praise or reproof as well as information about performance on the task. A study examining training practices in a safety program (Komaki, Heinzman, & Lawson, 1980) addressed the issue of feedback. Komaki and her colleagues specifically asked whether training alone was sufficient or if it was necessary to provide feedback in order to maintain performance on the job. This study was conducted in the vehicle maintenance division of a large city's public works department. The researchers selected a department which had high accident rates. The department was a vehicle maintenance division responsible for the repair and maintenance of vehicle equipment for the city. The researchers conducted a needs assessment, including examination of safety logs, to determine safety incidents that had occurred. With the help of supervisors and workers, they designed procedures to eliminate accident problems. Thus, if it was found that an accident occurred because a worker had fallen off a jack stand, an item was included in the training program related to the proper use of jacks and jack stands. These training items also formed the basis for a system for observing the effects of performance. The training program involved a number of procedures, including slides depicting posed scenes of unsafe behavior followed by discussions of safety procedures. For example, one slide depicted an employee working under a vehicle without appropriate eye protection devices. Komaki found that preceding training, employees were performing safely one- to two-thirds of the time. After training, performance improved about 9%. Komaki then added another condition, including feedback on a daily basis in the form of a graph showing the safety level of the group and the safety goals that the group was trying to achieve. This extra condition resulted in an improvement of 26% over the pre-training phase and 16% over the training-only phase. Komaki makes the point that training alone is not sufficient to improve and maintain performance. Rather, training plus feedback provides the most effective strategy.

The study of line drawing discussed above (Trowbridge & Cason, 1932), which added a group with specific knowledge of results, illustrates the informational function of knowledge of results. Of course, the extra information does not preclude the motivational aspects of the feedback. In most situations, it is difficult to separate the effects caused by the motivational qualities and the informational aspects of knowledge of results. Even the simple feedback of "right" versus "wrong" conveys some information. The important issue regarding the informational nature of knowledge of results involves specificity. Contrary to popular belief, increased specificity does not necessarily lead to improved performance. It can actually lead to performance deficits. While some increases in specificity may be helpful, a saturation point can be reached at which the information is too much for the subject to handle, and which simply leads to confusion. As the subjects become more proficient at a task, they may also be able to learn to integrate more specific feedback. For each task, it is necessary for the trainer to carefully design the feedback to fit that situation and the capabilities of the learner. Additionally, the feedback should be timed so that the information necessary to correct the subject's response is immediately available.

Most training analysts have placed considerable emphasis on the importance of knowledge of results in the learning process. Unfortunately, many of those who emphasize its importance simply assume that any form of feedback with any sort of timing will accomplish the purpose. The preceding discussion indicates that the application of feedback requires real sensitivity for the task and the learner. In addition, there appear to be some tasks, like tracking or trouble shooting, in which the utility of feedback is questionable (Gagné, 1962).

Retention

The utilization of previously learned materials in the transfer setting presupposes that the learner has been able to retain recently acquired skills; that is, the learner has not forgotten. Johnson (1981) makes the point that "the scientific community knows about retention about the same as what the man on the street knows; people can't remember what they didn't learn and they forget over time" (p. 258). A related criticism that Johnson makes is that most research has focused on laboratory tasks and there is little knowledge about retention on tasks that occur in real work settings. These criticisms have been voiced before and it is clear that research in field environments is badly needed in order to determine whether it is possible to be able to generalize our knowledge from laboratory settings to field environments. In that regard, it now appears that some researchers are taking that concern seriously. Thus, Hagman and Rose (1983) reported on 17 studies that examined retention of performance on military tasks. The results of their review are incorporated into the next section on the effects of variables on the retention process.

The degree of original learning.   Any of the variables that affect the degree of original learning also affect the retention of the material. The effects of overlearning are especially important in enabling the learners to retain their information over a long period of time. Other factors that should be examined include the motivational and informational character of the feedback and the distributed-practice methods. Hagman and Rose (1983) found in their review of military tasks that task repetition was especially effective in improving retention. This, of course, is consistent with the research on overlearning described in an earlier section. They note that repetition both before and after proficiency has been achieved increases the level of acquisition, which in turn is very helpful in maintaining performance during intervals when no practice takes place. They also note that training typically involves combinations where material is presented to be learned and then tests are given to recall information. The experiments they report indicate that repetitions of both the presentation and the testing are effective in promoting retention. The researchers also found that retention was better with spaced rather than massed training, again supporting the basic research literature.

The meaningfulness of the material.   There is extensive research to indicate that the more meaningful the material, the more easily it is retained. It is important to properly organize the material and to establish principles to retain information, even if the material appears to be meaningless. Music students are aided in their retention of the musical notes corresponding to the lines and spaces of the staff through the use of coding schemes that organize the information. For example, the lines of the treble staff are the first letters of *every good boy does fine,* and the spaces spell *face.*

Interestingly, Hagman and Rose did not find that the use of mnemonic techniques helped improve retention. However, in these experiments the task was relatively easy and the soldiers reported that it was not necessary to have a coding scheme in order to retain the material.

The amount of interference.   There are two types of interference that hinder the retention of material. In one type, proactive inhibition, previously learned material interferes with the recall of the new material. The other type, retroactive inhibition, pertains to activities that occur after the original learning (during the retention period) that interfere with the recall of the original material. Thus, proactive effects concern interference that results from materials learned before original learning, while retroactive effects relate to interference that occurs after original learning. These two interference problems are diagrammed in Figure 4.3.

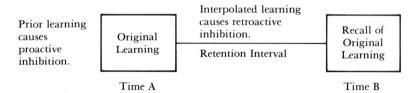

FIGURE 4.3   Interference theory. Material learned at Time A is tested for recall, after a retention interval, at Time B. Material learned prior to Time A (prior learning) produces proactive inhibition; things learned between Times A and B (interpolated learning) produce retroactive inhibition. (*From* Psychology: Its Principles and Meanings, *by L. E. Bourne, Jr., and B. R. Ekstrand. Copyright © 1973 by The Dryden Press. Reprinted by permission of The Dryden Press.*)

Interference relationships are often specified in terms of stimulus and response similarity. When the stimuli in the prior-learning and new-learning situations are the same but the responses required are different, strong proactive-interference effects in the recall of the new learning material can be expected.

Motives, perceptions, and retention.   There are many instances in which memory is affected by our perception of an event. Freud used the term *repression* to describe the tendency to forget events associated with fear and unpleasantness. Soldiers are sometimes unable to remember particular combat experiences because the events were frightening or because they were ashamed of their performance. Yet, these individuals are able to remember events of ordinary military life with ease. In a more common example, witnesses viewing the same accident give completely different descriptions of the events. In an experimental demonstration of the effects of perceptions on recall (Carmichael, Hogan, & Walter, 1932), subjects were presented with a stimulus figure. Some were told that it was a letter C, while others were told it was a crescent moon. When asked to recall the object, the subjects drew shapes that resembled the idea they had been given rather than the stimulus object. Thus, one group changed the figure toward a crescent and the other toward the letter C. This occurred for a variety of name pairs, including bottle-stirrup, eyeglasses-dumbbells, and gun-broom.

THE CONDITIONS OF TRANSFER

Although the previous sections emphasize basic learning principles and initial learning processes, the question of transfer is paramount, especially for those concerned with instructional programs. Evaluation designs and criteria are chosen to measure performance in the transfer setting as a function of initial learning in the instructional program. Trainees are expected to use the skills, knowledge, and attitudes developed in training in the transfer setting. The main problem is persistence of behavior from the learning setting to another setting.

An experiment by R. C. Atkinson (1972) illustrates the complexities of the transfer task and the necessity for closely examining the characteristics of the training and transfer environment. The task consisted of vocabulary learning, in which large sets of German–English items were to be learned. On each trial, a German word was presented, and the student responded with the English translation. The correct answer was then presented. Three strategies were utilized for the presentation of material. In the first strategy (random-order strategy), the items were randomly selected and presented by the computer. A second strategy (learner-controlled) permitted the student to decide which item was to be studied. A third strategy (response-sensitive strategy) utilized a mathematical model to compute, on a trial-by-trial basis, the individual's state of learning in order to optimize the final level of achievement. All instructions were administered by computer control, with each student being given 336 trials in an instruction session and a delayed test session one week later. Figure 4.4 presents the results of the experiment. During learning, the random-order procedure led to the best performance, followed by learner-controlled and response-sensitive strategies. However, the results on the final test, the transfer setting, were completely reversed. The random-order strategy resulted in good performance in training because it presented many items that had previously been mastered. The learner-controlled strategy allowed the students to concentrate on those items that they had not learned, which resulted in a relatively poor performance in training. The response-sensitive strategy successfully selected those items that had not been mastered by the student, leading to a high error rate in training. However, in the delayed test session, in which the students were examined on all of the material, the response-sensitive strategy produced the best performance, because the training procedure had maximized the amount of time spent on unlearned items.

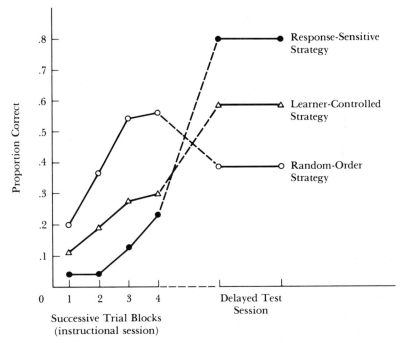

FIGURE 4.4 Proportion of correct responses in successive trial blocks during the instructional session and on the delayed test administered one week later. (*From "Ingredients for a Theory of Instruction," by R. C. Atkinson. In* American Psychologist, *1972, 27, pp. 921–931. Copyright 1971 by the American Psychological Association. Reprinted by permission.*)

Atkinson's experiment clearly warns against assumptions about transfer performance that are based only on initial learning scores. This experiment illustrates the necessity of carefully designing a training environment that will maximize transfer.

THE BASIC TRANSFER DESIGN

In order to determine transfer effects, we might compare an experimental group that learns one task and then transfers to a second task with a control group that performs only the second task. If the experimental group performs significantly better than the control group on the second task, *positive transfer* has occurred. It can be assumed that the learning that occurred in the first task has transferred and aided performance in the second task. This assumption would be valid only if the experiment were properly executed and if it accounted for the various forms of bias and error discussed in the chapters on criteria and experimental design. If the experimental group performs worse than the control group on the second task, *negative transfer* has occurred. The learning of the first task has resulted in poorer performance on the second task. When there are no differences in performance between the experimental and control groups on the second task, there is *zero transfer.*

While the basic paradigms of transfer of training have been examined for some time, the exact conditions leading to positive or negative transfer are not easily specified, because settings outside the experimental laboratory rarely lend themselves to the type of analysis necessary to accurately specify the degree of transfer. However, it is important to understand the theories that predict varying degrees of transfer, because they provide information about the type of environment necessary to achieve positive transfer. The two major viewpoints that describe the conditions necessary for transfer are the identical-elements and the transfer-through-principle theories.

Identical Elements

The theory of identical elements was proposed by E. L. Thorndike and R. S. Woodworth (1901). They predicted that transfer would occur as long as there were identical elements in the two situations. These identical elements included aims, methods, and approaches and were later defined in terms of stimuli and responses. Holding (1965) summarized the work on transfer by detailing the type of transfer expected based on the similarity of the stimuli and responses (see Table 4.3).

In the first case, the stimuli and responses are identical. If the tasks are identical in training and transfer, trainees are simply practicing the final task during the training program and there should be high

TABLE 4.3   Type of transfer—based on stimulus and response similarity

Task stimuli	Response required	Transfer
same	same	high positive
different	different	none
different	same	positive
same	different	negative

Adapted from *Principles of Training*, by D. H. Holding. ©1965 by Pergamon Press, Ltd. Adapted by permission.

positive transfer. However, it would be unusual for a training program to have the same characteristics as the transfer setting. The purpose of the training program is to provide an environment for learning because the trainee is not capable of performing the task as it exists in the transfer setting. Perhaps he or she requires special modes of feedback or a permissive atmosphere in which to learn new approaches. As instruction proceeds, many programs attempt to develop environments that are as similar as possible to the transfer surroundings. But some differences, however subtle, almost always remain. For example, airline trainees know that a serious pilot error on a well-designed simulator will not have the same disastrous consequences as a similar error in a real airplane.

The second case assumes that the task characteristics, both stimuli and responses, are so different that practice on one task has no relationship to performance on the transfer task. It would be farfetched, although not impossible, to design a training program that is totally unrelated to the transfer situation.

The third case is common to many training programs. The stimuli are somewhat different in training and transfer settings, but the responses are the same. The learner can generalize training from one environment to another. The person who has learned to drive one type of car usually has little difficulty switching to another (assuming the required responses remain the same), even though minor features may be different (for example, dashboard arrangement).

The fourth case presents the basic paradigm for negative transfer. A certain response to training stimuli is practiced so that the same response is given each time those stimuli appear. If the response becomes inappropriate, negative transfer results. As technology develops, producing continual modifications in control and display equipment without considering the role of human beings, there are frequent instances of negative transfer. Some airplane accidents provide a clear illustration of this effect (Chapanis, Garner, & Morgan, 1949). In one instance, a pilot attempted to correct for a landing, in which he was about to undershoot the field, by pulling back on the throttle and pushing the stick forward. However, this procedure was exactly opposite to the correct sequence of responses, and the pilot nosed his plane toward the ground. After the accident, the pilot (fortunately) was able to explain that he had been trained with planes in which the throttle was operated with the right hand and the stick with the left hand. In this plane, the positions of these controls were reversed. Thus, he used his left hand on the throttle and his right hand on the stick. When the emergency occurred, the pilot reverted to his old response habits—with disastrous results.

There is a tendency among some trainers to ignore stimulus and response elements as being too mechanistic and detailed. They make the assumption that analyses of stimulus and response elements are too difficult and that much of the research stems from the laboratory and therefore is not relevant. While these are difficulties, that is an unfortunate judgment. There are a large number of jobs that require responses to large, complex displays where such analyses would be extremely useful. An example of this situation is the nuclear power industry where there is extreme concern about transfer issues resulting from nuclear control room modifications. The life cycle of a nuclear power plant is approximately 40 years and in that time period there will be many changes in the control room. The concern is that the changes introduced must be carefully analyzed to avoid negative transfer effects.

An analysis of this problem (Sawyer, Pain, Van Cott, & Banks, 1982) noted that the most serious negative transfer problem was the situation where "new, conflicting responses on the transfer task are required while stimuli identical or similar to those used in the original task are retained" (p. 6). They performed an analysis of the potential changes in control room design and designated preferred versus less preferred solutions. An example of one of those situations is shown in Figure 4.5. Obviously, it would also be preferable to train operators on a display which, if not identical to the one that would be used, is at least as compatible as possible, thus preventing negative transfer.

Another important issue is the role of stress in effecting transfer performance. The popular idea is that increments of stress produce regression to prior habits, thus creating situations which are prone to negative transfer. While this might be true, there is not enough research evidence available to be able to determine the effects of stress on transfer performance in job situations.

Transfer through Principles

Critics of the identical-elements theory have argued that the analysis of transfer need not be limited to those situations in which there are identical elements. Actually, Thorndike and Woodworth did not intend for the identical-element view to be specific to stimulus and response components (Ellis, 1965). Their elements consisted of items like general principles and attitudes, as well as the more specific components. The principles theory suggests that training should focus on the general principles necessary to learn a task so that the learner may apply them to solve problems in the transfer task. An interesting experiment by

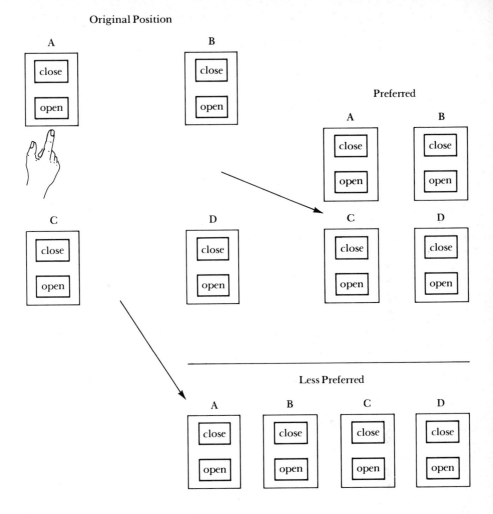

PROBLEM: The top legend-controls are difficult to reach and thus should be lowered.

EXPLANATION: The top alternative is preferable because it retains the basic perceptual relationship among the controls while at the same time moving the top controls within easy reach. Although the bottom alternative is not necessarily a bad one, because of prior experience (conditioning) operators may have some problem identifying the array rapidly.

FIGURE 4.5 Example of possible control board modifications. (*From Sawyer, C. R.; Pain, R. F.; Van Cott, H.; and Banks, W. W. Nuclear control room modifications and the role of transfer of training principles: A review of issues and research (NUREG/CR-2828, EGG-2211). Idaho National Engineering Laboratory.*)

Hendrikson and Schroeder (1941) demonstrated the transfer of principles related to the refraction of light. Two groups were given practice shooting at an underwater target until each was able to hit the target consistently. The depth of the target was then changed. One group was taught the principles of refraction of light through water. In the next session of target shooting, this group performed significantly better than the group not taught the principles.

This theory suggests that it is possible to design training environments without too much concern about their similarity to the transfer situation, as long as it is possible to utilize underlying principles. The primary concerns become which environmental design best helps the trainee to learn appropriate principles for application in transfer situations (Bass & Vaughan, 1966) and which design best avoids potential negative-transfer effects.

In recent years, researchers have begun to ask questions related to the transfer of performance based upon improving general abilities through training in related but non-identical tasks. The idea here is that if it were possible to identify broad abilities, it might be possible to train persons in these abilities and have performance transfer to a variety of different tasks, thus avoiding training for each specific task. As noted by Hogan (1978), the research question is whether training on tasks which require a particular ability will result in positive transfer to other tasks which are also known to require the same ability. There is no answer to this question yet. Based upon the work of Fleishman (1972), there is considerable evidence that basic abilities are related to performance in a wide variety of tasks. A few of the abilities specified by Fleishman include the following:

1. reaction time—speed required to respond to a stimulus;
2. multilimb coordination—the coordination of the movement of several limbs in the operation of a control;
3. gross body equilibrium—the control of balance with nonvisual cues.

Through a variety of studies, Fleishman found that the particular abilities required to perform a task were systematic and subject to change during practice. These changes have important implications for skill training at different stages of learning. For example, Fleishman (1972) analyzed a complex tracking task and found that spatial orientation was important early in the task and multilimb coordination was important later in the task. Fleishman used this information in a training program by first presenting special instructions about orientation and later providing information about coordination requirements. The trained group was found to be superior to several other groups when it was examined on the tracking task. Thus, Fleishman's approach presents an important methodology for the specification of particular abilities and their relationship to the most appropriate instructional technique. If it is found in future research that it is possible to train persons in specific abilities and have performance transfer to other tasks which use that same ability, it will be an important step forward.

In a broader context, the concept of occupational adaptability is based upon similar ideas. An adaptable individual is defined by Sjogren

(1977) "as one who can generalize, transfer, or form associations so that the skills, attitudes, knowledge and personal characteristics that have been learned or developed in one context can be readily used in a different context" (Pratzner, 1978, p. 13). Issues concerning this individual adaptability relate to both opportunities in career development and to opportunities for job transfers. Using this type of model, it is possible to conceptualize how easy or difficult it might be to transfer from one job to another based upon the similarities of the tasks, the knowledge, skills, and abilities, and the situation. Pratzner has attempted to outline some of these parameters for various jobs. Table 4.4 illustrates this approach. In this table, Pratzner has outlined how three parameters (methods used, content domain, context) change as you consider different jobs. If it were possible to establish measures empirically for each of these parameters and show how they vary from job to job, such a system would be very valuable to persons considering job or career changes.

Climate for Transfer

In the sections above issues involved in the specification of stimuli and responses and its relationship to the transfer issue were discussed. However, it is critical to remember that transfer of training from an instructional setting (such as a company training program) to a work environment involves all of the issues related to the necessity of having a positive transfer climate in the work organization. These concerns were discussed in the needs assessment chapter in the section on organizational analysis. However, it is appropriate to consider the issue again in this section since it is so clearly related to issues of transfer. It has become obvious that situations which should result in positive transfer have at best resulted in zero transfer because of a failure to consider issues related to the work organization. A number of empirical studies have begun to identify some of the factors that determine the extent of transfer support in the organization. Baumgartel and Jeanpierre (1972) found that persons who were in favorable organizational climates (freedom to set personal performance goals, risk-taking encouraged, growth-oriented, top management willing to spend money for training) were most likely to be able to apply knowledge gained in training programs. This effect was even more pronounced when the person was in a lower level position in the organization where the trainee did not have the influence to effect change unless there was a favorable climate. Other authors (Leifer & Newstrom, 1980; Michalak, 1981) make the following points:

1. We must have a system which unites trainer, trainee, and manager in the transfer process.
2. Before training, the expectations for the trainee and the manager must be clear.

TABLE 4.4   Examples of changes in job methods, content, and context as a function of changes in jobs

Methods Used (Tasks, Activity)	Content Domain (Concepts, Objects Acted upon)	Context (Work Situation)	Examples
Same	Same	Same	a. Change in rank from Junior Programmer, to Programmer, to Senior Programmer. b. Change in rank from Associate Professor to Professor. c. Clerk-Steno III to Secretary I.
Same	Same	Different	a. Design Engineer for government research, to Design Engineer for consumer product production, same employer. b. Navy Cook (retired) to Institutional Cook (civilian).
Same	Different	Different	a. Aerospace Systems Analyst for training requirements of new equipment, to Systems Analyst for Public Vocational Education Systems. b. Medical Secretary to Legal Secretary. c. Business Data Programmer to Scientific Data Programmer.
Same	Different	Same	a. Secondary English Teacher to Secondary Social Studies Teacher. b. Flying Instructor (single-engine prop) to Flying Instructor (2-engine jet). c. Truck Driver (light panel) to Truck Driver (heavy tractor-trailer).
Different	Same	Same	a. Skilled Craftsman to Foreman. b. Secondary Teacher to Assistant Principal.
Different	Different	Same	a. Progress upward through key rungs of career ladder, from Orderly, to LPN, to RN, to MD Intern. b. Flight Engineer to Commercial Pilot. c. Bricklayer (house construction) to Real Estate Agent.
Different	Same	Different	a. Liberal Arts Major in Psychology to Salesman. b. Business Major to Auditor.
Different	Different	Different	a. Liberal Arts Major in Philosophy to Broker. b. Housewife to Riveter. c. Electronics Technician to Developmental Psychologist.

From *Occupational Adaptability and Transferable Skills* (Information Series No. 129). Copyright 1978 by The National Center for Research in Vocational Education, Columbus, Ohio. Reprinted by permission.

3. We must identify obstacles to transfer and provide strategies to overcome these problems.
4. We must work with managers to provide opportunities for the maintenance of trainees' learned behavior in the work organization.

The importance of maintaining behavior and overcoming obstacles is clearly detailed in a model developed by Marx (1982). His model is based upon another model which was originally designed to examine relapse problems in addictive behavior such as smoking and alcoholism. The model as shown in Figure 4.6 outlines the importance of having coping responses in the repertoire of managers to prevent relapses in their learned behavior. Thus, as part of his training program, Marx makes managers aware of the relapse process. He also has them diagnose situations that are likely to sabotage their efforts at maintaining their new learning. For example, he notes in the model that if one problem is increased stress resulting from time pressure, then a coping skill such as time management techniques would be taught. As described in the model, these coping responses result in increased self-efficacy and decreased probability of relapse. The model also describes the situations that occur when no coping response is available. In this situation, the

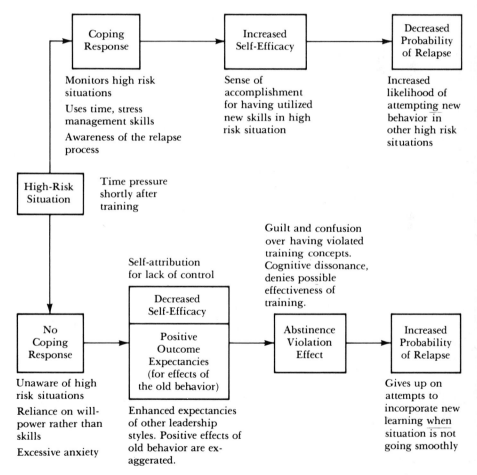

FIGURE 4.6 Cognitive-behavioral model of the relapse process. (*From "Relapse Prevention for Managerial Training: A Model for Maintenance of Behavioral Change," by R. D. Marx. In* Academy of Management Review, *1982, 7, pp. 443–441. Copyright 1982 by the Academy of Management. Reprinted by permission.*)

results can lead to giving up on attempts to incorporate new learning. Opportunities for positive transfer than disappear regardless of what has been learned in training. While many of the ideas in the model remain to be tested, it is clear that many researchers are beginning to investigate the important issues concerning a positive climate for transfer.

Training for Transfer

While the preceding issues regarding transfer difficulties are not yet completely resolved, there are guidelines from learning studies that suggest various ways of producing transfer to new learning situations. The following suggestions were adapted from Ellis (1965, pp. 70–72).

1. Maximize the similarity between the teaching and the ultimate testing situation.
2. Provide adequate experience with the original task. Most research shows that adequate practice in training is essential for positive transfer. This is especially true for new skills and concepts for which thorough training must be given early in the learning process.
3. Provide for a variety of stimulus situations so that the students may generalize their knowledge. One way of overcoming the constraints of a training setting is to provide a variety of stimulus situations so that the learners can begin to generalize their concepts to the many situations in which transfer must occur.
4. Label or identify important features of the task. Labeling helps distinguish the significant characteristics of the task. Thus, the learner is able to use the necessary cues to determine when transfer behavior is appropriate or inappropriate.
5. Make sure that general principles are understood. This can be accomplished by presenting a variety of situations and asking the learner to apply the general principle. If the program is based on the learning of principles and the trainees do not thoroughly understand them, they have gained little from the training program that will be useful in the transfer setting.

An additional series of recommendations can be added from points 1, 2, 3, and 4 in the preceding section (see page 95), concerning the importance of establishing a positive transfer of training climate in the work organization.

THE INSTRUCTIONAL ENVIRONMENT

Gagné's Instructional Theory

In the opening sections of this chapter, material is presented describing the development of a new approach to the study of learning environments known as *instructional theory*. As defined by Gagné and Dick

(1983), "theories of instruction attempt to relate specified events comprising instruction to learning processes and learning outcomes, drawing upon knowledge generated by learning research and theory" (p. 264). He also notes that these theories are often prescriptive in that they identify conditions of instruction which will optimize learning, retention, and transfer. It is also clear that such instructional theories often become the underlying foundation for instructional design procedures which will support the learning activities. One of the better-developed theories in this area has also been formulated by Gagné (1984). In this model, Gagné describes a set of categories of learning outcomes to organize human performance. He then related those learning outcomes to the conditions necessary to support learning performance. Gagné's learning outcomes are as follows:

> 1. *Intellectual skills.* These skills include concepts, rules and procedures. Sometimes this is referred to as *procedural knowledge.* The rules for mathematical computations are a good example of intellectual skills. Some further examples of types of intellectual skills and the tasks they emulate from can be found in Table 4.5.
> 2. *Verbal information.* This category is also sometimes called *declarative information* and it refers to the ability of the individual to declare or state something. In Table 4.5, the example is stating the main kinds of fire extinguishers and their uses.
> 3. *Cognitive strategies.* This refers to the idea that learners bring to a new task not only intellectual skills and verbal information but also a knowledge of how and when to use this information. In a sense, the cognitive strategies form a type of strategic knowledge that enables the learner to know when and how to choose the intellectual skills and verbal information they will use.
> 4. *Motor skills.* This skill refers to one of the more obvious examples of human performance. Examples of motor skills include writing, swimming, using tools, and the like.
> 5. *Attitudes.* Gagné notes that student preferences for particular activities often reflect differences in attitudes. He points out that persons learn to have these preferences and notes that the number of different commercial messages that we are bombarded by is evidence of the common belief that attitudes are learned.

It would be interesting to know what constitutes a category and why there are five categories instead of seven. Gagné's (1984) rules for the establishment of categories are as follows:

1. Each category should be distinguishable in terms of a formal definition of human performance.
2. The category should include a broad variety of activities that are not dependent upon intelligence, age, race, and so on. He excludes (while acknowledging) special categories such as musical virtuosity, wine tasting, and the like.
3. Each category should differ in terms of the basic learning processes, such as information processing demands.

TABLE 4.5   Examples of tasks reflected in target objectives and the learning categories they represent

Task	Learning Category
Discriminates printed letters *g* and *p*	*Intellectual skill* (discrimination)—perceiving objects as same or different
Identifies *ovate* shape of tree leaves	*Intellectual skill* (concrete concept)—identifying an object property
Classifies *citizens* of a nation, by definition	*Intellectual skill* (defined concept)—using a definition to identify a class
Demonstrates instances of the rule relating pressure and volume of a gas at constant temperature	*Intellectual skill* (rule)—applying a rule to one or more concrete examples
Generates a rule predicting the inflationary effect of decreasing value of currency in international exchange	*Intellectual skill* (higher-order rule)—generating a more complex rule by combining simpler rules
Originates a written composition on the cybernetic features of a bureaucracy	*Cognitive strategy*—inventing a novel approach to a problem
States the main kinds of fire extinguishers and their uses	*Information*—communicating organized knowledge in a way that preserves meaning
Chooses reading novels as a leisure-time activity	*Attitude*—choosing a course of personal action toward a class of events
Executes the tightening of a lag screw with a socket wrench	*Motor skill*—carrying out a smoothly timed motor performance

From *Principles of Instructional Design,* by R. M. Gagné and L. J. Briggs. Copyright ©1979 by CBS College Publishing Company, Inc. Reprinted by permission of Holt, Rinehart and Winston.

4. The learning principles should be similar for tasks within a learning outcome category but it should not be possible to generalize the principles across tasks from different categories.

Thus, Gagné and his colleagues have developed a set of learning categories which permits them to analyze tasks and code behavior into one of the learning outcomes. The most fascinating part of the system is that Gagné and Briggs (1979) have begun to examine each of the outcomes and determine the conditions of learning and instructional events which best support that learning outcome. This system is presented in Table 4.6. The behavioral learning outcomes (intellectual skill, cognitive strategy, and so on) are presented across the top of the table. Down the side of the table, Gagné and Briggs present a series of events which are considered important to the instructional system, such as gaining attention of the learner, providing feedback, and so on. The body of the table indicates how each instructional event is manipulated for each learning outcome. Thus, for the event presenting stimulus material, you would present examples of concepts or rules for intellectual skill development while you would present novel problems for the development of cognitive strategies. As more and more is learned about various ways to support learning performance, it is clear that such systems will be very important in helping us to design effective training environments.

TABLE 4.6 Instructional events and the conditions of learning they imply for five types of learned capabilities

Instructional Event	Intellectual Skill	Cognitive Strategy	Information	Attitude	Motor Skill
			Type of Capability		
1. Gaining Attention	Introduce stimulus change; variations in sensory mode				
2. Informing learner of objective	Provide description and example of the performance to be expected	Clarify the general nature of the solution expected	Indicate the kind of verbal question to be answered	Provide example of the kind of action choice aimed for	Provide a demonstration of the performance to be expected
3. Stimulating recall of prerequisites	Stimulate recall of subordinate concepts and rules	Stimulate recall of task strategies and associated intellectual skills	Stimulate recall of context of organized information	Stimulate recall of relevant information, skills, and human model identification	Stimulate recall of executive sub-routine and part-skills
4. Presenting the stimulus material	Present examples of concept or rule	Present novel problems	Present information in propositional form	Present human model, demonstrating choice of personal action	Provide external stimuli for performance, including tools or implements
5. Providing learning guidance	Provide verbal cues to proper combining sequence	Provide prompts and hints to novel solution	Provide verbal links to a larger meaningful context	Provide for observation of model's choice of action, and of reinforcement received by model	Provide practice with feedback of performance achievement
6. Eliciting the performance	Ask learner to apply rule or concept to new examples	Ask for problem solution	Ask for information in paraphrase, or in learner's own words	Ask learner to indicate choices of action in real or simulated situations	Ask for execution of the performance
7. Providing feedback	Confirm correctness of rule or concept application	Confirm originality of problem solution	Confirm correctness of statement of information	Provide direct or vicarious reinforcement of action choice	Provide feedback on degree of accuracy and timing of performance
8. Assessing performance	Learner demonstrates application of concept or rule	Learner originates a novel solution	Learner restates information in paraphrased form	Learner makes desired choice of personal action in real or simulated situation	Learner executes performance of total skill
9. Enhancing retention and transfer	Provide spaced reviews including a variety of examples	Provide occasions for a variety of novel problem solutions	Provide verbal links to additional complexes of information	Provide additional varied situations for selected choice of action	Learner continues skill practice

From *Principles of Instructional Design*, by R. M. Gagné and L. J. Briggs. Copyright 1979 by CBS College Publishing Company, Inc. Reprinted by permission of Holt, Rinehart and Winston.

Certainly, one of the points that instructional theorists are trying to make is that our traditional models of learning do not provide enough information for the design of instructional environments. They are not saying that feedback is unimportant or that massed versus spaced learning does not make any difference. They are saying that it is necessary to understand the type of learning involved and the instructional event being considered before it is possible to choose the most effective learning procedures. In addition to the work of instructional theorists, a number of other researchers have become concerned with various aspects of the instructional environment. Their contributions are discussed below.

Instructional Quality Inventory

A group of researchers (Wulfeck, Ellis, Richards, Wood, & Merrill, 1978) at the Navy Personnel Research and Development Center have concentrated on indicators of instructional quality. Utilizing information gained from research in cognitive and instructional theory, they have specified conditions concerning the adequacy of the course objectives, the test consistency, and the presentation consistency. Their work is based upon the idea that there is a task dimension and a content dimension to training. The task dimension refers to tasks a trainee can perform. The trainee can either remember information or use the information to do something. In addition, the trainee who uses information can either do it unaided, where there are no aids available except for memory, or do it aided, where some form of support is provided. The content dimension is divided into five types of content that can be provided in a training program: facts, concepts, procedures, rules, and principles. A matrix showing the task and content dimensions (with definitions) is shown in Table 4.7.

These researchers then use the dimensions to analyze the objectives, the presentation, and the tests used in a training program in order to establish the instructional quality. An example of their system for analyzing training presentations is shown in Table 4.8. Across the top of the table are content dimensions like facts, concepts, and so on. Along the side are various types of presentation components (statements, examples, and so on). The body of the table gives the appropriate presentation procedure. Thus, when presenting statements in a training program for a concept, all critical characteristics and their combinations are given. Similarly, when presenting statements for a procedure, all steps are given in the correct order. Wulfeck and his associates present similar rules for analyzing training objectives and training tests. For example, they ask questions concerning the conditions under which student performance is expected for each of the following:

TABLE 4.7 The task-content matrix of the instructional quality inventory

	FACT— recall or recognize names, parts, dates, places, etc.	CONCEPT— remember characteristics, or classify objects, events, or ideas according to characteristics	PROCEDURE— sequence of steps remembered or used in a single situation or on a single piece of equipment	RULE— remember or use a sequence of steps which apply across situations or across equipments	PRINCIPLE— remember, or interpret or predict why or how things happen, or cause–effect relationships
REMEMBER—recall or recognize facts, concept definitions, steps of procedures or rules, statements of principle					
USE-UNAIDED—tasks which require classifying, performing a procedure, using a rule, explaining or predicting with no aids except memory					
USE-AIDED—same as use-unaided, except job aids are available					

From Wulfeck, W. H., II; Ellis, J. A.; Richards, R. E.; Wood, N. D.; and Merrill, M. D. *The Instructional Quality Inventory: I. Introduction and Overview* (NPRDC SR 79-3). Navy Personnel Research and Development Center.

TABLE 4.8 Presentation consistency

Presentation Component	Content Type of the Objective				
	Fact	*Concept*	*Procedure*	*Rule*	*Principle*
Statement	complete fact presented	all critical characteristics and their combinations are given	all steps are given in the correct order	all steps and branching decisions are given in the correct order	all causes, effects, and relationships are given
Practice Remembering	recall or recognition required	recall of concept definition required	recall of all steps in correct order required	recall of all steps and branch decisions in correct order required	recall of all causes, effects, relationships required
For all content types:	Practice Remembering items must be the same as the test item. They must be the same format as the test item. All practice items must include feedback.				
Examples	not applicable	examples show all critical characteristics required for classification, non-examples show absence of critical characteristics	application of the procedure must be shown and steps must be shown in the correct order	application of each step or branching decision must be shown in the correct order	interpretation or prediction based on causes, effects, and relationships must be shown
Practice Using	not applicable	classification of both examples and non-examples is required	all steps must be performed in the correct order	all steps and branching decisions must be performed in the correct order	explanation or prediction based on the principle is required
For all content types:	Practice Using items must reflect what is to be done on the job or in later training. The task/content level, conditions, and standards must match the test item and objective. The practice item format must be the same as the test item format. All practice items must include feedback.				
For CONCEPTS, RULES, and PRINCIPLES:	Some practice items should be different than either the test items or the examples. (Common error items might be the same.)				

From Ellis, J. A., & Wulfeck, W. H., II. *The Instructional Quality Inventory: IV. Job Performance Aid* (NPRDC SR 79-5). Navy Personnel Research and Development Center, 1978.

Environment: Physical (weather, time of day, lighting, etc.)
                 Social (isolation, individual, team, audience, etc.)
                 Psychological (fatigue, stress, relaxed, etc.)
Information: Given information (scenario, formula, values, etc.)
                 Cues (signals for starting or stopping)
                 Special instructions
Resources: Job aids (cards, charts, graphs, checklists, etc.)
                 Equipment, tools
                 Technical manuals

Similarly, the Instructional Quality Inventory offers rules for test items. For example, all tests are judged according to the following criteria:

1. Determine whether each item is clear and unambiguous.
2. Determine whether each item is well constructed. For this criterion, separate instructions are given for different types of test items. For example, the criteria for tests that require trainees to list something are:

   The directions should specify the number of things to be listed (if appropriate for the objective, and if the number of things is not a hint).
   The directions should specify whether or not order is important. If so, the scoring key should score sequence separately.
   The scoring key should identify allowable synonyms of alternatives, and should specify different weights if appropriate.

3. Determine whether each item is free from hints.
4. Determine whether the items permit common errors to be made.
5. Determine whether there are enough items to test objectives adequately and whether it reflects the full range of performance expected on the job.

The development of test items reflects the use of criteria to measure training performance. This is a very important area which must examine a number of issues, such as the relevance of the criteria, types of criteria, and so on. Chapter 5 covers this topic.

In addition to developing the inventory and handbooks describing its use, these researchers have also begun to conduct research studies. They have generally found that when instructional materials have been modified according to the principles stated in the inventory increases in trainee performance results.

Other Instructional Considerations

There are many other instructional considerations that designers and trainers must attend to when designing training programs. Probably, one of the most important items is the role of the trainer, who typically makes the difference between a successful or unsuccessful learning experience. The potency of the trainer's role has been demonstrated in some very important research conducted by Eden and his colleagues (Eden & Ravid, 1982; Eden & Shani, 1982). In these studies, trainers were informed that they had trainees with very high success potential attending their course. Learning performance as measured by both weekly performance measures as well as instructor ratings was significantly higher for the classes with high success potential as compared to control groups. Interestingly, the control groups in these cases consisted of trainees with the same ability levels as the persons in the high success groups. The only difference was that the trainers were informed that one group had high success potential. Eden's analyses, which included reports from trainees, indicated that inducing high expectations in trainers similarly enhanced trainee performance. He feels that the high expectations communicated by trainers or immediate superiors leads trainees to expect more of themselves and to perform better. An interesting facet of his data is that several instructors were replaced in the middle of the training program. However, the performance differentials continued unabated. Eden believes that by this time the induction of high expectancy effects had occurred and the trainees continued to perform at a high level. The researchers have dubbed this the "Pygmalion effect" in honor of George Bernard Shaw's work, which demonstrated the powerful effect our expectations can have on us. Certainly, this research attests to the powerful role that the instructor can have on learning performance.

Many opinions are offered about the characteristics that an instructor in a training course should have. Unfortunately, there is not much research related to questions about the role of these characteristics in fostering learning. Most of the research that has occurred on this topic has evaluated teacher characteristics and the reaction of students in academic classrooms. While it is not possible to state that all of these characteristics would be equally important in training settings, it is probably a good guess that instructors who had these characteristics would positively benefit the learning environment. One such list developed by Bartlett (1982) includes the following items:

> Emphasized conceptual understanding.
> Presented points of view other than his/her own.
> Gave exams that revealed strengths and weaknesses.
> Gave lectures so well organized they were easy to outline.
> Related lectures to other aspects of course.
> Was accessible outside of class.
> Gave exams that covered the course material.
> Demonstrated an extensive knowledge of the subject.
> Presented an outline of the course.
> Answered questions clearly and thoroughly.
> Used examples.
> Was available for out-of-class consultation.
> Set difficult but attainable goals.
> Encouraged class discussions.
> Was available to explain difficult concepts.
> Made good use of class time.
> Presented recent developments in the field.
> Was well-organized.
> Explained how topics in the course were related to each other.
> Was well-prepared.
> Encouraged students to ask questions.
> Introduced many ideas during each class session.

Allowed students to express problems related to the course.
Gave exams that were fair.
Encouraged students to share their relevant knowledge or experiences.
Effectively used blackboard and/or audio-visual aids.
Accomplished the goals and objectives of the course.
Showed enthusiasm for the subject.
Stimulated interest in the subject.

Another important approach to instructor quality issues is described by Randall (1978). He emphasizes the importance of instructor preparation. Any of us who have at the last moment discovered that our visual equipment is not available can appreciate the importance of his concerns. Table 4.9 presents an instructor preparation and planning checklist. It is hoped that the use of such a checklist will improve instruction and result in a more effective learning environment.

TABLE 4.9 Instructor preparation and planning checklist

Have you:
1. Publicized the program or activity?
2. Informed everyone about the time, place, location and other meeting arrangements?
3. Arranged all details of the meeting room?
4. Checked the physical requirements for conducting the session?
   a. Seating arrangement
   b. Podium
   c. Ashtrays
   d. Drinking water
   e. Coat racks
   f. Ventilation, heat, light, class comfort
   g. Projectors, screens
   h. Blackboard, chart pad, easel
   i. Chalk, crayon, eraser
   j. Papers, pencils
5. Secured necessary aids and equipment?
   a. Charts
   b. Handouts
   c. Demonstration materials
   d. Record-keeping items
   e. Films
   f. Slides
6. Checked to be certain equipment is in working order and familiarized yourself with it?
7. Established the objective for the session?
8. Carefully studied the lesson plan?
   a. Determined important points to be emphasized?
   b. Considered anticipated responses and group reactions?
   c. Considered experiences, examples and stories to be used?
9. Developed enthusiasm for the program?

From "You and Effective Training," by J. S. Randall. In *Training and Development Journal,* 1978, *32,* pp. 10–19. Copyright 1978 by the American Society for Training and Development, Inc. Reprinted by permission.

Evaluation

The Criterion Choices:
Introduction to Evaluation

Evaluation is the systematic collection of descriptive and judgmental information necessary to make effective training decisions related to the selection, adoption, value, and modification of various instructional activities. The objectives of instructional programs reflect numerous goals ranging from trainee progress to organizational goals. From this perspective, evaluation is an information-gathering technique that cannot possibly result in decisions that categorize programs as good or bad. Rather, evaluation should capture the dynamic flavor of the training program. Then the necessary information will be available to revise instructional programs to achieve multiple instructional objectives.

There have been many innovations in the development of instructional methodologies in past decades, including techniques like computer-assisted instruction. However, the development of such a system does not guarantee that the appropriate knowledge, skills, and abilities necessary for job performance are being learned and used by trainees on the job. Indeed, as pointed out in the preceding chapters, it is possible that the required skills have not been included in the training program or that the required skills taught in the program are not accepted by the supervisor on the job. It is also obvious that the actual designing of training programs is an art. This is true even for instructional programs that are based on careful needs assessment procedures. Evaluation thus permits the systematic collection of information to permit decisions about the selection, adoption, value, and modification of the training program. This philosophy is particularly well stated by Stake (1967).

> Folklore is not a sufficient repository. In our data banks we should document the causes and effects, the congruence of intent and accomplishment, and the panorama of judgements of those concerned. Such

> records should be kept to promote educational action, not obstruct it. The countenance of evaluation should be one of data gathering that leads to decision making, not to trouble making. (p. 539)

Unfortunately, the past history of evaluation of training programs indicates that much more effort is necessary to acquire the information needed for the decision-making process. One of the first reviews (French, 1953) to address the subject found that only one company in forty made any scientific evaluation of supervisory training programs. Since that time, articles have appeared regularly lamenting the lack of evaluation efforts. These articles written by a variety of persons from many different organizational settings, including schools, government, training laboratories, military establishments, and private industry, are remarkably similar in their descriptions of the difficulties facing evaluation researchers. The following includes a summary of several of these views.

> 1. There has been considerable difficulty in finding acceptable criteria (MacKinney, 1957). This problem becomes more serious as researchers attempt to measure the achievement of organizational objectives. However, as we shall see, the measurement of behavior in any setting is difficult.
> 2. There is a serious lack of personnel trained in the methodology of evaluation. Guba (1969, p. 37) quotes a director of a research and development center.

> > We are having trouble finding people . . . with sufficient sophistication so that they can help with technical problems. We need an evaluator interested in measuring change, who is statistically competent and has all the characteristics of a stereotype methodologist in evaluation but who has a willingness to look at new kinds of problems.

> 3. Wallace and Twichell (1953) have lamented the difficulties in establishing meaningful relationships in industrial settings. Guba (1969) noted that school evaluation studies are frequently incapable of securing any significant information. Studies of different alternatives most often find no statistically significant differences, and, even when differences are established, researchers are uncertain about the variables that determine the effect.
> 4. The personnel responsible for training and educational research are often not responsive to the need for evaluation or are fearful of the entire process. In some cases, management is reluctant to expend effort to evaluate a program that it considers to be more than adequate (Wallace & Twichell, 1953). In other cases, the training or educational director is afraid of evaluation because, if his program were found to need modification, it might jeopardize the continuance of the program as well as his position as director (Howell & Goldstein, 1971). The latter view assumes that training programs that are not immediately successful will be dissolved; the theory that training programs should be continually evaluated in order to modify and improve the product is not recognized.

While all of these concerns represent real difficulties, it is important to note that there have been important advances in the development of evaluation models during the last ten years. Many of these advances have been spurred by demands for accountability in the areas of criminal and civil justice, social welfare, fertility control, mental health, and medical treatment. Many of the evaluation issues facing these evaluators, including the establishment of relevant criteria and innovative experimental designs, are exactly the same concerns facing the training evaluator. An evaluation will not solve all training problems, but it is an important step forward. In many instances, the utilization of a simple procedure—for example, giving participants a pretest that can be used in later comparisons—will dramatically improve the validity of the obtained information. The complexities of evaluation should not be underestimated; however, the most serious problem has been the failure even to consider examining the instructional methods. The following material focuses on various components of evaluation. This chapter discusses the criteria, and the following chapter presents methods and designs of evaluation approaches. Clearly, there are numerous interactions between the two topics; the chapters should be treated not as separate entities but as two parts of the same evaluation process.

INTRODUCTION TO CRITERION DEVELOPMENT

Industrial psychologists concerned with the selection of personnel have developed programs based on instruments (for example, paper-and-pencil tests) that predict a standard of success or criterion of the job. The last decade of research has attempted to resolve questions related to these measures of success. Unfortunately, designers of training and educational programs are still faced with the same questions—that is, the choice of measures against which they can determine the viability of their program. In some cases, the training program is the instrument utilized to predict job success. In this situation, the evaluator attempts to establish the relationship between performance in the training program and performance on the job. In a different model, the training evaluator attempts to determine if persons undergoing one form of training perform better on the job than those persons who have either been trained in another program or simply been placed on the job. In all of these situations, the measures of success are standards by which the value of the program can be judged. The most carefully designed study, employing all the sophisticated methodology that can be mustered, will stand or fall on the basis of the adequacy of the criteria chosen.

In Chapter 3, we traced the development of objectives through the techniques of organizational, task, and person analyses. These objectives stated the terminal behavior, the conditions under which the terminal behavior is expected, and the standard below which the performance is unacceptable. In other words, good instructional objectives clearly state the criteria by which the student is judged. At this point, it would be tempting to declare the problem solved and proceed to the next chapter. Unfortunately, that is not possible. First, the choice of criteria is complex. Finding adequate measures of the success of a training program begins with the specification of objectives. Just because there is a measure of success does not mean that it is reliable or free from bias. It is one matter to measure success in a training program that has a degree of control, but quite another to measure success on the job, where the environment often makes the collection of valid criteria a demanding chore. There is also the question of the relationship between the measures chosen in training and performance on the job. Wallace (1965) described life-insurance programs in which it was possible to predict training-school grades with considerable accuracy; however, the scores had no relation to selling performance on the job.

In addition, there is little doubt that the complex goals represented by organizational objectives are even more difficult to measure. Guion (1961) describes with pointed humor the whole sequence of criterion selection. The following is an abbreviated version.

1. The psychologist has a hunch (or insight) that a problem exists and that he can help solve it.
2. He reads a vague, ambiguous description of the job.
3. From these faint stimuli, he formulates a fuzzy concept of an ultimate criterion.
4. He formulates a combination of measures that will give him a satisfactory composite for the criterion he desires.
5. He judges the relevance of this measure—that is, the extent to which it is neither deficient nor contaminated.
6. He then finds that the data required for his carefully built composite are not available in the company files, and there is no immediate prospect of having such records reliably kept.
7. Therefore, he selects the *best available criterion.*

Similar difficulties plague all forms of organizational and educational research. Stake (1967) suggests that the more formal evaluations specify few criteria, with little concern for standards of acceptability. He notes that even the best-trained evaluators have used a microscope rather than a panoramic viewfinder in their examination of instructional methods. Stake laments the difficulty of finding adequate criteria to study the total complexity of the educational goals. However, he is also suffering from the evaluator's decision to choose the most available criterion. Wherry (1957) further warns us that this choice is often dictated by measurement considerations that are no more valid than an arbitrary choice. He notes that selecting a criterion just because it can be measured says "We don't know what we are doing, but we are doing it very carefully, and hope you are pleased with our unintelligent diligence" (pp. 1–2). Little understanding can be gained by carefully measuring the wrong thing. Thus, these researchers suggest that criteria must also be carefully evaluated so that a good indicant of the impact of our instructional program may be obtained. The following section considers these issues of criterion evaluation.

THE EVALUATION OF CRITERIA

Criterion Relevancy

One of the purposes of the needs assessment is the determination of the knowledge, skills, and abilities (KSAs) required for successful job performance. As shown in the instructional model developed in Chapter 2, that information must provide direct input into the training program to determine the actual content of the instructional material. The same information concerning the knowledge, skills, and abilities necessary for successful job performance should also provide the input for the establishment of measures of training success. Logically, we should want our training program to consist of the materials necessary to develop the knowledge, skills, and abilities to perform successfully on the job. Just as logically, we should determine the success of our training program by developing measures (or criteria) that tell the training evaluator how well the training program does in teaching the trainees the same knowledge, skills, and abilities necessary for job success. It is likely that we would want to use these criteria at the end of the training program to determine how well our program is doing at that time, and then we might also want to use these criteria later on when the trainee is on the job to determine how much of the knowledge, skills, and abilities learned in training transferred to the actual job.

The chosen criteria are judged relevant to the degree that the components (knowledge, skills, abilities) required to succeed in the training program are the same as those required to succeed at the ultimate task (Thorndike, 1949). It is important to recognize that evaluators often choose a criterion because of its immediate availability, so it must be examined for relevance, the fundamental requirement that transcends all other considerations related to criterion development. Accurate job analysis and the ensuing behavioral objectives suggest more clearly the actual criteria to be employed in achieving the behavioral objectives. This relationship between objectives and criteria is an exercise in determining relevance.

Figure 5.1 presents the relationship that can exist between items established by the needs assessment and the items represented in the criteria chosen to assess the training program. The degree of overlap between these two sets establishes the relevance of the criteria. The term *criteria* refers to the many measures of success that must be used to evaluate instructional programs and the numerous objectives of training programs. The set on the left side shown in Figure 5.1 refers to

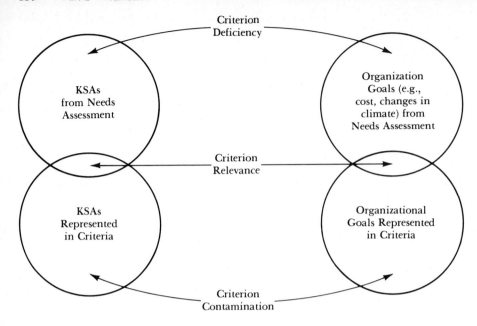

FIGURE 5.1 The constructs of criterion deficiency, relevance, and contamination.

characteristics of individual achievement for trainees as represented by the KSAs. However, it is just as possible to conceive of organizational goals established from the needs assessment and the degree to which these organizational goals are characterized in the criteria. Again, the degree to which they overlap determines the relevance of the criterion set. These relationships are represented on the right side of Figure 5.1.

Another way of conceptualizing these relationships is presented in Figure 5.2. In this case, to simplify the diagram, the relationships are just presented for KSAs. However, the reader should note that the diagram could be redrawn to show the same relationships for organizational goals such as cost. In this diagram, the horizontal axis across the top of the figure represents KSAs determined by the needs assessment. As indicated below that title, there are two possibilities, the KSAs either are or are not represented. Similarly, along the vertical axis, the KSAs are shown as either represented or not represented in the criteria. This results in the four boxes labeled ABCD in Figure 5.2. Using this method of conceptualizing, both boxes A and D are labeled criterion relevance. Box D identifies a situation where the KSAs are represented in the needs assessment and the criteria. Box A represents a situation where the KSAs are not identified by the needs assessment as being part of the situation being studied, and thus the criteria appropriately are not designed to represent these KSAs. Essentially, this point of view says that relevance is determined by making sure the criteria contain

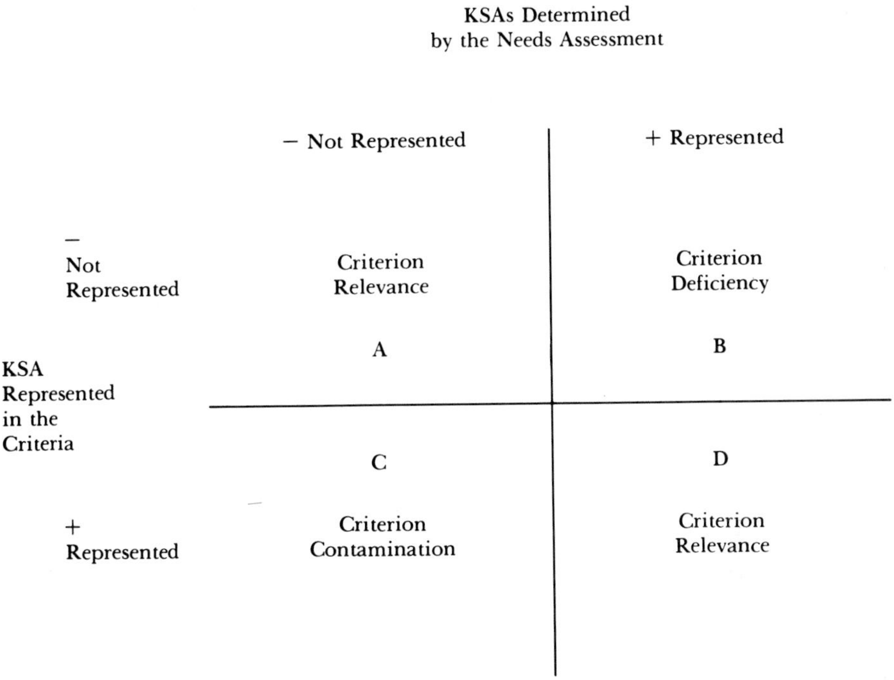

KSAs Determined
by the Needs Assessment

	− Not Represented	+ Represented
− Not Represented	Criterion Relevance A	Criterion Deficiency B
KSA Represented in the Criteria	C	D
+ Represented	Criterion Contamination	Criterion Relevance

FIGURE 5.2   The relationship between criteria and needs assessment.

the components identified as needed for job success, but do not include those components which have been determined as not relevant for job success. Of course, it is only fair to point out that while we have drawn this diagram as a four-part table, it is actually a continuum. Thus, particular KSAs may be identified by the needs assessment as particularly important, not at all important, a little important, and so on. However, the idea that the criteria should measure those KSAs determined as relevant and not measure those KSAs determined not to be relevant is still the essential point. Of course, the same point can be made about the contents of the training program. It also is supposed to contain materials related to the relevant component and not contain materials which are judged, as a result of the needs assessment, not to be relevant. The kinds of errors that can be made in this process are discussed in the next section.

Criterion Deficiency

Criterion deficiency is the degree to which components are identified in the needs assessment that are not present in the actual criteria. This situation is represented in Figure 5.2 as Box B. It is also represented in the upper circles in Figure 5.1. In many cases, it is necessary to make careful judgments about the relationship that is expected between the

KSA components established in the needs assessment and the criteria used in the training program.

Actually, there are several kinds of deficiency. The most obvious kind is the type represented in Figure 5.2. That is, an important KSA is identified but left out of the criterion constructs. It may also be left out of the training program itself. For example, an organization may expect all middle-level managers to be able to appraise the performance of their employees and provide feedback to the individual so each can improve his or her level of performance. However, as most managers have discovered, their training courses often give them a lot of general information about human relations but do not provide any instructional material on the complex process of appraising the performance of employees. The material is often not only left out of the training programs but also left out of the criterion development package; not only is the manager left in the position of not knowing how to perform the task—the organization does not even know that the manager cannot perform. Sometimes the material is included in the training program, but criteria are still not developed to measure the manager's performance either in training or on the job. This also represents a deficiency. Again, the organization does not even know that the manager cannot perform. Even though the organization provided training materials, it has no idea whether the manager has learned the material because there are no criteria available to measure the performance. The only solution is to determine, throughout the methodology of needs assessment, the most appropriate multiple criteria to measure success. The complexity of these criteria should be represented in those criteria chosen to judge the initial success of individuals in the training program and on the job. Of course, dependent upon the level of expertise expected by the organization, there will be many instances in which the trainee will not be able to perform with the same skill as an experienced worker. The criteria must be able to reflect these differences.

A system's perspective which regards training as one part of an organizational system suggests that there are probably other forms of deficiency. It is quite possible that the needs assessment indicates that particular KSAs are required for the job but that there is no intention for the material to be learned through training. For example, a salesperson could be hired with the understanding that the individual will already have all the necessary knowledge concerning the advantages and disadvantages of various advertising media. In this case, even though this knowledge component is identified as a critical item for job success, it is not to be learned in the training program. Thus, criteria developed for evaluation of the training program for the salesperson would not be deficient if criteria to measure this knowledge component were excluded. However, it should be represented in the selection system.

The issues related to deficient criteria are just as important to the measurement of organizational objectives. This adds a degree of complexity that some evaluators would prefer to avoid. It is one matter to specify all the components that determine the success of an individual on required tasks, but it is another matter to insist that all the components that determine the success of an entire training program also be specified in criteria that can be measured and evaluated. However, it should be clear that criteria representing organizational objectives provide information that is critical for the feedback and decision processes. It should not be avoided.

Criterion Contamination

Box C in Figure 5.2 and the lower circles in Figure 5.1 present a third construct–criterion contamination. This construct pertains to extraneous elements present in the criteria which result in the measure inaccurately representing the construct identified in the needs assessment. The existence of criterion contamination can lead to incorrect conclusions regarding the validity of training programs. For example, a supervisor may give better work stations to those individuals who have participated in the new training program because they are "better equipped" to handle the assignment than those persons who have simply been placed on the job. In this case, the training program may demonstrate its validity in that the participants have better assignments, but it is just as easy to describe situations in which the opposite phenomenon occurs. Bellows (1941) described some of the factors that contribute to criterion contamination. The following presentation adapts his concepts, as well as Blum and Naylor's approach (1968), to issues concerning instructional procedures.

Opportunity bias. This type of bias refers to situations in which individuals have differing opportunities for success, unrelated to the skills developed through their training program. The preceding example concerning work stations is an illustration of opportunity bias. In other instances, educators may provide more or less opportunity for students who have previously been instructed through innovative media like computer-assisted instruction (CAI). Thus, data may indicate that students from a CAI program do not perform well in a second course utilizing more traditional techniques because the educator does not provide the same opportunities for them as for the students educated traditionally. On the other hand, some educators have extraordinary faith in media like CAI and do not offer equal remedial help to more traditionally trained students. Any approach that treats individuals from various instructional conditions differentially will contaminate the criteria and lead to improper evaluation of the program. A study done by Dorcus in 1940 demonstrated that criteria-contamination problems were a serious concern even in the relatively simple job of door-to-door sales of bakery products. In order to reduce opportunity bias, Dorcus constructed economic maps of the city based on rental values of homes so that he could have an estimate of the effect of sales territory on sales volume. Another investigation by Ohmann (1941) underscores the large number of variables that could lead to opportunity bias. In order to establish territories with equal potential for each salesperson of construction materials, Ohmann considered the following factors:

1. sales volume for 1937
2. average number of calls per day
3. number of years worked at Tremco
4. salesman's net commission earnings for 1937
5. average size of order
6. average number of new accounts per month
7. average sales volume per year for length of time employed
8. sales volume for the first six months on the job
9. trend of sales volume over a period of years
10. amount of allowances to customers
11. amount of returned merchandise
12. classes of trade called on
13. classes of products sold. (p. 19)

Similar factors must be considered for any environment in which there is variability in the transfer setting.

Group-characteristic bias.   Another type of bias can result from the characteristics of the group in the transfer setting. In some instances, the trainees are not permitted to demonstrate the skills they have gained from the training program because of informal or formal regulations that do not permit them to work at capacity levels. Thus, experienced personnel often socially ostracize workers who produce at too rapid a rate, or regulations often restrict the use of particular equipment that might raise the level of production.

Knowledge of training performance.   The contamination occurs here because the person responsible for judging the capabilities of the trainees allows their knowledge of the training performance of the individual to bias their judgment of the individual's capabilities in the transfer setting—that is, on the job or in the next class. Thus, individuals who performed well in the training setting would be evaluated correspondingly well on the job. This problem becomes particularly serious when more subjective measures of performance, like rating scales, are used to determine capabilities.

It is important to be continually aware of the potential danger of criterion contamination because, in many instances, control is possible. For example, training designers should keep trainee scores confidential and should control for factors like trainee work assignments. There are other factors that interrelate with the criteria measures, including the experimental design utilized in the evaluation. These issues will be examined in the next chapter.

Criterion Reliability

Reliability refers to the consistency of the criteria measures. If the criteria are ratings of performance, and there is little agreement between two raters, then there is low reliability. Correspondingly, consistently different performance scores by the same individual at different times also reflect low consistency and thus low reliability. Reliability is a necessary condition for stable criteria measures, but it is important to recognize that it will not replace the need for relevant criteria. Because reliability can be measured statistically, some evaluators emphasize it rather than relevance, but as mentioned earlier there is no utility in carefully measuring the wrong indicant of success.

Nagle (1953) suggests that the instability of a given activity is the main limitation in achieving reliable criteria. He lists the following factors that affect the reliability of measures.

1. the size of the sample of performance
2. the range of ability among the subjects
3. ambiguity of instructions
4. variation in conditions during measurement periods
5. the amount of aid provided by instruments. (p. 277)

In addition, Nagle lists sources of unreliability that are peculiar to those situations in which ratings are used as criteria.

1. the competency of the judges
2. the simplicity of the behavior
3. the degree to which the behavior is overt
4. the opportunity to observe
5. the degree to which the rating task is defined. (p. 277)

Other Considerations

In addition to relevancy and reliability, there are several other considerations in the evaluation of criteria. These include acceptability to the organization, cost, and realistic measures. These factors cannot replace relevancy and reliability; they are of consequence only after the relevancy and reliability have been determined. If these latter factors have been established, the training analyst knows he is convincing the organization to accept criteria that may be costly but that are the most valid measures to judge the adequacy of the training program.

THE MANY DIMENSIONS OF CRITERIA

There are few, if any, single measures that can adequately reflect the complexity of most training programs and transfer performance. When all the facets of human behavior are considered, including satisfaction, motivation, and achievement, it is clear that there is a series of ultimate criteria from which actual criteria that are relevant and reliable must be obtained. A study by O'Leary (1972) further illustrates the importance of considering the many different dimensions of the criteria. She utilized a program of role-playing and group problem-solving sessions with hard-core unemployed women. At the conclusion of the program, the trainees had developed positive changes in attitude toward themselves but these were not accompanied by positive attitudes toward tedious, structured jobs. Rather, these trainees apparently raised their levels of aspiration and subsequently sought employment in a work setting consistent with their newly found expectations. In this instance, it was obvious that the trainees were leaving the job as well as experiencing positive changes in attitude. However, there are many other cases in which the collection of a variety of criteria related to the objectives is the only way to effectively evaluate the training program.

One treatment of criterion development argues that performance can best be approximated by a single measure or a group of measures combined into a single measure. This is known as the *composite view* of the criterion. The other side of the issue, known as the *multiple-criteria approach,* states that the various performance measures must be treated independently. Advocates of the multiple-criteria approach believe a single composite measure is invalid; criteria are multidimensional. Considering that training programs must be examined with a multitude of measures, including participant reactions, learning, performance, and organizational objectives, it is necessary for training evaluators to view the criteria as multidimensional. Training can best be evaluated by examining many independent performance dimensions. However, the relationship between measures of success should be closely scrutinized, as the inconsistencies that occur often provide important insights into training procedures. The collection of different criteria reflecting the many objectives of an organization leads to a more difficult decision process than the collection of a single criterion of performance. However, judgment and feedback processes depend on the availability of all sources of information. For instance, a particular instructional program might lead to increased achievement but dissatisfied participants. It is important to find out why the program is not viewed favorably so changes that might improve the reactions of the trainees may be considered. If the decision-makers are more concerned with achievement than with reaction, they might not be willing to institute changes. However, the decision-makers do have the information available to make the choice and can consider the possible consequences.

An illustration of the thoughtful development of multiple criteria is offered by Freeberg's (1976) study of youth work-training programs. Freeberg investigated training projects of the Out-of-School Program of the Neighborhood Youth Corps in thirteen different cities. Freeberg noted the importance of developing criteria based upon constructs chosen on a rational basis from the stated objectives of the program. In this case, the youth-training programs had goals related to trainee social, community, and occupational adjustments and attitudinal perceptions. The author examined the original manpower legislation and the standards of the sponsoring federal agency. He also interviewed the professionals running the training programs and directly observed the operational practices. Based upon this work, Freeberg established a number of measures for both short-term program criteria and more distal post-program criteria. He had a number of measures for each of the following short-term and long-term criteria. The short-term criteria were:

1. vocational awareness and planning skills (importance of various job characteristics, knowledge of relevant ways to seek a first job, rated quality of short-term and long-term job plans, and so on);
2. personal-social adjustment (with regard to family, police, people in the community, financial management);
3. work motivation (based on willingness to train full time and part time and to accept jobs under specified adverse conditions);
4. work-training program adjustment (for example, proficiency ratings by counselors, work site supervisors, and peers, and work-site absences);
5. vocational confidence (as measured by a seven-item scale).

The long-term criteria were:

1. extent and level of employment (for example, employment status, hours worked per week, rated "quality" of the job, starting salary);
2. job performance and adjustment (for example, salary raises, employer proficiency rating, number of jobs held);
3. personal–social adjustment (with regard to family, police, community members, financial management, personal health);
4. vocational motivation and planning (for example, time required to find the first job, number of sources used, level of short-term and long-term job plans).

The careful tracing-out process for each of the criteria listed above is made obvious by the measures chosen to reflect each of these criteria. For example, measures chosen for the construct of job motivation include the number of places interviewed, applications filed, sources used to find a first job, and visits to state employment service. In his study, Freeberg studied the relationship between his short- and long-term criteria. He found a number of strong relationships. For example, trainees who assessed themselves higher on the necessity for keeping out of trouble tended to have higher ratings from their employer, fewer actual police contacts, and families that had more positive feelings about the trainee. Similar relationships were found for trainees who had positive self-perceptions of employment capability, high proficiency ratings by counselors and peers, and a positive attitude toward further training.

As is made obvious by Freeberg's study, there are many different dimensions by which criteria can vary, including the time the criteria are collected and the type of criteria data collected. These dimensions are not independent. For example, learning criteria and behavior on the job not only are different types of criteria but also vary according to the time of collection. Some of the more important dimensions that should be considered are discussed in the following sections.

Levels of Criteria

Kirkpatrick (1959) suggests that evaluation procedures should consider four levels of criteria—reaction, learning, behavior, and results.

Reaction

Kirkpatrick defines reaction as what the trainees thought of the particular program. It does not include a measure of the learning that takes place. The following are suggested guidelines for determining participant reaction.

1. Design a questionnaire based on information obtained during the needs assessment phase. The questionnaire should be validated by carefully standardized procedures to be certain that the responses reflect the opinions of the participants.
2. Design the instrument so that the responses can be tabulated and quantified.
3. To obtain more honest opinions, provide for the anonymity of the participants. Often, it is best to provide for anonymity with a coding procedure that protects the individual participant but permits the data to be related to other criteria, like learning measures and performance on the job.
4. Provide space for opinions about items that are not covered in the questionnaire. This procedure often leads to the collection of important information that is useful in the redesign of the questionnaire.
5. Pretest the questionnaire on a sample of participants to determine its completeness, the time necessary for completion, and participant reactions.

The reaction of the participants is often a critical factor in the continuance of training programs. Responses on these types of questionnaires help ensure against decisions based on the comments of a few very satisfied or disgruntled participants. Most trainers believe that initial receptivity provides a good atmosphere for learning the material in the instructional program but does not necessarily cause high levels of learning.

It is important to realize that reaction measures, like any other criteria, should be related to the needs assessment. Thus, it does not make any sense to use reaction measures that ask if the trainee is happy (from agree to disagree) unless there is some relationship between happiness and the objectives of the course as established by the needs assessment. In this regard, Bartlett (1982) met with academic university departments, interviewed individual faculty members, and used questionnaires to develop a teaching evaluation instrument. Stemming from the needs assessment, one part of that instrument is a reaction and attitude measure which students filled out concerning the course. This part of the scale is shown in Table 5.1. Here, the students were not indicating how happy they were about the course, but rather their reactions to specific goals and objectives that stemmed from the needs assessment. Interestingly, a study using this scale with college students showed that favorable reactions were positively related to expected student grades and self-reported attendance in the course.

Learning

The training analyst is concerned with measuring the learning of principles, facts, techniques, and attitudes that were specified as training objectives. The measures must be objective and quantifiable indicants of the learning that has taken place in the training program. They are not measures of performance on the job. There are many different measures of learning performance, including paper-and-pencil test, learning curves, and job components. Again, the objectives determined from the needs assessment must be the most important determinants of the measure to be employed. The importance of developing good proficiency measures for training is illustrated in the work of Gordon and Isenberg (1975). These investigators noted that the growing concern in a program for machinist training was that the matter of passing or failing a particular trainee had become a matter of how lucky

TABLE 5.1   University teaching reaction measure

Use the rating scale below to respond to the remaining statements:

Strongly Agree A	Agree B	Neither Agree nor Disagree C	Disagree D	Strongly Disagree E

Reactions and Attitudes of Students
As a result of this course I believe that I . . .
   developed specific skills or competencies that can be used later in life.
   gained a greater understanding of the subject.
   gained factual knowledge (terminology, classifications, methods, trends).
   learned fundamental principles, generalizations, or theories.
   would like to take another course from this instructor.
   would recommend this course and instructor to others.
   was encouraged to think.
   really learned a lot.
   learned to apply course material to improve rational thinking, problem solving and decision making.
   gained a greater interest in this subject.
   developed skill in expressing myself orally and/or in writing.

From scale developed by C. J. Bartlett for Division of Behavioral and Social Sciences, University of Maryland. Copyright 1982 by C. J. Bartlett. Adapted by permission.

FIGURE 5.3 Realtrain simulation identification. (*From "Military Research on Performance Criteria: A Change of Emphasis," by J. E. Uhlaner and A. J. Drucker. In* Human Factors, *1980, 22, pp. 131–139. Copyright 1980 by the Human Factors Society, Inc. Reproduced by permission.*)

you were in having a particular trainer as your grader. These researchers developed standardized exercises based upon the goals of the training program. They developed a criterion based upon the difficulty of the machine operation, tolerance requirements, and finish specifications. For example, they developed a point system whereby the smoother the finish required for the part, the higher the points earned by the trainee for completing the work within the specified standards. As a result of this work, the investigators were able to develop a reliable system whereby judges strongly agreed on the scores earned by individual trainees.

There are many other imaginative examples of the development of relevant criteria. One of these examples is the measure used by the army to assess the performance of trainees involved in a two-sided exercise under simulated battlefield conditions. As described by Uhlaner and Drucker (1980), "Each soldier's weapon is equipped with a 6x telescope, and all participants wear black, three inch, two digit numbers on their helmets. Opponents try to read each other's numbers using the telescopes" (p. 134). This system is depicted in Figure 5.3. When opponents can identify the number, they fire a blank shot and radio a report to the controller which results in the person or equipment that has been observed being removed from the exercise.

Another illustration, involving peer evaluations of police trainees at the end of their 11-week training program, is offered by Goldstein and Bartlett (1977). Trainees were to rate each other based upon the following instructions.

RECRUIT BACK-UP QUESTIONNAIRE

Again, assume that your recruit class has graduated, and that all of you are regular police officers in X city. If you were to find yourself in a crisis situation (such as an armed robbery, a high speed chase, a domestic dispute, a drug raid, a multiple car accident, or a riot), which five members of your recruit class would you *most like to have* as your back-up?

On the following page is an alphabetical list of the members of your recruit class. *First,* find your own name and cross it off the list by drawing a line through it. *Second,* go through the remaining names and circle the five names you would most like to have as your back-up in a crisis situation. Make sure you consider all names before choosing. *Then circle five and only five names.*

It was found that these paper nominations did not correlate with grades and other learning measures at the end of the 11-week police academy training measures. However, the peer nominations did predict a later training performance measure. That is, the police trainees, after graduating from the academy, went into field training with each trainee assigned to an individual field-training officer. The length of time that the trainee stayed in field training was determined by each trainee's performance as judged by the training officer. The peer nominations at the end of field training correlated –.43 with the number of days that a trainee spent in field training. That is, the more positive the peer nominations, the fewer days were spent in field training. Evidently, the trainee's peers saw something in the performance of their fellow trainees that was not reflected in their grades in the police training academy.

Behavior

Kirkpatrick used the term *behavior* in reference to the measurement of job performance. Just as favorable reaction does not necessarily mean that learning will occur in the training program, superior training performance does not always result in similar behavior in the transfer setting. The significance of this point is emphasized by a review of research studies conducted between 1906 and 1952. In this investigation, Severin (1952) found that the median correlation between production records and training grades was .11. He concluded that training records did not always accurately represent performance on the job and should not be substituted for studies of on-the-job behavior without first determining that a strong relationship exists.

There are a large number of measures that can be employed to assess on-the-job performance. Measures employed during training frequently can be useful in measuring job performance. For example, the illustration offered by Gordon and Isenberg (1975) for machinist training, including finish specifications and tolerance requirements, is just as useful on the job as it is in training. In other cases, measures might be needed which reflect other skills which are expected to be developed on the job as a result of initial learning in training. Again, it is particularly important to make sure that the criteria fit the objectives of the training program as established by the needs assessment. Latham and Wexley (1981) offer a large number of behavioral rating item examples for a number of different jobs based upon careful needs assessment. For example, managers who had been trained in these areas could be rated from "almost never" to "almost always" on the following types of items based upon job performance:

> Establishes mechanisms for spotting trends/patterns in key departmental/functional areas.
> Clearly defines the role responsibilities of key managers.

A mechanic in a bowling alley might be rated on the following items:

> Asks the mechanic leaving the shift what machines need watching.
> Checks the tension of chains weekly and keeps them oiled.

Results

Kirkpatrick uses this category to relate the results of the training program to organizational objectives. Some of the results that could be examined include costs, turnover, absenteeism, grievances, and morale. An earlier chapter on needs assessment described the various components of organizational analysis, including goals and objectives, which in turn should suggest relevant organizational criteria. Again, it is important to emphasize the tracing-out process so that relevant criteria stemming from the needs assessment are developed. A criterion that has received increasing attention over the last several years is cost. Many organizations have designed instructional programs in the hope that it will reduce other costs. Thus, an entry-level sales training course is used in the hope that the trainee, upon beginning the job, is able to produce at a higher rate than might otherwise be expected. Obviously, these kinds of analyses require very careful detailing of all the costs and gains associated with training. Mirabal (1978) has outlined the costs associated with the actual instructional program. Table 5.2 shows some of these costs as related to the trainee, the instructor, and the facilities. Other charts developed by Mirabal address items such as the development costs of training.

An important addition to the concept of cost in evaluating training programs is the idea of utility. Most of the work involving utility has been applied to the usefulness of selection programs (Cascio, 1982a,b), but it is just as possible to apply the concepts to training programs. The basic idea is that the utility of a training program is the translation of validity information into cost figures that permit comparisons between different types of programs. The use of such concepts considerably increases the number of ways one would measure the success of a training program. For example, it is possible to ask what the training program will add to other interventions, such as a selection system, which itself has varying degrees of success. It is also possible to ask what the utility of a formal training program is as compared to expecting employees to learn on the job from other, more experienced, persons. Here, it becomes necessary to ask what differences in productivity for the new employee result from the two approaches, what is the loss in productivity from people on the job who have to teach the employee (compared to the cost of the formal training program), and what is the dollar payoff to the organization. If the cost of formal training is very great and the production return is very little, and if, in addition, the employee moves on to other jobs in a short time, a formal training program may not be worth it. Cascio (1982a,b) has demonstrated the use of such models. They will be explored further in the next chapter, on evaluation models.

While all four categories of criteria are important, research indicates that these data are usually not collected. One investigation (Catalanello & Kirkpatrick, 1968) found that, of 154 companies surveyed, the largest number (77%) stressed studies related to reactions. Even in those instances in which reaction data are collected, some investigators (Mindak & Anderson, 1971) have suggested that most of these measures are eyeball attempts to measure reactions. Few investigations have bothered to measure learning, behavior, or results, and those that have done so rarely stress proper evaluation procedures (for example, control groups). It is probably not unreasonable to suspect that these investigations also do not consider criterion relevance and reliability.

Kirkpatrick's analysis of criteria represents just one approach to different levels that could be examined. Other categories have been developed that are more specific to the particular program being evaluated. Thus, Lindbom and Osterberg (1954) suggest that three effective levels for examining the results of supervisory training are (1) supervisor's classroom behavior, (2) supervisor's behavior on the job, and (3) employee's behavior on the job.

Process and Outcome Measures

Outcome measures refer to criteria, like learning and performance, that represent various levels of achievement. While these measures are critical in determining the viability of instructional programs, strict reliance on outcome measures often makes it difficult to determine why the criteria were achieved. Thus, I have stressed the importance of process measures that examine what happens during instruction (Goldstein, 1978b). This emphasis is illustrated in the training instructional model in Figure 2.1 (p. 16) by the arrow between "training" and "evaluation."

It is not unusual for a training program to bear little relationship to the originally conceived format. One of my favorite examples occurred in a basic-learning laboratory, where the experimenter's ability to control the setting supposedly prevents these events. In this study, a pigeon was trained to peck at a key for food. Later in the experiment, the researcher noted that the response rate of the animal was surprisingly low. The researcher decided to observe the pigeon and discovered that it was not pecking the key to earn reinforcement. Instead, it was running across the cage and smashing into the wall that held the key, thereby setting off the mechanism and earning food! This example was

TABLE 5.2   Charts for specifying training costs

CHART I. TRAINEE COSTS

DATE:

Course Title	Trainees and Hours				Salary		Travel and Per Diem	Materials and Supplies	Total Trainee Costs	
	No. of Trainees	Level and Step	Curriculum Hours	Trainee Hours	Hourly Salary plus Benefits	Total Salary	Annual Travel and Per Diem	Annual Cost	Total Trainee Cost	Trainee Cost per Trainee Hour
	1	2	3	4	5	6	7	8	9	10

CHART II. INSTRUCTOR COSTS

Course Title	Agency Instructors							Non-Organization Instructors			Travel and Per Diem		Total Instructor Costs	
	No. Instructors and Level	Salary per Hour	Overhead per Hour	Salary Plus Overhead	Hours per Year	Annual Salary Plus Overhead Cost	Annual Salary Plus Overhead Cost per Trainee Hour	No. Instructors	Annual Salary or Fee	Annual Salary per Trainee Hour	Annual Travel and Per Diem	Annual Travel and Per Diem per Trainee Hour	Total Annual Instructor Costs	Annual Instructor Costs per Trainee Hour
	1	2	3	4	5	6	7	8	9	10	11	12	13	14

CHART III. FACILITIES COSTS

Course Title	Non-Organization Owned Space				Improvement to Space		Equipment and Furnishings			Total Facilities Costs	
	Annual Cost of Required Space	*% of Time Used for Course*	*Annual Cost of Space for Course*	*Cost per Trainee Hour*	*Cost per Year*	*Annual Cost per Trainee Hour*	*Total Cost of Items*	*Annual Cost of Items for Course*	*Annual Cost of Items per Trainee Hour*	*Total Annual Facilities Cost*	*Annual Facilities Cost per Trainee Hour*
	1	2	3	4	5	6	7	8	9	10	11

Adapted from "Forecasting Future Training Costs," by T. E. Mirabal. In *Training and Development Journal*, 1978, 32, pp. 78–87. Copyright 1978 by the American Society for Training and Development, Inc. Adapted by permission.

used in the first edition of this book and it often prompted readers to ask me if the incident was true or made up for the sake of the book. Sadly, I have to inform them that it is true! Even in basic research laboratories, complete reliance on outcome measures often misleads the investigator. In the next chapter, on evaluation models, it shall be noted that even the use of rigorous experimental designs does not necessarily provide the investigator with the degree of understanding that is anticipated.

Evaluation designs and specification of outcome criteria have often been based upon a product or outcome view of training validity. Thus, researchers collected pre- and post-criterion measures, compared them with control groups, and discovered that they did not understand the results they had obtained. This problem became especially apparent when the collectors of these data were outside consultants who appeared only to collect pre- and post-data but had no conception of the processes that had occurred in training between the pre- and post-measurement. An experience of mine illustrates this issue. In a study of computer-assisted instruction in a school setting (Rosenberg, 1972), two teachers agreed to instruct a geometry class by traditional methodology and by computer-assisted instruction (CAI). Each teacher taught one traditional and one CAI class. Further, the teachers agreed to work together to design an exam which would cover material that was presented in each of the classes. At the end of the first testing period, the traditional classes taught by each teacher significantly outperformed the CAI groups taught by the same teachers. However, at a later testing, one of the CAI groups improved to the extent that it was equivalent to the two traditional groups. The other CAI group performed significantly worse than the other three instructional groups. One reasonable conclusion for this series of events might be that one of the teachers learned how to instruct the CAI group so that it was now equivalent to the two traditional groups, but the other teacher had not been able to perform that task with the other CAI group. Indeed, if the investigators had only collected the outcome measures, this or other similar erroneous conclusions would probably have been offered as explanations for the data. In this case, the investigators also observed the instructional process to provide further information about the program. In this way, the evaluators learned that the instructor for the CAI group that eventually improved had become disturbed over the performance of his students. As a result, the teacher offered remedial tutoring and essentially turned the CAI class into a traditional group.

From an industrial psychology perspective, process measures might provide important insights for the analysis of instructional programs in organizations. As indicated, process measures can help determine the source of the effect. If it is found that the trainers' attitudes or the trainees' expectations account for a substantial portion of the variance in the outcomes, those variables must be considered in the design of instructional programs. The utilization of process measures may provide all sorts of unanticipated dividends. I will never forget the look of astonishment on the faces of a number of high-level executives who had just discovered that the reason entry-level grocery clerks could not operate the cash register was that the instructional sequence was no longer part of their carefully-designed instructional program. Another perspective on these events is that there are both intended and unintended outcomes which result from our programs. This view stresses the concern for side effects that is familiar to researchers in medicine but has been ignored by many training researchers. For example, criteria might be established to measure the side effects of a training program for hard-core unemployed workers. Since such a program would place more minority-group workers on the job, it might have the unintended and unwanted effect of increasing racial tensions by introducing workers with different sets of personal and social values. By carefully considering these possibilities, criteria could be established to measure these unintended outcomes so that information is available to determine side effects. In many cases, these criteria data become important elements in shaping policy and determining future objectives. Again, this view reinforces the belief that criterion development should be approached with thoughtful emphasis on broadly relevant criteria.

Time Dimension

Criteria also vary according to time of collection. Thus, learning-criteria measures are taken early in training, and behavior-criteria measures are taken after the individual has completed the training program and transferred to the new activity. Figure 5.4 depicts the time dimension of criteria. In this diagram, immediate criteria refer to those measures that are available during the training program. Proximal criteria are measures that are available shortly after the initial training program. They might include performance in an advanced section of the training program or initial success on the job. Distal criteria are available after considerable

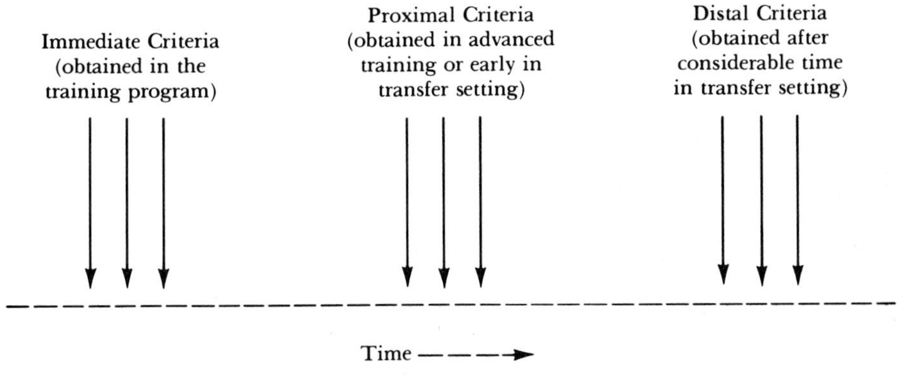
Immediate Criteria (obtained in the training program)
Proximal Criteria (obtained in advanced training or early in transfer setting)
Distal Criteria (obtained after considerable time in transfer setting)
Time

FIGURE 5.4 The time dimensions of criteria.

time in the transfer setting. There are no exact rules that tell when to measure or when a proximal criterion becomes a distal criterion. Several previously mentioned examples in this chapter illustrate the time dimensions of criteria. Thus, Freeberg's (1976) study of youth work-training programs (see section titled "Many Dimensions of Criteria") discusses the relationship between measures collected at the end of training and other criteria collected six months after training was completed. Similarly, Goldstein and Bartlett (1977) discussed the use of peer nominations collected at the end of a police academy training program and a later field training measure consisting of the number of days required to complete field training (see section on learning criteria).

Ghiselli (1956) introduced the concepts of static and dynamic dimensions to account for the changes in criteria that occur during the passage of time. The static dimension is used to describe criteria that do not change over time. The dynamic dimension indicates that successful performance is affected by factors that change with time. Thus, organizational objectives might change, in which case new criteria become necessary. The initial objectives might be growth and acquisition of new clients, while the later objectives might be stability and cultivation of present clients (Prien, 1966). New criteria will have to be developed to measure these objectives. A further implication is that the relationship between training performance and transfer performance is dependent on the time of measurement.

TYPES OF CRITERIA

This section provides a few general criteria categories that are meaningful for training research but have not been emphasized in previous sections. These categories include norm- and criterion-referenced measures and objective and subjective measures.

Criterion- and Norm-Referenced Measures

Criterion-referenced measures are dependent on an absolute standard of quality, while norm-referenced measures are dependent on a relative standard. Criterion-referenced measures provide a standard of achievement for the individual as compared with specific behavioral objectives and therefore provide an indicant of the degree of competence attained by the trainee. Norm-referenced measures compare the capabilities of an individual to those of other trainees. Thus, schools administer nationally standardized exams that determine the individual's standing in comparison with a national sample. The norm-referenced measures tell us that one student is more proficient than another, but they do not provide much information about the degree of proficiency in relationship to the tasks involved. Unfortunately, many training evaluations have employed norm-referenced measures to the exclusion of other forms of measurement. In order to properly evaluate training programs, it is necessary to obtain criterion-referenced measures that provide information about the skill level of the trainee in relationship to the expected program achievement levels. Data informing us that the student is equal to or above 60% of the population provide little information about his specific capabilities; thus, it is difficult to design modifications to improve the program.

While there are not many examples of the use of criterion-referenced measures in training settings, it is obvious that many of the rules for the development of test items follow the philosophy of the critical importance of criterion relevancy espoused in this chapter. Persons interested in the procedures necessary to develop criterion-referenced measures should consult an excellent book by Swezey (1981). One recent example of the development of such measures in a training situation is offered in a study by Panell and Laabs (1979). These investigators were interested in using criterion-referenced measures for a training program for navy boiler technicians. They designed a set of 186 items by setting up hypothetical job situations which required the knowledge and skills contained in each of the training modules. They then had job experts check the items to determine the correspondence between the job situations and the knowledge and skills, and to ensure adequate question representation for each module. The hypothetical job situations were also checked to determine that each situation was based on known job requirements and that each situation utilized job materials such as maintenance requirement cards, charts describing maintenance actions, and illustrations of tools and equipment. Panell and Laabs followed these procedures with empirical methods to establish the reliability of the items and cut-off scores for passing and failing. This resulted in 127 useable items. Then the investigators administered the test to 75 trainees who were about to enter the training course and another 75 trainees who had just completed the course. They then compared the results of the performance of the two groups on the test items. Those results are presented in Table 5.3. Using the cut-off scores established by these investigators, it is possible to see that in a large number of cases, the test items did differentiate between the two groups. For example, in module 1, 88% of the individuals who were in either the group entering training or who had completed training were identified correctly by their test score performance. That is, persons who had completed training knew the test items stemming from the needs assessment while persons entering training did not know the test items. For that same module, 4% of the pre-instruction group did well enough on the test that they were identified as not needing training and 8% of the group that had completed training was still identified as needing training. Of course, there could be many reasons why some persons were misidentified. It is quite possible that some trainees knew the

TABLE 5.3   Hits and misses in classification of trainees

Module	% false positives[a]	% false negatives[b]	% hits
1	8	4	88
2	22	0	78
3	16	16	68
4	8	6	86
5	12	14	74
6	2	6	92
7	8	6	86
8	18	10	72
9	12	10	78
10	16	4	80
11	10	2	88
12	8	4	88
13	12	2	86
14	8	2	90

[a] A false positive is diagnosing a preinstruction group member as not needing training.

[b] A false negative is diagnosing a preinstruction group member as needing training.

From "Construction of a Criterion-Referenced, Diagnostic Test for an Individualized Instruction Program," by R. C. Panell and G. J. Laabs. In *Journal of Applied Psychology*, 1979, *64*, pp. 255–261. Copyright 1979 by the American Psychological Association. Reprinted by permission.

materials before they entered and that some other trainees did not know the material after they completed the course. If that happened with large numbers of persons, it could also be possible that the test items were not very well constructed or that the training course was not doing its job. As Swezey (1981) points out, it is critical that the criteria be developed with an emphasis on criterion relevance. Otherwise, it is not possible to make any judgments about the training program or the level of knowledge of the trainees. As Swezey states it:

> First, it must be determined that objectives have been properly derived from adequate task analyses that prescribe clearly what an examinee must do or must know in order to perform the task under examination.
>
> Second, each item must be carefully evaluated against its associated objective to ensure that the performances, conditions, and standards specified in the item are the same as those required by the objective. (p. 151)

Objective and Subjective Measures

Measures that require the statement of opinions, beliefs, or judgments are considered subjective. For example, rating scales are subjective measures, while measures of absenteeism are more objective. (However, supervisors' ratings of the absenteeism level of employees could turn that measure into a subjective criterion.) Objective measures—for example, rate of production—are especially vulnerable to criterion contamination based on opportunity bias, whereas subjective measures are affected by the difficulties that one individual has in rating another without bias. For various reasons, rating scales have been the most commonly employed measures in applied settings. This appears to be the case partially because there are not many objective measures of the performance of individuals in complex jobs, such as that of manager. Unfortunately, another reason is that it is simple to throw together a rating scale with a few traits (such as honesty, interpersonal sensitivity), rate individuals, and delude yourself into believing that you have a useful measure of performance. Professionals who have developed relevant criterion measures know that the steps in the process are very similar for objective and subjective measures and that shortcuts do not work in either case.

For any criterion, the issues discussed in this chapter, such as relevance, deficiency, contamination, and bias, are critical. The tracing-out process from the needs assessment in order to develop relevant criteria is the same for both objective and subjective measures. As discussed earlier, Freeberg (1976) examined manpower legislation, interviewed persons running training programs, and directly observed the programs as input into the development of criteria. Some of the objective measures for job motivation for the trainees in youth work-training include number of places interviewed, number of applications filed, number of sources used to find first job, and the like. Goldstein and Bartlett have developed an approach for linking behavioral rating scale items directly to the needs assessment. They run workshops where job knowledge experts are trained to write rating scale items. As input, they are given task items and asked to write behavior items that reflect effective, ineffective, and average performance on the task. Thus, they tie the rating items directly to the needs assessment by using as-input tasks identified in the needs assessment as critical tasks. The instructions they use for this procedure are presented in Table 5.4. After the development of these behavioral items, they still have to be edited, judged to be certain they are important behaviors (as described in Chapter 3), and checked for reliability. However, one starting point is tied to important tasks for that job.

Unobtrusive Measures

Recent research (Webb, Campbell, Schwartz, & Sechrest, 1966) has seriously questioned the reliance of social science work on interviews and questionnaires. In comments relevant to training research, Webb and his associates suggest that these techniques create as well as measure attitudes and that they are chosen solely on the basis of accessibility and availability. While these authors agree that any method is subject to serious flaws, they are especially concerned because these methods are the only techniques being employed. Thus, they suggest that some measures that do not require the cooperation of a respondent and do not themselves contaminate the response should be examined. They offer two examples.

TABLE 5.4   Instructions for performance measurement workshop

Industrial/Organizational Psychology Program
Department of Psychology
University of Maryland
College Park, Maryland 20742

The industrial/organizational psychology program at the University of Maryland has agreed to help develop rating scales for the use of the Police Department. This rating scale will be used as part of the appraisal system for police officers. During the past several weeks, the personnel department has conducted a job analysis in order to obtain a list of job tasks performed by officers in X city. For example, a few of the many tasks include:

Check bars for liquor law violation.
Engage in high speed pursuit driving to apprehend suspects.
Administer first aid to injured persons.
Conduct bank security checks to determine level of protection.

The next step in obtaining relevant items for a rating scale is obtaining performance examples for each of these tasks. For example, consider the task of "conduct conflict resolution between members of the community." Performance examples for this task might be:

Effectively calms the emotions of others at the scene of an incident.
Demonstrates good self-control when harassed by the public.

Note that you would probably consider these performance examples to be illustrations of effective behavior. We would also like to have performance examples which might illustrate ineffective behavior. For example:

Makes insulting remarks to law violators.
Becomes belligerent when interacting with citizens.
Questions the sincerity of rape victims.

Finally, we would like to obtain some behavior statements which you would judge to be of average effectiveness. For example:

Discusses police actions with private citizens affected.
Explains court procedures to complainants.

Thus, we would like you to write out examples of behaviors according to the instructions that are given to you.

Instructions to job knowledge experts:
Please write out examples of effective behavior* for item _____ through _____ on the enclosed sheet. An example of effective behavior should be a sign of good performance in the sense that it contributes to the goals of good police functioning. The behavior should also have the following characteristics:

(a) The behavior should be realistic in the sense that this type of behavior has occurred in the police department.
(b) The behavior should be relevant to the jobs of police officers.
(c) The behavior should consist of specific behavioral examples that tell us what happened. For example, saying the officer "showed good judgment" does not tell us what the person did (or did not do) that made you feel it was effective. An effective example here might be "did not fire at an escaping criminal when it would endanger innocent bystanders."

*Similar instructions are used to obtain examples of ineffective and average performance.

Adapted from instructions developed by Goldstein, Irwin L., and Bartlett, C. J. Copyright 1982 by Irwin L. Goldstein and C. J. Bartlett.

1. The floor tiles around the hatching chick exhibit at Chicago's Museum of Science and Industry must be replaced every six weeks. Tiles in other parts of the museum need not be replaced for years. The selective erosion of tiles, indexed by their replacement rate, is a measure of the relative popularity of exhibits.

2. Library withdrawals were used to demonstrate the effect of the introduction of television into a community. Fiction titles dropped; nonfiction titles were unaffected. (p. 2)

Although it is difficult to imagine the use of the first example's measure as a criterion for a training program, the second example does suggest an interesting way to examine the implications of educational and training programs offered through television.

These methods are not without their own drawbacks and sources of bias. This is clearly indicated by D. T. Campbell's (1969) discussion of the use of archival methods.

> Those who advocate the use of archival measures of social indicators must face up not only to their high degree of chaotic error and systematic bias, but also to the politically motivated changes in record keeping that will follow upon their public use as social indicators. (p. 415)

With that warning taken into consideration, it still appears that the solution to the criterion problem will depend on the effective use of the analyst's imagination and willingness to work to uncover relevant measures of success.

CONCLUSIONS

In summary, the following suggestions about the determination of criteria appear relevant.

1. Place the greatest degree of effort on the selection of relevant criteria. Relevance should be conceptualized as a relationship between the operational measures (criteria) and KSAs determined from the needs assessment. Thus, several suggestions can aid in the selection of relevant criteria. First, carefully examine the behavioral objectives established from the needs assessment procedures. Since the objectives are statements about terminal performance, they suggest potential criteria. Next, carefully examine all the components suggested by the needs assessment so that the criteria are not deficient. For example, criteria utilized to measure the performance of grocery cashiers include not only measures of register skills but also ratings of various aspects of customer service. Finally, carefully reduce the extraneous elements that often cause criterion contamination. As described earlier, two contaminating factors that can be effectively eliminated are opportunity bias and pre-knowledge of training performance.

2. After establishing relevant criteria, statistically determine the reliability or the consistency of the measure. If the criteria are not measured reliably, they are useless as indicants of success. Several of the factors that affect the reliability of the measure are listed on page 121 of this chapter. Since ratings are often used as measures of success, consider the difficulties in rating a bus driver on a trait like "being careful." Compare that to the following rating statements utilized by a bus company.

Slowing and Stopping
1. stops and restarts without rolling back
2. tests brakes at tops of hills
3. uses mirrors to check traffic to rear
4. signals following traffic
5. stops before crossing sidewalk when coming out of driveway or alley
6. stops clear of pedestrian crosswalks

Note that the behaviors are overt, easy to observe, and well defined. Certainly, more reliable measures could be expected by utilizing these statements than by simply rating "being careful" or even "slowing and stopping" without further defining the behaviors.

3. Because of the complexity of most training programs and the corresponding evaluation efforts, criterion selection must reflect the breadth of the objectives. One especially useful paradigm is suggested by Kirkpatrick's (1959) measures of reaction, learning, behavior, and results. This particular analysis provides for measures of training performance, transfer performance, and organizational objectives. It is critical that the criteria chosen not only be relevant but also reflect the breadth of the program. Thus, it makes little sense to have measures that reflect training performance but not job performance. Similarly, it makes no sense to have measures of various types of performance without considering cost or utility factors that provide information about whether training offers more than other interventions. The criteria must be chosen so that they reflect the breadth of the approach. Thus, it is not only important to have measures that reflect the outcomes but equally important to collect data that provide information as to why those outcomes occurred. Also, there must be criteria that reflect the organizational objectives as determined by the organizational analysis. Otherwise, no matter how successful individual performance is, the organization might judge the training intervention as having failed.

Evaluation Procedures

As previously stated, evaluation is the systematic collection of descriptive and judgmental information necessary to make effective training decisions related to the selection, adoption, value, and modification of various instructional activities. The objectives of instructional programs reflect numerous goals ranging from trainee progress to organizational goals. From this perspective, evaluation is an information-gathering technique. Then the necessary information will be available to revise instructional programs to achieve multiple instructional objectives.

It is interesting to categorize the questions that are asked about training programs. I have indicated (Goldstein, 1978a) some of the kinds of concerns that evaluators are asked to respond to by trainees, trainers, and organizational executives. A close examination of these complaints reveals certain underlying evaluation questions that have to be asked in order to respond to the complaints. The complaints are as follows:

> 1. *The trainee complaint.* There is a conspiracy. I just finished my training program. I even completed a pretest and a posttest. My posttest score was significantly better than the scores of my friends in the on-the-job control group. However, I just lost my job because I couldn't perform the work.
> 2. *The trainer complaint.* There is a conspiracy. Everyone praised our training program. They said it was the best program they ever attended. The trainees even had a chance to laugh a little. Now, the trainees tell me that management won't let them perform the job the way we trained them.
> 3. *The organization complaint.* There is a conspiracy. My competition used the training program, and it worked for them. They saved a million. I took it straight from their manuals, and my employees still can't do the job. (p. 131)

Most persons concerned with training development and evaluation have heard these and other, similar statements a bewildering number of times. These complaints can be scaled on many dimensions, including who complains, the type of complaint, and the many potential sources of difficulty that resulted in the complaint. The dimensions that are of particular relevance for this chapter are the evaluation questions that must be asked and answered in order to respond to these complaints. Rational decisions related to the selection, .adoption, support, and worth of various training activities require some basis for determining that the instructional program is responsible for whatever changes occurred. Instructional analysts should be able to respond to the following questions:

1. Does an examination of the various criteria indicate that a change has occurred?
2. Can the changes be attributed to the instructional program?
3. Is it likely that similar changes will occur for new participants in the same program?
4. Is it likely that similar changes will occur for new participants in the same program in a different organization?

These questions could be asked about measures at each criterion level (reaction, learning, behavior, results). Thus, evaluations of training programs are not likely to produce dichotomous answers. However, training analysts who expect results to lead to a yes or no value judgment are unrealistically imposing a simplistic structure and are raising false expectations among the recipients and sponsors of training programs. While the answers to these questions provide information about the accomplishments of training programs and the revisions that may be required, it is important to bear in mind that there are other types of questions that investigators may be interested in asking. In some cases, they are interested in the relative accomplishments of two different training approaches. It is also possible to ask which training approach works best with what type of training participant or in what type of organization. Researchers may also be interested in testing various theoretical hypotheses which provide the foundation for the design of a new training approach. In this later instance, researchers will still want to know if a change has occurred and whether it can be attributed to the training program. However, they may also ask questions concerning the effects of the training program on trainees with varying characteristics (for example, high and low verbal ability). Before discussing particular methodologies for training evaluation which help answer these types of questions, it is important to recognize that there are many different viewpoints about the desirability of evaluation, the approach to evaluation, and the effects of evaluation. The following sections discuss the most prominent of these viewpoints.

VIEWS OF THE EVALUATION PROCESS
Phases of Evaluation

I have described efforts at evaluation as evolving through a series of phases (Goldstein, 1980). In the most primitive phase, appropriate methodology is ignored and decisions are at best based upon anecdotal trainee–trainer relations. Persons with these kinds of views are described by Randall (1960) as negativists. They are individuals who feel that evaluation of training is either impossible or unnecessary. Some negativists feel that the value of formal training programs cannot be demonstrated by quantitative analysis, while others feel that the positive effects of the training program will be so obvious that evaluation is unnecessary. This text argues that there are now many developing methodologies which permit the investigator to gain valuable information about the instructional program. In part, the reason that persons originally believed programs could not be evaluated is that many of the methodologies developed were relevant to studies conducted in basic laboratory settings but did not consider the demand characteristics of research conducted in work organizations. However, as the reader will see, there are now many researchers who are developing appropriate methodologies. Also, of course, the idea that the value of programs will be obvious without evaluation certainly fails to consider the complexity of the organizational environment and all the interacting forces that are acted out in training and on the job. A consideration of the difficulties associated with criterion contamination alone makes it clear that casual observations are not likely to provide much more than the observer's biased opinion. Also, the negativist's view that trainee improvements in the transfer setting will be obvious treats evaluation of programs in extremes—the program is either good or bad. Instead, training programs should be considered dynamic entities that slowly accomplish their purpose in meeting predesigned objectives. Without systematic evaluation, there is no feedback to provide the information necessary to improve programs or quality information to make decisions. Fortunately, the number of negativists appears to be diminishing.

A second phase in evaluation is represented by those persons who believe that only rigorous scientific evaluation of training is a worthwhile approach. Randall named these persons positivists. These individuals feel that anything less than an experimental study utilizing scientifically-established control groups is not worth the effort or resources. Interestingly, this phase, which is dependent upon strict adherence to the basic experimental methodologies of academic laboratories, can also be very unproductive in providing relevant information. This phase is characterized by designs which do not recognize constraints imposed by the environment or the influences of the multitude of organizational variables. Researchers discover that these types of studies come to a screeching halt because of organizational constraints, or because a technology has been applied which does not answer the questions being asked. Even worse, advocates of this approach would have the researcher avoid studying a situation where the sample size is too small for traditional designs. This view, if carried to extremes, could result in research only in academic laboratories where systematic control of the environment can be maintained. While the data collected in these settings are important, the approach could have the undesirable effect of reducing our understanding of training programs in real settings.

Fortunately, fewer researchers are feeling constrained by the views of positivists. Instead, evaluation research is evolving into a third phase. Persons who have reached this phase recognize that training programs must be evaluated but are concerned with the methodology necessary to perform the evaluation. This group recognizes that all programs will be evaluated, either formally or informally; thus, it is concerned with the quality of the evaluation rather than with the question of whether to evaluate. Randall has named this group *frustrates* in recognition of their continuing battle to work out designs appropriate for that environment; I prefer the term activists. My support goes to the activists. It is important to use the most systematic procedures available that fit the particular setting being investigated, to control as many of the extraneous variables as possible, and to recognize the limitations of the design being utilized. Thus, the better experimental procedures control more variables, permitting a greater degree of confidence in specifying program effects. While the constraints of the environment may make a perfect evaluation impossible, an awareness of the important factors in experimental design makes it possible to avoid a useless evaluation. The job of the training analyst is to choose the most rigorous design possible and to be aware of its limitations. These limitations should be taken into account in data interpretation and in reports to the program sponsors.

Values and the Evaluation Process

Before beginning a discussion of evaluation models and strategies, it is important to consider the context in which evaluation occurs. There are a whole set of values and attitudes which belong to the evaluator, the trainees, the decision-makers in the organization, the trainers, and so on. It would be naive to suggest that these values and attitudes don't affect many of the decisions involving both the evaluation and the resulting data interpretations. Some of the more obvious factors can be controlled by some of the evaluation designs. Thus, medical researchers use designs so that the investigator does not know which subjects were given the experimental drug and which subjects were given a placebo. However, it is useless to pretend that all values and attitudes which affect our research are controlled, much less that the factors are even recognized. Researchers are now beginning to acknowledge these variables and are designing research to study the outcomes that occur when these variables are manipulated. Thus, J. P. Campbell (1978) warns us that the choice of criteria is a value judgment which all concerned parties should examine and discuss; otherwise, when the results are in, there will be widespread disagreement about the outcome. In this regard, Weiss (1975) notes that decision-maker values often determine how data are interpreted. For example, if the decision-maker is concerned about trainees holding on to skilled jobs, then negative evaluations about the impact of instructions are treated with alarm. However, if the evaluator is interested in keeping the ghetto quiet, negative training evaluations might be treated as irrelevant and be ignored. At the very least, the organizational analysis part of the needs assessment should provide the opportunity for these value systems to be made public so that their potential interaction with the evaluation is explored. Ball and Anderson (1975) have made up a chart of some of the predispositions and preferences of evaluators and how they might affect decisions about the design and interpretation of evaluation studies. As an illustration of this concept, a few of these dimensions are presented in Table 6.1. My view is that it is often quite useful to consider both sides of some of these dimensions. Thus, in the first dimension, well-done case-study and process measures are as useful in providing information as experimental-design and objective-measurement methods. However, that is a statement about my value system and there is no doubt that there are other evaluators who espouse different values. It is important to understand the value system of all parties and its effects on evaluation choices before the investigation begins. It is also important to warn the reader that the categories represent extreme points on a continuum and that many investigators fall somewhere between these dimensions. However, the table is still useful in pointing out some of the ways that the predispositions of evaluators affect some very important choices.

TABLE 6.1 Predispositions and preferences of evaluators

	PHENOMENOLOGICAL	BEHAVIORISTIC
Design	Clinical or case study	Experimental or quasi-experimental design
Measurement	Subjective measurement methods, content analyses, self-reports	Objective measurement methods, tests, systematic observations
Interpretation	Judgmental, value-laden	Nonjudgmental
	ABSOLUTIST	COMPARATIVE
Design	One-group design	Experimental or quasi-experimental design with comparison group(s)
Interpretation	Standard-referenced	Comparison-group-referenced
	PRAGMATIC	THEORETICAL
Design	Widely varying	Experimental or quasi-experimental design (hypothesis testing)
Measurement	Ad hoc measures, records	Established measures, construct validity emphasized
Interpretation	Program-specific conclusions, little generalization (ideographic)	Hypothesis confirmation, generalization (nomothetic)
	NARROW SCOPE	BROAD SCOPE
Measurement	Few and specific measures	Many and global measures
Interpretation	Oriented toward component functioning	Oriented toward system functioning

From *Professional Issues in the Evaluation of Education/Training Programs,* by S. Ball and S. B. Anderson. Office of Naval Research, Arlington, Va. 1975.

In addition to realizing that values affect evaluation efforts, there is a growing recognition that all of our decisions in conducting research have an affect on the study itself. This point of view is often described as the philosophy of intervention. It recognizes that even the decision to evaluate affects the data collected. Cochran (1978) makes this point with the following tale about Grandma Moses.

> It is reported that Grandma Moses told an art dealer who purchased one of her early paintings from a gallery exhibit that there were 15 more like it at home. He bought them sight unseen and paid the same price for each as he paid for the one on display. Arriving at her home the next day to pick them up, the dealer found Grandma Moses with a saw, cutting one of her paintings in half. It seems that when she got home she found she had only 14 paintings and, not wanting to fall back [sic] on her agreement, she was correcting the discrepancy. (p. 366)

In an example that may be more relevant to work organizations, Cochran has also pointed out that there are changes in the use of criterion data when organizations discover that these data are being used in an evaluation study. For example, when there are programs to lower crime, the criterion data often consists of the number of larcenies of $50 or more which are counted in the Uniform Crime Act. One result of programs to lower crime is that the statistics give the appearance of a decrease in crime when none actually exists. In some cases, this comes about because of outright falsification of data. In other cases, it is more subtle. Larceny figures are based upon stolen goods, which are used items. Thus, there is some value judgment in setting the actual dollar value of a stolen item. There are many psychological studies which indicate that the criteria used in making these judgments are often altered by the context and purposes of the study. A dramatic illustration of this is described by Rosenthal (1978), who examined over 140,000 observations in various psychological studies. He discovered that 1% of the observations were in error. Two-thirds of all errors favored the hypotheses of the observer.

An important warning statement about the consequences of conducting research is provided by Argyris (1968b) in an article with the very descriptive title "Some unintended consequences of rigorous research." Argyris makes the point that our empirical-appearing research tends to treat research subjects in an authoritarian manner as passive, predictable creatures. He feels that subjects do not simply accept deception research and less-than-meaningful control procedures. Instead, they try to second-guess the research design or, in some cases, to circumvent the study in some other fashion. Thus, the result of these well-controlled studies may be behavior which is not representative of what happens in that organizational situation. Support for Argyris's concerns is offered by Hand and Slocum's (1972) study which speculates that decrements in control group performance occur as a consequence of their being upset over more favorable treatment being given to the training group. In another study (Pfister, 1975), the researchers' procedure of assigning 24 of 78 police officer volunteers to a control condition resulted in officers becoming angry and withdrawn, and making unpublishable comments regarding the research investigators. Argyris suggests that the meaningful inclusion of research subjects in the design and evaluation of programs which will ultimately affect their lives is one important way to avoid such problems. One way of doing this is to set up representative steering committees in the organizational analysis phase of the needs assessment. Some researchers have resolved some of the problems of the control group by eliciting the cooperation of the trainees based upon an understanding that the control subjects will be trained after the experimental group has completed their training. The most important aspect of the issue is the understanding that trainees are cognitive and emotional human beings with concerns about their relationship to the organization in which they live. The development or the evaluation of a training program is an intervention in their lives. Researchers who ignore these concerns are likely to suffer the consequences. Many evaluation models discussed in this chapter reflect these types of issues.

Formative and Summative Evaluation

As originally conceived by Scriven (1967), formative evaluation is utilized to determine if the program is operating as originally planned or if improvements are necessary before the program is implemented. The major concern of summative evaluation is the evaluation of the final product with the major emphasis being program appraisal. Thus, formative evaluation stresses tryout and revision processes, primarily using process criteria, while summative evaluation uses outcome criteria to appraise the instructional program. However, process criteria (such as daily logs of activities) are also important in summative evaluation, because they supply the information necessary to interpret the data. Of course, both formative and summative evaluations can lead to feedback and program improvements. Design changes based on summative evaluations are determined by the degree to which program objectives are achieved. Improvements based on formative evaluations are related more to how close to the original design the program is operating. The formative evaluation should be completed and judged adequate before summative evaluations are begun. Many research problems result from one-shot evaluation studies that attempt to combine formative and summative evaluations. Thus, the program is often appraised as if it is a completed product when it has not been implemented as originally designed.

A false concern with formative evaluations is that methodological difficulties might be caused by the continual changes adopted from collected data. But that constant modification is exactly the purpose of the formative period, and experimental design considerations should not prevent the necessary changes. Once the formative evaluation is completed, experimental design provides the foundation for the summative evaluation. On the other hand, satisfactory formative data indicating that the program is operating as designed do not mean that summative evaluations are unnecessary, just as the satisfaction of the personnel responsible for the implementation of the program does not mean that the program is meeting the stated objectives.

Practical, Statistical, and Scientific Significance

Analysts sometimes overemphasize the importance of statistically significant changes. It is quite possible to achieve statistically significant changes so small that they have virtually no bearing on the organization's objectives. On the other hand, the achievement of practical significant changes assumes that the differences are indeed reliable and will recur when the next instructional group is exposed to the treatment. Interacting with both ideas is the concept of scientific significance—that is, the establishment of meaningful results that permit generalizations about training procedures beyond the immediate setting being investigated. As Campbell, Dunnette, Lawler, and Weick (1970) suggest for managerial training, "Once the effects of such a program are mapped out for different kinds of trainees and for different types of criterion problems under various organizational situations, the general body of knowledge concerning management training has been enriched" (p. 284). If the instructional program is well designed, it should contribute to the solution of organizational goals, as well as add to the body of instructional knowledge.

METHODOLOGICAL CONSIDERATIONS IN THE USE OF EXPERIMENTAL DESIGNS

Each research design has different assets and liabilities in controlling extraneous factors that might threaten the evaluator's ability to determine (1) if a real change has occurred, (2) whether the change is attributable to the instructional program, and (3) whether the change is likely to occur again with a new sample of subjects. Specific research designs will be discussed in a later section, but several general design concepts, including control groups and pre/posttesting, are mentioned here as background for the presentation of the sources of error that can affect the validity of the experimental design.

Pre/Posttesting

The first question is whether the participants, after exposure to the instructional program, change their performance in a significant way. A design to answer this question would use a pretest administered before the instructional program begins and a posttest given after exposure to the instructional program. The timing of the posttest for the evaluation of an instructional program is not easily specified. A posttest at the conclusion of the training program provides a measure of the changes that have occurred during instruction, but it does not give any indication of later transfer performance. Thus, other measures should be employed after the participant has been in the transfer situation for a reasonable time period. Comparisons can then be made between (1) the pretest and the first posttest, (2) the pretest and the second posttest, and (3) the first and second posttests. For convenience, this section will refer only to pre- and posttests, but it is important to remember that one posttest immediately after training ordinarily will not suffice. An additional factor in the analysis of pre- and posttest scores is how scores on the pretest affect the degree of success on the posttest. One possibility is that the participant who initially scored highest on the pretest will perform best on the posttest. In order to examine this effect, some researchers (Mayo & DuBois, 1963) have suggested that the pretest scores should be partialed out of the posttest.

The variables measured in the pre- and posttests must be associated with the objectives of the training program. The expected changes associated with the instructional program should be specified so that statistically reliable differences between the pre- and posttests can confirm the degree to which the objectives have been achieved. This text does not attempt to treat the statistical considerations in instructional evaluation analyses except to warn the reader that statistical expertise is necessary to properly evaluate programs.

Control Groups

The specification of changes indicated by pre- and postmeasurement is only one consideration. It must be determined that these changes occurred because of the instructional treatment. To eliminate the possibility of other explanations for the changes between pre- and posttest, a control group is used (treated like the experimental group on all variables that might contribute to pre/post differences except for the actual instructional program). With control procedures, it is possible to specify whether the changes in the experimental group were due to instructional treatment or to other factors, like the passage of time, maturation factors, or events in the outside world. The kinds of errors that can occur will be specified in the next section, but, as an example of the necessity for control groups, we can consider the placebo effect. As mentioned earlier, the placebo is an inert substance administered to the control group by medical research so that subjects cannot distinguish whether they are members of the experimental group or the control group. This allows the researcher to separate the effects of the actual drug from the reactions induced by the subjects' expectations and suggestibility. In instructional research, similar cautions must be taken to separate the background effects sometimes employed in the experimental setting and the actual treatment. It is possible that treatment effects in an experimental group in which videotape feedback is being investigated are caused by the presence of recording equipment and numerous observers (Isaac & Michael, 1971). Thus, the control group should be presented with similar attention. As discussed in the section on values and evaluation, it is also becoming increasingly obvious that the use of experimental design, including the assignment of persons to control groups sometimes produces profound changes in the behavior of participants, with consequences that can include the sabotaging of outcomes of programs. Obviously, if these effects are not detected by the investigators, misinterpretations of the results of the study are very likely. Before discussing specific research designs, it is necessary to consider those factors that contribute sources of error. D. T. Campbell and J. C. Stanley (1963) originally organized and specified these threats to experimental design. Cook and D. T. Campbell (1976, 1979) have updated this text and include discussions of many of the intervention threats stemming from a growing appreciation of the values of trainees, trainers, evaluators, and organizational sponsors. For the most part, Cook and Campbell's labels and organization are used in this text.

INTERNAL AND EXTERNAL VALIDITY

Internal validity asks the basic question, "Did the treatment make a difference in this particular situation?" Unless internal validity has been established, it is not possible to interpret the effects of any experiment, training or otherwise. External validity refers to the generalizability or representativeness of the data. The evaluator is concerned with generalizability of results to other populations, settings, and treatment variables. External validity is always a matter of inference and thus can never be specified with complete confidence. However, the designs that control the most threats to internal and external validity are, of course, the most useful.

Threats to Internal Validity

These threats are variables other than the instructional program itself that can affect its results. The solution to this difficulty is to control these variables so that they may be cast aside as competing explanations for the experimental effect. Threats to internal validity include the following.

History. History refers to specific events, other than the experimental treatment, occurring between the first and second measurements that could provide alternative explanations for results. When tests are given on different days, as is almost always the case in instructional programs, events occurring between testing periods can contaminate the effects. For instance, an instructional program designed to produce positive attitudes toward safe practices in coal mines may produce significant differences that have no relationship to the material presented in the instructional program because a coal-mine disaster occurred between the pre- and posttest.

Maturation. Maturation includes all biological or psychological effects that systematically vary with the passage of time, independent of specific events like history. Participants become older, fatigued, or more or less interested in the program between the time of the pretest and the time of the posttest. Thus, performance can change for reasons unrelated to the instructional material.

Testing. This variable refers to the influence of the pretest on the scores of the posttest. This is an especially serious problem for instructional programs in which the pretest can sensitize the participant to search for material or to ask friends for information that provides correct answers on the posttest. Thus, improved performance would occur simply by taking the pre- and posttests, without an intervening instructional program.

Instrumentation. This threat to validity results from changes in the instruments that might result in differences between pre- and posttest scores. For example, fluctuations in mechanical instruments or changes in grading standards can lead to differences, regardless of the instructional program. Since rating scales are commonly employed as a criterion in training research, it is important to be sensitive to differences related to changes in the rater (for example, additional expertise in the second rating, bias, or carelessness) that can cause error effects.

Statistical regression. Participants for instructional research are often chosen on the basis of extreme scores. Thus, students with extremely low and extremely high intelligence-test scores may be chosen for participation in a course using programed instruction. In these cases, a phenomenon known as statistical regression often occurs. On the second testing, the scores for both groups regress toward the middle of the distribution. Thus, students with extremely high scores would tend toward lower scores, and those with extremely low scores would tend toward higher scores. This regression occurs because tests are not perfect measures; there will always be some change in scores from the first to the second testing simply because of measurement error. Since the first scores are at the extreme ends, the variability must move toward the center (the mean of the entire group). Students with extremely high scores might have had unusually good luck the day of the first testing, or students with extremely low scores may have been upset or careless that day. On the second administration, however, each group is likely to regress toward the mean.

Differential selection of participants.   This effect stems from biases in choosing comparison groups. If volunteers are used in the instruction group and randomly chosen participants are used in the control group, differences could occur between the two groups simply because each was different before the program began. This variable is best controlled by random selection of all participants, with appropriate numbers of participants (as determined by statistical considerations) for each group. Random selection is a particular problem in educational settings where one class is chosen as the control group and another class as the experimental group. Establishing experimental and control groups by placing individuals with matched characteristics (for example, intelligence, age, sex) in each group is still not the best alternative. Often, the critical parameters that should be used to match the participants are not known, and thus selection biases can again affect the design. One alternative is a combination of matching and randomization in which participants are matched on important parameters; then, one member of each pair is assigned randomly to the treatment or control group.

Experimental mortality.   This variable refers to the differential loss of participants from the treatment or control group. In a control group of volunteers, those persons who scored poorly on the pretest may drop out because they are discouraged. Thus, the group in the experimental program may appear to score higher than the control group, because the low-scoring performers have dropped out.

Interactions.   Many of the above factors—for example, selection and maturation—can interact to produce threats to internal validity. When younger students are compared with older students over a period of a year, there are differences in initial selection and differences in maturation changes that could occur at varying rates for each of the different groups.

The following threats to internal validity can be labeled intervention threats because they stem mainly from the decision to evaluate a program. Interestingly, many of the internal threats to validity discussed above can be constrained by the use of experimental design procedures. For example, the internal threat of history effects can often be constrained by having an experimental and a control group so that whatever the historical occurrence it affects both groups. However, most of the next set of threats cannot be constrained by experimental methodology. Rather, as discussed in the section on values and evaluation, it will take other approaches—for example, working with the participants as part of the evaluation model so that they do not feel threatened by events such as being assigned to a control group. Many persons in organizations are interested in achieving success. Therefore, it should not surprise anyone that a mysterious announcement from a training analyst that assigns only certain individuals to a training program might be viewed by the control subjects as a message that they are not in favor with the organization. Also, as described below, some organizations tend to interfere with the assignment of treatment effects because they are certain that training will work, and they want the control group also to have the benefit of the effect even while evaluation is proceeding. Some of these types of threats to validity (adapted from Cook and D. T. Campbell, 1976, 1979) include the following.

Diffusion or imitation of treatments.   In organizations where members of the experimental and control treatments know each other, information passed on to the controls by members of the group being trained can diffuse the effects of training. Thus, members of the training group tell control individuals how to use this wonderful new procedure. As a result, differences between the two groups based upon the training treatment disappear and the evaluator does not learn whether the program accomplished its goals.

Compensatory equalization of treatments.   When the training treatment is perceived to produce positive benefits, there is often a reluctance to permit perceived inequalities to exist. Thus, administrators or trainers provide control subjects with similar or other benefits that wipe out any measured differences between the control and experimental groups in the evaluation. Cook and Campbell note that in several national educational experiments so-called control schools tended to be given other federal funds by well-meaning administrators. This of course resulted in these control schools actually being another form of experimental condition. Unfortunately, as later analyses indicated, it also wiped out the differences between the experimental and "control" treatments, leaving many individuals thoroughly confused as to why their training treatments had no effect.

Compensatory rivalry between respondents receiving less desirable treatments.   In some situations, competition between the training group and the control group may be generated. This is more likely to occur when the assignments are made public or when intact units (like a whole department or work crew) are assigned to a particular condition. The problem is that this special effort may wipe out the differences between the two groups but not be a reflection of how control subjects would ordinarily perform. This kind of effect is also possible where the control condition is the old training procedure. Here again the controls might work extra hard so that their performance would be equivalent to the persons assigned to the new treatment condition. Saretsky (1972) labels this type of effort the "John Henry effect." As memorialized in the folk song, John Henry competed against a steam drill. He worked so hard that he outperformed the drill and died of overexertion.

Resentful demoralization of respondents receiving less desirable treatments. In some instances, persons selected for a control condition can become resentful or demoralized. This is especially possible when control subjects believe that the assignment might be a message that they are not as highly valued by management. This can result in the person not performing as capably as possible. In this instance, the control subjects' drop in performance could result in differences between the treatment and control that leads to the incorrect conclusion that the training program has been successful.

Threats to External Validity

External validity refers to the generalizability of the study to other groups and situations. Internal validity is a prerequisite for external validity, since the results for the study must be valid for the group being examined before there can be concern over the validity for other groups. The representativeness of the investigation determines the degree of generalizability. For example, when the data are initially collected in a low socioeconomic setting, it is difficult to claim that the instructional program will work equally well in a high socioeconomic area. The following external validity threats which are potentially relevant to the evaluation of training programs are adapted from the original text by Campbell and Stanley (1963).

Reactive effect of pretesting. The effects of pretests often lead to increased sensitivity to the instructional procedure. Thus, the participants' responses to the training program might be different from the responses of individuals who are exposed to an established program without the pretest; the pretested participants might pay attention to certain material in the training program only because they know it is covered in test items. Usually, it is speculated that pretest exposure will improve performance. However, Bunker and Cohen (1977) discovered that the posttest scores of persons low in numerical ability were hindered by exposure to the pretest. They offer several possible reasons for this development. The trainees may mistakenly have attended to only the limited sample of material appearing on the pretest. Another possibility is that the trainees who were low in numerical ability may have become quite anxious because of the pretest and that might have interfered with later learning. Further research will be needed to explore that possibility. However, generalizations to later training populations that would not be exposed to a pretest would be in error. Interestingly, however, the problem occurred only for low ability students. Thus, the external validity threat of pretesting interacted with the selection of the participating group. That type of threat is discussed next.

Interaction of selection and experimental treatment. In this case, the characteristics of the group selected for experimental treatment determine the generalizability of the findings. The characteristics of employees from one division of the firm may result in the treatment's being more or less effective for them, as compared to employees from another division with different characteristics. Similarly, characteristics, such as the low numerical ability example just discussed, may make trainees more or less receptive to particular instructional programs.

Reactive effects of experimental settings. The procedures employed in the experimental setting may limit the generalizability of the study. Observers and experimental equipment often make the participants aware of their participation in an experiment. This can lead to changes in behavior that cannot be generalized to those individuals who will participate in the instructional treatment when it is not the focus of a research study. The Hawthorne studies have become the standard illustration for the "I'm-a-guinea-pig" effect. This research shows that a group of employees continued to increase production regardless of the changes in working conditions designed to produce both increases and decreases in production. Interpreters believe that the experimental conditions resulted in the workers' behaving differently. Explanations for the Hawthorne effect include: novelty; awareness of being a participant in an experiment; changes in the environment due to observers, enthusiasm of the instructor, recording conditions, and social interaction; and daily feedback on production figures. The important point is that, since the factors that affect the treatment group will not be present in future training sessions, the performance obtained is not representative of that of future participants.

The potency of these types of variables was demonstrated by Eden and Shani (1982) in a study of military combat training for the Israeli Defense Forces. Instructors had been led to expect that some of these trainees were better students than others, although actually there were no greater ability differences for the person chosen. The individuals for whom trainers had high expectancies scored significantly higher on objective achievement tests, exhibited more positive attitudes toward the course, and had more positive perceptions of instructor leadership. These types of variables become an external validity threat because there is often more enthusiasm when courses are first being offered (and evaluated). However, that enthusiasm sometimes disappears when the course becomes more routine. To the extent that the training effect was due to enthusiasm, it will disappear with the more routine course. On the other hand, if organizations can learn to use and maintain variables underlying factors such as enthusiasm, there are indications that training performance will improve. It is hoped that the positive attitudes and performance generated in the Eden and Shani study will continue on the job. However, further studies will be needed to make that determination.

Multiple-treatment interference. The effects of previous treatments are not erasable; therefore, threats to external validity occur whenever there is an attempt to establish the effects of a single treatment from studies that actually examined multiple treatments. Thus, trainees exposed to role playing, films, and lectures may perform best during the lectures, but that does not mean that they would perform in a similar manner were they exposed to lectures only.

EXPERIMENTAL DESIGN

This section presents some of the many designs that examine the effects of experimental treatments. The previous sections on internal and external validity discussed some of the factors that make it difficult to determine whether the treatment produced the hypothesized results. As we shall see, these threats are differentially controlled by the various designs. Given a particular setting, the researcher should employ the design that has the greatest degree of control over threats to validity. Certainly, it is possible to avoid choosing a useless design. In many cases, the main difficulty has been the failure to plan for evaluation before the program was implemented. In these instances, the utilization of a few procedures—for example, pre/posttesting and control groups—could dramatically improve the quality of information.

For convenience in presenting the experimental designs, T_1 will represent the pretest, T_2 the posttest, X the treatment or instructional program, and R the random selection of subjects. Cook and Campbell (1979) have organized a detailed examination of the variables that should be considered when choosing a research design. The designs in this test, organized into several different categories, provide examples of the numerous approaches available. The first category includes pre-experimental designs that do not have control procedures and are more difficult to use in analyzing cause-and-effect relationships. Experimental designs, the second category, have varying degrees of power that permit some control of threats to validity. The third category includes quasi-experimental designs that are useful in many social-science settings where investigators lack the opportunity to exert full control over the environment.

Preexperimental Designs

1. The one-group posttest only design:

$$\boxed{X \qquad T_2}$$

In this method, the one group posttest only design, the subjects are exposed to the instructional treatment (without a pretest) and then are tested once at the completion of training. Without the pretest, it is not possible to be certain that there is any change as a result of the training treatment from before to after training. Also, without the control group, it is difficult to infer that the cause of the change is the training treatment rather than an internal threat to validity such as history. Thus, the limitations include the lack of hypothesis testing and problems in generalizability. However, the reader should realize that valuable information can be obtained from this method. It is possible to have very rich descriptions stemming from this type of design. For example, case study approaches used in the social sciences often employ a posttest-only design that provides considerable information based upon the collection of a large number of measures at the posttest time. This information can provide very important hunches and hypotheses which can be used as input for another study. Replications with more controlled conditions which are based upon hypotheses stimulated by the case study method and previous theory development is a powerful methodology. However, interpretations of causality and generalizability in a single posttest-only design are precarious.

2. The one-group pretest/posttest design:

$$\boxed{T_1 \qquad X \qquad T_2}$$

When this design is employed, the participants are given a pretest, presented with the instructional program, and then given a posttest. This design is widely utilized in the examination of instructional settings, because it provides a measure of comparison between the same group of subjects before and after treatment. Unfortunately, without a control group, it is difficult to establish whether the experimental treatment is the prime factor determining any differences that occur between the testing periods. Thus, the many threats to internal validity, including changes in history, maturation, testing effects, changes in instrumentation, and statistical regression, are not controlled. This design does, however, control biases due to subject mortality.

Research Example of Preexperimental Designs

Golembiewski and Carrigan (1970) carried out a training program that utilized a pre/post design without a control group in one of a series of investigations designed to change the style of a sales unit in a business organization. They had a series of goals, including: the integration of a new management team, an increase in congruence between the behaviors required by the organization and those preferred by the men, and a greater congruence of individual needs and organizational demands. The training program consisted of a laboratory approach using sensitivity training to encourage the exploration of the participant's feelings and reactions to the organization. The program also included confrontation in which management of various levels were given an opportunity to discuss their ideas and feelings. The instrument used to measure pre- and postexperimental changes was Likert's profile of organizational characteristics, which includes items related to leadership, character of motivational forces, communication, interaction influence, decision making, goal setting, and control.

After statistical analyses, the authors concluded that the learning design had the intended effect in terms of the measured attitudes. Golembiewski and Carrigan indicated that they had included all the managers in the treatment and so did not have a control group. Thus, their design did not permit them to be certain that the effects were a result of the training program rather than of random factors or the passage of time. This design uncertainty is expressed by Becker (1970) in an article entitled "The Parable of the Pill":

> There once was a land in which wisdom was revered. Thus, there was great excitement in the land when one of its inhabitants announced that he had invented a pill which made people wiser. His claim was based on an experiment he conducted. The report of the experiment explained (1) that the experimenter secured a volunteer; (2) the volunteer was first given an IQ test; (3) then he swallowed a pill which he was told would make him more intelligent; (4) finally he was given another IQ test. The score on the second IQ test was higher than on the first, so the report concluded that the pill increased wisdom.
>
> Alas, there were two skeptics in the land. One secured a volunteer; gave him an IQ test; waited an appropriate length of time; then gave him another IQ test. The volunteer's score on the second test exceeded that of the first. Skeptic One reported his experiment and concluded that taking the first test was an experience for the subject and that the time between the tests allowed the subject to assimilate and adjust to that experience so that when he encountered the situation again he responded more efficiently. Time alone, the skeptic argued, was sufficient to produce the increase in test score. The skeptic also pointed out that time alone could have produced the change in test score reported in the experiment on the Wisdom Pill.
>
> Skeptic Two conducted a different experiment. He held the opinion that most people were to some extent suggestible or gullible and that they readily would accept a suggestion that they possessed a desired attribute. He further believed that people who accept such a suggestion might even behave in a way such as to make it appear, for a time at least, that they indeed did possess the suggested ability. Therefore, the skeptic secured a volunteer; gave him an IQ test; had him ingest a pill composed of inert ingredients; told him the pill would increase his intelligence; then gave him another IQ test. Skeptic Two dutifully reported his subject

achieved a higher score on the second test and, based on his hypothesis, explained how the disparity arose. He also pointed out that the increase in test score in the Wisdom Pill experiment could have been due to the taking of the pill and expectations associated with taking the pill rather than to the ingredients in the pill.

The inventor of the wisdom pill drafted a reply to the two skeptics. He wrote that, although he did not employ a control group or a placebo group, he is confident that the pill's ingredients caused the observed change because that change is consistent with the theory from which he deduced the formula for his pill. (p. 94)[1]

The point in the parable is that Skeptic One, Skeptic Two, or the inventor of the pill may be right. There is no way of being certain, given the present design, what was responsible for the effect.

The next group of designs shows how easily many of the pre-experimental designs can be improved. Design 1 can be strengthened by adding a pretest, and both Design 1 and Design 2 can be improved by adding a control group. Even where the environment makes a control group impractical, these designs can be improved by using the approaches described in the section on quasi-experimental designs.

Experimental Designs

3. Pretest/posttest control-group design:

Experimental Group (R)	T_1	X	T_2
Control Group (R)	T_1		T_2

In this design, the subjects are chosen at random from the population and assigned randomly to the experimental group or control group. Each group is given a pre- and posttest, but only the experimental group is exposed to the instructional treatment. If there is more than one instructional treatment, it is possible to add additional experimental groups.

This design represents a considerable improvement over Designs 1 and 2, because many of the threats to internal validity are controlled. The differential selection of subjects is controlled by the random selection. Variables like history, maturation, and pretesting should affect the experimental group and the control group equally. Statistical regression based on extreme scores (if subjects are chosen that way) is not eliminated but should be equal for the two groups because of the random selection procedures. However, any effects not part of the instructional procedure that are due to differential treatment of subjects in the control and experimental groups must still be controlled

---

[1] From "The Parable of the Pill," by S. W. Becker. In *Administrative Science Quarterly,* 1970, *15,* pp. 94–96. Copyright 1970 by Administrative Sciences Quarterly. Reprinted by permission.

by the experimenter. This includes the problems of intervention threats such as compensatory rivalry or resentful demoralization of control groups. This design is affected by external threats to validity, which are not as easily specified as the threats to internal validity. The design does not control the effects of pretesting; thus T_1 could have sensitized the participants to the experimental treatment in a way that makes generalizations to future participants difficult. Generalizations would also be hampered because subjects in the experiment might be different from those who will participate at later times and because the guinea-pig effect could lead to differences between the experimental and control groups. This latter concern is dependent on the ingenuity of the experimenter in reducing the differences between groups by treating the control group in the same manner as the experimental group (except for the specific instructional treatment).

The difficulties associated with external validity should not freeze the researcher into inactivity. While most threats to internal validity are reasonably well handled by experimental designs, generalizations, which are the core of external validity, are always precarious. As Campbell and Stanley point out, experimenters try to generalize by scientifically guessing at laws and by trying out generalizations in other specific cases. Slowly, and somewhat painfully, they gain knowledge about factors that affect generalizations. (For example, there is now ample evidence that pretesting does sensitize and affect participants.) As shown in the following design, a control for pretest sensitization is relatively easy to achieve by adding a group to Design 3 that is exposed to the treatment without first being presented with the pretest.

4. Solomon four-group design:

Group

1 (R)	T_1	X	T_2
2 (R)	T_1		T_2
3 (R)		X	T_2
4 (R)			T_2

The Solomon four-group design represents the first specific procedure designed to consider external validity factors. This design adds two groups that are not pretested. If the participants are randomly assigned to the four groups, this design makes it possible to compare the effects of pretesting. (Group 4 provides a control for pretesting without the instructional treatment.) It also permits the evaluator to determine the effects of some internal validity factors. For example, a comparison of the posttest performance for Group 4, which was not exposed to pretesting or instructional treatments, to the pretest scores for Groups 1 and 2 permits the analysis of the combined effects of maturation and history.

Research Example of Experimental Designs

Goodacre (1955) reported on an evaluative study of a supervisory training program at B. F. Goodrich Company that fits into the classification of experimental designs. The program consisted of conferences, lectures, and discussions for different supervisory and managerial personnel on topics related to the understanding of human behavior, decision making, employee selection, employee progress, and job evaluation. The experimental design was developed in conjunction with the program and built into the instructional procedure. The 800 participants were randomly placed into two groups—an experimental group and a control group. As Goodacre notes, random selection was necessary to assure that the groups would be comparable on variables like age, length of service, job level, and intelligence. The control group did not participate in the training program, but, in all other regards, it was treated similarly to the experimental group. Various criterion measures, including attitude scales, achievement tests, and ratings by immediate supervisors, were administered both before and after training.

As reported by J. P. Campbell et al. (1970), the control group did not show any significant changes, but the experimental group improved on the achievement tests, self-confidence ratings, and post-training performance measures. This is one of the few studies that not only used a rigorous design but also attempted to measure performance on the job and in the training program. Goodacre and Campbell et al. note that one problem with the performance ratings was that the raters knew who participated in the training program. Yet, even with that difficulty, the experimental design permitted the control of many threats to internal validity that plague preexperimental designs. However, it did not control for the external validity threats of pretest sensitization.

Quasi-Experimental Designs

5. The time-series design:

$$\boxed{T_1 \quad T_2 \quad T_3 \quad T_4 \quad X \quad T_5 \quad T_6 \quad T_7 \quad T_8}$$

This design is similar to Design 1, except that a series of measurements are taken before and after the instructional treatment. This particular approach illustrates the possibilities of utilizing quasi-experimental designs in situations in which it is not possible to gain the full control required by experimental designs. An examination of the internal validity threats shows that this design provides more control than Design 1. If there are no appreciable changes from pretests 1 to 4, it is unlikely that any effects will occur due to maturation, testing, or regression. The major internal validity difficulty with this design is the history variable; that is, events that may happen between T_4 and T_5 (such as environmental changes and historical occurrences) are not controlled by this procedure.

The use of the time-series design does not control most of the external validity threats. Thus, it is necessary to be sensitive to any relationships between the treatment and particular subject groups (like volunteers) that might make results difficult to generalize to other groups, and it is also necessary to be aware that subjects might be sensitized to particular aspects of the instructional program through the use of pretests.

6. The nonequivalent control-group design:

Experimental Group	T_1	X	T_2
Control Group	T_1		T_2

The nonequivalent control-group design is the same as Design 3, except that the participants are not assigned to the groups at random. (The choice of the group to receive the instructional treatment is made randomly.) This design is often used in educational settings where there are naturally assembled groups, such as classes. If there is no alternative, this design is well worth using and is certainly preferable to designs that do not include control groups (such as Design 2). The more similar the two groups and their scores on the pretest, the more effective the control becomes in accounting for extraneous influences—for instance, internal validity factors like history, pretesting, maturation, and instrumentation. However, the investigator must be especially careful, because this design is vulnerable to interactions between selection factors and maturation, history, and testing. Since the participants were not chosen randomly, there is always the possibility that critical differences exist that were not revealed by the pretests. For example, some studies use volunteers who might react differently to the treatment because of motivational factors. Thus, the investigator must be sensitive to potential sources of differences between the groups. The dangers of instrumentation changes and of differential treatment of each group (unrelated to the treatment) remain a concern for this design as well as for Design 3.

Although the external validity issues are similar to those for Design 3, the nonequivalent control-group design does have some advantages in the control of the reactive effects of experimental settings. The utilization of intact groups makes it easier to design the experiment as part of the normal routine, thus reducing some of the problems associated with the guinea-pig effect. Since this design is not as disruptive, it is also possible in some settings (for example, educational systems), to have a larger subject population, thus increasing generalizability.

Research Example of Quasi-Experimental Designs

A study by Canter (1951) illustrates a quasi-experimental design employing pre/post measures with nonequivalent control groups. The purpose of this investigation was to train supervisory personnel in human relations—that is, to establish facts and principles so that supervisors could become more competent in their knowledge and understanding of human behavior. The criteria consisted of a test battery including measures of supervisory behavior, social judgment, and logical reasoning.

The experimental group contained supervisors from one department, and the control group contained members from two other departments. Since the participants were not randomly chosen, Canter checked variables like age, sex, mental alertness, and years of service. While there were no statistical differences due to considerable variability in the scores, the author indicated that differences in number of years of service and mental alertness were discernible. The results of the study indicated that changes in performance favored the trained group.

While this design controls history and maturation factors reasonably well, there are problems related to selection interactions and factors like history and testing. The participants in this program worked under different supervisors and in different psychological and physical environments. The effects of these selection factors are unknown, but of special concern is the fact that the department heads for these participants did observe certain aspects of the training.

Another ingenious example of the use of quasi-experimental design is offered by the research of Komaki, Heinzmann, and Lawson (1980). This study was described briefly in Chapter 4 in the section on knowledge of results. Since it is a good illustration of quasi-experimental designs, it will be described here in more detail. These investigators were studying safety problems in the vehicle maintenance division of a city's department of public works. The department being studied had one of the highest accident rates in the city. Komaki and her colleagues performed a needs assessment including an analysis of the factors that led to unsafe practices and hindered safe acts. They examined safety logs for the previous five years to determine what type of accidents occurred and then wrote safety behavioral items that would have prevented that accident. Throughout this procedure they interacted with supervisors and workers on the specification and development of safety procedures. Some examples of safety items generated for the vehicle maintenance department are:

1. Proper use of equipment and tools. When reaching upward for an item more than 30 cm (1 ft.) away from extended arms, use steps, stepladder, or solid part of vehicle. Do not stand on jacks or jack stands.

2. Use of safety equipment. When using brake machine, wear full face shield or goggles. When arcing brake shoes, respirator should also be worn.

3. Housekeeping. Any oil/grease spill larger than 8 x 8 cm (3 x 3 in.) in an interior walking area (defined as any area at least 30 cm [1 ft.] from a wall or a solid standing object) or an exterior walking area (designated by outer white lines parallel to the wall and at least 30 cm [1 ft.] from the wall) should be soaked up with rice hull or grease compound.

4. General safety procedures. When any type of jack other than an air jack is in use (i.e., vehicle is supported by jack or off the ground), at least one jack stand should also be used. (pp. 262–263)

Komaki and her colleagues designed a training program that used slides to depict the unsafe practices employed in the department, examined the trainees on their knowledge of appropriate safe behaviors, discussed correct safety behaviors, and then showed the same slides but this time demonstrated safe practices. Also, the employees were given copies of the appropriate safety rules to take with them. This procedure was designated the Training Program. Another procedure used later in the program was called Training and Feedback. In this procedure, in addition to the training given earlier, the employees were informed about realistic safety goals that were set on the basis of their previous performance. Then, randomly timed daily safety observations were made and the results were posted on a graph so that the employees could see how they were progressing toward their goals.

The design of this study was a time series with at least four or five observations for each of the first three phases of the study and an average of three observations per phase for the last two phases. The phases are depicted in Figure 6.1. The first phase, referred to as baseline, consisted of the collection of data before any training or feedback. It essentially consisted of multiple pretests. The second phase was the training program, and the third phase added feedback to the already-trained employees. The fourth phase went back to training only with no feedback being given, and the final phase reinstituted feedback to the already-trained employees. Note that all persons proceed through the entire sequence of five phases and that there are multiple data collection points in each phase. The data collected consisted of the number of incidents performed safely. It was collected by trained observers and there was a high level of agreement between the observers. In the data shown in the graph for two departments (preventive maintenance and light equipment repair), performance improved from baseline to after training and then improved more when feedback was added. When feedback was taken away performance went down, but performance improved again when feedback was put back in the last phase of the study. Komaki's point is that, in addition to training, feedback on employee performance is a critical component of the program. In two other departments, Komaki obtained similar data for the first four phases, but improvement did not occur again as a result

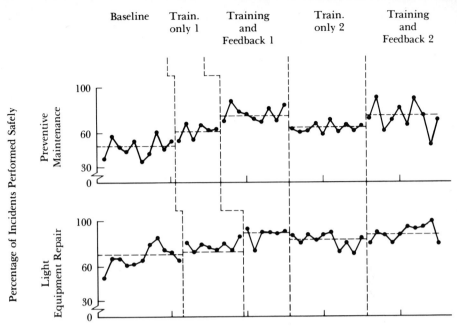

FIGURE 6.1 Percentage of incidents performed safely by employees in vehicle maintenance departments under five experimental conditions. (*From "Effect of Training and Feedback: Component Analysis of a Behavioral Safety Program," by J. Komaki, A. T. Heinzmann, and L. Lawson. In* Journal of Applied Psychology, *1980, 65, pp. 261–270. Copyright 1980 by the American Psychological Association. Reprinted by permission.*)

of the fifth phase. The investigators in this study considered the various threats to validity and how their quasi-experimental accounted for these factors. They noted:

> Plausible alternative hypotheses (history, maturation, statistical regression) were ruled out because the two phases were introduced to the sections at different points in time and improvements occurred after, and not prior to, the introduction of these phases. History was ruled out as a source of internal invalidity because it is not likely that an extraneous event would have the same impact in separate sections at different times. If maturations were responsible, performance would be expected to improve as a function of the passage of time; however, improvements occurred, with few exceptions, after the introduction of Phase 3. The effects of statistical regression were ruled out because regression effects would be seen in any series of repeated measurements and not just after the introduction of the two phases.
>
> Reactivity of measurement was also not likely to be a plausible explanation for the improvements obtained because the observers were present during all phases. Therefore, improvements in performance during any one phase could not be due to the reactivity of the measure per se. Questions concerning reactivity and external validity, however, were

not so straightforward. Although the issue of the generality of improvements was not addressed directly in the present study, support was provided by accident records, which showed that injuries were reduced by a factor of seven from the preceding year. Since the observers were present during a relatively small percentage of working hours, it is unlikely that improvements were confined to these times. (p. 267)

UTILITY CONSIDERATIONS

As mentioned in the chapter on criterion issues, an important consideration in the evaluation of training programs is the concept of utility. As noted by Schneider and Schmitt (1986) in their discussion of utility and selection procedures, psychologists act as if a significant validity coefficient relating a test and criterion measure was proof of the test's usefulness. However, meaningful terms for management usually involve monetary considerations. They note that when a production manager requests a new piece of machinery, it is usually supported by projected increases in productivity and resultant decreases in unit cost of production. Maintenance managers support hiring requests with figures showing decreases in downtime due to equipment problems and the resulting savings. As Schneider and Schmitt note, this means translating our validity coefficients into dollar values even if the translations are crude. These kinds of translations are called *utility analysis*. The analysis not only enables researchers to have information about the costs of their programs but also permits comparisons between the costs of different programs—for example, a formal training program versus on-the-job training, or a training program versus a selection program.

Cascio (1982b) has written a book titled *Costing Human Resources: The Financial Impact of Behavior in Organizations* which describes the various procedures and issues involved in utility analysis. While many of the details are beyond the scope of this volume, it is possible generally to describe its use as an evaluation technique for examining training programs. A distinction is made between cost benefit (CB) analysis and cost-effectiveness analysis (CE). Cost benefit analysis is the examination of "training costs in monetary units as compared to benefits derived from training in nonmonetary terms" (Cascio, 1982, p. 208). Some examples include trainee attitudes, health, and safety. Cost effectiveness is the examination of training costs in monetary units as compared to the benefits of training, also in monetary units. Some examples here include production waste, production increases, downtime, and so on.

The use of utility approaches in the examination of structured training versus unstructured training for a production worker is presented in the work of Cullen, Sawzin, Sisson, and Swanson (1978), illustrated in Figure 6.2. Training costs in that figure would include training development, training materials, training time, and produc-

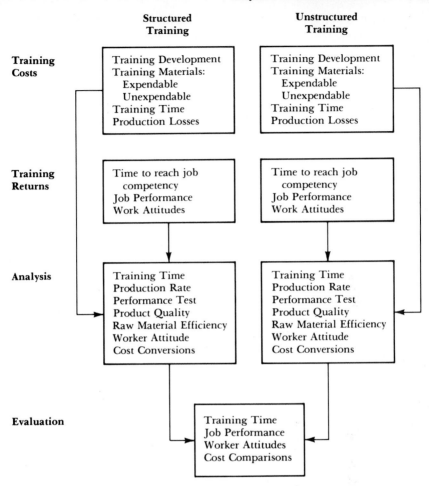

FIGURE 6.2 Industrial training cost-effectiveness model. (*From "Cost Effectiveness: A Model for Assessing the Training Investment," by J. G. Cullen, S. A. Sawzin, G. R. Sisson, and R. A. Swanson. In* Training and Development Journal, *1978, 32, pp. 24–29. Copyright 1978 by the American Society for Training and Development, Inc. Reprinted by permission.*)

tion losses. Each of these variables would be detailed. For example, time would involve trainee time, including total hours and resulting salary for the trainee to reach competency. It would include the total hours and resulting salary for the trainer until the trainee reached competency. The complexity of the cost analyses for specifying training costs is illustrated in Table 5.2 (p. 130) in the chapter on criterion measures.

The analysis requires that measures be developed for each of the categories (training costs, training returns, and training analysis listed in the figure). This involves all the criterion issues (relevancy, reliability, and so on) discussed in the previous chapter. The final stage of assessing the cost effectiveness (as shown in the figure) is called evaluation. Here, the structured and unstructured training methods are compared on all the variables in the diagram. Each variable must be translated into monetary terms. Thus, each of the factors in the analysis would be specified and translated. For example, raw material usage would be specified as the "weight of the raw material supplied to the machine versus weight of scrap and amount of quality product produced" (Cullen et al., 1977, p. 27). The translation of these measures into monetary figures includes the conversion of variables such as worker attitudes. As Cascio (1982) notes, this is difficult to accomplish, but the failure to analyze our programs in dollars ensures that training will continue to be viewed as a cost rather than as a benefit to the organization. For information about how to measure variables such as attitudes in monetary terms, the reader is directed to Cascio. It is clear that utility analyses will become an increasingly important part of evaluation analyses.

OTHER METHODS OF EVALUATION

The experimental models of evaluation which center on pre- and post-tests, control groups, threats to validity, and so on, represent the traditional models used to assess the effects of training programs. The reader should be aware of the fact that there are a large number of other evaluation models. For example, there is the adversarial model (Levine, 1974) which stems from a criticism of the classical experimental model. This point of view maintains that the traditional point of view is not well-suited to decision-making and does not focus well on questions of the value or worth of the program being evaluated. The adversarial model is developed around a system similar to a court of law. The model takes the point of view that all researchers are biased and the best way to counteract this problem and determine the value of the program is to have two sets of researchers. Each group gathers its own data to support its viewpoint and advocates a point of view to a judge or jury, who then renders a decision about the value of the program. Many of the rules of data gathering, analysis, and so on, are similar to the experimental model. However, the final decision is based on a judge's or jury's determination of worth based upon the evidence presented by the advocates.

There are many other evaluation models, but unfortunately it is not possible to discuss them all in this book. However, there are a few other models which are particularly relevant to the evaluation of training programs. They are individual differences models and content validity models.

Individual Differences Models

Many industrial psychologists have emphasized the use of training scores as a way to predict the future success of potential employees. Figure 6.3 presents a hypothetical set of scores on a sales training test and a criteria consisting of sales volume at the end of one year on the job. One way of characterizing the relationships between these two variables is by the statistical determination of the correlational coefficient. The value of the correlational coefficient ranges from +1.00 for a perfect positive relationship to –1.00 for a perfect negative correlation. A .00 correlation indicates that there is no evidence that the two variables are associated.

In this example, persons with higher scores on the training test also tended to perform better on the job in terms of sales volume. Thus, the better performers in training were better performers on the job, and the poorer performers in training were poorer performers on the job. There are a number of these types of studies showing meaningful relationships between training performance and on-the-job performance. For example, Kraut (1975) found that peer ratings obtained from managers attending a month-long training course predicted several criteria, including future promotion and performance appraisal ratings of job performance. Other investigators have used early training performance to predict performance later on in more advanced training. An example of this approach is offered by Gordon and Cohen (1973), whose study involved a welding program that was part of a larger manpower development project aimed at training unemployed and underemployed individuals from the eastern Tennessee area. The program consisted of 14 different tasks that fell into four categories

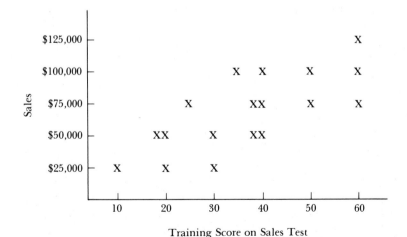

FIGURE 6.3 Hypothetical scores on a sales test at the end of training and sales volume after one year on the job.

and ranged in difficulty from simple to complex. Advancement from one task to the next was dependent upon successful completion of all previous tasks. Thus, trainees progressed at a rate commensurate with their ability to master the material to be learned. For each trainee, data were collected on the amount of time spent on each of the tasks. The correlations between the completion times for the four categories of tasks and total time to complete the plate welding course are given in Table 6.2.

Gordon and Cohen (1973) indicate that the results show "that early performance in the lab generally is an excellent predictor of final performance. Furthermore, the greater the number of tasks included in our predictor, the better our prediction will become. It is possible, therefore, to identify those trainees who will take longer than average to complete the plate welding course by simply examining their performance on the first few tasks" (p. 268).

These investigators understood that they were predicting the performance of individuals on a later task—for example, on the job or later in training—based upon performance in the training program. As a matter of fact, once these relationships have been established in an appropriately designed study, it is possible to select individuals for a job or for later training based upon these training scores. In other words, the training score serves as a validated predictor of future performance. However, caution should be used when this technique is considered as an evaluation of the training program. The relationship between training performance and on-the-job performance simply means that persons who perform best on the training test also perform

TABLE 6.2 Correlations between the time to completion for various segments of the course and total time required to complete the plate welding course

	Correlation of Task			
	1 with finish	*1 & 2 with finish*	*1–3 with finish*	*1–4 with finish*
I (N = 21)	0.55	0.76	0.81	0.84
II (N = 19)	0.70	0.83	0.94	0.96
III (N = 18)[a]	0.09	0.18	0.77	0.78
Total (N = 58)	0.69	0.79	0.87	0.87

Note—Groups I, II, and III differed in their starting dates.

[a] A word of explanation is due regarding the poor predictability of tasks 1 and 2 in Group III. Discussion with the training supervisor of the welding program indicated that illness had caused two of his three instructors to be absent for most of the period during which Group III was learning tasks 1 and 2. Consequently, the amount of supervision and guidance provided was necessarily below normal. It is probable that this temporary understaffed situation changed the usual conditions of learning, and caused the correlations observed in Group III to be unlike those recorded for Groups I and II.

From "Training Behavior as a Predictor of Trainability," by M. E. Gordon and S. L. Cohen. In *Personnel Psychology,* 1973, *26,* pp. 261-272. Copyright 1973 by Personnel Psychology, Inc. Reprinted by permission.

well on the job. This does not necessarily mean that the training program is properly designed or that persons learned enough in training to perform well on the job. It is entirely possible that the training program did not teach anything or that the trainees did not learn anything. In those cases, there would still be individual differences on the training test. Even if the training program did not teach the relevant material for the job, there would still be a strong relationship if the persons who performed well on the test also performed well on the job and the persons who performed poorly on the test performed poorly on the job. That is, the training program might not have achieved anything except to maintain the individual differences between trainees that might have existed before they entered training. There are two solutions to this problem. First, the use of appropriate pretests and control groups will establish whether learning has occurred and whether it is likely to be a result of the training program. In other words, even when the purpose is to use the training scores as a predictive device, it is useful to use experimental methodology evaluation to ensure that the training program has actually accomplished its learning objectives. Another procedure that lends some credence to individual difference methodology is to demonstrate that the training program and the criteria used to evaluate training are based upon a thorough needs assessment so that the training program really does reflect the required KSAs. This later procedure introduces another evaluation methodology—content validity.

Content Validity Models

If the needs assessment is appropriately carried out and the training program is designed to reflect knowledge, skills, and abilities, then the program will be judged as having content validity. That is, the training program should reflect the domain of KSAs represented on the job that the analyst has determined should be learned in the training program. An interesting question is whether it is possible after the design of the training program to determine if indeed it has content validity. Another question is whether it is possible to determine if a training program designed several years ago is content-valid in the sense that it reflects the content established by a recently completed needs assessment.

One way of conceptualizing the content validity of a training program is presented in Figure 6.4. In this figure, the horizontal axis across the top of the figure represents the dimension of importance or criticality of the KSAs as determined by the needs assessment. While the diagram only presents KSAs as being important or not important, it is vital to realize that this is an oversimplification of a dimension with many points. The vertical dimension represents the degree of emphasis for the KSAs in training. Again, to simplify the presentation, the dimension is presented as indicating that the KSA is or is not

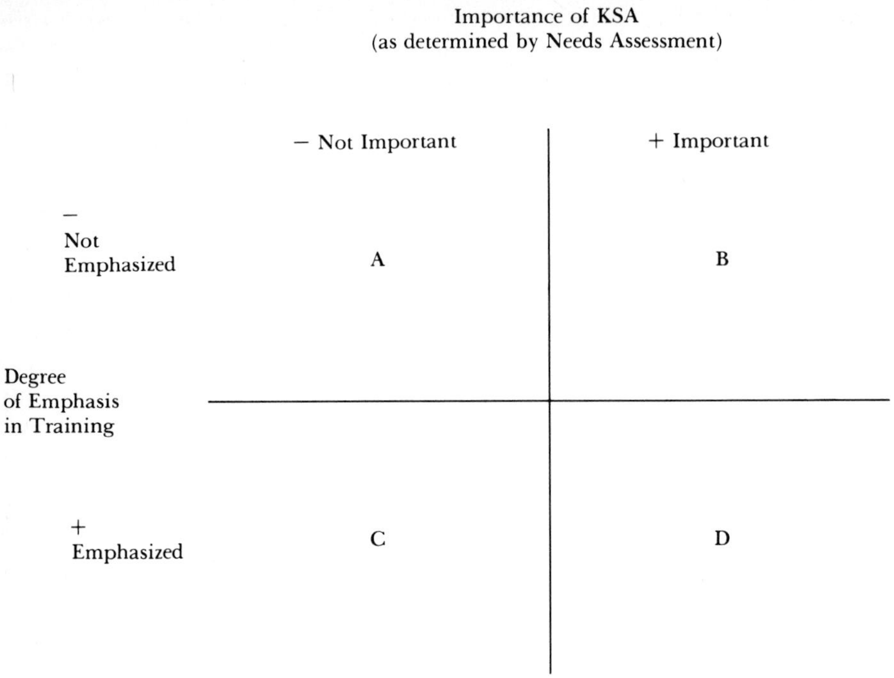

Importance of KSA
(as determined by Needs Assessment)

	− Not Important	+ Important
− Not Emphasized	A	B
Degree of Emphasis in Training		
+ Emphasized	C	D

FIGURE 6.4   A conceptual diagram of content validity of training programs.

emphasized in the training program. This results in the fourfold table presented in Figure 6.4. Using this approach, both Boxes A and D provide support for the content validity of the training program. KSAs that fall into Box D are judged as being important for the job and are emphasized in training. Items in Box A are judged as not important for the job and are not emphasized in training. Conceptually, to the degree to which KSAs fall into categories A and D, it is possible to think about the training program as being content-valid. Of course, this is an oversimplification. There will be KSAs which are judged as moderately important for the job or KSAs which are moderately emphasized in training. However, it is possible to conceive of this type of relationship and to actually measure the degree to which those KSAs judged as important are emphasized (and hopefully learned) in training. Very few persons would be unhappy with a training program that tended to emphasize the objectives associated with KSAs that are judged critical or important for job performance.

Box B represents a potential error and could affect the degree to which a program is judged content-valid. KSAs falling into the B category are judged as important for the job but are not emphasized in training. From a systems perspective, these items must be analyzed to determine whether the organization intends for these KSAs to be gained as a result of training. If that is the case, then there is a problem. However, it is also possible that individuals are expected to be selected with that particular KSA or that the individual is expected to learn the material related to that KSA on the job. To that extent, the training program should not be expected to emphasize the item and its content validity would not be questioned. However, it would still be important to determine that KSAs judged as important or critical are covered in another system, such as the selection of employees. If the item is not represented, then the organization must decide whether revision of the training program is necessary or if some other system must be designed to cover that material.

Box C represents KSAs that are emphasized in training but are judged as not being important for the job. This is often a criticism of training programs. That is, they tend to spend time emphasizing material that is not job-related. Most analysts agree that the use of needs assessment procedures and examination of training content results in a decrease in the amount of training time necessary to complete the training program. This usually occurs because of a reduction in the program based upon an elimination of the types of items present in Box C. Interestingly, a systems view of this process might even suggest a reduction of items that would appear in Box D. Selection experts like Bartlett (1982) might suggest that sometimes KSAs included in Box D are unnecessary because they have already been used as a basis for selection. Thus, if such materials are included in the training program, trainees are again subjected to materials on KSAs which are already in their repertoire.

As noted in the introduction to this section, there are very few analyses in the research literature based on these types of content-validity strategies. Ford and Wroten (1984) did explore some of these strategies in an examination of police officer training programs. On the basis of needs assessment procedures, these investigators identified 383 KSAOs (the O stands for other personal characteristics—for example, attitudes—determined in the needs assessment in addition to knowledge, skills, and abilities which are used to define the content training domain). They then had 114 experts independently rate the importance of each of the items for job performance. Basically, these investigators have taken items which would be identified as emphasized and determined whether the item fell into category C (not important for job performance) or category D (important for job performance). They discovered that 237, or 62%, of the KSAOs met the criteria they specified as being important for job performance. In another analysis, these investigators also found 57 items which were rated as important for job performance but which were not included in the training program. A few of those items were judged to be KSAs that were trainable and important, and they were thus added to the program.

As part of a research program involving our attempts to develop content validity models to understand training, Newman (1985) conducted research examining the implications of the diagram in Figure 6.4. His study was conducted on the job of cook foreman for the Federal Bureau of Prisons. First, a needs assessment was conducted to determine the KSAs needed for the job. In addition, since the training program was already in existence, another, separate, needs assessment was conducted to determine the KSAs taught in the training program. The training program is a two-week course covering the basics of institutional cooking and baking for cook foremen who supervise inmates in the preparation of meals in the federal prisons. Trainees come from 45 institutions across the country. The reason that a KSA analysis was done for the training program as well as the job is that it would thereby include the possibility that there might be KSAs emphasized in training which are not important on the job (Box C in Figure 6.4).

Both sets of KSAs were combined in an inventory. Newman then had 87 job subject matter experts (SMEs) rate the KSAs in terms of importance on the job, difficulty of learning, and where best acquired. The same KSAs were also rated by two training SMEs (the training director and the course instructor) on importance on the job, difficulty to learn, and time spent in the program teaching the KSA.

As an indicator of content validity, Newman correlated the KSA job importance ratings and the training emphasis ratings (as reflected by time spent). For the cooking and baking KSAs the correlation was .52. For another set of KSAs related to supervision and administration the correlation was .55. These data provided some evidence that KSAs judged higher in job importance were KSAs most emphasized in training. Interestingly, the trainer SMEs and the job SMEs also agreed on what was important with a correlation of .59 for cooking and baking KSAs and .76 for supervision and administration KSAs.

As a result of this study, it was also possible to do an analysis of where KSAs should be learned and which KSAs fell into the four boxes diagrammed in Figure 6.4. Newman also collected other quantitative and qualitative data about the program. For example, he found improvement from pre-training to post-training based on test scores and found that trainees as compared to a control group received higher performance ratings on training-relevant dimensions.

A final word of caution should be added to any conclusion about the use of content validity of training programs. Obviously, content validity is very important and all training programs should be content-valid. It makes no sense to have training programs that do not cover the KSAs necessary for the job. The whole purpose of performing a needs assessment and then tracing out the training program objectives based on the needs assessment is to have a content-valid program. If the reader reexamines Chapter 5 (see Figures 5.1 and 5.2), the concept of criterion relevance is based on exactly the same idea. Also, if the criterion is based on the needs assessment and the training program is based on the needs assessment, then the criterion should form a good basis for the evaluation of the training program. However, the point is that the reason for concern about the development of criteria is the importance of having a measure of trainee performance both in the training program and on the job. That is why using only the concept of content validity in the evaluation of a training program is a problem. The program may very well be content-valid, but that does not provide information about whether the trainees learned the material in the training program and whether the trainee was also able to transfer that knowledge to the job. Some of the additional data that Newman collected about pre/post differences allow stronger inferences about training program effects than content validity information by itself could permit. Information concerning that issue requires the use of principles of experimental design and quasi-experimental design to ensure that learning occurs and that it transfers to the job. For these types of reasons, some researchers (for example, Guion, 1977) have argued that the term *content validity* should not be used. Rather, they prefer that a term be employed which reflects the fact that the important domains are present in the instrument or program but that assumptions about validity are weak. That view makes sense, and it should be clear from the above discussion that there are various things that can be done to strengthen or weaken the inferences that can be made. However, for want of a better term I have chosen to continue to use *content validity*. Persons who prefer a different term might consider *content relevance*. In any case, the important point is not the terminology but an understanding of the strength of the inference that can be made based upon the procedures used.

The same point might be made about the use of individual difference methodology described in the preceding section. As described in that section, a correlation between scores in training and on the job does not guarantee that the program is doing the job. It does mean that persons who perform well on the test in training also perform well in job performance, and those persons who perform poorly on the training test perform poorly on the job. These same relationships may exist regardless of whether the training program accomplished anything. If the training program was also shown to be content-valid, then there is reason to be more optimistic. It is also possible to consider training evaluation as a succession of steps which provides information of better and better quality. Thus, as a next step, it is possible to add a pre- and posttest on relevant criteria. It is then possible to be more certain because there will be information on changes in trainee performance from before to after training. If, in addition, it is possible to add a control group, there will be more information about ruling out other reasons for the changes from pre- to posttest. The point is that establishing the validity of training programs involves building a network that gives more and more information with better and better controls so that the evaluator has more faith in the information. In some cases, it may be possible only to start with an individual difference methodology. On that basis, the investigator will know whether persons who perform well on training test measures also perform well on the job. Then, it might be possible to obtain a pretest, then content validity, and so on. As I have stated previously (Goldstein, 1980), "In order to gain an appreciation for the degree to which training programs achieve their objectives, it is necessary to consider the creative development of evaluation models. The models should permit the extraction of the greatest amount of information within the constraints of the environment. . . . Researchers cannot afford to be frozen into inactivity by the spectre of threats to validity" (p. 262).

FROM NEEDS ASSESSMENT TO TRAINING VALIDITY: SOME CONCLUDING WORDS

This chapter began with a number of complaints concerning training made by trainees, trainers, and organizations. Answers to these complaints require the analyst to examine various components of the training systems approach, including needs assessment, criterion development, and evaluation models. One way of conceptualizing responses to these complaints is to ask what is the actual purpose of the instructional system. Is there interest in having a program where trainees perform better at the end of the training program? Or is there interest in trainees who perform better at both the end of the training program and on the job? Goals might include all of these considerations, but an additional goal might be knowledge about how another group of trainees (after the program has been developed and evaluated) are going to perform. Then again, someone might be interested in how the program might work in another organization with other trainees. The answers to these questions require the analyst to consider what system training issues must be addressed. It is possible to characterize instructional design as an attempt to achieve one of the following types of validity (Goldstein, 1978a):

> 1. *Training validity.* This particular stage refers only to the validity of the training program. Validity is determined by the performance of trainees on criteria established for the training program.
> 2. *Transfer validity.* This stage of analysis refers to the validity of the training program as measured by performance in the transfer or on-the-job setting. Ordinarily, training and transfer validity are both considered indicators of internal validity. That is, they indicate whether the treatment made a difference in a very specific situation. Here performance validity is considered an external validity concept, because training programs are typically developed in a particular environment that is different from the organizational settings in which the trainee will eventually be expected to perform.

3. *Intra-organizational validity*. This concept refers to the performance of a new group of trainees within the organization that developed the original training program. In this instance, the analyst is attempting to predict the performance of new trainees based upon the evaluated performance of a previous group.

4. *Inter-organizational validity*. In this instance, the analyst is attempting to determine whether a training program validated in one organization can be utilized in another organization.

The first two stages, training validity and transfer validity, have been the topics of the first five chapters of this book. Thus, training validity begins with the needs assessment process and continues with criterion development, evaluation, and the feedback necessary to revise the program. Transfer validity requires attention to all aspects of training validity but must include the idea that the trainee must perform on the job. Considering the needs assessment procedures and evaluation procedures necessary to establish training validity, it would seem that there is little to add to a section on transfer validity. Unfortunately, this is not the case. In a sense, this is now a discussion of external validity operations which involve the transfer of performance in one environment (training) to another environment (on-the-job). As noted in Chapter 5, the tracing process from needs assessment to criterion development must now be concerned with relevant on-the-job criteria while avoiding deficiency and contamination. Also, transfer validity is affected by the fact that the trainee will enter a new environment to be affected by all the interacting components that make up organizations today. Certainly, there are some aspects of the environment which contribute to the success or failure of training programs beyond the attributes the trainee must gain as a result of attending the instructional program. For example, as described in Chapter 3 in the section on organizational analysis, the training program and the organization often specify different performance objectives, and trainees are caught in a conflict which sometimes results in failure. Thus, the trainee and the training program are declared inadequate because the training analyst never considered the relevant variables which determine success or failure at each of the four stages of validity. I have become convinced that many training programs are judged failures because of organizational systems constraints. Transfer validity thus requires the use of organizational analysis as a critical component of program development. Most of these concepts have been discussed in the preceding chapters in this book. However, the concepts of intra- and inter-organizational validity prompt several new considerations. These are discussed in the next section.

Intra-Organizational Validity

Intra-organizational validity presupposes that the trainer has established training and performance validity and is concerned now with the performance of a new group of trainees. Just as performance validity presupposes the consideration of the points established for training validity, intra-organizational validity presupposes that the points discussed for training and transfer validity have been established. It should be noted that the previously-expressed view concerning evaluation stated that evaluation is considered an information-gathering process which provides feedback about the multiple objectives of most training programs. Thus, it becomes apparent that evaluation should be a continual process that provides data as a basis for revisions of the program. New data should be collected based upon the performance of a new group of trainees which provides further understanding about the achievement of objectives or about the variables which affect the achievement of objectives. That does not mean that each effort must start from the very beginning. However, it should be possible to collect further new information about the effects of revisions. Also, it should be possible to collect data that can be checked against previously-collected information to make sure that the instructional program is having the same effect.

Given the above philosophy, it is still possible to ask how dangerous it is to generalize results from the previous training program to a new group of trainees in the same organization. The answer to that question stems from a consideration of many of the factors already discussed. First, it is necessary to consider the components of the needs assessment process, including task, person, and organizational aspects. If the job tasks and resulting KSAs have been revised, or if their frequency, importance, or degree of difficulty have changed, then the training program requires revisions. In these cases, generalizations based on the old program are speculative at best. These kinds of task changes can occur for a variety of reasons, including technological developments or revisions in jobs being performed at various levels in the organization. Similarly, if the kinds of persons entering the organization are different, then it is difficult to generalize from the old program. These kinds of changes also occur for a variety of reasons, including moving the organization from an urban to suburban environment or market and career shifts that result in differences in the KSAs of individuals desiring particular types of employment. Also, of course, modifications in the organization or constraints that affect the organization also affect the degree to which generalizations are safe. While time itself is not ordinarily considered a variable, it is also apparent that these types of changes eventually occur in all organizations, rendering long-term generalizations of training results to new populations increasingly suspect. A good procedure might be to recheck the needs assessment for applicability before attempting to generalize to new trainee populations. If needs assessment procedures are not carried out, the original program is questionable and generalizations are treacherous.

A second factor to consider before generalizing is how well the evaluation was performed in the first place. If the data upon which the generalizations will be based are only the reactions of the trainees to the instructional program, then the original evaluation is suspect as well as any future generalizations. In the same sense, properly evaluated instructional programs will provide a variety of information about the achievement of multiple goals. It is necessary to consider what has been achieved and what remains questionable before deciding whether to generalize to new trainees.

A third consideration is whether the training program will be the same. This factor is misleadingly simplistic. Almost everyone would agree that it is dangerous to generalize to new trainee populations when they are not being instructed in the same training program. However, most training analysts fail to realize how different established training programs tend to be from the original training program from which evaluation data was collected. Some of these difficulties generally can be labeled problems of reactivity. Observers, experimental equipment, and questions being asked often result in changes in behavior that are not a result of the actual training program. To the extent that these variables are a source of training results and to the extent that these variables are not present the next time training is offered, it is difficult to generalize. There is a certain aura of excitement surrounding new instructional treatments or training programs that simply disappears over time. In some studies (Rosenthal, 1978), researchers have specified how the expectations of the experimenters (or trainers or teachers) themselves have an effect upon the performances of individuals. To the extent that these factors change over time, the training program has changed, and it is difficult to generalize. Also, programs tend to change over time as trainers and managers add to and delete from the originally-designed program. Sometimes changes in carefully-designed programs radically alter the training system. One of the most compelling reasons for the use of process criteria is to attempt to specify these variables and their effects. When the process criteria indicate that the training programs have not changed, then it is obviously safer to generalize.

From a consideration of the needs assessment component, the quality of the evaluation, and the similarity of the training program, the decision of whether to generalize becomes easier. It should also be clear that the more the confidence in training and transfer validity, the easier it is to generalize. Even so, my personal choice will always be to collect some evaluative information to make sure that the program continues to work.

Inter-Organizational Validity

In this instance, the analyst is attempting to determine whether a training program validated in one organization can be utilized in another organization. All of the factors discussed in training validity, performance validity, and intra-organizational validity affect this decision. As indicated in the section on intra-organizational validity, when the needs assessment shows differences (that is, the task, person, or organizational components), or the evaluation is questionable, or the training program will differ, then generalization is dangerous. In this instance, the needs assessment and evaluation have not been performed for the organization that desires to use the training program. Clearly, the more similar the organizations, as shown by a needs assessment, the more likely similar results will occur. Still, considering the incredible number of ways organizations differ, it is dangerous to attempt to generalize the training results in one organization to trainees in another organization. On the other hand, it is entirely appropriate to borrow needs assessment methodologies, evaluation strategies, and training techniques to try out in different organizations. Through these procedures organizations can establish techniques that work, and perhaps it will be possible to begin to understand what variables affect the success of programs across organizations. However, given the present state of knowledge, simply borrowing results from another organization as a shortcut in the training process is asking for trouble.

Instructional Approaches

A Variety of Instructional Techniques

A complete systematic needs assessment procedure includes a set of learning objectives that determines the type of learning necessary to achieve the goals. The instructional designer is then able to examine the media and techniques available and to choose the method most appropriate for the behaviors being considered. This procedure should be appropriate for all different types of objectives, from motor-skill specifications in pilot training to styles of managerial behavior in various organizations. At a molar level, there is basic knowledge that helps specify the appropriate technique for particular behaviors. For example, machine simulators are used for the development of motor skills, while role playing is designed to acquaint managerial trainees with a variety of interpersonal situations. Unfortunately, there has been no advancement beyond molar generalities. In part, this is due to the difficulties encountered in the development of a comprehensive set of categories to describe the type of learning underlying the behavioral objectives. Another dilemma is the determination of the behaviors that are likely to be modified by the various techniques. J. P. Campbell (1971) expressed this dilemma by noting that it is not possible to organize the empirical research around dependent variables. He believes in examining which kinds of experiences produce particular outcomes and which variables affect the relationship between treatments and outcomes. However, for a variety of reasons, instructional designers have not arrived at that state of knowledge. First (as stated many times before), the empirical research necessary to establish these relationships has been insufficient. Second, most research efforts have emphasized reactions and learning in the training setting rather than performance in the transfer setting. Third, empirical studies have tended to cluster around demonstrations of the value of the technique, rather than the nature of the learning activities for which the method is useful. Thus, this material is organized around instructional approaches, with the hope that future texts on instructional procedures might be able to choose a different format.

This section is titled instructional approaches (rather than media or techniques) because some of the topics are clearly not dependent upon a particular method. Some topics focus on particular groups of trainees, like managers, police, the hard-core unemployed, or individuals searching for second careers, rather than on particular methods. Also included in this multitreatment category are studies of individual differences in which investigators have attempted to match the abilities of the learner to a variety of different instructional approaches.

Part 3 also includes material devoted to particular methods, like programed instruction, computer-assisted instruction, business games, behavioral role modeling, role-playing, and behavior modification. It is not possible to examine every training technique or the many variations of each technique. The criteria for inclusion are almost as complex and difficult to express as the criteria for most training programs. I have selected techniques that have aroused the interest of the training community and that appear likely to be used in the coming decade. I have also favored approaches that elucidate the topics presented in the first six chapters. For example, behavior modification represents a technique that is a direct development of the learning literature on operant conditioning. Other approaches are included because they represent attempts to deal with today's serious social problems. Thus, there are sections devoted to training and fair employment practices, training the hard-core unemployed, and training for second careers. In some instances (notably, training for second careers), there is very little information to offer the reader, but the seriousness of the problem demands its exploration.

The tremendous variety of approaches requires a flexible format for the presentation of techniques. In those cases in which the technique consists of well-defined approaches, such as programed instruction, descriptive background material and specific research examples are included. In those approaches that do not have well-defined characteristics, such as on-the-job instruction, only general descriptions can be included. Where enough empirical information is available, there is a general discussion of the evaluation data, with particular emphasis on the problem areas that must be faced by the researcher and the practitioner. Finally, there is a summary of the advantages and limitations of the approach, based on evaluation studies whenever possible.

The grouping and ordering of techniques was another judgment call. This chapter consists of a variety of techniques, including programed instruction, machine simulators, behavior modification, audiovisual and so on. Most of the techniques described are related to knowledge (for example, learning math) and skills (for example, flying an airplane) training. Of course, many of the techniques can be used for a variety of situations. Thus, programed instruction can be used to teach interpersonal skills to managers and audiovisual techniques are often used in role-playing as a basis for examining interpersonal behavior. However, granting that there are lots of exceptions, most of the techniques in this chapter are designed to teach skills and provide knowledge. The training programs discussed in the next chapter (Chapter 8), including techniques such as role-playing, sensitivity training, are more often related to interpersonal interaction situations, like responding to a complaining employee or customer, or teaching managers how to supervise employees. As a matter of fact, many of these techniques are employed in management or supervisory training programs.

Chapter 9 presents special issues, including individual differences approaches and treatment interactions, training for those looking for second careers, training for the hard-core unemployed, training and fair employment practices issues, and training and socialization issues.

CONTROL PROCEDURES—ON-THE-JOB TRAINING AND THE LECTURE METHOD

Before beginning a discussion of the more specific instructional approaches, it is important to consider the two general procedures that are most frequently used—on-the-job training and the lecture method. Valid information about the utility of these two procedures is not readily available. Everyone uses these methods, but they are rarely investigated except when they are employed as a control procedure for research exploring another technique. Even in those cases, the discussion of results centers on the "new" technique. This is especially shortsighted since many research investigations have not found any differences in achievement between control techniques and other methods, such as films. The "no differences" results have led many investigators to believe that films and television are at least as good as the more traditional lecture method. Thus, they suggest focusing attention on those situations that are particularly appropriate for films. However, the question could be reversed to determine what lectures and on-the-job training can offer the learner. For example, it could be asked whether there are particular learning behaviors that are especially well-taught by on-the-job training. Since these control methods are used so often and are relatively inexpensive compared to methods like computer-assisted instruction, some research effort in this direction would appear to be advantageous. It is certainly ironic that the best information available about the two most frequently used techniques is a series of generalizations based mainly on intuition.

On-the-Job Training

Almost all trainees are exposed to some form of on-the-job training. This form of instruction might follow a carefully designed off-the-job instructional program, or it might be the sole source of instruction.

There are very few, if any, instructional programs that can provide all the required training in a setting away from the job. At the very least, provisions for transfer to the job setting must be part of the initial learning experience of the actual job environment. Unfortunately, an on-the-job instructional program is usually an informal procedure in which the trainee is simply expected to learn by watching an experienced worker. This informal approach reflects the main argument against the use of on-the-job training as the fundamental instructional system. While there is no reason why a carefully designed on-the-job instructional system should not be as successful as any other approach, the success of the program still demands that the objectives and the training environment be carefully prepared for instructional purposes. Given the proper conditions, there are certain advantages to on-the-job training. For example, the transfer problem becomes less difficult, because the individual is being trained in the exact physical and social environment in which he is expected to perform. There is also an opportunity to practice the exact required behaviors. As far as evaluation is concerned, on-the-job instruction could result in the collection of more job-relevant criteria.

Unfortunately, most on-the-job training programs are not planned and thus don't work well. Too often, practicality is the main reason that this form of training is chosen. It is cheap and easy to implement with no planning at all. The simple instruction to any employee "Help John learn the job" fully implements the training program. The entire instructional process is placed in the hands of an individual who may or may not be capable of performing the job and who probably considers the entire procedure an imposition on his time. Under these conditions, training takes second place to the performance of the job. Even if the "instructor" is capable, it may not be possible to slow down the pace, appraise the responses, and supply feedback to the trainee in a job setting where performance is the criterion for success. Simply put, the job environment may not be a good learning environment. While this point is obvious when very complex behaviors must be learned (for example, flying an airplane), it is too often neglected for other behaviors that appear easy enough to learn on the job.

Many of these difficulties plague on-the-job training programs that have attempted some systematic form of instruction. Apprenticeship systems provide a good example of the difficulties in implementing on-the-job programs. These formal programs are used to teach various skilled trades. Typically, the trainee receives both classroom instruction and supervision from experienced employees on the job. At the end of a specified period of training, the apprentice becomes a journeyman. This system is employed in a wide variety of skilled trades and is commonly accepted as a valid mode of instruction for large numbers of trainees. For example, in 1966, Chrysler Corporation employed

10,600 individuals in the apprenticeable skilled trades (Irwin, 1967). At that time, 2000 of these employees were apprentices. Despite the size and scope of these programs, analyses indicate that the on-the-job portion of the training is not easily adapted into a good learning environment. Strauss (1967) described the problem as follows:

> 1. While apprenticeship systems are assumed to provide systematic on-the-job training, the sad fact is that they actually provide little systematic guidance by the journeymen or supervisors. Exposure to a broad range of pertinent experiences appears to be mainly a matter of dumb luck.
> 2. Learning in school systems may be more effective than on-site training simply because learning on the job is secondary to the employer's insistence that the trainee put in a full day's work.
> 3. On-site training often results in learning sloppy ways of doing things.
> 4. Many of the newly developed skills, such as electronics, have an intellectual component that is difficult to teach on the job.

However, these difficulties should not lead the reader to conclude that on-the-job training programs cannot produce well-trained employees. A study (Lefkowitz, 1970) of the effects of a training program on the productivity and tenure of sewing-machine operators demonstrated that on-the-job training programs can produce direct benefits. The experimental program integrated off-site simulation training, which was instituted in a room off the assembly line, with on-site training. Some training groups were exposed only to varying lengths of off-site simulation. The group experiencing both off- and on-site training achieved the best balance of productivity and employee retention. Employee retention had been a serious problem before the study, with turnover as high as 68% in one year. Lefkowitz noted that the on-the-job phase of the training program provided for job-oriented discussion following the first exposure to the factory. Thus, the trainees were able to discuss various difficulties, like scheduling and job-related tension, and to reach solutions to the problems that led to the high turnover of previous employees. Lefkowitz also noticed that the first-line supervisors paid greater attention to these trainees during their first days of integrated training. He suggested that this occurred because the trainees would be returning to the off-site simulation and reporting their experiences to the trainer.

While on-the-job training can work, as demonstrated by this study, it is not usually successful when it is used to avoid the necessity of designing a training program. As long as programs are designed solely for that purpose, they will face difficulties of incompetent instructors, priority production schedules, and a generally poor learning environment. On-site training must be treated like any other method; the technique should be chosen because it is the most effective way of implementing certain behaviors. Once the training analyst ascertains that on-site training is the most effective technique to teach the pertinent skills, the environment must be designed as carefully as any other in-structional environment (Mosel, 1957). This procedure is equally appro-priate for on-site training that follows an off-the-job instructional program. Sometimes a trainee completes a carefully-designed instruc-tional program, only to be confronted by a bewildering environment on the job. Often, the trainees are not even accorded the benefit of an orientation program that might at least provide an introduction to the individuals with whom they will be working.

Lecture Method

While on-the-job training is the most extensively used procedure in industrial settings, the lecture method enjoys that status in educational environments, from primary school to evening-division programs for employed workers. In addition, the lecture method is the most fre-quently employed control procedure in the analysis of recently de-veloped techniques, like films, television, and programed instruction.

Many authors (McGehee & Thayer, 1961; Bass & Vaughan, 1966) question the usefulness of the lecture method as an instructional tech-nique. Their criticisms focus on its one-way communication aspects. Too often, the lecture method results in passive learners who do not have the opportunity to clarify material. In addition, it is difficult for the lecturer to present material that is equally cogent to individuals who have wide differences in ability, attitude, and interest. By the time a criterion test is employed, some individuals may be hopelessly behind. Many of these difficulties can be overcome by competent lecturers who are able to make the material meaningful and who remain aware of the reactions of their students by effectively promoting dis-cussion and clarification of material.

Many studies have compared programed instruction or televised instruction to the lecture technique. The results indicate that these newer techniques do not necessarily lead to superior student achieve-ment, although there is some evidence that the student completes the material faster. Thus, there appears to be little empirical reason for the bias against the lecture procedure. Yet, one survey (Carroll, Paine, & Ivancevich, 1972) found that training directors ranked the lecture method last among nine techniques as a procedure for the effective acquisition of knowledge. The other techniques included case studies, conferences, business games, films, programed instruction, role-playing, sensitivity training, and television. Interestingly, these authors also found that the research does not support the poor opinions of the lecture technique as an instrument in the acquisition of knowledge.

Certainly, the lecture method has shortcomings. It is insensitive to individual differences, and it is limited in providing immediate feedback to the learner. However, considering the low cost of the lecture method, it is important to determine empirically when and how it can be used. There is already evidence that the technique is not appropriate when complex responses (for example, motor skills) are required but may be quite applicable to those situations in which acquisition of knowledge is the goal. There is general uncertainty about the benefits of the lecture method for other behaviors, such as attitude change. Most authors and training directors feel that the lecture method is not useful in promoting attitude change, but, again, there is little empirical evidence to support their view. Actually, several studies conducted by Miner (1961, 1963) suggested that the lecture was appropriate as an attitude-change technique. One study examined 72 supervisors in the research and development department of a large corporation. These employees had been neglecting their supervisory activities in favor of their scientific interests. Miner developed a course that placed considerable emphasis on scientific theory and research findings relevant to supervisory practices. He found that the experimental group developed more favorable attitudes toward supervisory training as compared to a control group that did not participate in the lecture program. Interestingly, the control group developed negative feelings during the training period because of the threat of department reorganization.

Unfortunately, few studies have examined lecture courses that are specifically designed as part of a training program. Usually, when the lecture method is employed as a control procedure, most of the effort is devoted to the development of the experimental technique. Almost all other techniques have a large number of proponents who excitedly proclaim the validity of their procedure with little, if any, empirical evidence. On the other hand, the lecture technique is viewed with disdain without much empirical evidence. The lecture is still used, however, in a wide variety of settings. It would be interesting to learn which conditions help determine the usefulness of this technique. Is the method of instruction important? Is discussion necessary? What determines the quality of the instructor? Lectures are unlikely to disappear. It would be most appropriate to gain some knowledge concerning their potential.

PROGRAMED INSTRUCTION

Since the mid-1950s, a large number of devices, such as self-instructional materials, automated teaching machines, and programed texts, have been developed. These programed materials systematically present information to the learner while also utilizing the principles of reinforcement (Silverman, 1960). Programed instruction (PI) is dependent not on the physical characteristics of the display (for example, a book, a computer, or a mechanical apparatus) but on the quality of the program.

In 1962, Bass and Vaughan (1966) found that there were 165 commercial programs available. More recent estimates from educational, industrial, and government sources signal an astounding increase in the number and kinds of programs available. For example, a U.S. Civil Service Commission survey (1970) identified over 2300 programs being used in various government installations. Contrary to the original expectations that PI would prove useful only for basic subjects in the school classroom, the topics of instruction include such diverse subjects as air traffic control, blueprint reading, food-borne disease investigation, and analyses of tax returns. A survey of educational institutions reveals that there are few students graduating today who have not been exposed to programed devices as teaching aids. Surveys in work organizations would also indicate that PI is being used in an ever-increasing number of activities. For example, the Life Insurance Marketing and Research Association has a variety of texts to train new agents in areas such as the purpose of life insurance, use of mortality tables, types of policies, and so on. This company also has PI texts on sales skills, including the use of the telephone, prospecting for clients, and the like. Wexley and Latham (1981) report on a gift shop retail chain that uses PI to train their Christmas rush sales force. The material consists of self-paced texts and diagnostic pretests that permit trainees to skip material that they know. This is especially valuable for this organization because many of their Christmas employees return year after year. These employees can skip over material that they remember from their last tour of work. The PI material covers many work-related topics, ranging from customer relations to operating the cash register, handling refunds, and cashing checks. Why have these programs been adopted by many institutions? What is expected from programed learning that is not available from other techniques? In order to answer these questions, it is necessary to examine the historical development and objectives of PI.

Approaches to Programed Instruction

Autoinstructional method. In the early 1900s, Thorndike introduced the *law of effect.* This law states that stimulus–response associations that are followed by a satisfying state of affairs are learned, while those that are followed by unsatisfying states of affairs are weakened and eliminated. In the 1920s, Pressey (1950) applied Thorndike's principles of learning to the classroom environment by utilizing the feedback from examinations. He argued that exams that are scored immediately can provide the feedback necessary to help the student determine his strengths and weaknesses; thus, he developed *auto-instructional* programs to supply immediate feedback. In this system, the student reads a question and chooses the appropriate response from a series of multiple-choice answers. If the student is correct, he is immediately reinforced by a light or a buzzer, which "stamps in" the correct associations. If the response is incorrect, the learner is not re-inforced, thus weakening the incorrect association. The student then must respond with one of the remaining alternatives. This process continues until the students pick the correct answer, at which time they are reinforced and proceed to the next question. Although a number of studies conducted by Pressey indicated that the technique was promising, a movement favoring the use of PI never developed. A variety of reasons have been offered for this lack of interest. Some commentators (Lysaught & Williams, 1963) suggest that the onset of the Depression created an unfavorable social climate for an "industrial revolution" in the schools. Other educators believe that Pressey's autoinstructional system was really a testing device that did not provide for systematic programing of materials. Thus, they contend that the method had little new to offer.

Linear programing.   Opinions about PI changed radically when B. F. Skinner (1954) published his article "The Science of Learning and the Art of Teaching," which applies his models of operant conditioning to the educational process. Skinner argues that a program could successively shape the learner by reinforcing the achievement of small steps in the same way that the pigeon is conditioned by the reinforcement of successive approximations to peck a key. Since Skinner believes that positive reinforcement of correct responses is the most efficient way to produce learning, he designed his programs to condition the learner through a series of small steps so that few errors occur. Thus, the learner is expected to continually earn positive reinforcement. If errors are made at a particular point in the program, there is a problem with the program, not the student. The only variability that is permitted among learners is the speed with which they complete the program. Since a student proceeds through each successive step, the technique became known as *linear programing.* Its essential parameters include the following characteristics (Bass & Vaughan, 1966; Fry, 1963):

1. All material is presented in small units called frames. Each frame varies in size from one sentence to several paragraphs, depending on the amount of material necessary to guide the learner.
2. Each frame requires an overt response from the learner. The student reads the frame and then constructs a response by filling in the blank. Thus, the learner is actively involved in the learning process.
3. The learner immediately receives feedback indicating the correctness of his response. Since the program is constructed for a minimum number of errors, the learner usually receives immediate positive reinforcement.
4. The program is predesigned to provide proper learning sequences. Since the units must be presented in small steps to achieve low error rates, the programer must carefully analyze both the material and the learner's characteristics in order to obtain the most appropriate step size and sequence. This process requires pretesting of the program and revisions based on student

responses. If a criterion of approximately 90% correct by all trainees is not met, the material must be rewritten.

   5. Each trainee proceeds independently through the program at a pace commensurate with his own abilities.

A sample of a program that discusses two of the principles of linear programing, self-pacing and small steps, can be found in Table 7.1.

   Intrinsic or branching programing. In branching programs, correct responses by the learner lead directly to the next step of the program, while incorrect answers lead to a branch designed to correct the mistake. The branches can vary in complexity from a few short frames to an elaborate subprogram. Intrinsic programs (Crowder, 1960) have had the greatest impact on the development of branching techniques. These programs have relatively long frames followed by a series of multiple-choice answers. If the program is in text form, the learner turns to the page number associated with his answer choice. There, the trainee is presented with another series of frames based on his previous answer. If the chosen answer is correct, the response is simply confirmed, and the learner is directed to the next frame. If the answer is incorrect, the learner proceeds to a remedial set of frames designed to

TABLE 7.1   Sample of a linear program

	1. You are now beginning a lesson on programed instruction. The principle of *self-pacing* as used in programed instructions allows each trainee to work as slowly or as fast as he chooses. Since you can control the amount of time you spend on this lesson, this program is using the principle of self- _____.
pacing	2. People naturally learn at different rates. A program that allows each trainee to control his own rate of learning is using the principle of _____.
self-pacing	3. If a self-pacing program is to be successful, the information step size must be small. A program that is self-pacing would also apply the principle of small _____.
steps	4. The average trainee will usually make correct responses if the correct-size step of information is given. This is utilizing the principle of small _____.
steps	5. A program that provides information in a step size that allows the trainee to be successful is applying the principle of _____.
small steps	6. A trainee knows the material being taught but has to wait for the remainder of the class. What programing principle is being violated? _____.
self-pacing	7. Two principles of programed learning are: (1) _____. (2) _____.
1. *self-pacing* 2. *small steps*	

Note—For practical reasons, the frames are arranged on one page rather than on succeeding pages. The answers should be covered until the preceding frame has been answered.
Adapted from U.S. Civil Service Commission. *Programed Instruction: A Brief of Its Development and Current Status.* Washington, D.C.: U.S. Government Printing Office, 1970.

correct the previous response. Table 7.2 presents an example of an intrinsic branching program. Branching programs cannot eliminate all errors; however, the students do not proceed until they can demonstrate by their performance on the branching step that they understand the concept previously missed. Crowder designed his steps so that they are larger than those that appear in linear programming. The superior student can then proceed through larger steps, while the student experiencing difficulty is directed into branching programs with smaller steps. Crowder believes that this procedure permits the designer to consider the individual differences and backgrounds of the students. The superior student is able to progress through the program without be-

TABLE 7.2   Sample of an intrinsic branching program

Definition of the term "teaching machine"

Page 8

In 1924, Dr. Sidney L. Pressey invented a small machine that would score a multiple-choice examination automatically at the time the answer-button was pushed.

Although he designed it as a testing machine, he perceived that by a simple expedient he could use the machine as a teaching device. All he had to do was design it so that, for each question, the correct answer-button had to be pushed before a subsequent question would appear in the window.

From this simple beginning, the concept of *teaching machines* has grown until now the educator is faced with many types and styles, from the simplest cardboard device costing pennies to incredibly complex electronic wonders costing thousands of dollars.

But don't despair. All teaching machines have three characteristics in common:

1. They present information and require frequent responses by the student.
2. They provide immediate feedback to the student, informing them whether their response is appropriate or not.
3. They allow the student to work individually and to adjust their rate of progress to their own needs and capabilities.

Now, based on the three criteria listed above, is the educational motion picture, as it is normally used, a teaching machine?

YES   *(Turn to page 6.)*
NO   *(Turn to page 4.)*

Page 6

The educational motion picture, as it is normally used, *does* present factual information but does *not* satisfy any of the other conditions set down for a teaching machine; no response is called for, no feedback is given, and the student has no control over his rate of progress.

The standard educational motion picture, then, is similar to a well-prepared lecture but is not a teaching machine.

Please read the conditions on page 8 again, and then select the other alternative.

Page 4

Right! The educational motion picture, as it is normally used, is not a teaching machine.

1. Although the motion picture presents information, it does not require periodic responses from the student in the form of answers, selections, or motor responses.
2. Since it does not ask for responses, it does not indicate whether the responses are appropriate or not.
3. It does not allow the individual class member to adjust their rate of progress to their own needs and capabilities.

Adapted from *Explaining Teaching Machines and Programming* by D. Cram. Copyright © 1961 by Fearon Publishers. Adapted by permission.

coming bored, and the slower student is given special attention. Of course, most branching programs have limited flexibility. Only a certain number of branches can be designed for the individual student without the whole project becoming cumbersome. However, computer-assisted instruction (discussed later in this chapter) does offer increased flexibility for branching. Most educators (DeCecco, 1968) agree that there is little empirical justification for a choice between linear or branching techniques. It has become increasingly popular to utilize both techniques within the same program. The particular instructional objectives, entering behavior of the students, and material to be learned should determine the most appropriate procedure at any point in the program.

Evaluation of Programed Instruction

A large number of programs remain unevaluated; however, as compared with research on most other training methods, the evaluation data available on PI represent a storehouse of knowledge. Holt's studies (Holt, 1963; Shoemaker & Holt, 1965) provide good examples of and illuminating commentary about the utility of PI as a training technique. In one investigation, he compared the standard lecture–discussion method to a pretested linear PI course in basic electricity for telephone electricians. The main criteria were tests examining facts and concepts given at the completion of training and six months later. The assignment of trainees to treatment conditions was based on when the employees reported for training. The first set of trainees to arrive completed the course using the standard lecture procedure, consisting of ten days of class work. The next group of trainees was assigned to a PI group that attended only for as many days as were necessary to complete the program. Although this procedure does not utilize random assignments, good sampling is achieved if the variation for individuals assigned to training is not biased across time periods. This assumption is reasonable, but, as a further check, Holt compared the experimental and control groups on a number of factors, including intelligence, knowledge of basic electricity, years of experience, and course work in electricity and math. There were no pretraining differences between groups on these measures. This method provides a good illustration of the procedures that can be employed even when strict randomization cannot be achieved. Holt's study also attempted to control for the Hawthorne effect by treating both groups as part of the experiment. This treatment included informing all trainees of the nature of the experiment as well as instituting similar procedures for both groups regarding pretesting, questionnaires, interviews, and other parameters that were not strictly part of the treatment procedure.

The data analyses indicated that the PI groups achieved superior performance on the immediate posttest and on the six-month retention test. However, on the six-month test, both groups' scores decreased substantially. While this study represents one of the few efforts that examined performance at later time intervals, the retention loss raised some question about the relevance of the training program to job performance. Holt examined the use of PI in a situation in which there was an already existing lecture course. Thus, the needs assessment procedure did not directly precede the development of the PI program. An analysis indicated that the retention loss for both groups occurred because the course itself was not relevant to the technician's job, and thus, the knowledge gained was not utilized in the transfer setting. A good needs assessment could avoid this difficulty by implementing courses that are job-relevant and also by helping in the development of job-performance criteria that could establish the utility of the procedure. While there is ample reason to believe that the course was not relevant, there is also the possibility that the criteria were not relevant. There may be many instances in which the six-month retention tests would show a decrease in performance, whereas more job-oriented criteria would not.

Holt's investigations also explore some questions about the time needed to complete the course. In his study, there were no differences between the two groups, but the common finding is that PI groups complete the program more quickly than do traditional groups that are locked into set time intervals. However, Holt noted that the traditional group in his study had materials available for home study, while the PI group did not. Most other investigations do not comment on the availability of opportunities outside the training setting that can contribute to time differences or changes in achievement scores. So that the outcomes of experiments can be understood, the data must be related to process-oriented criteria that provide information about the procedures employed during training. Otherwise, the interpretation of data remains tenuous.

A study (O'Brien & Plooij, 1977) involving cultural training for nurses being trained for work with Aborigines in Australia presents another fascinating example of some of the principles of programed instruction. Much of this work was based upon a program known as the cultural assimilator (Fiedler, Mitchell, & Triandis, 1971). The principle is that individuals who work in a culture different than their own need information about the differences that will help facilitate cooperation with the host country. The main characteristic of the cultural assimilator training program is the presentation of cultural knowledge through specific situational contexts preceding the use of a programed format for self-instruction. The main aspects of the O'Brien and Plooij (1977) study were:

> 1. The investigators interviewed persons who had worked in these communities and asked them to describe positive and negative incidents. An incident was considered positive if it facilitated job performance and coopera-

tion with the Aboriginals. The interviewers obtained information about the place of the incident, tasks being performed, the exact behavioral outcomes, and so on. This is, of course, a needs assessment technique which is called the critical incident technique.

2. The incidents were grouped and selected on the basis of frequency of occurrence and agreement about the interpretation of the event. They were also selected on the basis of their relevance to the role of medical workers and they were checked by medical authorities and anthropologists for interpretation difficulties.

3. A programed manual was written containing 41 incidents that began with the simplest ones and proceeded to the more complex. The manual and feedback about the incidents were also checked by experts for potential problems.

Based upon the development of the manual, studies were designed that tested retention of material, generalization of appropriate responses to other cultural incidents not in the manual, and attitudes and motivation to work with Aboriginals. One of the studies involved 74 qualified nurses attending postgraduate studies at the Australian College of Nursing. The study used a pretest/posttest design with subjects being assigned to either the programed condition, no training, or an essay condition. The essay condition consisted of the nurses reading a series of essays that were comparable in content to the manual in terms of the topics and cultural principles.

Basically, the results showed that the programed manual had a stronger effect than essay training or no training on both retention and generalization of cultural knowledge. Interestingly, the programed manual group became much more cautious about wanting to work with Aboriginals. Previous work on the cultural assimilator had identified a similar effect. The authors felt that in part this was due to the sobering effect of the realistic job preview provided by the programed manual, which was based upon the needs assessment. Some researchers maintain that one of the advantages of well-designed training programs is that they will provide a realistic job preview and thus prepare the individual for entry into the work organization. Others maintain that such realistic previews might even dissuade persons who are not interested in that job situation. The use of training techniques as socialization to the work place will be examined further in the last chapter of this text. Since the present study did not examine actual job performance, it is not possible to determine whether these effects would generalize to the work setting. However, it does give a fascinating example of the use of needs assessment and a training program based upon the principles of programed instruction.

Since there are a number of studies that have investigated PI, it is possible to ask what generalizations can be gained from this research. Early analyses (Briggs & Angell, 1964; Schramm, 1964) of the literature that compared student achievement in PI and in more traditional methods (for example, the lecture method) found that the majority of studies showed no significant differences between methods. Of the remaining studies, most favored PI. These analyses also tended to indicate that PI groups required less learning time. A review by Nash, Muczyk, and Vettori (1971) examined the relative effectiveness of PI in both academic and industrial settings. The largest proportion of these studies had been performed in academic settings, although there was no evidence of differential data due to location. Table 7.3 presents the Nash et al. data for three different criteria, including training time, immediate learning, and retention. These authors included an important additional criterion in their review: in order for the technique to be judged the more effective, the statistical test had to be significant and

TABLE 7.3 Comparisons of programed instruction versus conventional methods for each criterion in studies that include two or more criteria

	Conventional method superior	*No significant difference between methods*	*Programed instruction superior*
Training time	1	2	29
Immediate learning	3	20	9
Retention[1]	5	16	5

[1] Of the 32 studies that included measures of both training time and immediate learning, only 26 also had a measure of retention.

From "The Relative Practical Effectiveness of Programed Instruction," by A. N. Nash, J. P. Muczyk, and F. L. Vettori. In *Personnel Psychology*, 1971, 24, pp. 397–418. Copyright 1971 by Personnel Psychology, Inc. Reprinted by permission.

the differences between the techniques had to exceed 10%. Nash et al. argued that the development of PI is an expensive endeavor; thus, they felt that new techniques with differences in overall effectiveness of only a few percent would not be worth considering for institutions that had less expensive techniques available. Their analyses of the statistical data (excluding the practicality criterion) supported earlier reviews stating that most studies examining achievement (immediate learning and retention) showed no significant differences, and the remaining studies favored PI. However, when the authors examined those studies in which the statistical differences were significant but the practical effectiveness was not above 10%, the trend toward no differences between techniques was even stronger. The analysis of learning-time data supported the established trend, indicating that PI students learn faster (the average reductions often approaching one-third). While the data concerning learning time have generally been consistent, they must be interpreted cautiously. The programed-instruction group is self-paced, and the learner may leave the program whenever he has completed the material. However, the more traditional programs have a fixed time limit, and the superior learners cannot leave even if they have learned enough material to achieve the objectives. Of course, that is one of the advantages of programed learning, but it might be interesting to discover what would happen if the learner in the control condition could take their achievement test when they have completed the program to their own satisfaction.

The thoroughness with which Nash and his colleagues performed their review raised one other serious question about the effects of PI on achievement level. These authors divided the studies into effectively and less-effectively controlled studies. Effectively controlled studies included the investigations that had (1) experimental and control groups selected by random assignment or a pretest measure used for adjustments when the groups varied on significant variables, and (2) a sample average of 20 subjects, with a minimum of 15 in each group. These, of course, are minimum standards and do not go so far as to require controls for pretest sensitization or a consideration of Hawthorne effects. However, many of the studies that did find that PI resulted in superior achievement levels were "less-effectively controlled" studies.

Advantages and Limitations of Programed Instruction

Advantages

1. Properly designed PI follows the basic steps necessary for an effective training program. It is more difficult to build frames, provide feedback, and design sequences without analyzing the instructional content. The procedure also includes objectives with built-in checks to make sure that the learner understands the material.

2. The evidence indicating that trainees learn more using PI techniques is mixed but they appear to learn at least as much as trainees in control procedures such as lecture groups. There is sufficient evidence to conclude that training time is effectively reduced for PI groups.

3. Programed materials are easily packaged and can be sent to widely dispersed training centers. In addition, individual students may take the course when it is deemed most appropriate.

4. Many trainers believe that the reinforcement provided by programed learning leads to a more highly motivated learner.

5. The individualization of instruction is an important aspect of PI. The self-pacing procedure permits learners to proceed at the rate most comfortable for their ability level and even permits them to take pretests and skip material which they have already learned. Thus, the training program for Christmas sales employees described above allowed trainees to concentrate on materials they still needed to learn. In the Nash et al. (1971) review, the authors found a number of studies that show that high- or low-ability trainees, who might be expected to benefit most from self-pacing, perform in a superior manner on immediate-learning criteria. Individual modes of instruction will be treated more fully in the next section on computer-assisted instruction.

Limitations

1. The major limitation of PI is the expense and preparation necessary. An examination of the requirements necessary to develop a linear or branching program clearly indicates that it is a time-consuming task involving considerable analysis and pretesting.

2. One limitation noted early in the history of PI is that, even with the increasing variety of programs, the emphasis of PI is on factual materials. Basically, that is still true, since PI cannot as easily simulate the interactions between employees and managers that can be performed in role-playing training. On the other hand, materials regarding principles related to personal interactions can be presented. An example of this is described above in the programed material for training nurses to learn cultural material related to working with Australian Aboriginals.

3. Student-reaction data have indicated that PI by itself may not be an acceptable mode of instruction. Several early studies (Patten & Stermer, 1969) have indicated that the learner is more satisfied with a combined technique, such as a conference or discussion along with programed instruction. More recently, similar comments have been made about other technologically-based programs such as computer-assisted instruction. School systems have often stated that PI has permitted their instructors to spend more time with individual students or small groups of students. It may be equally important for the adult in industry to have similar human interaction.

COMPUTER-ASSISTED INSTRUCTION

One of the more recent innovations in instructional technology is computer-assisted instruction (CAI). With the advent of microcomputers, there is clearly a revolution occurring, exemplified by the number of primary schools teaching computer programing and the move toward office automation systems. This revolution is also affecting computer-assisted instruction. It is not unusual to use computer-assisted instruction to educate students on the use of the computer and employees on the use of office automation systems. In CAI systems, the student interacts directly with the computer, which has stored within its systems information and instructional materials necessary for the program. The degree of computer interaction with the student varies with the individual system. In 1969, Cooley and Glaser developed a general model that described the processes in the design of CAI systems.

1. The goals of learning are specified in terms of observable student behavior and the conditions under which this behavior is to be manifested.

2. When the learner begins a particular course of instruction, the initial capabilities—those relevant to the forthcoming instruction—are assessed.

3. Educational alternatives suited to the students' initial capabilities are presented to him. The student selects or is assigned one of these alternatives.

4. The students' performance is monitored and continuously assessed as they learn.

5. Instruction proceeds as a function of the relationship between measures of student performance, available instructional alternatives, and criteria of competence.

6. As instruction proceeds, data are generated for monitoring and improving the instructional system. (pp. 574–575)

At that time, this description was more of a hope of things to come. Now it appears to be a rapidly developing reality. It is also interesting to note that many of these steps parallel the instructional model in Chapter 2.

State of the Art

The excitement about the development of CAI is based on the storage and memory capabilities of the computer, which in turn provide the potential for true interaction with the individual student. The proponents of this system believe that this potential provides the ultimate in branching programs. The computer records the individual's previous response, analyzes its characteristics, and determines the next presentation to the student on the basis of the learner's needs. Developments are beginning to occur. However, there are still relatively few systems that actually utilize CAI technology. Most of the large number of press releases, research articles, and institutional reports present vague speculations and still dwell on hardware development. For example, there are typewriters tied to computer devices, pens that draw curves on cathode-ray tubes, and devices that present auditory material and score student answers. Sometimes the sophisticated instrument is simply a PI device that uses electronic presentation instead of textbooks. Also, an examination of the use of these devices rarely presents validation data or cost estimates. These misguided efforts should not detract from the tremendous possibilities of computer technology in instructional systems and the fact that there are a number of actual programs being used. In 1968, R. C. Atkinson participated in a carefully developed system at Stanford University. He suggested that "the problem for someone trying to evaluate developments in the field is to distinguish between those reports that are based on fact and those that are disguised forms of science fiction" (p. 225). In 1984, P. Galagan wrote the following in an editorial for the *Training and Development Journal.*

> Personal computers will soon be a mass market appliance. They are tools that training cannot afford to ignore. When a technology appears, it will be used, and the time is ripe for trainers to influence the potential of this powerful medium to monitor, promote, encourage and reward not just learning but human development.
>
> Then, for instance, my computer/teller could train me to manage my cash flow or to understand its record-keeping system, rather than leaving me broke without warning or explanation. But I guess one can't expect money from a machine and training too. (p. 4)

Those who are concerned with the development of useful instructional techniques must be concerned with the distinction between fact and fiction. CAI has tremendous potential but it requires valid instructional research before the publication of glowing publicity reports. An example of a system for which extensive research and development is taking place is known as PLATO (Programmed Logic for Automated Teaching Operations). Its system includes capabilities for displays of all kinds, modifiable graphics, and touch-panel inputs. For example, the touch-panel graphics were used in one study of a pilot trainer where sets of push-buttons were graphically simulated. The system provides control and monitoring of student progress and has the capabilities to maintain student and evaluation data. The system can also handle large numbers of students. For example, PLATO IV at the University of Illinois has capabilities for handling 950 terminals for students as nearby as the university and as far away as San Diego. Training programs on topics as diverse as remedial math, oscilloscope preparation, recipe, and conversion (Hurlock & Slough, 1976) have been designed and evaluated. The researchers found the system to be highly effective for training, especially for performance involving sequencing and procedural learning. The next section provides further information about a few examples of these systems which are likely to affect us all in the future.

Examples of CAI Systems

The preceding discussion implies that CAI is not a single method. It can involve drill-and-practice, tutorial programs, simulations, and so on. Two of the most well-developed systems are drill-and-practice and tutorial.

Drill-and-practice.   The simplest of the two systems is drill-and-practice, which is ordinarily used as a supplement to conventional instruction (Suppes & Jerman, 1970). The program is usually controlled by a teacher, who first introduces the material in class and then specifies the topics that are to be practiced by the students individually at instructional terminals. This CAI system permits the teacher to present creative material in the classroom but also provides immediate feedback to large numbers of students on various sets of problems. The computer can present individualized material to a number of students simultaneously, as well as provide feedback to the individual student and records of progress to the teacher. One of the earliest drill-and-practice programs was developed at Stanford.

The Stanford (Suppes & Morningstar, 1969) drill-and-practice program in mathematics has 20 to 27 concept blocks for each grade level. Each concept block contains a pretest, five days of drill, a posttest, and review drills. This system has provisions for administering the following program: (1) a pretest, which determines the student's entering ability for that concept block; (2) the assignment of a series of lessons (which vary in difficulty) according to the student's ability; (3) a compilation of records on the student's performance on each lesson; (4) the determination of the appropriate lesson as a function of the student's progress on the previous material; (5) a posttest, which assesses the student's progress. Suppes and Morningstar (1969) have reported on a series of research investigations that analyzed the effectiveness of the mathematics program. The data from these studies, which included primary-school students from California and Mississippi, generally favored the CAI group, although there were some criteria on which the traditionally educated students performed better than the CAI students. More interesting was the relative superiority of the experimental group in Mississippi as compared to its control group. An analysis of these data indicated that the differences occurred because the control group in Mississippi was not improving at the same rate as the one in California. This result led the authors to speculate that these programs will have striking benefits in environments that are not socially and educationally affluent. It is in these situations that the student benefits most from the opportunity to learn from effectively designed programs. Considering the difficulties that many industrial institutions have in designing basic instructional material, the opportunity for their employees to work at a terminal that is coordinated with a central instructional system must certainly be appealing. The Stanford project utilized a central computer in California for primary-school students in California, Kentucky, and Mississippi. The usefulness of drill-and-practice programs has also been established at the college level. In another Stanford project, Suppes and Morningstar (1969) reported on a study indicating that CAI students were superior to a traditional class in the first-year Russian program. There were also fewer dropouts in the CAI group, and a greater percentage of the CAI group enrolled in the second year of Russian.

The military (McCann, 1975) has also developed a drill-and-practice program to teach remedial math. This program utilizes the PLATO system described above. The program teaches basic math for trainees in the Basic Electricity/Electronics School. The research here investigated different types of feedback systems as a way of reinforcing learning. The reinforcement system was the opportunity to make play movements in a game after correct performance on practice problems. Receiving game moves did not change student test performance or training time. As one might suspect, however, students indicated strong and favorable preference for practice having feedback with games.

Tutorial.   The tutorial program, as compared to drill-and-practice, assumes the responsibility for most, if not all, of the information incorporated into the program. Most CAI programs are tutorial in nature and may be complete course sequences or special supplementary units. If they are supplementary units, the teacher incorporates the material into the course program. Such programs are especially useful when expertise for a particular unit of subject matter is not readily available. These programs have the capability for real time decisions, with branching contingent upon the student's previous responses or set of responses. The numerous branching patterns often result in students following diverse paths.

The most creative work involving CAI stems from researchers investigating the possibilities of tutorial instruction. Collins (1977) has been exploring the Socratic method of teaching as a way of understanding the dialogue that occurs between teachers and students in a learning situation. Collins and his colleagues have analyzed dialogues between tutors teaching different subjects, including medicine, geography, and so on. The strategies involve entrapping the students into different kinds of mistakes and then confronting the students with examples that show the error. In this system, the student is required to derive general principles from specific cases and then learn to use these principles to make predictions about new cases. These analyses have led to the development of a set of rules. For example, one rule used to point out irrelevant factors is as follows:

> If
> (1) the student asks about the value of an irrelevant factor in trying to make a prediction,
> then
> (2) point out the factor is irrelevant, or
> (3) ask whether the irrelevant factor affects the dependent variable.
> *Example:* If the student asks whether Denver or Salt Lake City is further west in trying to decide which has the colder temperature, then point out that longitude does not matter, or ask whether longitude affects temperature.
> *Reason for Use:* This forces the student to learn what is irrelevant, as well as what is relevant, in making any decision. (Collins, 1977, p. 348)

Collins and his colleagues (Collins & Adams, 1977) have used these rules to develop tutorial strategies for CAI. One such system is known as SCHOLAR. This system is capable of carrying out a tutorial dialogue with a student. Various procedures are used to present information to the student, ask questions, assess the answers, correct mistakes and answer the questions of the student. The idea here is that the system is not confined to the more rigid modes of interaction typical of programed instruction. Rather, it is based upon the type of interaction which is more typical of human tutors. Some dialogue generally representative of the interactions using this system is presented in Table 7.4. The annotated comments refer to comments about the interaction provided by Collins and Adams for the reader's benefit.

The flexibility of such programs was demonstrated by the work of Collins, Adams, and Pew (1978) in a program called Map-SCHOLAR. In the program, the system was further developed to permit the integration of graphic information with verbal information. The graphic information consists of map capability; the display can be referred to by the student by either inputting names of geographic areas or by pointing to the area. Figure 7.1 shows one of the displays and the dialogue between the student and the system. The author describes the activity of the dialogue as follows.

> Figure 1 illustrates how Map-SCHOLAR asks map-related questions, evaluates the student's answers, and corrects any mistakes. First, the dots indicating the location of the cities appear unlabeled on the map of Brazil and start blinking. Then SCHOLAR asks the student to name the blinking cities. When the student responds, it indicates which answers were

correct and prints their names on the map. Because Lima was given erroneously as an answer (see Figure 1), Map-SCHOLAR pointed out that Lima is in Peru and showed where Lima is on the map. Thus, Map-SCHOLAR gives both verbal and visual feedback to help the student learn the material. (p. 2)

These investigators have combined their development work in CAI with a program of research to help determine the effectiveness of the systems they are designing. Thus, Collins and Adams (1977) examined the effectiveness of the program illustrated in Figure 7.1 when compared to a linear method derived from programed instruction in systems. These authors generally found the SCHOLAR program to be more effective in promoting student learning. In addition to studying the effectiveness of the technique, the investigators designed studies to help them understand the characteristics of the system and its effects on learning performance. Thus, an investigation of the system displayed in Figure 7.1 (Collins, Adams, & Pew, 1978) was designed to study the effects of the Map-SCHOLAR program with its interactive map display when compared to static labeled maps or unlabeled maps. They found that the interactive map was more effective. They believe that the reason for this is that the map changes with relevant information. It also permits questions to be posed in a visual form not possible with static map displays. A final general comment about tutorial systems is that it

TABLE 7.4 An annotated excerpt of the dialogue between tutorial mode of SCHOLAR and a student (the student's inputs are between asterisks)

Dialogue	*Annotated comments*
WHAT IS CHILE? *COUNTRY IN SOUTH AMERICA* VERY GOOD.	This is the most important property of Chile. (A tutor would suppress it on the assumption that the student knows the answer.) In evaluating the answer, it looks for "country," ignores the rest.
CORRECT OR INCORRECT? CHILE IS IN NORTHERN SOUTH AMERICA. *INCORRECT*	Location is the next most important attribute under Chile.
YOU ARE CORRECT. CHILE IS IN SOUTHWESTERN SOUTH AMERICA.	The student answers correctly, so SCHOLAR will go deeper into Location.
THE EASTERN BORDERING COUNTRY OF CHILE IS— *I DON'T KNOW*	This is the most important Bordering-Country of Chile.

THE ANSWER IS: ARGENTINA.
THE BOUNDARY OF THE EASTERN
    BORDERING COUNTRIES OF
    CHILE IS THE ANDES.
THE NORTHERN BORDERING
    COUNTRY OF CHILE IS PERU.
THE NORTHEASTERN BORDERING
    COUNTRY IS BOLIVIA.
	Since the student has missed the question, SCHOLAR presents some related information about Bordering-Countries.

From "Comparison of Two Teaching Strategies in Computer-Assisted Instruction," by A. Collins and M. J. Adams. In *Contemporary Educational Psychology*, 1977, *2*, pp. 133–148. Copyright 1977 by Academic Press. Reprinted by permission.

Now let's see what you remember about the cities of Brazil.
Please name the principal cities of Brazil now blinking on the
display screen.

Manaos, Sao Paulo, and Lima.

Manaos and Sao Paulo are correct. Lima is in Peru, not in Brazil.
The principal cities of Brazil are blinking on the screen.

Rio de Janeiro is in Southeastern Brazil. It is on Guanabara Bay
and the Atlantic.

Brasilia is in Central Brazil. It is far from the ocean.

FIGURE 7.1 Interactions with Map-SCHOLAR showing answer evaluation and error correction. (*From "Effectiveness of an Interactive Map
Display in Tutoring Geography," by A. Collins, M. A. Adams, and R. W.
Pew. In* Journal of Educational Psychology, *1978, 70, pp. 1–7. Copyright 1978 by the Journal of Educational Psychology. Reprinted by permission.*)

is still possible to cite easily most of the operational systems in a very
short summary chapter. However, it is also obvious that if CAI will
really effect the development of training programs in work organizations, it will occur because of the potential power of tutorial programs.

Evaluation of CAI

CAI research began in the mid-1960s but initially was hampered by
hardware and software difficulties. While recent efforts have resolved
many of those problems, every new system development seems to

underestimate these difficulties as well as the time necessary to resolve them. Many of the studies reported above reflect well-designed and creatively-conceived research investigations. None the less, most CAI investigations have been little more than demonstrations of technology with an occasional posttest after the treatment. This one-shot case-study approach is ordinarily useful only for the collection of information preliminary to more thorough investigations. The following section discusses trends and generalizations based on a limited number of well-conceived studies. Due to the scarcity of research, the reader should be somewhat wary of attempts to predict future developments. However, it is important to consider the present state of development. In some of these studies the authors have specified particular evaluation problems, related to criterion contamination or experimental design, that have plagued their research. The following tentative statements are offered.

> 1. From the beginning of its development, a substantial number of studies have indicated that CAI requires less time than more traditional methods to teach the same amount of material. For example, studies by the U.S. Army Signal Center and School (U.S. Civil Service Commission, 1971b) found that the CAI course took 11% less time than instructor-controlled methods. A revision of this program resulted in further time savings, raising the average savings of all groups to 20%. Davis (1977) described a number of efforts in the navy training systems which cited savings time ranging from 27% to 50%, and Dossett and Hulvershorn (1983) cited similar savings for the air force in electronics training. The latter investigators also described research where air force trainees were assigned in pairs to CAI training. They referred to this as a peer-training system and compared it to an individually-trained CAI group and a traditional training group. They found no differences in achievement level between the three groups but both CAI groups took less training time. They also found that the peer group took less time than the individual CAI group. The authors note that, if the peer results hold up in future studies, training time will be even further reduced since two trainees receive instruction at one terminal. Clearly, more research is needed on that effect but even so, research data consistently points to decreased training time when utilizing CAI techniques.
>
> 2. The achievement data appear to parallel programed-instruction analyses. A number of studies have indicated that CAI students perform better than traditionally-educated students and very few studies have shown CAI students perform more poorly, but the largest number of investigations found no significant difference between the two groups.

Most of the studies that were used as a basis for the preceding statements would be included in the Nash et al. (1971) category of effectively-controlled studies. Yet, the authors of this research describe a variety of difficulties that hindered the interpretation of their data. One source of difficulty was criterion contamination. The criteria utilized for many of the studies conducted in school settings were originally designed for traditional-instruction classes. Often, they were nationally standardized exams constructed years before CAI existed. Some investigators have stated that the behavioral objectives specified in the design process of CAI systems are not appropriately measured by these standardized exams. They believe that the CAI method has unique features that should lead to the specification of new behavioral objectives. For example, CAI tutorial programs might permit students to learn certain concepts that could not be taught by a group lecture; the test of these programs should therefore include measures that adequately reflect the new objectives. Many of the studies described above, especially those in work organizations, use measures that reflect the objectives of CAI instruction. Unfortunately, there are some administrators who are unwilling to accept innovations unless the students perform adequately on the traditional normative measures, which may not be a good indicant of course objectives. One apparent solution to this problem is careful needs assessment procedures that establish the objectives and the criterion measurements before the instructional program begins. A related concern is the appropriate timing of the criterion measurements. Students in traditional methods are given their exams when they complete all of their course material. In many studies, CAI students are also required to take the examination at one specified time, although they may have completed the course material days earlier or may not even have finished it. Thus, the self-pacing procedures of CAI place the student at a disadvantage. The solution to this problem depends on effective testing procedures that are used when the trainee finishes the required material. There is little sense in a system in which students are permitted to pace themselves through the entire program only to await mass testing at one designated time.

Threats to external validity resulting from the Hawthorne effect are also a problem in CAI research. While control students remain in their traditional school setting, the CAI students are placed in a unique situation with new equipment, observers, and a generally experimental atmosphere. Seltzer (1971) notes that the superior performance of the Mississippi group in the Stanford study occurred in a poor socioeconomic environment where the students tend to be deprived of learning materials. Thus, it is necessary to speculate on the Hawthorne effect generated by the computer terminals and experimental environment. As mentioned earlier, some researchers (such as Atkinson, 1968) have attempted to partially overcome this problem by having the control group in one study participate as CAI students in another subject.

Another concern is the interactive effects of program and teacher quality (Rosenberg, 1972). In most studies, there is little attention paid to the quality of the traditional instructors or to the quality of the program. The interactive effects are especially apparent in the Suppes and Morningstar (1969) Mississippi study. The authors suggest that the superior effect of CAI may have been related not to the program but to poorer teacher preparation or training that adversely affected the traditional group. In order to assess the results of any particular instructional program, it is necessary to examine the quality of the traditional and innovative methods.

Advantages and Limitations of Computer-Assisted Instruction

Advantages

1. The major advantage of CAI is the individualization of instruction. PI can adapt to the gross characteristics of a specific individual, but CAI has the potential for responding to detailed characteristics of trainees and their needs at a precise moment in time. An illustration of this is apparent in the studies described above that utilize the SCHOLAR system. CAI programs can attend to individual attributes—that is, demographic information, previous performance, most recent response, and any other variable that can be programed for and stored in the computer.

2. The reinforcement provisions of the CAI systems are a real benefit to the learner. As Singer (1968) noted, "The program has infinite patience. It does not have preconceived notions about a student. . . . Mistakes are not penalized by scorn or sarcasm, successes are marked by positive reinforcement" (p. 3).

3. CAI systems present teachers with a new role. The role-keeping is performed by machine, and complete analyses of student performance are readily available. This gives the instructor time to spend with individuals or small groups of students. Dossett and Hulvershorn (1983) noted that the required student–instructor contact time in their CAI electronics course was less than 2% of the total training time in the study. They feel that that permits the following activities:

(a) an instructor can provide individual student help when required
(b) the instructor's role may include the management of individualized instruction and
(c) more training can be conducted with a smaller staff. (p. 558)

4. Due to the data-collection provisions, CAI offers the researcher a good opportunity to gain knowledge about techniques and the instructional variables which can support their systems.

Limitations

1. At the present time, a restraining factor in the use of CAI is the limited state of knowledge. The small number of empirical studies makes generalizations about the utility of CAI extremely hazardous. In 1968, DeCecco expressed the fear described below about the emphasis on technology leading instructional efforts astray. In 1985, his fears are still well-founded.

All these facilities and equipment, I must remind you, are much more sophisticated than any theory of teaching we presently have. The temptation in a technological society is to allow our fantastic machines to determine our research problems and our educational practice. It is far more important that we subordinate the machines to the theoretical and practical instructional problems which, undoubtedly, the machines can help us solve. (p. 539)

2. The cost of CAI systems remains a serious obstacle. It is true that the cost of hardware is decreasing significantly, but there are still large costs related to development, communications and maintenance. The navy (Hurlock & Slough, 1976) provided some cost estimates for their PLATO system based upon the following assumptions:

(a) terminals are purchased and used for ten years;

(b) fixed costs for time sharing, maintenance, and communications remain the same each year;

(c) each terminal is used 2000 hours per year.

Under these conditions, the cost was $3.90 per student contact hour. What is interesting about these estimates is how complicated the cost issues are. For example, it was noted that the system was so expensive that unless large numbers of persons were being trained the cost was too high. On the other hand, the $3.90 cost was for terminals located in San Diego 1800 miles from the University of Illinois System. If the terminals were installed closer, the corresponding reduction in phone costs would reduce the cost per student by $1.67. However, there is no doubting that these systems are expensive. System management and maintenance alone is estimated at $170,000 a year. Clearly, the answer to the cost effectiveness issue includes many complicated issues, like the cost of the alternative and how the savings in training time gets translated into dollars. In any case, the development costs of CAI programs make it unlikely that smaller organizations will participate until the system is fully developed. This may result in the development of prepackaged programs that do not consider the particular needs of the organization. Of course, this is a danger with all packaged materials that are simply sold off the shelf without any consideration of the needs assessment characteristics of the individual buyer.

3. One remaining question concerns the effects of a machine-oriented learning environment on satisfaction, motivation, and development. As noted in the discussion of programed instruction, there have been several studies suggesting that adult learners do not prefer to be taught exclusively by machine. At the present time, students still spend very little of their time in a CAI environment and most students like CAI instruction. However, if the technique becomes widespread, it will become necessary to ask if a rich enough stimulus environment is being provided. Systems like CAI cannot be evaluated just in terms of learner achievement. CAI leads to new environments that must be investigated in relation to attitudes and the socialization process.

AUDIOVISUAL TECHNIQUES

Both television and films extend the range of stimuli that are normally brought into the training environment; they display events and sequences of events rather than simply present objects. The implementation of this instructional technique is extensive in scope with a variety of topics covered and studies performed. Topics include such subjects as automobile dealer training sessions, customer engineering, dentistry, driver education, literacy training, and a variety of other topics. For example, Wexley and Latham (1981) report that the Weyerhaeuser Company uses entertainment films such as the *Bridge on the River Kwai* and *Twelve O'Clock High* as a basis for discussing interpersonal and social relationships in their management school. With the increasing technology and size of organizations, many are finding that the live lecture method is inadequate to handle the number of people who need to be trained. Also, organizations are finding that bringing persons from very diverse locations to live training programs is extremely expensive. The use of audiovisual techniques is considered by some organizations as a partial solution to this problem. Originally, audiovisual techniques were criticized because it was not possible to be responsive to the needs of individual students in diverse locations. However, developing technology has begun to resolve many of those problems. For example, a basic audiovisual system now utilizes standard telephone transmissions, allowing students and instructors to share the same basic materials, including questions, written materials, voice communications, and so on. Many systems have electronic blackboards and slide projection equipment at each site. One major organization expects to cut its travel budget by 50% for its technical training by the use of audiovisual systems (Bove, 1984). The use of techniques combining audiovisual systems such as closed circuit television and telephone communications has spawned a new term for this type of training—*teletraining.* The following examples are chosen from a number of diverse settings to illustrate the considerable variety of approaches to audiovisual techniques.

CIGNA, a large insurance company, faced the problem of delivering training to members of their property and casuality group, which consists of 20,000 employees at more than 200 locations (Kung & Rado, 1984). Their training sessions were based upon a job analysis which was used to develop the knowledge and skill requirements for employees. The purpose of the training session was to teach managers how to use the knowledge and skill guide with their employees by comparing actual knowledge and skill profiles with job requirements. The teletraining system used permitted active participation. Lectures were minimal, and a number of other activities such as exercises were used to keep participation active. The system also used local facilitators who were also trained using teletraining.

Chu and Schramm (1967) reported on a study in American Samoa designed to implement a modern educational program for a traditional rote-learning system through the use of television. Almost all of the teachers were trained under the traditional system, and the educational administrators realized that it would take a century to proceed through the normal evolutionary process. Thus, they consolidated their one-room schoolhouses, installed a six-channel television system, and brought in expert teachers to train new instructors and to help the established instructors adapt to the innovations. Similar developments are being implemented in other countries where teachers are not available to instruct the hundreds of thousands of children who are presently without any educational facilities.

One of my favorite examples of this technique comes from the television program *Sesame Street* (Ball & Bogatz, 1970). The reason I enjoy this example is that many readers of this book learned basic concepts from *Sesame Street,* and very few people realize that this entertainment show was really a carefully designed training program. Basically, research on this program showed that (1) the children who watched the program learned more than those who didn't; (2) those skills that were emphasized on the program were learned best; and (3) disadvantaged children as compared with middle-class children began the program with lower achievement scores on the topics being emphasized, but their performance surpassed middle-class children who watched the program infrequently. Viewers who were not part of the experimental design often did not realize that this creative and entertaining program was an experiment designed to achieve specific behavioral objectives. These objectives were carefully determined in a series of workshops attended by representatives of all the pertinent fields, including psychologists, sociologists, teachers, film-makers, writers, advertising personnel, and evaluators. They established objectives related to symbolic representation, cognitive processes, and physical and social environments. For example, behavioral objectives for symbolic representation might include: "Given a set of symbols, either all letters or all numbers, the child knows whether those symbols are used in reading or counting," or "Given a series of words presented orally, all beginning with the same letter, the child can make up another word or pick another word starting with the same letter" (Ball & Bogatz, 1970).

The evaluation design and criteria for *Sesame Street* were developed as part of the entire instructional program. The measures included outcome criteria, such as degree of learning, as well as process measures, which assessed what occurred during instruction. The process measures included the number of hours that the child viewed the program and the child's reactions while viewing. These measures also permitted the investigator to relate the number of hours of viewing to other criteria like learning. The pretests indicated that older children performed better than younger children. However, after viewing the program, the younger children who watched regularly often scored higher than older children who were infrequent viewers. This program is a fine example of the information that can be gained by the utilization of a variety of criteria developed from carefully defined goals and objectives.

Evaluation of Audiovisual Techniques

Most of the recent work on the use of audiovisual techniques, including the teletraining programs, remains unevaluated. As indicated below, most of the evaluation work on audiovisual techniques was conducted many years ago. However, the results of those studies were quite consistent.

Many evaluation studies compare audiovisual techniques to conventional lecture-type instruction. However, there are a surprising number of studies that compare techniques to control groups that receive no instruction at all. The investigators are asking whether the student or trainee learns anything from media like television and films. As reported by Chu and Schramm (1967), these studies showed that the audiovisual groups systematically improved their performance over that of control groups. Several of these studies compared the experimental groups' scores to national scores on standardized tests, with the audiovisual groups again performing in a superior manner.

The results of the studies that compare audiovisual to other techniques are consistent. Two major reviews that analyzed 393 comparisons (Schramm, 1962) and 421 comparisons (Chu & Schramm, 1967) showed few significant differences in achievement, with those differences present favoring audiovisuals. From another perspective, Schramm (1962) notes that in well over 80% of the cases, the audiovisual technique was as good as or better than the conventional technique. Thus, the majority of "no significant difference" cases should not lead to a rejection of the technique but rather to a determination of where and how it can be utilized effectively. For example, audiovisuals are extremely useful when good teaching is not immediately available or where courses or materials cannot be presented in the traditional instructional mode. The identification of other effective ways to utilize audiovisuals will undoubtedly contribute to the implementation of the technique. For example, several studies have found that audiovisuals are more effective if the learner is active rather than passive. In one study (Lumsdaine, May, & Hadsell, 1958), the participants' performance was improved by splicing questions about the material into the film. In summary, most studies indicate that the effective use of television is dependent on the basic qualities of good teaching. Chu and Schramm (1967) feel that the important qualities are "simplicity, good organization, motivation, practice, knowledge of results, rest pauses at appropriate points, cues that direct the pupil to the essential things he is to learn . . . " (p. 100).

Unfortunately, many of the studies have not provided useful information for reasons similar to those affecting PI and CAI. The research efforts for these media have been especially victimized by sampling procedures in the selection of subjects, by the Hawthorne effect, and by inadequate criteria. However, there is one interesting factor that should be mentioned because of its implications for all training procedures. Chu and Schramm (1967) discovered that almost all of the investigations compared instructional groups taught completely by television to those taught completely by conventional methods. However, they contend that this is not a realistic comparison "because almost nowhere in the world is television being used in classrooms without being built into a learning context managed by the teacher" (p. 6). Thus, the technique should be examined in the context of how it can fit into the total learning environment as part of the instructional process. In the previous discussion of external threats to validity, it was indicated that it is difficult to generalize from multiple-treatment environments to environments where a single treatment is used in isolation. The opposite problem is present in this discussion. It is difficult to generalize from the application of a single treatment to situations in which the media are combined with other treatments. The only solution is to begin investigations that examine combinations of treatments.

Advantages and Limitations of Audiovisual Techniques

Advantages

1. The results of a large number of experiments indicate that audiovisual techniques can be effectively utilized for a wide variety of subjects.

2. Audiovisual techniques are especially useful for those situations in which competent instructors are not immediately available or in which travel costs make instruction prohibitive. It is reported that American companies spend 35 billion dollars a year on training and that more than 25% of that is spent on airfare, lodging, and meals for trainees. Obviously, this makes the use of audiovisual training programs very appealing to organizations (Bove, 1984).

3. Audiovisuals are uniquely appropriate for presenting dynamic events that unfold over time. Thus, it is possible to demonstrate the terminal performance expected in a complex motor sequence (Gagné, 1970). Pictures used in learning sequences can also provide effective feedback to the participant. This medium can be utilized to control time by speeding up or slowing down particularly important aspects of behavior and by instant replay. Good editing can highlight crucial aspects of performance.

4. This particular medium is useful for presenting events that cannot be recreated in the traditional classroom. For example, films of simulated accidents can vividly demonstrate what happens to individuals who are not wearing a seat belt.

Limitations

1. Previously, the technique used to be only a one-way communication device. While many of the new uses, including teletraining, make the technique into a two-way communication system, most audiovisual systems in use today are still one-way communication systems. Thus, it is often necessary to use individual facilitators at the site to overcome this problem. Also, there is still not much research on the effectiveness of the two-way communication systems or their effects on learning. Finally, audiovisuals are not easily adaptable to those situations in which there are great differences in the ability levels or interests of the participants. Programed instruction or CAI is more effective in such cases.

2. Audiovisuals often involve complex arrangements. For example, the CIGNA teletraining program involves distribution of a national implementation schedule, arrangements with operators to initiate all phone communications, training of facilitators, and so on. Clearly, scheduling and preparation become very important factors in these types of systems. Also, while many firms are finding these systems to be cost effective because of the large number of trainees in diverse locations, it is also true that audiovisuals are expensive and may not be cost-effective in all situations.

MACHINE SIMULATORS

Training simulators are designed to replicate the essential characteristics of the real world that are necessary to produce learning and transfer. These efforts can vary from flight simulators, which have a substantial degree of *physical fidelity* (that is, representation of the real world of operational equipment), to role-playing methods, in which the degree of physical simulation is minimal. In any case, the purpose of the simulation is to produce *psychological fidelity*—that is, to reproduce in the training tasks those behavioral processes that are necessary to perform the job. There are a variety of simulators that have been designed for specific training purposes, including skills development, decision making, and problem solving. In this section, simulators designed for skills training will be discussed. Most of these types of devices are called machine simulators. They are more likely to be found in flight training, maintenance training, and the like. Simulations which are designed for training interpersonal skills or management skills, such as role-playing, will be saved for the next chapter which focuses more on management and leadership training. However, before beginning a discussion of any type of simulation, it is important to discuss the reasons that simulation is considered a very important training method.

Reasons for Simulation

Controlled Reproducibility

Simulations permit the environment to be reproduced under the control of the training analyst. They represent a training laboratory outside the real-world setting, where uncontrolled parameters make it difficult to produce the desired learning environment. By careful design and planning, environments can be created that supply variation in the essential characteristics of the real situation. In addition, simulation permits the trainer to expand, compress, or repeat time, depending on the needs of the trainees. A business game designed to simulate market and supply conditions can present six weeks of essential financial operations in six hours, and an airline simulator can provide months of aircraft landing experience in several hours.

Safety Considerations

In many cases, the required terminal behavior is too complex to be safely handled by a trainee. The simulator permits the learner to be slowly introduced to the essential task characteristics, without any danger to himself, his fellow workers, or the expensive equipment. While many observers recognize the validity of carefully planned introductions to complex tasks, like flying an airplane, they fail to realize that many jobs, like assembly-line operations, also require considerable pretraining. Some industrial firms solve this problem by a *vestibule* training program, which consists of a simulation, off the production line, of the equipment and materials utilized on the job. Simulations also permit the trainee to practice emergency techniques before being exposed to hazardous situations in real settings. The focus of safety should not be narrowed to skills development. It is also reasonable to consider the psychological safety of a manager required to face the problems of racial strife on the job. Role-playing several solutions to that situation in the comparative safety of the training environment could have some benefits.

Utilization of Learning Considerations

Most simulations permit the effective utilization of learning principles. Since the environment is carefully controlled by the trainers, they can easily (1) introduce feedback, (2) arrange for practice, (3) use part or whole and massed or spaced methods, and (4) design the environment according to the best-known principles of transfer. Thus, careful design of simulations can produce an environment conducive to positive transfer.

Cost

The acquisition of skills requires practice, and if practice is not feasible in the real world, simulation provides a viable alternative. While most simulation efforts are expensive, they are often an economical alternative to using high-priced, on-the-job equipment. For example, Americans being trained to assume vital roles in overseas environments are being exposed to simulated training settings because trial-and-error performance in foreign countries is too expensive. And, quite probably, the behavior of a beginning trainee handling a multimillion-dollar jet might quickly convince passengers to make donations to simulation training programs.

All of the previously mentioned reasons for simulation have prompted the development of skill simulators. These simulators are utilized when the required skills are quite explicit and the behavior can be measured objectively. Frequently, these simulations have extensive physical fidelity and can represent a large number of potential environmental situations. Flight simulators are becoming so complex that many airlines expect to be in a situation soon where all flight training will be done on a simulator. While simulators are very expensive to manufacture, estimates in 1976 (*Human Factors Society Bulletin*) were that a DC-10 simulator runs at a cost of $500 per hour, while the actual aircraft costs $2300 per hour in direct costs without including any lost revenue. Obviously, increases in fuel costs magnify those differences. Research flight simulators are just as complex. For example, the navy's primary jet trainer is simulated for research purposes at the Naval Training Equipment Center in Orlando, Florida. This simulation includes all normal operations, including carrier arrest landing, and carrier simulation, including provisions for ship pitch, roll, and heave, as well as variations in sea conditions, wind conditions, and turbulence. I have flown the simulator and can attest to the complexities of landing a plane on an aircraft carrier. In my weaker moments, I might even mention that in numerous tries I never even hit the carrier but rather managed continually to land in the ocean. Just how complex a flight simulator can be is made clear in the following description provided by J. A. Adams (1961).

> Most commonly, the term "flight simulator" refers to a complex electronic device designed to reproduce with considerable fidelity, for one or more aircrew stations, the location and physical features of controls and instruments, the aerodynamic response of instruments and controls under various conditions of flight and operator response, switches, warning lights, radio and navigational aids, and sometimes auditory stimuli. If a combat aircraft is simulated, there usually will be armament controls, radar controls and displays if required, and target stimuli for combat problems. (p. 88)

The design of machine simulators need not be limited to expensive, large-scale operations. Many efforts are part-simulations, which replicate a critical or difficult portion of the task without attempting to provide a complete environment. Also, simulators are not just useful in large-scale system training such as that found in flight simulation. A good example of another use of simulation is provided in a study by Salvendy and Pilitsis (1980) which investigated its use in teaching medical students suturing techniques needed in surgical operations. The traditional method consists of a lecture–slide and videotape describing the technique. Included in the instructions were materials related to the general geometry of the suture path, descriptions of the instruments and their functions, and general guidelines. The student then utilized these instructions while practicing on pigs' feet until the instructor determined that the student was performing the task appropriately. One of the simulators used as an alternative to the above procedure is known as the "inwound" procedure simulator. A description of this device and its characteristics is as follows:

> The "Inwound" procedure simulator . . . assists the student in acquiring the manipulative motor skills during the inwound procedure phase by puncturing a simulated tissue with an electrically activated needle holder. . . . The simulated tissue contains related wound path geometry such as "entry" and "exit" points. The overall unit is mounted on a revolving fixture located in a mannequin-type arm. The student is able to monitor his/her progress by gaining information as to correctness of motions through the student feedback console. This console consists of 11 clearly marked amber and red lights that correspond to correct and incorrect motions. Both audio and visual channels are activated by the suture needle as the needle is guided by the student through the "wound." If the various phases (entry, depth, exit) are performed correctly, the amber lights are activated. . . . An incorrect needle motion while the

needle is in the wound causes a corresponding red light and tone genera-tor to be activated momentarily. When the needle is corrected in its path, the related visual and auditory feedback is discontinued. Number of errors, time in the wound, and number of cycles performed for each of the procedure phases are recorded individually on the monitoring con-sole. (pp. 155–156)

These investigators also designed a knot-tying simulator. In addition to the simulators, another training condition in this study consisted of a perceptual training method where students observed filmed perfor-mance of experienced surgeons and inexperienced medical students in addition to traditional techniques.

Generally, the investigators found that simulation training and perceptual training improved the performance of the medical students beyond the traditional training methods. In addition, the investigators collected psychophysiological measures of stress such as heart rate variance, muscle tension, and so on. The data also tended to confirm that students trained by simulation method showed less stress when they were required to perform new suturing tasks.

Another interesting and more amusing study of part-simulators in a laboratory study is provided by Rubinsky and Smith (1973). They examined simulated accident occurrence in the use of a grinding wheel. Traditionally, teaching the operation of power tools relies on written or verbal instructions, with an occasional demonstration. These authors devised a task that exposed operators (college students) to a simulated accident (a jet of water). The "accident" was designed to occur when the operator stood in front of the grinding wheel during the starting operation—that is, the time when there is the greatest danger of the wheel exploding. The investigators found that those subjects who ex-perienced a simulated accident as part of their training program were less likely to repeat the hazardous behavior than those who were given written instructions or demonstrations of safe procedures. The results were maintained over a series of retention tests. The authors suggest that simulated accidents might be effective in reducing power-tool accidents. Certainly, this procedure provides an interesting form of feedback for incorrect responses.

Due to the large scale of many of these simulation efforts and investigator concerns about the adequacy of simulation, there are a number of topics that are often discussed whenever simulators are being considered. These are discussed below.

Fidelity of simulation. Most researchers maintain that simula-tion efforts must have psychological fidelity (that is, the representa-tion of the essential behavioral processes necessary to perform the job) as their chief objective. However, the question of how much physical representation is necessary in order to achieve psychological fidelity remains. The entire task is rarely produced in a simulation. In some cases, it is simply too expensive or dangerous, while in other instances, certain factors are judged as not important to the learning of the task (for example, training the pilot in opening or closing the door to the aircraft). However, the choice is not always clear. For example, it is still not certain whether the simulation of motion is a necessary aspect of pilot training. In addition to the question of whether such variables contribute to learning, this becomes an important question because of the extra cost involved. It costs at least a quarter of a million dollars extra to include motion as a part of flight simulation (Orlansky & String, 1977). However, there is little gained in the production of expensive simulators in which tasks that are critical for positive transfer are being excluded. These issues reflect the same problems faced in the design of all training programs. Initially the only solution is careful design based on needs assessment techniques. After accomplishing that part, questions about the relationship of certain components to training effectiveness can only be determined by a careful program of empirical research.

Team training.   Due to their task complexity, machine simulators often require the coordinated performance of several individuals. This includes simulations of jobs such as those of air traffic controllers, nuclear plant operators, and the like. Thus, they are sometimes utilized to investigate *team training,* with a team being defined as a group working together to achieve a common goal (Blum & Naylor, 1968). Of course, the term *team training* could apply equally well to other group instructional efforts, like organizational development and business games. Interestingly, most training efforts have not considered whether teams require special considerations beyond the principles utilized in the training of individuals. The intricacies of the team situation are exemplified by the complexities in providing feedback. Glanzer (1965) noted that errors caused by members of a team were especially burdensome because it was not always possible to determine who caused the error. Even if the source was discovered, considerable delay had occurred before feedback could be given. In addition to these difficulties, there is the question of what type of feedback should be presented— team, individual, or both. If given individual feedback, the team members might concentrate more on their own, rather than their team's, performance. However, team feedback does not provide direct information about an individual's performance. Perhaps the best solution is a combination of both types of feedback; but the empirical literature has little to offer in the way of advice. Unfortunately, similar difficulties in resolving issues concerning team training have plagued this area since it was identified as an important area of study. Thus, after a thorough review of the literature, Denson (1981) noted that there were at least two serious problems. One was the need for adequate assessment/measurement techniques for team behavior. The other was the need for identification of team performance parameters that describe team functioning such as communication, coordination, and decision making. The only unfortunate aspect of this statement is that it is no different from the needs that were specified decades ago. However, researchers have not been able to conceptualize the problem and resolve the issues.

Transfer of training issues.   It is important to remember that simulation efforts are directly related to transfer of training. Individuals are trained on a simulator so that they will perform better in the work situation. Many of the parameters involving transfer were considered in the transfer of learning section in Chapter 4. However, despite accomplishments in the literature and laboratories, the degree of understanding that might be expected has not been achieved. In part, the limitations are a result of inadequate evaluation efforts. For example, Blaiwes and Regan (1970) suggest that evaluation efforts must consider three criteria: (1) original learning efficiency, (2) transfer of learning to the new task, and (3) retention of learning. Yet, in the area of flight simulation (the most advanced simulation effort to date), the emphasis has been on the most immediate criterion—original learning efficiency. Even these original-learning studies have been plagued by serious problems. Williges, Roscoe, and Williges (1972) note that there is little agreement on what constitutes ideal pilot performance, since the reliability of most pilot-performance grading systems has been disappointing. Thus, the studies are difficult to evaluate because there is little agreement on what constitutes terminal performance. Studies investigating the transfer of skills from simulation to on-the-job efforts are less frequent and suffer from serious design flaws, usually caused by the lack of a control group. Studies concerning retention measures are virtually nonexistent. Thus, there is little information on whether skills obtained through simulation efforts are maintained over a period of time or whether certain learning variables (for example, massed versus spaced practice or amount of original learning) make any difference in long-term retention. Williges, Roscoe, and Williges (1972) describe the research difficulties in the following manner:

> Measurement of retention is hindered by such problems as variations in the original training of subjects, difficulty of controlling the amount of flying experience each individual receives during the retention period, and unavailability of subjects after a sufficiently long retention period. The lack of simulator studies using a retention measure reflects the general insufficiency of information relating to retention of pilot skills or, for that matter, retention of any complex motor skills. (p. 13)

Researchers are attempting to design systems that permit predictions concerning whether a particular device will lead to positive transfer. For example, Swezey (1982–83) applied a model of the transfer process developed by Wheaton and his colleagues (1976) to two different training devices in order to predict which one would lead to more transfer. Some of the parameters of the model include:

1. task commonality—whether the device permits the trainee to practice skills required for actual performance on the real task;
2. equipment similarity—whether the equipment involves physically similar equipment and the same information requirements.
3. learning deficit analysis—an examination of the task to determine its relationship to the input repertoire of trainees and the difficulty level of training the necessary skills and knowledges;
4. training technique analysis—an estimate of the instructional effectiveness of the device based upon the degree to which relevant principles of learning are utilized.

Research involving models like this one are an encouraging sign that it may soon be possible to understand what variables contribute to transfer of learning. Simulator training for complex skills, motor or otherwise, offers a real opportunity for research that will contribute to an understanding of the learning process. Most sponsors prefer to have their trainees learn skills on simulated instruments rather than on original equipment. Thus, the research opportunities are there; it is not necessary to sell anyone on the need for training. Rather, it is necessary to produce the carefully designed research that contributes to understanding and knowledge.

The importance of gaining this understanding is further illustrated by a problem which up to now has received very little attention. That is, there is increasing evidence that persons become ill in simulators. The term *simulator sickness* is now being used to describe this phenomenon. Symptoms include disorientation, dizziness, nausea, spinning sensations, and confusion. McCauley (1984) has found that such disturbances can occur during simulation trials and often continue for hours afterwards. He notes that the sickness can result in a number of serious problems, including such post-effects as placing the individual at risk when in such real life situations as driving a car.

BEHAVIOR MODIFICATION

Behavior modification is a direct application of the principles of reinforcement developed by B. F. Skinner in his operant-conditioning studies. Originally, behavior modification was utilized in clinical settings as a change technique for maladaptive behavior. Some training analysts (Nord, 1970; Feeney, 1972) suggested that the principles of behavior modification might be effectively utilized in the design of training programs. The basic procedures suggested by this approach can be summarized in the following way.

1. An assessment is performed to specify where problems exist and to help in the determination of precise behaviors that require elimination, modification, or development.

2. Reinforcers appropriate to the situation and to the individual are selected.
3. The implementation of the actual program consists of a variety of different procedures dependent on the behavior of the trainees.
4. Desired responses are immediately and continuously reinforced. Once the behavior is established, intermittent programs of reinforcement are instituted.
5. Evaluation procedures are employed to determine the degree of change.

The original efforts describing these techniques actually consisted of a reinterpretation of previous work into a reinforcement framework to demonstrate the potential value of the system. For example, Nord (1970) describes a program instituted by a retail firm to reduce tardiness and absenteeism. The absenteeism problem affected secretaries and sales and stock personnel at the firm's stores, warehouses, and offices. The firm instituted a program whereby monthly drawings were held for prizes, which were appliances worth approximately $25. There was one prize for each 25 employees. In order to be eligible, the employee had to have a perfect attendance and punctuality record for the preceding month. Similar drawings for a major prize (such as a color television) were based on performance over a six-month period. After one year, absenteeism and tardiness were reduced to about one-fourth the level prior to the program. Sick-leave payments were reduced approximately 62%. Nord concludes that the lottery system served as a stimulus to reinforce punctuality and attendance at work.

Feeney (1972) noted that particular responses and associate contingencies represent the core of the behavior-modification system. Proponents of the system, like Feeney, criticize other training efforts for emphasizing the teaching of processes like general management skills with the hope that the knowledge gained will solve a problem. Instead, Feeney suggests a performance audit to define a particular difficulty, followed by the reinforcement of the appropriate responses necessary to overcome the problem. These principles were demonstrated by Feeney in a widely publicized project conducted at Emery Air Freight, which drew attention to the possibilities of behavior modification as a training technique. A performance audit indicated that the employees believed that, nine out of ten times, they were responding to customer inquiries within 90 minutes. Emery Air Freight was also committed to combining small packages into large containers. The employees believed that they were effectively using containerized shipments 90% of the time. Feeney's data showed that the responses to customer inquiries were occurring within 90 minutes only 30% of the time and that the use rate on shipments was actually 45%. Focusing on these particular problems, Feeney instituted a program based on the principles of positive reinforcement. He talked with employees and found out their needs. Then, he used positive reinforcers to reward early approximations of the desired terminal responses. He focused on frequent reinforcement at the onset of the program and later switched to more intermittent programs. In all cases, the reinforcement was directly related to the performance. This emphasis on performance and feedback is illustrated by one aspect of the program, called the feedback system. The key elements are:

1. Find out what people think they should be doing.
2. Find out what they are doing—not by asking but by getting the raw data and comparing that with their perceptions.
3. Be sure feedback is measurable and that it gives comparisons to performance in previous similar periods.
4. Ensure that feedback gets to the proper unit in the organization—to the people who need it, as well as to their supervisors and intermediate management levels.
5. Make certain the feedback is timely—provided as soon after the performance as possible. The best procedure is to have the worker measure his own performance. That way, feedback is immediate; the employee is more likely to accept it and more likely to react favorably to it.
6. Design feedback in positive terms; even if there is no performance improvement, at least the employee can be complimented on his honesty in reporting accomplishments. (p. 8)

Feeney estimates that Emery Air Freight saved several million dollars in a three-year period because of the changes in performance resulting from the application of reinforcement principles.

While Feeney's study received considerable publicity because of the estimates of savings produced by the technique, it is really only possible to suggest that this method has potential as a behavior-change technique. The demonstrations and reinterpretations of previous programs do not permit any powerful statements about the accomplishments of the program or about the important parameters of the technique. When a program like the one used at Emery Air Freight is introduced there are many variations in the environment that could be responsible for changes in behavior. Unfortunately, the lack of scientific procedures makes it difficult to ascertain why changes occurred. It has already been mentioned that on-the-job training is often employed to avoid the development of training programs and generally indicates a lack of commitment by the organization. Perhaps the use of any method, including behavior modification, with appropriate fanfare and commitment by management could result in changes similar to those achieved by Emery Air Freight. Any real gains in understanding await the employment of procedures beyond anecdotal case studies without control procedures.

Unfortunately, as noted by Wexley (1984), the actual implementation and evaluation of behavior modification techniques in work organizations remains quite limited. For example, a review by Andrasik (1979) found about 20 applications for such techniques. However, those studies did not stand up well in Andrasik's evaluation of their work. He points to a number of problems with the studies, including measurement reliability, lack of systematic interventions, and failure to provide post-training followup. However, there are a few examples of well-conceived and thoughtful studies which do demonstrate the possibilities of behavior modification techniques. One set of these studies is demonstrated by the work of Komaki and her colleagues (1980) in reducing accidents. That work is described in Chapter 6 (p. 163) as an example of quasi-experimental designs and in Chapter 4 in the section on feedback. The reader should reexamine those studies because they provide a fine illustration of the possibilities of behavior modification as well as a good illustration of the use of effective research designs.

Certain aspects of behavior modification promise that careful attention will be paid to some of the most important determinants of program success. First, the emphasis on program audits before and after the implementation of the technique suggests that the proponents of behavior modification will look at the accomplishments of their program rather than assume that success will follow automatically. Also, the concern with particular performance problems and associated behaviors requires careful needs assessment procedures before the design of the program. If this technique follows a path that includes needs assessment and evaluation, there is reason for an optimistic outlook. On the other hand, the identification of positive reinforcers in complex organizations represents a serious obstacle.

In any particular job, it will be necessary to determine which stimuli serve as reinforcing agents. These reinforcers may be attention, status, privileges, promotion, and recognition, as well as the more obvious reinforcers such as bonuses, pay raises, and vacation time. McIntire (1973) cautions us that the determination of reinforcers for adult behavior is a complex task. For example, he suggests that it is difficult to modify safety practices in certain high-accident industries (for example, coal mining) by having contests and awarding lapel pins, because these stimuli are typically not viewed as positive reinforcers. More likely, peer approval and the social reinforcers controlled by experienced workers would be effective. These reinforcements can be established by having respected and experienced workers serve as models to demonstrate the safe approach or by pairing a new trainee with an individual who uses correct procedures, thereby providing peer approval of the safe approach. The various views on motivation and learning (see Chapter 4) suggest that the reinforcing stimuli will be viewed differently by different individuals. In these cases, the treatment of individual differences results in additional complications for behavior modification. If different reinforcers are needed for different responses for different learners, the implementation of this technique in an on-the-job setting or in a training environment will present a real challenge.

One criticism often made about behavior modification in clinical settings (and likely to be repeated in training environments) is related to the manipulation of human behavior by reward systems. Actually, any training technique is designed to modify human behavior, and it is

unreasonable to single out behavior modification if the method suc-
ceeds in changing behavior. The key issue should be the careful determination of individual and organizational goals. Where conflict exists,
the issues must be resolved before training begins. A sure way to fail,
no matter what the technique, is to proceed with a training program
when there is wide-scale disagreement about the goals and objectives.
If behavior modification requires the organization to face these problems, it has a definite advantage.

Training Techniques Emphasizing Managerial and Interpersonal Skills

This chapter deals with training techniques which are related to interpersonal skills. Some of the strategies emphasize self-awareness, while others focus on skills for establishing communication and relationships with others. As such, many of the techniques are used with persons who supervise others, such as managers in work organizations. Of course, these types of techniques are also used in a variety of settings where persons interact, such as school principals and teachers, hospital administrators and staff, and even school teachers and students. It is also clear that in part the grouping of techniques in this and the preceding chapters is arbitrary. Thus, as with most techniques, behavioral role-modeling involves knowledge components as well as the practice of interpersonal skills. I chose to include it here because of the technique's emphasis on learning interpersonal strategies.

SIMULATIONS

In Chapter 7, simulations oriented toward skills training were presented as important components of simulation training. This presentation also applies to simulations involving interpersonal skills. It would, therefore, be useful for the reader to reexamine that material before continuing with this section.

The use of simulations in interpersonal skills training involves a variety of techniques and procedures. Sometimes the simulation forms the foundation for the entire training program, as in the technique called *business games*. In other cases, the simulation is one part of a much larger training exercise. In a technique called behavioral role-modeling, particular situations are simulated; however, a variety of other procedures, including audiovisual presentations, role-playing in simulations, obtaining group feedback on role-playing performances, and trying out behavior on the job, are also involved. In that sense, labeling sections "simulations" or "role-playing" is a simplification for presentation purposes.

Business Games

Business games are a direct outgrowth of the war games that are used to train officers in combat techniques. One military war game developed in 1798 used a map with 3600 squares, each representing a distinctive topographical feature, on which pieces representing troops and cavalry were moved (Raser, 1969). After visiting the Naval War College in 1956, members of the American Management Association developed the first business game. It is estimated that over 30,000 executives participated in the large number of games that were developed in the following five years (Stewart, 1962). A general description of business games is given by Dill, Jackson, and Sweeney (1961).

> A business game is a contrived situation which imbeds players in a simulated business environment where they must make management-type decisions from time to time, and their choices at one time generally affect the environmental conditions under which subsequent decisions must be made. Further, the interaction between decisions and environment is determined by a refereeing process which is not open to argument from the players. (pp. 7-8)

Most business games include the following steps (Greenlaw, Herron, & Rawdon, 1962; Moore, 1967):

> 1. The participants are first oriented to the simulated game by instructions describing the business objectives, decisions required, and rules of the game.
> 2. The competing teams then organize themselves and become cognizant of background information on the operations of the business. Then, the first series of decisions is made. Depending on the simulation, the decision may be based on one day or several months of operations.
> 3. After the first period is completed, the decisions for the competing teams are given to the game administrators.
> 4. The results are tabulated, manually or by computer, and are returned to the team participants along with other information that describes changes in their operating environment.
> 5. The cycle is repeated a number of times. Usually, at the completion of the game, the results are analyzed in a critique session. While this description is appropriate for most business games, there are many variations. For example, the complexity of the games in terms of days played and variables implemented as part of the gaming process varies greatly.

The early business games were nearly all designed to teach basic business skills. For example, the following is a description of one of the more complex games, known as the Carnegie Tech Management Game (Cohen, Cyert, Dill, Kuehn, Miller, Van Wormer, & Winters, 1962).

> The packaged detergent industry has served as a general model for the industry of the game. The selection of this industry for our model was primarily one of convenience. Its advantages included the existence of a national market, a small number of firms, and a set of differentiated

products. . . . There are three companies in the game. The players have the role of executives in the three competing companies. Each firm consists of one factory, located in one of the four geographical territories that comprise the total detergent market. At this factory, there are the following facilities: (1) a raw-materials warehouse, (2) production facilities that can be used to produce different mixes of product, (3) a factory warehouse for the storage of finished product, and (4) offices and facilities for new-product research and development. (pp. 105–106)

The players receive realistic and copious data in almost all areas of operations, including finance, sales, production, and marketing. They are expected to make realistic decisions based on this information. The computer processing of players' decisions, based on a programed economic model, results in a new supply of data, and the cycle repeats.

Interestingly, while most of the early games involve skills similar to those necessary for the Carnegie Tech Management game described above, some of the newer games are just as concerned with interpersonal skills such as the ability to communicate effectively. Some of these types of simulations are spin-offs from the concept of an assessment center. The term *assessment center* refers to a standardized set of simulated activities of the role of manager. The activities, which should be based on a careful needs assessment of the job, could include business games, leaderless group discussions, and so on. The original purpose of these activities was to assess individuals for management jobs under controlled testing conditions. Typically, candidates for these jobs would be assessed in groups of six or seven by a highly trained group of assessors. They might be assessed on anywhere from 10 to 15 dimensions, such as oral communication skill, organization and planning ability, and decision making. A small part of a description of an individual's performance in an assessment center is presented in Table 8.1. Even from the short summary provided of Mr. Smith's performance, it is clear that there are at least two types of organizational questions that can be asked as a result of such activities. There is an assessment question, which refers to who should be selected, and there is a development question, which refers to how persons can be trained to perform better on these job-relevant activities. Bray (1976) notes that it is now quite common for organizations to spend several days in assessment activities. Several more days are then spent in developmental activities, which include training sessions and feedback to participants. While the latter activity is more relevant to our purposes, the fact that assessment centers can be used for these multiple objectives again speaks to the complex systems nature of most organizational activities. Unfortunately, as noted by Wexley and Latham (1981), there are no published evaluation studies of the developmental learning part of assessment centers. However, there has been increasing effort in the area of using simulations as a learning technique.

One of the most carefully developed simulation efforts is known as Looking Glass, Inc. (McCall & Lombardo, 1982). Its purpose is the

TABLE 8.1   Sample of descriptions and strengths and weaknesses from a candidate in an assessment center

Smith's overall performance in the Management Development Centre (MDC) was average or below average on most exercises. He showed strengths in energy and initiative.

In the background interview, Smith was extremely open in discussing his problems and hopes in detail. He came across as a loyal, hard-working, highly motivated person who had a strong desire to do a good job, but he was weak in creativity, initiative, independence, and leadership skills. He appeared to be tenacious and have a high stress tolerance but to be weak in problem analysis. He struck the assessor as being overwhelmed by his job, where his efforts are not bearing the fruit he would like. He may well have feared for his job, given the division's performance. Delegation seemed weak, as was subordinate development. He felt the only way to train was to teach by example. Sensing poor morale, he did not know how to improve it.

Questioning in the 'research budget' fact-finding exercise was not well organized, but effective. He appeared to find decision making difficult, but once the decision was made, he stuck to his idea. Slightly nervous, he was not stressed by the resource person.

Writing seemed to be a weak area. Smith's financial presentation was hard to read and disorganized. Similar observations were made about his creative writing assignment, and his in-basket.

Strengths

Work Standards. Tried hard in every exercise; worked very hard on job; did not want to settle, personally, for less than the best. Was disappointed by own performance, as indicated by his self-evaluation.

Intelligence. Fast reader, caught on fast.

Corporate Thinking. A company man, very loyal.

Integrity. Will not compromise convictions, e.g., copy-machine discussion.

Energy. Active in all exercises.

Weaknesses

Use of Delegation. Not effective on job, average in in-basket. He reported he did a lot of work that should be done by subordinates.

Financial Analytical Ability. Below average on financial problems, e.g., missed opportunity to change product mix.

Temper. When he did not get his way in discussion, he became obstructive to leader.

Impact. Good first impression—after that, would not stand out in a crowd.

Adapted from "The Use of Assessment Centres in Management Development," by W. C. Byham. In B. Taylor and G. L. Lipitt (Eds.), *Management Development and Training Handbook*. Copyright 1975 by McGraw-Hill Book Company (UK) Limited. Adapted by permission.

development of management teams, which of course is most relevant to the questions of training addressed here. A brief description of Looking Glass follows.

> Looking Glass, Inc. is a hypothetical medium-sized glass manufacturing corporation. . . . For a simulation, Looking Glass is quite realistic. Complete with annual report, plausible financial data and a variety of glass products, the simulation creates the aura of an authentic organization. Participants are placed in an office-like setting, complete with telephones and an interoffice mail system. The positions actually filled in the simulation are the top management of the corporation, including four levels ranging from president to plant manager. . . . The company consists of three divisions whose environments vary according to the degree of change, with one division's environment being relatively placid, another turbulent, and the third a mixture of the two.
>
> Lasting six hours, the simulation is intended to be a typical day in the life of the company. It begins by placing each participant face-to-face with an in-basket full of memoranda. Together with background information common to all participants, this information, which differs

somewhat from division to division, level to level, and position to position, constitutes the stimulus. Participants spend the rest of the day responding to these interlocking sets of stimuli, acting and interacting as they choose. Contained in the collective in-baskets of the 20 participants are more than 150 different problems that participating managers might attend to. The problems vary in importance, and they also vary, realistically, in how apparent or hidden they are to the one or more individuals who ought to be concerned about them. Also true to life, the number of problems far exceeds the time available to deal with them. (Kaplan, Lombardo, & Mazique, 1983, p. 29)

The purpose of this simulation is management development, both as individual members and as members of a team. It involves capturing communication and group dynamics in a way that permits the managers to learn both by doing and by the feedback provided at the end of the exercises. While what happens during this simulation varies somewhat with each group, there are several stages.

1. *Preparing for the simulation.* This stage starts with meeting the team and assessing both their willingness and readiness to participate in the simulation. During this period, the group also tries out experiential methods and begins with low to moderate risk situations. Since simulations involve public scrutiny, it is necessary to spend time understanding group functioning, building relationships between teams and staff. This also involves feedback to individuals and to the team.

2. *The simulation.* During this stage, the group spends a complete day in the Looking Glass, Inc., simulation. The participants begin by reading a thick set of materials, including annual reports, job descriptions, and memos that they "wrote or received." As described above, the participants spend the rest of the day reacting to the 150 or so problems and running the company. They work in an office-like setting and can hold meetings, call each other on the phone, write memos, read, plan, and so on.

3. *Feedback.* Debriefing sessions involving participants and consultants are designed to provide both individual and group learning. Kaplan et al. (1983) describe the performance of one group of 17 managers who came from the same organization. At the time of their attendance at the simulation, their organization, which was a public agency in a midwestern city, was besieged by problems. At the end of this group's participation, the members of the team and the consultants reached the following conclusions about themselves as a team.

(a) Most of the team members spent their time sitting alone at their desk doing paperwork in a cloud of cigarette smoke. This was contrasted with other groups who usually spent their time tracking down information and fighting fires.

(b) The group wrote over 150 memos, which was about twice as many a group that size usually wrote.

(c) In general, the managers did not choose well between high and low priority items.

As a result of these and other, similar patterns, the team reached conclusions about how their individual behavior was hurting their performance as a team. They also discussed their simulated performance and its relation to their on-the-job performance.

4. *Application.* After the simulation and debriefing, the procedure calls for the application of what the team has learned. One way this is done in this

program is to resolve one of the problems identified by the team. This is known as a breakthrough project. The consultants try to help the group choose a project which is both important and resolvable with the belief that, if the breakthrough occurs, the group will achieve both a tangible result and a real boost in self-confidence.

The advantages and disadvantages of business games such as those described above are similar to those expressed for other types of simulation efforts. Thus, experience is necessary in order to have the opportunity to develop the capabilities to perform. Yet, most firms cannot afford the trial-and-error learning period necessary for the development of such skills. Simulations and business games are seen as the solution to this problem. The games provide practice in decision making, interaction among various components of the firm, and interaction among participants. Similar to machine simulations, business games permit control over time. Thus, numerous samples can be presented in a short period of time. Furthermore, most games place a premium on planning that requires the participants to consider objectives, long-term plans, and overall point of view. The feedback provisions and dynamic quality of the play are seen as being intrinsically motivating to the participant.

Some writers (Bass & Vaughan, 1966) warn that the dynamic quality of the environment makes it difficult to use effectively as a teaching tool. In some games, the participants may become so involved in the excitement and in the competitive aspects of the game that they lose sight of the principles and evaluations of consequences that are its most important aspects. Instead, the participants tend to become more concerned with beating the system and one another. Clearly, this is a serious danger unless the game involves careful feedback sessions. Also, of course, it depends on the design of the game, which should itself be based on careful needs assessment. If the purpose of the game based upon the needs assessment is to provide a competitive atmosphere, then it should be designed that way. The Looking Glass, Inc., simulation obviously has goals related to team development, and thus the game is designed to foster cooperation. There is no reason for a business game to have competitiveness as an inherent aspect, unless that is its purpose. Another issue relates to the fidelity of the simulation. Most business games are not based on a real business enterprise, but (ideally) on psychological fidelity principles. Of course, this is simply another way of saying that the design of the simulation must be based upon the same careful needs assessment procedures as any other training technique. The problem here is that the simulation is designed to be relevant to the large number of organizations who send participants. Very complex needs assessments are required to prevent particular solutions rather than basic principles and concepts being carried away from the game and inappropriately applied in the real organizational setting. As a step in this direction, McCall and Lombardo (1979) have analyzed Looking Glass by directly observing the participants. The research tracked various activities, including amount of paperwork, telephone time, time in meetings, and the like, and found it to be very similar to the composition of tasks in managers' jobs. In a sense, that type of analysis provides information about physical fidelity. Of course, the most interesting questions are whether psychological fidelity is produced and whether learned behavior actually transfers to the job. The issue of evaluation has a long but not very productive history.

Shortly after business games first became popular, McGehee and Thayer (1961) stated that there was no research on the relative effectiveness of games as compared to other techniques. There also were no data on the utility of various approaches, like competition or no competition and complex or simple games. These authors concluded: "For all we know, at this time, there may be a negative or zero relationship between the kinds of behavior developed by business game training and the kinds of behavior required to operate a behavior successfully" (p. 223). Since these authors stated their opinion, other investigators have expressed concern about the cost of gaming (for example, Raia, 1966) and the continued lack of descriptive and statistical information. In 1971, J. P. Campbell concluded, "There have been almost no recent attempts to study the development of problem-solving and decision-making skills, even though a number of strategies exist for developing these skills" (p. 585). At this point in time, the 1961 and 1971 comments of McGehee and Thayer and J. P. Campbell continue to provide an accurate description of the vast number of business games. One hopeful sign is the careful developmental work involving Looking Glass, Inc. Kaplan et al. describe an evaluation effort involving the 17 managers from the public agency described above. In that case, the authors presented process data describing the qualitative changes the observers had noted during the simulation. They also collected questionnaire data from the managers, who self-reported their responses on a variety of issues, including trust within management team, their own management effectiveness, and so on. Those data are presented in Table 8.2. As shown in the table, these data were collected before the simulation, three weeks after the simulation, and six months after the simulation. As can be seen, there were a large number of reported positive changes from before the simulation to the three-week period following the program. This was also supported by the qualitative reports. Six months afterwards, the reports were still positive as compared to before the program, but there was a falling-off of reported effects from the data collected at three weeks. The qualitative data also supported these findings and identified some of the issues. Three months after the simulation, the company laid off one-third of its 180 employees, and the insecurity created among the managers (none of whom were actually laid off) was quite high. Also, there was no one in the organization responsible for making changes. One comment was "No one is carrying

TABLE 8.2   Questionnaire results before, three weeks after, and six months after Looking Glass*

Variable	Before	Three Weeks	Six Months	Significant Effect Before—Six Months	Significant Effect Three/Six Weeks/Months
	(n = 15)	(n = 14)			
Management Effectiveness	3.12	4.17	4.00	Yes	No
Trust (within the management team)	2.85	4.43	3.50	No	Yes
Cooperation (among different functions)	3.00	4.30	3.79	Yes	Yes
Agreement on Goals	3.47	4.03	4.00	Yes	No
Belief that CES Can Improve	3.35	4.53	4.21	Yes	No
Competence of Managers	3.47	4.53	4.11	Yes	No
Absence of Stress	2.47	2.60	2.25	No	No
Agency Held Accountable	2.44	3.60	3.36	Yes	No

*The scale ranged from 1 (strongly disagree) to 6 (strongly agree).

Adapted from "A Mirror for Managers: Using Simulation to Develop Management Teams," by R. E. Kaplan, M. M. Lombardo, and M. S. Mazique. Copyright 1983 by the Center for Creative Leadership, Greensboro, N. C.

the ball for change, and old habits are returning" (p. 26). On the other hand, as shown in the data, improvements were still noted when six-months scores were compared to pre-simulation scores. Some comments supporting those differences were "The changes are very much alive" and "There's a lot more direct communication, a lot less memos, and a lot more interaction among staff at all levels. We're not as concerned about turf as we used to be" (p. 26). Clearly, there are other data that could be collected to strengthen this type of evaluation, including on-the-job observations by other employees of the changes in the managers' behaviors. However, the efforts at examining the effects of this simulation should be praised and encouraged. Unfortunately, efforts to examine business games are few and far between, and efficacy of the technique is typically based on the proponents' hard-sell verbal approach. Investigations of other media, like PI and audiovisuals, have not always produced definitive results. However, the empirical research already accomplished on PI, CAI, and audiovisuals has resulted in an appreciation for their advantages and limitations that does not exist for business games.

Case Study

The conditions of an organization are sometimes simulated by a case study. The trainee receives a written report that describes an organizational problem. He or she is then expected to analyze the problem and offer solutions based on a number of factors, including people, environment, rules, and physical parameters. The trainee usually studies the case individually and prepares solutions. He or she then meets with a group that discusses the various solutions and tries to identify the basic principles underlining the case. The group procedure is designed to promote feedback and allow the individual to learn by observing others developing their respective solutions. It is generally recognized that there is no correct solution; the trainees are thus encouraged to be flexible.

Critics of this approach feel that the method is not useful for learning general principles and that the lack of guided instruction that generally characterizes the group process is detrimental. The proponents of this technique feel that the self-discovery occurring during these sessions is likely to lead to longer retention of the principles generated by the trainees. (For a discussion of these views, see Campbell et al., 1970.) As discussed earlier, Raia (1966) found that business games, as compared to the case-study method, led to superior performance on several criterion measures, including standardized case studies and the final exam. Moore (1967) also examined business games and case studies. Essentially, he found no differences between the two groups on a series of criterion measures. However, he suggests that one disadvantage of business games was the preoccupation of the participants with beating one another instead of learning the basic concepts. Thus, he suggests that the case study, with the more static setting, provides an atmosphere more conducive to the examination of general principles and issues.

The validity of Moore's point depends on the ability of the participants or the leaders (if they are included) to evaluate and reinforce one another. Participants in the case-study technique can become entangled in the large amount of information presented and never find the basic issue; the technique cannot work unless the group focuses on the issues. Also, the principles learned from the case study should be applied to everyday situations on the job to avoid the danger of the trainees becoming so engrossed in the case study that they never see the relevance of the principles to everyday life.

A more interesting criticism of the case-study method is provided by Argyris (1980). He believes that there are two types of learning. First, there is the form that involves the detection and correction of error. An example of this type of learning, known as single-loop, is a thermostat, which detects when a room is too hot or cold and corrects that situation. Argyris describes the second form of learning as double-loop; this involves changes and corrections in underlying policies, assumptions, and goals. In this case, the thermostat would be a double-loop learner if it questioned why it was set at 65 degrees or even why it was measuring heat. Argyris's concern is that the case method may unintentionally undermine double-loop learning. Specifically, this view about case studies stems from his observations and tape-recordings of a three-week management development program for a multibillion-dollar company, which used the case-study method as its major form of instruction. He observed that the trainers dominated classroom activities, designed procedures to save face for trainers and participants, and generally designed the atmosphere to avoid confrontation and open discussion of new ideas. Argyris also noted that the trainers espoused views such as "People should expose their ideas, maps, strategies for solving the problem; yet faculty members do not expose many of their ideas and strategies about the case" (p. 295). He also felt that there was little time or effort spent on ensuring that learning transferred back to the organization environment, a criticism which is common to most training programs. Argyris argues that trainers should be taught to be less dominating, that open discussion should be encouraged, and that cases from their own organization should be used to enhance transfer.

Argyris's view concerning transfer is a continual issue and is one of the reasons that evaluation is so important. His views concerning single- and double-loop learning remain controversial. He strongly believes in experiential learning and group confrontation as a way of unfreezing old values. Some of these issues will be discussed again in the section on sensitivity training. However, in part, the answer is very dependent on the needs assessment and the training objectives. There may be instances where single-loop learning is the goal. However, even if it is not, the training environment must still be designed to achieve the appropriate goals and must be analyzed to determine if the goals are realized. Actual studies demonstrating both the need for and the achievement of double-loop learning remain an important agenda item.

Role-Playing

In this technique, trainees act out simulated roles. Role-playing is used primarily for analyses of interpersonal problems and attitude change and development of human-relations skills (Bass & Vaughan, 1966). This technique gives the trainees an opportunity to experience and explore solutions to a variety of on-the-job problems. The success of the method depends on the participants' willingness to actually adopt the roles and to react as if they were really in the work environment (Campbell et al., 1970). There are many different role-playing techniques. In one variation, trainees who disagree are asked to *reverse roles* (Speroff, 1954). This procedure is intended to make a person more aware of the other's feelings and attitudes. In another variation, called *multiple role-playing* (Maier & Zerfoss, 1952), a large number of participants are actively involved in the role-playing process. The entire group is divided into teams that each role-play the situation. At the end of a specified period of time, the participants reunite and discuss the results achieved by each separate group.

One of the more recent and unique uses of role-playing is called self-confrontation. In this procedure, the trainee is shown a videotape replay of his entire performance. While viewing the tape, he is given a verbal critique of his performance by the trainer. One set of studies exploring this technique was prompted by the image of American advisers and officers overseas (King, 1966). Researchers feel that a lecture on how to behave in a foreign country is equivalent to a lecture on how to fly an airplane. With the self-confrontation technique, the trainee is first given information about the culture and the desired general behavior. Then, the learner plays the role of an adviser in a foreign country. Typically, the trainee interacts with a person from the foreign country who is a confederate of the trainer. After role-playing, the trainee views the tape and is given a verbal critique of the performance by the trainer. Several studies have indicated that the videotape and feedback session does result in changes in behavior. In one study (King, 1966), the subjects played the role of a United States Air Force captain who was required to report to a foreign counterpart. They were required to reprimand the counterpart on one aspect of the behavior and to commend another aspect. This conversation was to take place in a highly prescribed way, consistent with the culture and containing 57 different behaviors, ranging from gross motor movements to subtle voice cues. The results of this study indicated that trainees who participated in self-confrontation performed consistently better than another group of subjects who had spent an equivalent amount of time studying the behavioral requirements outlined in the training manual. Retention tests given two weeks later indicated that the self-confrontation group maintained their skills. While self-confrontation techniques can be applied as a feedback supplement for a variety of training techniques, a number of studies (Haines & Eachus, 1965; Eachus & King, 1966) have demonstrated that it is especially useful with interaction procedures like role-playing. It has already been mentioned that the key to techniques like role-playing and business games is the feedback and critique session. The self-confrontation method provides accurate and detailed feedback, and, when it is combined with sensitive analyses of performance, it appears to be a very useful procedure.

In a study which provides an important illustration of the unintended consequences of interventions, Teahan (1976) reported on a study that investigated role-playing effects on the attitudes of police officers. As part of their academy training, both white and black police officers role-played sensitive racial situations. Attitude-change scores indicated that black officers became more positive in their views of whites. However, white officers, while becoming more sensitized to the presence of black–white problems, became more prejudiced toward blacks. The author's interpretation of these results indicated that white officers had the perception that the program was intended for the benefit of blacks rather than whites. Independent of the interpretation, the results underscore the importance of examining the outcomes of our interventions rather than simply assuming that all is well.

Besides the few studies mentioned above, there are relatively few research efforts available on role-playing. Interestingly, one reason is that role-playing by itself does not seem to be used very frequently. Rather, it has become part of other techniques such as behavioral role-modeling, which will be discussed next. Early concerns about the technique were that participants might find the role-playing childish (Liveright, 1951) and that they might have a tendency to put more emphasis on acting than on problem solving (Bass & Vaughan, 1966). If the emphasis is on the acting of roles, there is a possibility that participants will behave in a manner that is socially acceptable to other members of the group but not reflective of their actual feelings. In this case, the role-playing may not lead to any behavioral changes outside the role-playing environment (Ingersoll, 1973). In the traditional format, the feedback is controlled by the participants in the role-playing setting. If the feedback focuses more on the acting ability of the participant than on the solution to problems, the entire learning process can be circumvented. Again, the leader becomes the key element to a successful training session. Later techniques such as behavioral role-modeling have focused on specific problem situations in the work environment in order to avoid such difficulties.

Behavioral Role-Modeling

In the past decade, the technique that has generated the most excitement has been behavioral role-modeling. This approach is based on Bandura's (1969, 1977) social-learning theory, which stresses the use of observing, modeling, and vicarious reinforcement as steps for modifying human behavior. This theory as an approach to learning is presented in Chapter 4 (p. 74). As described, Bandura's theory focuses on the acquisition of novel responses through observational learning. He notes that evidence for this form of imitative learning consists of persons exhibiting novel responses which have been demonstrated by observers and which are not likely to have occurred without such a demonstration. Also, the responses of the observers should be quite similar in form to the response of the model. Bandura obtained these types of effects in a number of studies, many of which focused on children demonstrating highly novel responses. As a result, Bandura (1969) suggested a number of subprocesses which are important parts of the observation learning process. They are:

> 1. *The attentional processes which relate to the ability of the observer to attend to and differentiate between cues.* Bandura notes that some of the factors which can influence these attentional characteristics include variables like model characteristics and the ease with which modeling conditions can be discriminated. As noted by Wexley and Latham (1981), these factors include evidence that modeling increases when the model is perceived as relevant in terms of variables such as age and sex. If the observers see very little similarity between themselves and the model, they are less likely to imitate the behavior. Also, greater modeling will occur when the behavior is demonstrated in a clear and detailed manner.
>
> 2. *The retentional processes which have been characterized as the capability required to remember the stimuli over a period of time.* Bandura points out that this factor is likely to be affected positively by covert and overt rehearsal and negatively by factors like interference from previously learned material.
>
> 3. *The motor reproduction processes which refer to the physical abilities needed to acquire and perform the behavior portrayed by the model.* Most of the constraints related to this process refer to physical abilities. Thus, without considerable amounts of practice and skill, it might not be possible for an observer to imitate the behavior of a skilled craftsperson such as a carpenter even if the behavior had been modeled appropriately.
>
> 4. *The incentive and motivational processes which have been defined as the reinforcement conditions that exist at the time the observed behavior is performed.* Bandura's theory argues that reinforcement is not a necessary condition for the learning of models' responses, but he does note that it is important in getting persons to actually exhibit the behavior which has been learned. There is also evidence that observers are more likely to retain those modeling sequences which are seen as likely to have some utility at a later time.

In 1974, A. P. Goldstein and Sorcher published a book called *Changing Supervisory Behavior,* which adapted many of the principles of Bandura's social-learning theory into a training approach, their goal being to improve interpersonal and related supervisory skills. These authors criticize other approaches to training managers as focusing on attitudes and not on the behaviors necessary to carry out their work. Thus, they argue that training programs typically tell managers that it is important to be good communicators, with which almost everyone agrees (and probably knows before coming into the training program). However, the programs do not teach the manager how to become a good communicator or motivator or whatever. Also, as described by Moses (1978), most training programs do not appear to have any use-fulness for later job performance. Thus, the adult learner tends to be turned off by the artificial atmosphere of a training program that doesn't seem to be job-relevant. In contrast, the A. P. Goldstein and Sorcher approach consists of

> providing the trainee with numerous, vivid, detailed displays (on film, videotape or live) of a manager–actor (the model) performing the specific behaviors and skills we wish the viewer to learn (i.e., modeling); giving the trainee considerable guidance in and opportunity and encouragement for behaviorally rehearsing or practicing the behaviors he has seen the model perform (i.e., role playing); providing him with positive feedback, approval or reward as his role playing enactments increasingly approximate the behavior of the model (i.e., social reinforcement). . . . (A. P. Goldstein and Sorcher, 1974, p. 37)[1]

A. P. Goldstein and Sorcher's approach stimulated the imaginations of a number of persons and resulted in a symposium (Kraut, 1976) reporting on a number of preliminary studies that showed promise for the vitality of the approach. As often happens, practitioners were excited by the approach and started using the method, without much empirical evidence for evaluating the technique or for determining the important characteristics of the technique and under what conditions it is effective. As a result, McGehee and Tullar (1978) wrote an article criticizing the growing support for these new methods before further empirical developments had been reported.

While the number of studies reported since their critique has not been great, several carefully carried-out empirical research efforts have been reported. One of the best of these studies was reported by Latham and Saari (1979). Their study involved 100 first-line supervisors who would all receive training. Since it was not possible to train everyone at once, they randomly selected 40 supervisors and randomly assigned 20 of them to a training condition and the other 20 to a control group. The control group knew that they would be trained and were actually

---

[1] Scattered quotations from *Changing Supervisor Behavior,* by A. P. Goldstein and M. Sorcher. Copyright 1974 by Pergamon Press, Inc. This and all other quotes from the same source are reprinted by permission.

unaware of the fact that they were serving as a control. In this clever design, they simply assumed that for logistical reasons it was not possible to train everyone and thus they would be trained afterwards. (As a matter of fact, they were trained at a later time, but in the interim they served as a control condition for the study.)

The training program was based upon nine training modules developed by Sorcher on the basis of the work by A. P. Goldstein and Sorcher (1974). These modules were designed to increase the effectiveness of first-line supervisors in working with their employees. The topics included orienting a new employee, motivating a poor performer, correcting poor work habits, handling a complaining employee, overcoming resistance to change, and the like.

Each of Latham and Saari's training sessions for the topics followed the same procedure:

> (a) introduction of the topic by two trainers (attentional processes); (b) presentation of a film that depicts a supervisor model effectively handling a situation by following a set of 3 to 6 learning points that were shown in the film immediately before and after the model was presented (retention processes); (c) group discussion of the effectiveness of the model in demonstrating the desired behaviors (retention processes); (d) practice in role playing the desired behaviors in front of the entire class (retention processes; motor reproduction processes); and (e) feedback from the class on the effectiveness of each trainee in demonstrating the desired behaviors (motivational processes). (p. 241)

During the practice sessions involving role-playing, one of the trainees took the role of the supervisor and another trainee had the role of the employee. The trainees did not use prepared scripts. Instead, they were asked to recreate an incident that had occurred during the past year which was relevant to the training topic for that week. During the session, the learning points which were emphasized in the film were posted so that the person playing the role of supervisor could make use of the principles. An example of the learning points for one of the programs—handling a complaining employee—consisted of the following:

> (a) Avoid responding with hostility or defensiveness, (b) ask for and listen openly to the employee's complaint; (c) restate the complaint for thorough understanding; (d) recognize and acknowledge his or her viewpoint; (e) if necessary, state your position nondefensively; and (f) set a specific date for a follow-up meeting. (p. 241)

Trainees playing the role of supervisor had no idea what the employee role-player would do. He simply responded as best he could using the learning points and information gained from watching the role models in the film carry out the learning points. Two trainers were present at all sessions, with the first trainer supervising the role-playing practice. The second trainer worked with the group to teach them how to provide constructive feedback that would enhance the confidence and self-esteem of the person receiving feedback. At the end of each session, the trainees received printed versions of the learning points and were sent back to their jobs with instructions to use the supervisory skills they had gained. The purpose here was to facilitate transfer of the learned skills back to the job. At the next session, the trainees reported their experiences. In situations where the supervisors had difficulty, they were asked to report it back to the class. Then they role-played the situation, with the class providing feedback on desired behaviors and the supervisor again practicing the appropriate behaviors. Latham and Saari also noted that some of the learning points for some of the programs did not fit their specific situation, and so the points were revised by the trainees and the investigators. Latham and Saari also provided training for the supervisors of the trainees to ensure that the trainees would be rewarded for their on-the-job behavior.

In addition to carefully designing a training program, Latham and Saari evaluated the results using reaction measures, learning measures, behavioral measures, and job-performance measures.

1. The reaction measures were collected immediately after training and consisted of information on items such as whether the training was helpful for performing the job better and for interacting more effectively with employees. These indicators came out quite positively. A follow-up 8 months after training had been completed also indicated that there was no difference in response immediately after training and eight months later.

2. The learning measure consisted of a situational test with 85 questions developed from critical incidents found in the job analysis. An example of one situational question is:

You have spoken with this worker several times about the fact that he doesn't keep his long hair confined under his hard hat. This constitutes a safety violation. You are walking through the plant and you just noticed that he again does not have his hair properly confined. What would you do? (p. 243)

The trainees were asked how they would handle each of the situations. A scoring response was developed based upon the training program for each of the situations before the test was administered to the trainees. The test also contained items for behavioral situations that were not covered in the training program so that trainees had to generalize what they had learned to new situations. The data indicated that the mean score for the training group was significantly higher than the score for the control group.

3. The behavioral measure consisted of trainees rating the tape-recorded behaviors of supervisors resolving supervisor–employee problems. These were based upon scripts that had been developed to reflect job situations and use of learning points as presented in the training programs. None of the situations presented had previously been described during training, nor had they been shown in the training films. The researchers again found that the performance of the trained group was superior to that of the control group even when some of the controls were given the learning points (but not the rest of training) to use in making their ratings.

4. The job-performance measure consisted of ratings by the supervisors of the trainees on rating scales based upon a job analysis which produced critical

incidents depicting effective and ineffective supervisory behavior. The investigators found no difference between pre-measures of the training and control group. Posttest measures indicated that the training group performed significantly better than the control group.

As a final step, Latham and Saari trained the control group. After their training was complete, all the differences between the control group which was now trained and the original training group on all four measures disappeared. This kind of careful implementation and evaluation in a real work environment should serve as a model for what can be accomplished with some thoughtful effort.

Since the Latham and Saari study, there have been a number of research efforts demonstrating the effects that a well-designed program can have on performance. An even more positive sign is that various researchers have begun to examine aspects of the technique to determine what contributes to performance. For example, Decker (1980) has examined a number of components, including the effects of symbolic rehearsal upon performance. In order to induce symbolic rehearsal, he asked the trainees to close their eyes and picture themselves actually performing the modeled behavior. This was done while the trainees used a number of descriptive codes which provided a summary of the model's key behaviors. He found that symbolic rehearsal, with or without the use of codes, enhanced reproduction of modeled events and generalization of the observational learning to other problem situations for which training had not been provided. Through research efforts such as those of Latham and Saari and Decker, it is possible that behavior role-modeling will not only be used but will actually be understood.

LABORATORY TRAINING

Laboratory training refers to a variety of techniques, such as T-group training, encounter groups, L- (for learning) groups, and action groups. This approach originated in an intergroup community-relations workshop held in Connecticut in 1946. The learning results of this group-interaction meeting stimulated the participants to organize the first formal sensitivity-training session in Bethel, Maine, during the summer of 1947. From this session, a group known as the National Training Laboratories (NTL) was formed to promote and investigate sensitivity training. This group is still active today presenting programs which vary in length from a few days to several weeks, on topics such as power in organizations, supervisory relationships, and personnel development for executives and managers. In addition to NTL, there are hundreds of other organizations sponsoring similar laboratory training. The large number of laboratory techniques vary not only in length but in focus (from personal growth to the building of teams), qualifications of the trainer (from individuals trained at NTL to self-designated leaders), and type of participants (strangers, members of the same firm, married couples) (Buchanan, 1971).

Characteristics and Objectives of Laboratory Training

Laboratory training is characterized by face-to-face interaction among individuals in a group. In addition, Blumberg and Golembiewski (1976) describe the elements of laboratory groups as follows:

> 1. There is a concern for the here-and-now. The basis for this is the belief that the data which will most help persons learn about themselves are those which are most available.
> 2. Feelings are both appropriate and important material for analysis. This is based on a belief that feelings must be part of the learning process.
> 3. There is frequent feedback and analysis, including self-disclosure involving here-and-now events that occur during group interactions. This is considered an important part of the development of self-awareness based on reality testing.
> 4. It is important to have a climate that permits individual choice. That is, it is the choice of the individuals who receive feedback whether or not they will do anything to change.

The setting is designed to foster psychological safety where members are away from their organizations and free to voice their opinions. Some of the remarks may cause hard feelings, but Argyris (1964) feels that any pain caused must be viewed from the perspective of personal growth. In order to be effective, the experience should be gut-level and emotional. Anxiety is viewed as useful in creating an atmosphere in which individuals examine interpersonal and group problems in order to gain a deeper understanding of their own reactions toward colleagues and supervisors (Burke & Bennis, 1961).

As an example of the processes that occur during a laboratory session, we can examine Argyris's (1967) sample of a group experience. The president and nine vice-presidents of a large corporation attended a retreat for a week to discuss their problems. The seminar leader defined the objectives of the educational experience and prompted the group to begin. There was a long period of silence that was eventually broken by individuals who asked what was going on and who was in charge of the meeting. Then one participant began:

> "You know, there's something funny going on here."
> "What's funny about it?"
> "Well, up until a few minutes ago we trusted this man enough that all of us were willing to leave the company for a week. Now we dislike him. Why? He hasn't done anything."
> "That's right. . . . He's the leader and he ought to lead."
> " . . . I honestly feel uncomfortable and somewhat fearful. . . . "
> "That's interesting that you mention fear, because I think that we run the company by fear."

The president turned slightly red and became annoyed: "I don't think that we run this company by fear, and I don't think you should have said that."

A loud silence followed. The vice-president thought . . . and said, "I still think we run this company by fear, and I agree with you. I should not have said it."

The group laughed, and the tension was broken. (p. 66)

At this point, the president apologized for his remarks and indicated a desire to achieve an open and trusting relationship. He went on to say that he always had an open door and that it wasn't easy to hear his company described as being run by fear. The group members discussed how they judged the openness of a person and how they had all inhibited one another.

These types of educational experiences are designed to achieve a variety of different goals. The following, summarized by Campbell et al. (1970), lists most of the objectives:

1. To give the trainee an understanding of how and why he acts toward other people as he does and of the way in which he affects them.
2. To provide some insights into why other people act the way they do.
3. To teach the participants how to "listen"—that is, to actually hear what other people are saying rather than concentrating on a reply.
4. To provide insights concerning how groups operate and what processes groups go through under certain conditions.
5. To foster an increased tolerance and understanding of the behavior of others.
6. To provide a setting in which an individual can try out new ways of interacting with people and receive feedback as to how these new ways affect them. (p. 239)

The Controversy over Laboratory Training

It is clear that laboratory training often utilizes anxiety-provoking situations as stimulants for learning experience. Many observers (for example, House, 1967; Odiorne, 1963) feel that these experiences are disruptive to the health of some of the participants. Critics also feel that it is one matter to express true feelings in the psychological safety of the laboratory but quite another to face fellow participants back on the job. These views are buttressed by reports that some individuals are hurt by the emotional buffeting experienced during the session and that more than one person has left the group feeling disturbed. For example, Klaw (1965) reports that some people return from these sessions liking themselves less and feeling unsure what to do about it. His survey of 100 graduates from Western Training Laboratories revealed that one in ten graduates felt that way. The views of these critics are expressed by Kirchner (1965):

Do we really want to rip off the "executive mask," which hides from the individual his true feelings, desires, and knowledge of self? Most people have taken many years to build up this "mask" or to build up their psychological defenses. While it can be very enlightening to find out that nobody loves you and that some people think that you have undesirable traits, this can also be a very shocking experience to individuals and not necessarily a beneficial one. (p. 212)

These early reports continue to appear, but they are being countered by a number of investigators who maintain that figures citing high rates of casualities are misleading. Cooper (1975) reports on a number of studies where the rates of problems are low. Cooper also notes that few studies control for the possibility that reported problems may be reflecting increases in willingness to self-disclose rather than increases in disturbances. However, Cooper does agree that disturbances are more likely to occur when individuals are randomly assigned to groups without prescreening to assess an individual's capability for participating in the give and take of laboratory sessions. Also, some of Cooper's research (1977) indicates that both positive and negative effects in groups are strongly related to the trainer's behavior and personality, with trainers who are relaxed, self-sufficient, and tranquil producing the most positive benefits. Given the potential for problems, several suggestions made by Jaffe and Scherl (1969) seem very sensible. They are:

1. Participation should be completely and truly voluntary.

2. Participation should be based upon informed consent with complete information about purposes and goals provided for each person. For example, potential participants should be warned that these groups are not intended for therapy or for persons who feel a need for treatment.

3. Participants should be screened, preferably through an interview procedure.

4. Participants should be advised about what types of behavior are acceptable during the group session.

5. Follow-up help for all persons should be available to deal with any issues stemming from group termination.

It is important to note that these suggestions result in some evaluation difficulties. If the participants are all volunteers, there will be limited generalizability because of the threat to external validity resulting from possible interactions for the selection of subjects and the experimental treatment. However, until the effects of laboratory training are more certain, it is safer to accept limited generalizability. Also, studies which compare the characteristics of persons who do or do not volunteer to participate in laboratory-training exercises are needed for understanding the volunteer effect in this situation.

Some observers believe that controversies about the use of laboratory training are related to the lack of evaluative studies. At best this is only partially true. While there have been questions regarding methodology and doubts about what is transferred to the job, there are more studies of laboratory training than of any other managerial-development technique. Yet other training procedures have not suffered the criticism leveled at laboratory training. The controversy is really related to concerns about the psychological safety of individuals who participate in T-group experiences.

Evaluation of Laboratory Training

Early in the history of the application of laboratory training, Dunnette and Campbell (1968) criticized the work in this area for its failure to meet basic scientific standards. Due to concerns over both ethical issues and the welfare of individual participants, their comments attracted considerably more attention than most remarks about poor evaluation, although the standards they stressed were certainly quite reasonable. They included pre- and postmeasurement, a control group, and some procedures to control for interaction between the pretest and behavior in the training program. This latter point is often referred to as the *reactive effect* of pretesting and results from increased sensitivity to the training program caused by exposure to the pretest. This effect is a special concern in human relations–type training in which the participants' expected changes do not concern complex motor skills but rather attitudes and social skills. Several techniques can be used to provide some estimate of the presensitization effect. For example, a group can be given a pretest with feedback and then a posttest after an intervening period that does not include training. Any changes in the scores provide an estimate of the sensitization effect, although there is also the possible contaminant resulting from specific events that occur between pre- and posttesting. A second procedure can have one group undergo training and the posttest without even taking the pretest. It is then possible to compare those scores to scores of the group that participated in the pretest, training, and posttest. These control procedures are not especially demanding, but, as we have already noted in our discussion of other training techniques, they are not often adopted.

At the time that Dunnette and Campbell (1968) presented their criticism, there were virtually no studies that even employed pre- and postmeasurement and a control group. While it is not possible to be sure why, a large number of studies were conducted in the years following the criticism. In an excellent review, Smith (1975) found 95 studies which met the following criteria:

1. The measures were administered pre- and posttraining.
2. There was a control group that did not receive training.
3. Training lasted at least 20 hours.
4. Training was done in small groups and involved the examination of the interpersonal relations of those persons in training with one another.
5. Groups included persons not undergoing psychotherapy.

The studies included were not limited to management training but also included students in schools, counseling center groups, business school projects, and the like. Table 8.3 summarizes the results of these studies on seven different types of measures. As can be seen, about three-quarters of the studies detected some changes immediately following training that were not found in the control group. Among studies that examined follow-up data at least one month after training, the effect rate dropped to about two-thirds of the studies. However, it is not always easy to evaluate the changes which have been found. For example, when observers are being used from the everyday setting, they tend to know who has and has not been trained, and thus they are not impartial observers. These are, of course, the problems of doing research in field settings. Interestingly, Smith in his review examined the more rigorously-designed studies and did not find any changes in the pattern of results.

One concern expressed by Dunnette and Campbell is that while training may produce observable changes, the utility of these changes for the individual and the organization remains in question. As an example of this issue, Underwood (1965), describing changes found for his training groups, noted that 15 incidents indicated increased supervisory effectiveness, while seven indicated decreased effectiveness. He pointed out that the decreased effectiveness changes revealed a heavy emotional loading. He speculated that "these subjects were venting emotion to a greater degree than usual, and to the observers, operating in a culture which devalues such expression, this behavior yielded a negative evaluation" (p. 40). Whether such changes are acceptable is dependent on the organization's objectives. At the present stage of development, it appears that laboratory training has the potential to modify the behavior of at least some of the participants. It would be very interesting to learn if there are particular characteristics of individuals that make them more amenable to change, but that is a research issue that remains to be explored. In any case, each organization and individual must explore the potential changes. They must then decide whether to participate based on their own personal and organizational objectives. At least there is a growing research base to help in making those choices.

ACHIEVEMENT MOTIVATION TRAINING

A number of leadership training approaches have been developed based on theoretical models of the leadership process. Most of these approaches are at best characterized by efforts concerning theory and conceptual development but include virtually no empirical research which would permit tests and modification of the theory. Two of these approaches have provided the basis for some empirical efforts. They are achievement motivation training, which is discussed in this section, and leader match training, which is discussed in the following section.

TABLE 8.3   Changes found with different criterion measures

Types of measure	*Changes immediately after training*			*Changes at follow-up*		
	Intended effects found	*Total N*	*Percent successful*	*Intended effects found*	*Total N*	*Percent successful*
Global self-concept	17	28	61	2	6	33
Self as the locus of causality	10	17	59	1	3	33
Prejudice and open mindedness	10	20	50	2	5	40
Orientation toward participative behaviors	14	22	64	2	9	22
Other aspects of personality	9	19	47	2	5	40
Perception of other	5	13	38	1	2	50
Others' perception of trainees	18	22	81	2	4	50
Organizational behavior	10	13	77	10	11	90
Total sample	78	100	78	21	81	68

McClelland (1976) has been studying the idea of need for achievement as a construct for over 25 years. He has symbolized the term "nAch" and defines it as the urge to improve or a desire to excel. McClelland and his associates (McClelland & Winter, 1971) have identified individuals who have high nAch as persons who have a drive to persist in attaining goals and who seek challenging tasks and responsibility. However, these researchers also estimate that only 10% of the population is high in nAch. On the other hand, they have identified situations where high nAch is particularly important for success. One such situation is the small business organization. As McClelland (1978) states,

> It was concluded on the basis of evidence, that entrepreneurs needed high n Achievement; therefore they were taught to think, talk and act like a person with high n Achievement as that behavior has been worked out by years of empirical research in the laboratory and in the field. (p. 205)

The training program (McClelland & Winter, 1971) consists of a variety of training materials, including business games, paper-and-pencil exercises, outside readings, and tests. However, the researchers organize their description of the program under four main headings.

1. *The Achievement Syndrome.* The purpose of this part of the training program is to teach participants how to both recognize achievement fantasies and then produce those fantasies themselves. They start by taking the Thematic Apperception Test, which requires that they write imaginative stories about a series of pictures. The trainees are then taught how to code what they have written according to a standardized scoring system for identifying nAch. That is, they learn when a statement in their story refers to "doing better" or competing with a standard of excellence. They are taught the difference between the desire to accomplish something, the act required to accomplish it, and blocks to accomplishment which can either be personal or in the environment. Then the participants are taught to rewrite the stories so that they can achieve the maximum points for need achievement. The purpose of this part of the training program is to form the associative network so that they begin to know what achievement is and how to think along those lines.

During the next phase of the achievement-syndrome part of the training program, the participant is taught to tie the new cognitions to action. In this phase, they are taught how high nAch persons behave. For example, they are taught that high nAch persons like to take personal responsibility for the performance necessary to achieve a goal. These various action patterns are taught partially through involvement in business games where they have the opportunity to both practice these actions and observe others performing the actions. The final part of this stage of training is the use of cases similar to those discussed earlier in this chapter. The purpose of this part of the training program is to illustrate how nAch thoughts and actions can be displayed in everyday business life. After the cases have been discussed, participants are asked to bring in their own problems from their business environment for analysis in terms of the achievement syndrome.

2. *Self-Study.* The authors note that up to this point the goal of the training program is to teach participants what nAch is and how it influences behavior. In this next section of training, the participants are asked to confront

the ways in which need achievement relates to their own lives, careers, goals, and values. All of this is explained through the use of outside readings, lectures, group discussions, and films. The participants now decide whether they want to become that type of person, what this all means to them in terms of their self-image, and how it will affect them in their job and life. In this part of the program, an analysis is conducted using children's stories, myths, and customs to identify conflicts and issues between value systems and the achievement syndrome.

3. *Goal Setting.* The authors note that many persons arrive with rather vague hopes and expectations as to what they will achieve in the course. The purpose of the training during this phase now shifts toward more precisely defining the goals for each participant and determining ways that each participant can measure his or her progress toward these goals. Toward the end of the course, each participant is asked to fill out a detailed achievement plan for the next two years. This consists of specifying what the participant wants to accomplish, the blocks each individual will have to overcome, and where he or she will seek help in accomplishing these goals. The plans are also reviewed in small group discussions, where participants assist one another in formulating their goals. The participants are told to consider themselves in training for the next two years and that the ten- to fourteen-day course is too short to do more than present a new way of acting. The instructors help the participants during the next two-year period by contacting them every six months, obtaining reports on progress, and working with them in the specification and achievement of goals.

4. *Interpersonal Support.* The authors note that many parts of the course could have been taken by correspondence. However, they point out that one of the distinguishing features of the actual training program is the degree of warmth and interpersonal support that is provided for participants. The group leaders are there to help clarify what the person wants and provide information that will make the self-study more complete, while at the same time providing the warmth and respect that is needed while the participant goes through individual soul-searching.

McClelland and his colleagues have studied the effects of these programs in a variety of settings. McClelland and Winter (1971) report on the effects of achievement development courses in a number of small cities in India. In general, course participants showed improved performance as compared with their own pretest measures and with a number of matched control groups. The participants generally participated more in development activities in the community, began more new businesses, and invested more in expanding their businesses. The results of a two-year follow-up period indicated they employed over twice as many new people as did the untrained businessmen. Miron and McClelland (1979) report on other training programs similar to the one described above. The first was conducted through the business school at Southern Methodist University and another was conducted through the Small Business Administration in eight cities. A third program was designed to help mostly black business firms in Seattle that were experiencing business difficulties. The authors examined financial data for periods preceding training and for periods after training for all three programs. In general, all three programs resulted in increased profitability. For example, in the SMU training program there were increases in sales, profits, and number of employees.

Before completing a discussion of this program, it is important to note that systematic evaluation efforts, including those for this program, are not easy to accomplish. These are large-scale programs where it is often difficult to obtain all of the pre- and post-data, and many times control groups are also difficult to either obtain or find. Of course, random assignment to treatment and control conditions is often nonexistent. In many cases, the investigators are forced to examine many factors and treat each finding as a piece of a puzzle. Often, the researchers take a look at the consistency and direction of many different pieces of data to support their views on the value of their programs. There are many different strategies to consider in evaluating such efforts. One must ask the investigator to collect multiple criteria, including both process and outcome data, examine the relationships, and realize that no single study is going to provide extensive information about the value of the program. Also, it is important to recognize the limits of interpretation based upon the threats to validity which result from the design utilized. It is also important to utilize the designs which control as many threats to validity as possible given the constraints of the environment.

Finally, it is critical that the researchers share issues and problems in research so that the reader can make a reasoned judgment about the viability of the results and gain an understanding of the parameters which limit the interpretation of the data. Such analyses sometimes provide the most interesting and thought-provoking information about the entire study. In that regard, Miron and McClelland (1979) frankly discuss some of the problems they have in interpreting their research data. Some of the problems include the following.

1. It is sometimes difficult to interpret the criterion data because it involves complex analyses that require finding matching groups or interpreting data across time periods. Thus, in the studies in India, overall business employment in the treatment group was compared to a city that was matched on a number of demographic and economic variables. Clearly, it is hard to know whether you have matched on the right variables and whether the comparison city might have changed at different rates for other reasons. In some ways, this is similar to the problem of using a matched control group rather than random assignment. However, here it becomes increasingly complex because there are so many factors that can affect the performance of both the control and experimental groups, especially when dealing with indicators like unemployment factors, profitability, and so on.

2. A particularly vexing problem in these studies is whether some of the results could be due to a selection rather than training effect. Maybe the businessmen who have higher nAch are the ones who tend to respond to recruitment efforts to participate in the training efforts. Thus, they would have performed better, anyway.

3. Another problem for the interpretation of results is that the opportunity for success is different for persons who participate in training. Participants

might become aware of consultant assistance or access to money resources because of the training program. Thus, success is not directly related to what they learn in training but rather to factors that result from their being in the training program.

For many of these factors, Miron and McClelland provide analyses and strategies which lead them to believe that these factors do not account for their data. However, by providing access to both the problems and their interpretations, it is possible for the outside observer to make his or her own judgment.

LEADER MATCH

Leader Match Training is based upon a Contingency Model of leadership which has been developed by Fiedler and his associates (Fiedler, 1964, 1967, 1971). The theory states that effective leadership depends upon a proper match between the leader's style and situational characteristics. That is, in certain situations one kind of leader might be most effective while other situations might require another kind of leader. Fiedler defined the leadership situation according to three major dimensions.

1. *Leader–Member Relations.* This dimension simply refers to whether or not the members of the group like or trust or have loyalty to the leader. Thus, leader–manager relations measures the managers' perceptions of the amount of loyalty and support that the leader expects to receive from the group.
2. *Task Structure.* This dimension measures how clearly items such as goals, procedures, task requirements, and so on are specified for the manager.
3. *Position Power.* This refers to how much authority the manager perceives the organization has given in terms of control for dispensing rewards and punishments.

Fiedler dichotomized each of these dimensions so that leader–member relations could be considered good or bad, task structure could be high or low, and position power could be strong or weak. To the extent that a leader has good member relations, high task structure, and high position power, the situation is considered favorable. If there are poor member relations, the task is unstructured, and there is limited control or authority, the situation is considered unfavorable.

The second aspect of the match between a leader's style and situational characteristics refers to leader characteristics. This is measured on a scale known as the Least Preferred Co-worker (LPC) scale. This index requires a leader to rate the very worst person he has ever worked with on a number of traits. The traits include dimensions on a scale such as pleasant versus unpleasant, sincere versus unsincere, nice versus nasty, cheerful versus gloomy, and so on. In Fiedler's terms, if you are a high LPC leader, you will have values toward the positive end of the scale and will call your least-preferred worker sincere, nice, cheerful. On the other hand, the low LPC leader would describe the least preferred co-worker in terms such as insincere, uncooperative, nasty, and the like.

On the basis of his research, Fiedler maintains that low LPC leaders perform well in situations that are either highly favorable or highly unfavorable. The point is that low LPC leaders, who are characterized as having a nonparticipative, direct, structured style, work best in extremely favorable or unfavorable conditions, while high LPC leaders, who are characterized as participative, democratic, and relationship-oriented, tend to perform well in situations of moderate control.

Since there are two aspects of the match, the leader's style and the situational characteristics, any attempt at change which is related to this model would have the option of either changing the leader's personality to more precisely match the situation or change the situation to more precisely match the leadership style. Fiedler and his co-workers maintain that changing the leader's basic style is a difficult and demanding chore. Essentially, he argues that organizational engineering which changes the nature of the situation to better match the style of the particular leader is the more fruitful approach. Thus, he has designed a training program which shows the prospective leader how to increase or decrease the closeness of his interpersonal relations with his subordinates, how to structure the task, and how to change the various aspects of position power. It is this approach which forms the foundation for his training program, known as Leader Match (Fiedler, Chemers, & Mahar, 1976).

The training program itself consists of a self-administered programed workbook which trainees can complete on their own time and which can be augmented by lectures, discussions, or films. The program takes anywhere from four to twelve hours to complete, and it is recommended that this be done over several days to obtain maximum benefit. The first part of the workbook is designed to enable trainees to identify their own leadership style. Thus, they complete the LPC scale and interpret their own scores. The second part of the training program has the participants determine their own situational aspects. This is accomplished by filling out the scales and measuring their perceptions of leader–member relations, task structure, and position power. They are given information on how to change or modify situational factors in order to match the situation to their leadership styles. For example, depending on the situation judged most desirable, changes could consist of requests for more routine assignments or less structured assignments. It could also consist of the leader developing more or less formal relationships. The important point is that, depending on whether you are a high or low LPC leader, you will choose differently in modifying your situation to fit your leadership style.

Each chapter of the workbook consists of a short presentation that explains the basic aspects of the contingency model and how it can be applied. Essays are followed by several short problems called probes, which consist of leadership episodes. The trainees are asked to select the best solution for each probe. Then they are given feedback on the correct response. If the participant makes an incorrect response, the trainee is required to review the material to make sure that the chapter is understood. Each chapter closes with a summary. There are several short tests throughout the program, and a final exam.

The evaluation of the training program has mixed results. In part, there are difficulties similar to those experienced by McClelland which stem from conducting research in environments with many constraints and difficulties. It is possible to make the following points:

1. Fiedler and his associates have conducted more extensive research and evaluation studies than almost anyone else. Also, the studies tend to collect multiple criteria from different sources, and some of the studies have designs which include pre- and postmeasurement and control groups. Indeed, Fiedler correctly notes that many of his studies have employed rigorous procedures, including the random assignment of participants to training and control groups, which are not typical in complex environments.

2. The results of the studies are somewhat of a mixed bag. For example, Fiedler and Mahar (1979) reviewed 12 validation studies that they had conducted. Five of the studies examined participants in civilian occupations such as police sergeants, managers in county government, public service, and public health. In three of the studies, there were serious problems in attrition which made the results difficult to interpret. For example, in the police study, only seven of the 15 sergeants completed the training book. In most of the studies, rating scores were in the predicted direction but were often not statistically significant. Thus, in the study of middle managers in county government, two superiors rated each manager on the organization's 16-item rating scale three months after training. Eleven of the 16 items were in the predicted direction, but only two of the scales (cost-consciousness and dependability/reliability) were statistically significant. In the study on public works supervisors, 14 of 16 were in the right direction but only two were significant (makes decisions within the scope of the job and oral communication). The other studies were conducted in military settings involving either active duty personnel, military college students, or ROTC students. In those studies, there were fewer problems with the conduct of the studies and the data were more consistent in supporting training program effects.

3. While Fiedler and Mahar strongly believe that these data support the vitality of their training program, they do share concerns about threats to viability that might lead some readers to be less certain. The first serious issue discussed above is the problem of subject attrition. Of course, one concern about attrition is that it is not random. Thus, it is possible that persons who did not feel they were getting much from training were those subjects who managed not to continue participating. Also, in addition to subjects disappearing, data sometimes also disappeared. In one study of volunteer public health personnel in Central and South American villages, only 11 of 25 persons completed the program; in addition, some performance evaluations were lost in transit from Central America. Another issue of concern is rater bias. That is, raters tend to know who did and did not participate in training and that can effect their ratings. Fiedler and Mahar point out that they tried to check that point in some of their studies. In one study involving six-month followups, supervisors could not remember who did or did not complete

training. Since training in these studies often consisted of reading the programed manual on site, it is entirely possible that they had forgotten who had participated.

Another very interesting issue is the source of the effect. Is it Leader Match that makes the difference, or would any special treatment produce effects? Some persons note that a positive benefit of this program is its cost effectiveness. Most programs require considerable amounts of time (consider McClelland's nAch program or the Looking Glass, Inc., simulation). However, here all that is required are four to 12 hours of reading. Others question how this minimum effort can achieve substantive benefits for such complex behavior. Fiedler argues that some of his studies do involve comparisons to other training. Further, he did an analysis that indicated that persons who showed on a test that they knew more about the program tended to perform better. Also, those cadets who self-reported that they more often applied the principles also had higher performance ratings. On the other hand, Fiedler also reports that 36 cadets stated that they did not use the program on any occasion, but this group also performed significantly better than the control group.

It is hard to reach a final conclusion regarding the training program. The degree of effort must certainly be applauded. Also, as in the McClelland studies, the difficulties of the environment must be recognized. No investigator asks to be blessed by samples that disappear. There are some data that support the efficacy of the training. Given the threats to validity, however, these data must be treated with caution. Certainly more research which carefully specifies exactly how persons changed the environment to match their leadership styles would be extremely helpful. Since this technique is related to a theory of leadership, specific hypothesis concerning these situational changes and how leadership effectiveness is changed is important. Otherwise, questions remain as to what happens in training to produce these effects.

RATER TRAINING

In Chapter 5, information was presented on various types of criteria used to measure the effectiveness of individuals in work environments. One type of criteria discussed was rating scales, which are used in many organizations by managers to rate their subordinates on various job-relevant performance dimensions. Table 5.4 in Chapter 5 (p. 138) presents an illustration of the procedures used in developing rating scale items and examples of behavioral items that make up rating scales. While most textbooks recommend that raters be trained in the use of rating scales to appraise employees, until recently there has not been much systematic study of such programs. When the first edition of this book was written in 1974 there was not enough information available to make it feasible to include a section on rater training. A number of studies have been published on the topic since then, and, more interesting, controversies have developed that mirror the issues involved in the design, analysis, and interpretation of most training programs.

Most of the first set of studies focused on issues related to reducing errors made by managers in the rating process. Some of the kinds of errors that research focused on included the following:

1. *Halo error.* This is a tendency to rate a person high or low on all dimensions because of a global impression. In this instance, an impression that an employee is an effective performer tends to result in the individual being rated highly on all performance dimensions, including report-writing items, whether work is produced on time, whether work has quality defects. Similarly, a person considered an ineffective performer might be rated low on all dimensions, even though the employee might perform some aspects of the job well and others poorly.

2. *Leniency error.* In general this is a tendency to give everyone higher ratings than are warranted. The opposite dimension is a *severity error,* where there is a tendency to give everyone lower ratings than are warranted.

3. *Central tendency.* For this type of error, there is a tendency to give everyone scores in the middle of the scale and avoid extreme ratings. This can occur across dimensions for the single individual and/or across individuals for all dimensions.

4. *Contrast effects.* This is a situation where a rating of performance is given on two successive individuals. For example, a rater is asked to rate an individual who is an extremely effective (or extremely ineffective) performer, and then to rate a second individual. If the rating of the second individual is affected by the rating of the first, the error is known as a contrast effect.

An illustration of the type of training program developed to reduce rating errors is provided in the work of Latham, Wexley, and Pursell (1975). These authors noted that earlier work indicated that lectures on the problems of rating errors did not seem to have much of an effect on reducing the problem. They concluded that an intensive workshop which would give subjects a chance to practice observing and rating actual videotaped candidates along with immediate feedback regarding the accuracy of their ratings might be more effective. In order to study this problem, the authors randomly assigned 60 managers in a large corporation to one of three conditions: a workshop, a group discussion, or a control group that received no training. The workshop group viewed videotapes of hypothetical job candidates being appraised by a manager. The trainees then gave a rating indicating how they thought the manager would have rated the candidate and how they themselves would have rated the candidate. Group discussion concerning the ratings followed. As the authors note, this gave trainees the opportunity to observe videotaped managers making observational errors, find out how frequently they themselves made such errors, receive feedback on their own behavioral observations, and practice to reduce their own errors. The workshop group worked on a variety of rating errors, including contrast effects and halo errors, as well as errors such as first impressions, where judgments are made based on initial observations rather than the behavior which follows.

The group discussion format consisted of trainers first defining the various types of errors and providing examples for each error being presented. They then generated personal examples involving the various kinds of rating errors. They also divided into subgroups so that they could share examples, discuss them, and generate solutions to each of the rating problems. The control group did not have any form of training.

The testing of the effects of the various forms of training was conducted six months later. Members of all three groups were given video-tapes to observe. They also were given detailed job descriptions and lists of requirements for the job. They were then asked to rate the individuals in the videotapes in terms of the degree of job acceptability based upon the job descriptions and requirements provided for them. Basically, the results showed that the workshop group was no longer prone to any of the types of rating errors examined in the study. The group discussion trainees also performed well and exhibited only a tendency toward last-impression errors, which are errors that result from evaluating someone on previous behaviors based on the last impression of the person. The control group made a number of errors, including halo and contrast effects. The authors also collected data on trainee reactions to the training. They found that trainees reacted more favorably toward the workshop program than toward the group discussion. Trainees reported that the structured workshop format, including the video-tapes, made them feel that their time away from the job was being used wisely. The only disadvantages that the authors noted for the workshop procedure were that it is costly and time-consuming to develop. They also indicated that where these costs are important factors, the discussion-group technique could be used, since it also worked quite well.

Interestingly, even though the study by Latham, Wexley, and Pursell was well done, there are a number of heated controversies surrounding the rater training literature. In some cases, the controversy relates to the fact that most studies are not well done. A review by Spool (1978) of 25 years of research literature on training observers of behavior (of which rater training is one category) found a number of problems, including the designs of the studies, the criteria employed, and the fact that some interventions can be called training programs only by the most liberal of interpretations. However, even when obviously poor studies are eliminated from consideration, controversy continues. Speculation on why this might be the case will be saved for the conclusion of this section. Some of the issues which researchers are discussing include the following:

1. There are a number of design issues which severely limit the interpretation of rater training studies. These issues limit the external validity of the

generalizations that can be made as a result of the research. One serious issue is raised by an analysis of 22 rater-training studies by Bernardin and Villanova (in press), which indicated that 17 involved students doing the rating in an experimental context. Further, all but two of the studies involved ratings done in an experimental situation. In addition, I. L. Goldstein & Musicante's (in press) analysis of rater training studies indicates that only three studies have investigated the effects of rater training over time, and that two of these studies suggest that the positive effects associated with rater training may diminish over time.

2. There are serious questions about whether the criteria being chosen to analyze the results of rater training studies really reflect what should be measured. In many ways, this issue is related to the concepts of criterion relevance discussed in Chapter 5. Spool (1978) argues that "accuracy in observation can be improved by training observers to minimize rating errors." However, as noted by Bernardin and Beatty (1984), researchers seem to have focused on minimizing rating errors (like halo error or leniency error), but have forgotten that the actual goal is accuracy in observing. These authors further argue that training programs which focus on reducing one set of errors simply exchange one response set for another and thus may only substitute one set of errors for another without improving the accuracy of observations. They note that only three studies have actually studied the accuracy of observations and that in those studies reducing errors did not actually result in more accurate observation. Bernardin and his colleagues feel that there are more important issues which should be addressed in rater training, including giving raters a common frame of reference for defining the importance of the behaviors being observed and training raters on techniques of information gathering. He also believes that systems such as formal diary keeping should be developed as another way of standardizing observations of behavior and improving the accuracy of ratings. Some examples of suggestions provided by Bernardin and Beatty for writing descriptions of behaviors for diary keeping are presented in Table 8.4.

3. Some authors (Bernardin & Beatty, 1984; I. L. Goldstein & Musicante, in press; Warmke & Billings, 1979) have begun to suggest that other variables, such as the context or boundary conditions which surround the training situation, may have more influence on performance than originally thought. A consideration of organizational analysis questions such as those described in the chapter on needs assessment would probably be helpful. Just as the transfer of training into the organization must consider items such as the willingness of supervisors to appropriately model the learned behaviors, the transfer of trained rating behavior may involve issues such as political and union pressure on raters, whether the raters trust that the ratings will be used appropriately, to what ends the ratings will be used, etc. If problems are discovered, they must be resolved before a training program will work. Of course, that principle is the same for all training programs.

It is interesting to note the amount of controversy surrounding rater-training studies. As was the case with sensitivity training, it is somewhat difficult to determine why so much heat has arisen over these particular training programs. It is clear that the issues being discussed are important, but they are issues that should be of concern in the analysis of any training program. Here, however, they are treated with a special degree of emotion. If forced to venture a guess as to why this should be, I would speculate that it is necessary to understand the context of the use of rating scales in organizations. First, even though all criteria have problems related to relevance and contamination

TABLE 8.4   Suggestions for writing descriptions of behavior

1. Use specific examples of behavior, not *conclusions* about the "goodness" or "badness" of behavior.

   Use this: Gwen told her secretary when the work was to be completed, whether it was to be a draft or a final copy, the amount of space in which it had to be typed, and the kind of paper necessary.

   Not this: Liesa gives very good instructions to her secretary. Her instructions are clear and concise.

2. Avoid using *adjective qualifiers* in statements; use descriptions of behavior.

   Use this: Aimee repeated an employee's communication and its intent to the employee. She talked in private, and I have never heard her repeat the conversation to others.

   Not this: Kelly does a good job of understanding problems. She is kind and friendly.

3. Avoid using statements that make *assumptions* about an employee's *knowledge* of the job; use descriptions of behavior.

   Use this: Sarah performed the disassembly procedure for rebuilding a carburetor by first removing the cap and then proceeding with the internal components. When she was in doubt about the procedure, she referred to the appropriate manual.

   Not this: Sam knows how to disassemble a carburetor and does so in an efficient and effective manner.

4. Avoid using *frequencies* in statements; use descriptions of behavior.

   Use this: Patrol Officer Garcia performed the search procedure by first informing the arrested of their rights, asking them to assume the search position, and then conducting the search by touching the arrested in the prescribed places. When the search was completed, Garcia informed the arrested. He then proceeded to the next step in the arrest procedure.

   Not this: Patrol Officer Dzaidzo always does a good job in performing the search procedure.

5. Avoid using *quantitative values* (numbers); use descriptions of behavior.

   Use this: Nancy submitted her reports on time. They contained no misinformation or mistakes. When discrepancies occurred on reports from the last period, she identified the causes by referring to the changes in accounting procedures and the impact they had had on this period.

   Not this: Mr. Goebel met 90% of deadlines with 95% accuracy.

6. Provide sufficient detail so that an assessment can be made of the extent to which characteristics of the situation beyond the control of the ratee may have affected the behavior.

   Use this: Mr. Dzaidzo's failure to hit the "target date" for the sky-hook quota was caused by the failure of Mr. Ressler's department to provide the ordered supply of linkage gaskets. Mr. Dzaidzo submitted four memos in anticipation of and in reference to the gasket shortage.

   Not this: It wasn't Dzaidzo's fault that he didn't hit the deadline.

From *Performance Appraisal: Assessing Human Behavior at Work,* by H. J. Bernardin and R. W. Beatty. Copyright © 1984 by Wadsworth, Inc. Reprinted by permission of Kent Publishing Company, a division of Wadsworth, Inc.

(discussed in Chapter 5), rating scales are called subjective, and there is the suspicion that somehow they are easier to manipulate than other so-called hard criteria. Also, the use of rating scales in measuring behavior in organizations has become more prevalent as our sophistication in designing rating scales has increased. In addition, there are many inadequate rating scales where attempts to make them job-relevant have not even been considered. This results in unsophisticated users concluding that rating scales are inherently poor devices. Finally, in many fair employment practices lawsuits, performance differences between minorities and majorities as measured on rating scales have been a focal and volatile issue. Since training raters is considered a major way to improve the use of rating scales in organizations, training itself is right in the middle of these concerns. One can only hope that these pressures result in better needs assessment, better design and better evaluation. The entire training field can then benefit regardless of the origins of all this activity. Actually, that is a good concluding statement for all the training techniques discussed in the last two chapters. It is a hopeful sign that much of the research describing these techniques has occurred in the last ten years. Many of the studies involve innovative designs in an attempt to study important learning and training phenomena. One can only applaud these efforts and hope they continue.

Special Approaches to Training Issues

This chapter focuses on general approaches to training problems rather than on analyses of specific techniques. The first topic is an examination of individual differences and their relationships to learning and training, with emphasis on selecting techniques that fit the individual characteristics of different learners. Next, the use of individual differences in training and learning as a predictor of later performance either in advanced training or on the job are discussed. The third topic concentrates on fair employment practices issues, including the importance of training in civil rights litigation. The next topic concentrates on instructional programs for the hard-core unemployed, where training in the traditional sense will not work because of the diverse values and attitudes of individuals raised in different cultural environments. These programs must consider many aspects of a complex system, including the support services (for example, counseling and job placement) necessary for individuals who frequently have never been employed. It is also clear that training programs are only part of an answer to a complex problem. Next, retraining for second careers is discussed. Some of the individuals in this group have been placed out of work by technological changes, while others have decided that they are no longer interested in their first career. As an additional barrier, these potential employees face the hurdle of age discrimination. The hard-core unemployed and the second-career groups present a complex social problem that cannot be resolved by narrowly examining specific techniques of training. The final topic in this chapter considers organizational entry, training, and socialization, thus coming back to the entry of people into organizations.

INDIVIDUAL DIFFERENCES INSTRUCTIONAL APPROACHES

The current emphasis placed on the examination of individual-difference parameters in learning and training represents a merger between two separate camps that previously had rarely recognized each other's existence. Until recently psychologists concerned with learning and training examined the effects of their treatments and considered individual differences an annoyance that made the establishment of general laws of behavior difficult. Differential psychologists ignored treatment effects and busied themselves with the study of individual variability. For example, applied psychologists concerned with selection used measures of individual variability to predict future performance on various measures of success.

The reason for the current interest in individual differences and learning behavior is difficult to ascertain. Melching (1969) feels that it is related to a desire for education for the masses without mass education. He suggests that our society does not approve of lock-step educational procedures in which all students are treated as having equal ability and the same learning needs. While some commentators might argue that societal pressure prompted the development of instructional technology, there is also little doubt that hardware developments stimulated the instructional community to be responsive to individual differences. Thus, CAI has storage capabilities that permit consideration of many demographic variables, and PI and CAI have branching and self-pacing options. For whatever reason, a growing group of educators and psychologists are espousing the viewpoint that the design of instructional programs for the average participant is not the most efficient learning procedure. This view is especially well expressed by Lawrence (1954).

> Studies on training methods concerned with spaced versus massed practice, motivational level, and the like are primarily directed at modifying the average rate of learning. Normally, however, a standardized procedure for the spacing of practice and like factors is adopted for all individuals of the group. It is doubtful if this produces the optimum effect for each individual. The optimum value for one individual might well differ considerably from the optimum value for other individuals in the group, depending upon the variability in levels of performance at any given time, the rates of learning, and other characteristics of the individuals involved. (p. 374)

There are several different approaches that can be utilized in the treatment of individual differences (Cronbach, 1967). The following presentation discusses these approaches as applied to instructional programs.

Fixed-Program Approach

One method for treating individual differences is to design a single program with fixed objectives and to require the trainee to continue in the program until the criteria are achieved. Essentially, this procedure permits the individual learner rate to vary but requires that each participant eventually meet the criteria. This type of program is very much in evidence in primary-school systems in which children are not promoted until they learn to read. Similarly, the linear-programing approach to PI is designed to allow the individuals to proceed through the material at his own pace until they complete the program. There are several problems in the employment of this method. One administrative concern is that many types of training programs are likely to be prohibitively expensive and unwieldy if it becomes necessary to extend the instructional time for many trainees beyond minimal limits. Another problem is whether the attainment of certain skills can be accomplished by manipulating the learning time. While this is an empirical issue that cannot be resolved at the present time, some investigators (for example, Cronbach, 1967) feel that psychologists will achieve more by altering the technique than by just extending the duration.

Adapting-Goals Approach

This method utilizes separate programs to achieve the differential goals of the learner. Cronbach notes that this approach can be traced to the time when high schools stopped viewing the dropout problem as a way of reducing an undesirable population that was not interested in an academic education. Thus, different types of programs (for example, vocational instruction) were introduced based on decisions regarding the hypothesized role that the student might have as an adult. There is some recognition of this approach in industrial selection and placement programs. On the basis of employment tests and interviews, the applicant may be assigned to an instructional program that matches their needs. However, in most instances, the recognition of individual differences is more apparent in decisions that specify who should undergo training than in decisions that indicate which form of training is best (Howard, 1971). Thus, laboratory education is not recommended for individuals who have weak egos or who have a history of emotional disturbances. Unfortunately, when a laboratory-education program is instituted for managerial personnel, alternatives are not likely to be offered to those who are poor candidates for the original approach.

Erasing-Individual-Differences Approach

In this approach, the instructional system is designed to minimize individual differences by offering remedial branches. For example, PI branching programs are based on a diagnosis of the type of learner errors that occur in the instructional sequence. In industrial training programs, this approach is illustrated by the design of remedial sequences for those trainees who are not prepared for the fixed instructional programs—for example, remedial reading instruction for the hard-core unemployed.

All the preceding approaches are potentially useful in the treatment of individual differences. Future developments in instructional media, such as PI and CAI, are likely to contribute information about the most effective procedures in the implementation of these approaches. However, the most intriguing approach is the determination of instructional programs on the basis of individual characteristics.

Altering-Instructional-Methods Approach

The goal of this approach is to match alternate modes of instruction to the different characteristics of the individual so that each person utilizes the most appropriate learning procedure. This approach is often called Aptitude-Treatment Interaction (ATI). Figures 9.1 and 9.2 illustrate two types of ATI relationships. Figure 9.1 shows that all persons, regardless of aptitude level, improve with treatment A. In that case, there is no reason to use treatment B; thus, all individuals should be presented with treatment A. Figure 9.2 illustrates an interaction called the disordinal aptitude-treatment interaction. In this case, individuals to the right of the cutoff line (those with higher aptitude levels) perform best with treatment A. Persons to the left of the cutoff line (those with lower aptitude levels) perform best with treatment B. Thus, the aptitude level of the individual determines the form of treatment that will lead to superior performance. In these cases, aptitude refers to any personal characteristics that relate to learning and, thus, can include a broad range of variables, such as styles of thought, personality, and various scholastic aptitudes. The variety of factors that have

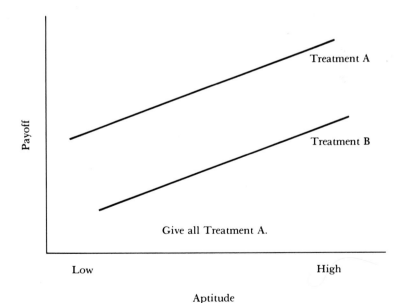

FIGURE 9.1 Illustration of no aptitude-treatment interaction. (*From "The Two Disciplines of Scientific Psychology," by L. J. Cronbach. In* American Psychologist, *1957, 12, pp. 671–684. Copyright 1957 by the American Psychological Association. Reprinted by permission.*)

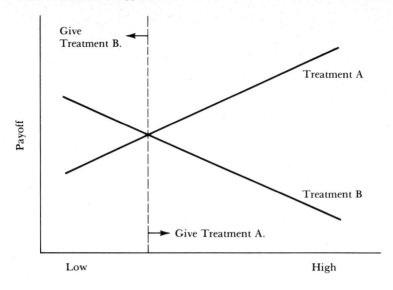

FIGURE 9.2 Illustration of a disordinal aptitude-treatment interaction. (*From "The Two Disciplines of Scientific Psychology," by L. J. Cronbach. In* American Psychologist, *1957, 12, pp. 671–684. Copyright 1957 by the American Psychological Association. Reprinted by permission.*)

been considered in the aptitude-treatment dimension is illustrated by the following partial list of variables (Howard, 1971).

Aptitude

Scholastic aptitude
Spatial aptitude
Verbal reasoning
Intelligence
Deductive/inductive reasoning
Cognitive style (analytic/nonanalytic)
Mathematics ability
Interests
Ascendancy, dominance
Introversion/extroversion
Need for achievement
Motive to avoid failure
Anxiety
Overachievement/underachievement
Sociability
Attitudes to instruction or subject
Need for autonomy
Miscellaneous personality characteristics

Treatment

Visual presentations
Verbal presentations
PI difficulty or complexity

Multiple-choice versus constructed PI responses
Classroom social change
PI—knowledge of results
PI—overt/covert responding
PI—immediate feedback
Verbal-figural material
Inductive/deductive method
Step size
Praise/blame as reinforcement
Lecture/PI text/teaching machine
Bypassing versus linear programing
PI sequencing (standard/random order)
Rote versus conceptual instruction

As an illustration of this type of research, we can consider a study of navy technical training made by Edgerton (1958) and reanalyzed by Cronbach and Snow (1969) for ATI effects. Two methods of instruction were utilized in a course for aviation mechanics. In one method, which was essentially rote learning, the trainees were told to memorize the material and reproduce it on examinations. In the second method, the instructor presented explanations and stimulated students to ask questions. This procedure was dubbed the "why" method. The test predictors taken by the 150 trainees in each group were the Tests of Primary Mental Abilities. The interaction analyses showed that those individuals who scored highly on the verbal-abilities tests were more likely to perform well under the rote treatment. However, a similar relationship was not found for the "why" group. Cronbach and Snow suggest that the explanations in the "why" condition overcame some of the potential learning difficulties for those trainees who scored poorly on the test. Another interesting interaction was established between scores on an interest test and performance in the course. Those individuals who performed best in the rote treatment had previously expressed interest in the kind of content being taught. There was no relationship between interests and performance in the "why" treatment. In this instance, the more meaningful treatment in the "why" condition may have compensated for whatever handicaps were established by the lack of interest.

Early analyses by some researchers (Bracht, 1970) found little evidence for ATI effects. However, those reviews often involved the examination of research where the studies were not planned for an analysis of ATI effects and the control conditions and choice of variables were not consistent with well-planned ATI studies. An exhaustive review of ATI strategies by Cronbach and Snow (1977) led them to conclude that the interactions are real phenomena. They noted that the findings which most clearly suggest ATI effects are those dependent upon prior learning experience. Thus, treatments work best for persons who have already experienced that particular type of instructional technique. However, ATI effects have not often generalized or been replicated. Thus, little sound advice can be offered beyond saying that systematic empirical and theoretical research which matches individual differences among learners to various instructional strategies is required. The use of randomly chosen abilities with whatever instructional technique happens to be available is not likely to produce any dividends. This advice is best characterized by the following quote from Cronbach and Snow (1977).

> The substantive problem before us is to learn which characteristics of the person interact dependably with which features of instructional methods. This is a question of awesome breadth. In principle, it calls for a survey of all the ways in which people differ. It requires that individuality be abstracted into categories or dimensions. Likewise, it calls for abstractions that describe instructional events in one classroom after another. The constructs descriptive of persons and instructional treatments pair up to form literally innumerable ATI hypotheses. It is impossible to search systematically for ATI when the swarm of hypotheses is without order. (p. 493)

These remarks are very important. A long history of trial-and-error empirical studies is not likely to produce any dividends. Rather, it is necessary to examine the processes in the various forms of learning. The choice of aptitude variables can then proceed from an analysis of strategies utilized in each form of learning rather than from measures of aptitudes that happen to be available. Thus, it is possible to ask which learning processes are utilized in problem-solving and which aptitude variables are likely to interact with those processes.

If this research does begin to produce consistent interaction data, there is another problem that has serious implications for training research. Cronbach and Snow (1969) warn us that particular training conditions that result in poor performance in one type of short-term treatment should be examined further. It must be determined how a particular problem (for example, inability to cope with a discussion method) can be rectified, because it is likely to limit the individual in other types of social and work situations. Thus, the problem for the trainer will be to design an instructional program that will allow the learners to profit from group discussions so that they will not suffer from that inadequacy in a job setting. In this way, interaction research may eventually offer another important tool by identifying problem areas that require further training. It is clear that individual-differences research needs further development before it can offer consistently useful information for instructional technology. Whether the research will occur and whether the outcomes will be consistent enough to be useful remains to be seen.

TRAINING AND LEARNING PERFORMANCE AS A PREDICTOR

Measures of performance in training have been used in several different ways. One approach is to use training scores to predict how trainees will perform later on the job in the work organization. In Chapter 6, on evaluation, the use of individual differences models was discussed and it was noted that such models did not provide information about the benefits of the training program itself. Trainees may vary in how well they perform in training. It may also be the case that trainees who tend to perform well in training also tend to perform well on the job. In that case, a relationship will be found between training performance and on-the-job performance. That does not tell the analyst much about the instructional program. The training program may be very well designed or poorly designed but it is still possible for persons who perform well in training to perform well on the job. However, even if the individual differences model does not help much in evaluating training programs, it is possible to predict how well trainees will perform on the job from their performance in training. There have been a number of studies that have demonstrated that it is possible to predict job performance from training performance. Kraut (1975) used peer nominations obtained from managers attending a month-long training program to predict later promotions and performance appraisal ratings. Peer nominations consist of selections by trainees of who they think will be successful. Mayfield (1972) used peer nominations, also obtained in training, to predict the sales performance of life insurance agents at the end of six months and one year on the road. Bartlett and Goldstein (1974) found that a road test which was part of a bus driver training program predicted accidents on the job for those same trainees. Also, some investigators have used early performance in training to predict later performance in training. In that case, early training scores were used as predictors to make inferences about later training performance scores which served as criteria. An example of such a study is the work by Gordon and Cohen (1973), who were able to predict performance in a plate-welding course by examining trainee performance on the first few tasks in the training program. That study is described in Chapter 6 (p. 170).

These types of studies have led some researchers to consider another use for the learning that occurs in training situations. Investigators (Siegel, 1983; Robertson & Downs, 1979) interested in predicting job performance have suggested that a person who is able to demonstrate proficiency in learning to perform on a job sample will be the same individual who will be able to learn and perform on the job (assuming appropriate training). Thus, the measure consists of a trainability test which is used to predict later performance. Note that the trainability test is not the entire training program but rather a sample of the tasks which reflect some of the required KSAs which are needed for job performance. Clearly, this sample must be based upon a careful needs assessment and does not serve in lieu of a training program. Rather, the purpose is to use a learning measure based upon performance on a relevant sample of tasks to predict later performance either in the full training program or on the job.

An example of this type of work is described by Siegel (1983). He describes the development of a battery of nine miniature job training and evaluation situations for navy recruits. For example, one of the trainability tests was the Computation and Projection (CAP) test, which included instruction in how to read a simplified plot diagram describing the position of two ships and their headings and speeds. Instructions included information on how to extrapolate the new position of the ships after an hour and how to evaluate the danger of a collision. After training and practice, problems were administered to the trainees and scores of performance on the miniature task were obtained. The battery of nine training tests was given to 1034 males who were later assigned to several navy jobs, including seaman, airman, and fireman. The individuals tested in the program were persons who had low aptitude scores on traditional tests and thus would not have been selected for those specialized career choices. In order to assess the training battery, Siegel and his colleagues performed two follow-ups, one at nine months and the other at 18 months. The follow-ups were done using job-technical forms which consisted of the different tasks performed in each of the three jobs. For example, tasks for a seaman might be "steer by compass," for a fireman "use lubricating oils and greases," for an airman "make aircraft tiedown lines." Each of the persons in the study was rated by a supervisor on the tasks with scores that could range from one (very poorly) to seven (very well). Siegel found that all nine of the trainability tests predicted performance for the seaman and fireman groups. However, for the airman group, only a few of the tests predicted performance. Seigel indicated that the job requirements for the various jobs were different but that the battery of trainability tests was originally constructed to be applicable to the jobs of seaman and fireman. A more relevant battery might also predict for airmen.

Most of the trainability test work involves psychomotor performance. A good example of the variety of such tests that have been developed is provided by Robertson and Downs (1979), who reported on over 20 years of research using trainability tests to predict later training performance. They found it possible to predict training success in a large number of jobs, including carpentry, welding, sewing, forklift operating, dentistry, and bricklaying. In some studies they even found that persons who performed poorly on the training tests were less likely to turn up for training and more likely to leave in the first month. Thus, the test might have provided some realistic expectations about what the training and job would be like.

Robertson and Downs followed a similar procedure for the use of the trainability test. First, they selected relevant sample activities based upon what is taught in training. Thus, the carpentry test involved making a certain kind of T-joint and the welding test consisted of several straight runs along chalk lines on steel. The procedure consisted of the following:

1. Using a standardized procedure, the instructor provides training and demonstrations with the applicant free to ask questions.

2. The applicant is asked to perform the task unaided.
3. The applicant's performance is recorded according to a standardized checklist.

It is important to realize that there is a distinction between predicting training performance and job performance. Some of the studies discussed at the beginning of this section, such as Kraut's use of peer ratings, were used to predict on-the-job performance. Some of the trainability test research, such as the study described above by Siegel, also predicted on-the-job performance. However, most of the Robertson and Downs studies used trainability tests to predict training performance. Studies which have employed this type of design do not necessarily offer data about the relevance of the training and its relationship to on-the-job performance. On the other hand, Ross (1974) argued that the use of appropriate selection devices could substantially reduce the cost of instruction. This view is supported by Reilly and Manese (1979), who employed a short, self-paced training course as a sample to predict trainee performance for programs in electronic switching systems for Bell Systems employees. The average cost for this six-month course was $25,000 per trainee. It is obvious that procedure is most cost-effective when the training program is also demonstrated to be as job-relevant as possible. This also has implications for work in fair employment practices. This will be discussed in the next section.

TRAINING AND FAIR EMPLOYMENT PRACTICES

In 1964, President Lyndon Johnson signed the Civil Rights Act into law. One section of that act, Title VII, has had a dramatic effect on employers, employees, job applicants, labor unions, lawyers and industrial-organizational psychologists. Title VII refers to employment and makes it illegal to discriminate on the basis of race, color, religion, sex, or national origin. The categories of the aged and handicapped were not included in this particular act but were added later on the basis of other legislative action. The 1964 act resulted in the establishment of the Equal Employment Opportunities Commission (EEOC) as an enforcement agency for fair employment practices. Since that time, numerous events have affected practices in this area. In 1972, an amendment to Title VII broadened its coverage from employers with 15 employees to state and governmental agencies, as well as educational institutions. The amendment also extended the authority of EEOC to bring court actions against organizations. EEOC had published a set of guidelines in 1970 and EEOC, the Civil Service Commission, the Department of Labor, and the Department of Justice published a new set of guidelines in 1978, all of which have had effects on personnel practices. Also, scientific and professional associations such as the Society for Industrial and Organizational Psychology (1980) have published principles to help clarify and develop guidelines for the field. Court actions ranging from district court decisions to those of the United States Supreme Court have added to the complexity. A review of all this material is beyond the scope of this text. However, an excellent summary of the basic issues is provided by Arvey (1979) in his text titled *Fairness in Selecting Employees.*

In order to understand the issues concerning training and fair employment practices it is important to understand several basic ideas. First, there is the principle of discrimination. As noted by Arvey (1979), the basic object in selection is discrimination. That is, the employer uses some instrument by which some employees will be selected and others rejected. Similarly, some persons on the basis of their training scores might be selected for promotion to a new job. The problem occurs when unfair discrimination or bias enters into the situation. While these terms are complex and subject to many interpretations, Arvey's definition makes the point clear:

> Unfair discrimination or bias is said to exist when members of a minority class have lower probabilities of being selected for a job when, in fact, if they had been selected, their probabilities of performing successfully in a job would have been equal to those of nonminority group members. (p. 7)

These kinds of issues often translate into court actions when a lawsuit is filed by an individual (called a plaintiff) against an organization (known as the defendant). Plaintiffs attempt to establish that there has been adverse impact against an individual. The demonstration of adverse impact relates to unfair discrimination. It is necessary to show that a person from a protected class (such as race, as defined in Title VII of the U.S. Civil Rights Act) is treated unfavorably as compared to persons in the majority group. While the exact procedures are complicated, an example might be where 100 whites out of 100 applicants were hired while only 5 of 50 blacks or females were hired. Once adverse impact has been demonstrated, the burden of proof shifts to the defendant. Now, the organization must show that the test or instrument being used which results in adverse impact is job-related or valid. Some additional complexities are that even if the instrument is job-related or valid, the defendant might be asked to show that other devices which do not have as much adverse impact have been considered and/or that the instrument is required for business necessity.

It should be clear from the examples used above that most of the original controversy involves questions concerning the selection of persons into work organizations. Thus, it is possible to ask what this has to do with training issues. The answer is that fair employment practices and training issues are becoming increasingly important. The following points should be considered.

   1. First, it is necessary to realize that in addressing the issue of testing in Title VII of the 1964 Civil Rights Act, the EEOC guidelines (1970) define a

test ". . . as any paper-and-pencil or performance measure used as a basis for employment decision." This means that if adverse impact is established, it will be necessary to establish the job-relatedness of any instrument used in the personnel decision. Almost all of the original legal actions decisions in the short history of fair employment practices involved persons attempting to enter the job market. Thus, the cases concerned the job-relatedness of selection tests such as paper-and-pencil, application blank, interviews, etc. More recently, as persons from protected classes successfully enter the job market, the issues have shifted to concerns about opportunities to move up the organizational ladder. Given these developments, cases concerning opportunities for promotions have become more frequent, and mixed-up right in the middle of these issues are training programs. For example, one target of litigation has become programs which determine who is given the opportunity to attend a training program so they can be selected for promotion to a managerial job. Those personnel decisions are subject to the same laws as personnel decisions for entry into the job market. Bartlett (1978), in an insightful analysis, listed some of the kinds of decisions involving training programs that were likely to be involved in litigation. His 1978 prognosis turned out to be extremely accurate. Some of the decisions he listed are presented below.

a. use of training as a job prerequisite
b. use of instruments to select persons for training
c. use of training performance, retention, or graduation as a criteria for another job or for entry into another training program
c. use of training as basis for advancement or increased compensation

Of course, any reader of this book knows that its author would insist on demonstrations of job relevancy regardless of whether there is adverse impact. However, the courts would not be interested unless adverse impact had been established.

2. In civil rights cases, if adverse impact is determined, the question becomes one of whether the program itself is job-relevant. In other words, what is the validity of the training program? In these cases, as described in Chapter 6, there are a number of evaluation methods each permitting varying degrees of confidence about inferences of the validity process. Thus, experimental designs (assuming that threats to validity are controlled) permit the strongest inferences with quasi-experimental designs also permitting inferences assuming reasonable control of threats to validity. Also described in that chapter are content validity models. Here, you are only able to show the content of training as matched with the important KSAs on the job. Thus, the model for inference is weaker because you cannot be sure that learning or transfer takes place. The point is that there are a variety of models which can be used to make inferences about the job relevancy of the training program. The models can, in varying degrees, permit inferences to be made about validity. Also, of course, the procedures used in carrying out each of the evaluation models also affect the strength of the inferences. Thus, content validity with a poor needs assessment further weakens the inference.

3. It is extremely important to specify the inferences you want to make. Thus, if the goal is to make inferences about whether training programs provide the appropriate instruction to improve performance, then appropriate experimental design evaluation models can provide that information. Even content validity models can indicate whether the important KSAs from the job are represented in training, although they cannot specify whether trainees learn or transfer learning to the job. On the other hand, you might want to know if persons who performed better in a training module also perform better on the job. This directly relates to the preceding section on individual

differences and training predictions. Here the question is whether training performance can predict job performance. As described in Chapter 6, this requires an individual differences evaluation model which specifies whether persons who perform better in training tend to perform better on the job. However, as noted in Chapter 6, this does not tell us anything about the quality of the training program. Of course, if the goal is to make inferences about the training program, there are wrinkles that can be added. Thus, it is possible to add pre- and posttests in training or content-validate the training program. In the latter instance, you have at least established that the important KSAs are included in training and that persons who do well in training do well on the job. As far as evaluation of training, it may not permit as strong an inference as an experimental design but it permits a stronger inference than an individual differences model without a content validity component.

4. Another way that training scores are used in fair employment practices cases is as criteria. For example, a selection test or an interview score is used to predict training performance. Here again, the question becomes one of what inferences can be made. It is clear that this model is being used to predict which persons, based upon the selection test, will perform well in training. Again, this does not provide any information about the quality of the training program. As a matter of fact, it is extremely difficult to make any inferences about job performance from evidence relating selection measures and training performance. There is some confusion about this point. Some persons have made the assumption that if a selection test predicts training performance, it should tell us something about job performance. Everything we have learned in this text about transfer and so on should warn against making that assumption. Again, the question is one of strength of inferences. If there is a strong relationship between selection and training and the training program is content-valid that permits slightly stronger inferences.

In conclusion, it is important to note that training is now in the middle of fair employment practices issues and many of these issues will be in front of the public over the next decade. Readers interested in an overall review of training and fair employment practices up to this time should read an excellent review by Russell (1984). Other articles providing insight into training and fair employment practices issues include material by Gordon (1978) and Sharf (1977).

TRAINING FOR THE HARD-CORE UNEMPLOYED

The civil disorders of the 1960s prompted a reconsideration of our poverty-ridden communities. In the cities alone, there were 500,000 unemployed persons (Report of the National Advisory Commission on Civil Disorders, 1968). Many of the members of these communities are hard-core unemployed (HCU); that is, they are not regular members of the work force, and, in many cases, they have been without employment for more than six months. The HCU are usually young, members of a minority group, and lacking a high school education. In addition, they are below the poverty level specified by the Department of Labor (Goodman, Salipante, & Paransky, 1973). Recent estimates support the fact that the HCU remain a serious problem. For the last decade, the jobless rate for black teenagers seeking employment has been two and three times the national unemployment rate.

Solutions to the problems of the HCU focus on training programs in remedial education, specific job skills, and motivational or attitudinal factors. Although some programs emphasize only one of these areas, most programs combine them. For example, remedial education and specific job skills are interwoven because many investigators have found that the HCU are limited by their educational background in programs that stress only skill proficiency. The need for sensitivity in designing programs is illustrated by the semantic differences that disrupt communication between trainees and employers. "Words that sound the same have different meanings. Sentence structure is different. Business and technical terms comprise another language. Thinking that they (minority-group trainees) understand, they often find that they really don't know what is wanted" (Van Brunt, 1971, p. 2). The seriousness of these issues is apparent from the research of Triandis and his colleagues (Triandis, Feldman, Weldon, & Harvey, 1975) on ecosystem distrust. This concept refers to distrust of people, things, and environment. The authors note that the environment for many persons in the ghetto is unpredictable and cannot be controlled. Ecosystem distrust is presumed to operate in an environment where negative reinforcements predominate, where parents have few financial resources, and where public authority figures are bureaucratic and tend to dispense few positive reinforcements. Results of these factors are that there is less trust for people, suspicion of motives, and a sense of individual powerlessness, as well as a feeling that if you are not careful you will get into trouble. This leads persons from these environments to have different interpretations of events. Thus, the reactions of middle-class whites to items such as "to do your own thing" have to do with self-improvement and self-actualization. The responses of ghetto minorities to doing your own thing have to do with getting into trouble, because that is the result of such behavior in the ghetto. The implications of many of these findings is that blacks from the ghetto are likely not to trust an authority figure and may misinterpret behavior that is intended to be friendly. Thus, a smile is interpreted as "He is trying to rip me off" and helpful behavior is perceived as being done only because the government forces it. Triandis notes that, unless supervisors and trainers are aware of ecosystem distrust, they fail to modify their behavior so that it cannot be misinterpreted. Unfortunately, there are few HCU programs that include motivational and attitudinal considerations; however, research indicates that programs that do not consider such factors are often doomed.

It is important to note that some training analysts have attempted to modify traditional techniques by applying information about the characteristics of their trainee population. For example, one program revised the characteristics of the traditional role-playing exercise for members of a group of HCU (Kennedy, 1970) in an effort to develop their interpersonal skills in dealing with customers and other personnel in the retail industry. In this program, the trainee is given a situation like "Your manager is impatient with you and won't give you an even break." The trainee then role-plays that situation while a videotape records the performance. Kennedy suggests that the replay of the videotape for the trainee reduces the threat of feedback that is ordinarily provided by other observers. In this situation, the trainee has an opportunity for self-criticism during the replay. Also, the videotape permits the trainee to view certain cues that can result in interpersonal difficulties, such as a loud voice or a facial sneer.

Another example of the adaptation of training techniques is the use of simulations to provide work samples for the HCU. Here, the simulation is designed not to teach job skills but to acquaint trainees with various aspects of the job. Thus, individuals are given information to help them decide which types of employment might serve their interests and aptitudes. One study of this program (Seiler, 1969) reported that trainees provided with initial orientation through work samples are less likely to switch or drop out of training programs.

The dangers in using any instructional technique without considering the characteristics of the trainees are made particularly obvious in a study that utilized PI materials as part of an instructional program for automobile mechanics and general machine operators. The program for each job was 225 hours long and was designed to prepare youths for job entry. During the PI program, the trainees continually checked one another's work to see who was proceeding fastest. Also, there was persistent peer pressure to work as quickly as possible; thus, the self-pacing aspect of PI was nonexistent. The speed pressure led to a tendency to cheat by looking at the next page of the programed text for the answer. In spite of these difficulties, the trainers judged the program a success because 80% of the PI group, as compared to 60% of the earlier traditional group, completed the program. Also, considerably more PI trainees were placed on the job. How much of this success was due to the student-modified PI section of the training curriculum is hard to ascertain.

It is possible to describe a vast number of techniques that have been applied to the problems of the HCU. However, if we concentrate on studies that emphasize only remedial programs or job skills, there are few programs that have any demonstrable utility. This is partially due to the now-familiar lament that there are many reports of programs but few reports of research studies focusing on results. However, another basic consideration is that programs that concentrate just on job skills, whether auto mechanics or retail selling, don't seem to work very well. This is evident in a study (Miller & Zeller, 1967) that followed 418 trainees who had graduated from a training program for highway-construction–machinery operators. The authors were able to obtain information from 279 graduates. Of these graduates, 61% were employed and 39% were unemployed at the time of the interview. In addition, more than half of the total group said they were without jobs more than 60% of the time. Some of the reasons for the unemployment situation related to inadequacies in training, which included limited task practice and insufficient training time. One trainee noted that "the contractors laughed when I showed them my training diploma and said 'Come back after you get some schooling, buddy'" (pp. 32–33). However, the inadequacies of the training program were only one of the problems faced by the potential employees. Miller and Zeller state the problem this way: "It might have been helpful to have included, within the training experience itself, practice in job hunting, assistance in contacting employers before the end of training, follow-up counseling, and job-placement help" (p. 31).

Research regarding these types of issues is not commonplace. An exception is an interesting study by Barbee and Keil (1973) which examined interview job training for the disadvantaged. They noted that culturally disadvantaged persons often present themselves passively in job interviews. Training was provided for persons who were enrolled in HCU training programs in interviewing skills. One training procedure which was most successful consisted of a combined videotape feedback and behavior modification program. In this procedure, trainees first participated in a simulated job interview, which included filling out an application and being interviewed by a researcher who previously had been a personnel interviewer. The initial interview was taped. Then subjects in the training program were asked to look at the tape, and search for behaviors they might change. The trainer helped with this process. An example of a sample behavior item to change could be "Clarify the exact kind of work you did on your last job" (p. 21). The trainer suggested ways of responding, indicating what kinds of behaviors interviewers looked for. The trainer also helped the trainee rehearse and then reinforced behavior changes. The trainee then went through a second interview with the person simulating the role of personnel interviewer. That interview was also videotaped. All videotaped interviews were presented to a group of five judges who were persons responsible for entry-level hiring in government agencies and the business community. The judges were not told which tapes were pre-training and which were post-training. Also, they were not told which tapes came from the training condition described above and which came from a control group that also had pre- and post-interviews but without any training. A second training condition, where participants had the opportunity to view the tape of their pre-training performance but did not receive any other instruction before the second interview was also included as part of the study. The trainees had been randomly assigned to those conditions. The study found that the performances of groups that had received the combined treatment of watching interviews and receiving behavior modification treatment were more improved than those of the other groups (control condition or just viewing the tape) on several measures, including assertiveness and initiative, asking about job tasks and conditions, and probability of hire. Unfortunately, the study did not provide data about the transfer of these skills to actual job-seeking behavior. Also, of course, the study does not tell us whether the acquisition of these skills resulted in improved job performance once a job was obtained. Some might argue that teaching interview behaviors which might not be related to successful job behavior characteristics is somehow not appropriate. On the other hand, others would argue that if one cannot obtain a job, successful job behavior is a moot point. Also, it seems to make sense that good communication skills should be useful both in the interview and on the job. However, given the problems in HCU programs, it is critical to conduct research on this issue so that trainees can avoid the problems exemplified in the Miller and Zeller study discussed earlier.

Job placement and counseling are two indicants of a common theme in HCU research; that is, training systems must be examined from a much broader perspective than just the trainee, the trainer, and the necessary job skills. A program that considers job training as only one aspect of the instructional program was developed at the Pittsburgh Technical Institute (Nester, 1971). The lengths to which this program goes to gain the trust of the trainee are extraordinary. The trainers not only call the trainee if they do not report by 9:00 A.M., but they also arrange for special tutoring, babysitters, and a variety of incentives to motivate the trainee. Most interesting is the approach taken by the staff to ensure the success of the trainee on the high school equivalency exam. In addition to tutoring the students, they arrange for a special testing, pay for the exam, provide transportation, and have two staff members present so that the student who looks up sees a familiar and friendly face. Another aspect of the total approach is a counseling program. Nester notes that some of the students have deep-rooted personal problems that make it difficult to learn or to keep a job. Therefore, it is necessary to have counselors available from the beginning of the program to gain insights into the causes of the problems and to suggest effective ways of coping. At the time of the author's report, the training program in drafting had resulted in 40 of 52 trainees being successfully placed, with eight possibilities pending. The commitment toward job placement is apparent from the 135 interviews that were arranged for the trainees.

The same themes of job placement, counseling, and attention appear in most programs that have evidence of success. In some cases, the attention is manifested in health care for individuals who were not able to attend training previously because of their ills. In other cases, the attention is focused on careful transportation directions to aid the trainees in finding their way to the training or job site. These factors make careful organizational analysis and needs assessment mandatory. For example, conflicts among government sponsors, employers, and training institutions can completely disrupt a program (Goodman, 1969). Many of these conflicts are based on differing goals and expectations. For example, the community training organizations are concerned with introducing people into the world of work, while the employer is concerned with obtaining and retraining people at a minimum cost. When these clashes remain unresolved, there is a situation with conflicting goals and objectives that eventually undermines the potential success for the HCU.

While training analysts are still struggling with the factors that determine the success of HCU instructional programs, the emerging emphasis on the nonskill variables suggests that the original analyses of the trainee population were not very astute. The important issue of motivation was rarely considered. One framework that can be utilized to examine this issue is the instrumentality theory of motivation (Goodman et al., 1973). This view states that the HCU expectancies about reward contingencies and attractiveness of these rewards determine whether the trainee will remain in the instructional program and on the job. From this framework, Goodman and his colleagues have interpreted some of the results of HCU research. They note that older workers are more likely to be successful than younger workers. This suggests that younger workers are more distrustful of the system and therefore perceive lower expectancies, while older workers have higher expectancies and greater desires for rewards. This particular hypothesis receives additional support from data indicating that male HCUs who have family responsibilities are also less likely to drop out. Proponents of behavior modification would probably say that, for these conditions, salary operates as a positive reinforcer. Regardless of the theoretical framework, the point is that a multitude of factors determine the success of the HCU, including the treatment that they receive from other employees and supervisors on the job. Thus, supportive behavior by the supervisor (Friedlander & Greenberg, 1971) relates to more effective HCU performance. "An important inference is that programs geared primarily toward adapting the HCU's work attitudes to the predominant social structure in the organization are far less potent than those that also incorporate the adaptation of the organizational climate" (p. 287).

The work on ecosystem distrust discussed above by Triandis and his colleagues is consistent with these viewpoints. They point out that with appropriate training members of different cultures would be more understanding of their own behavior and the responses their behavior is likely to evoke. As part of their research (Triandis, Feldman, Weldon, & Harvey, 1974), they describe a training approach called a culture assimilator. It is a programed-learning sequence where incidents of cultural conflict are described and trainees are asked to judge which factors are likely to be the cause. Then answers are discussed with references to the norms and values of the group being discussed. This approach is also presented in Chapter 7 in the section on programed instruction. In that study, the cultural assimilator involved nurses being trained to work with Australian Aboriginals. The approach described by Triandis and his colleagues for work with the hard-core unemployed is similar, although of course the types of incidents and references to cultural norms and values change as the cultures differ.

The work by researchers like Goodman, Friedlander, and Triandis makes it obvious that training programs must be considered in the context of the environments in which they operate. Some training analysts have concluded that training programs designed for remedial work or job skills do not work. They must realize that training programs need to include a number of factors, like job placement, counseling, health needs, and the training of supervisors. Future gains in this area of training are dependent on the careful specification of these variables, including those motivational factors that are important to the younger trainee and to the person without family responsibilities.

TRAINING FOR SECOND CAREERS

Another serious employment problem that has drawn considerable attention in recent years concerns individuals who had previously been employed but for any of a variety of reasons find themselves seeking retraining for new jobs or careers. While unemployment rates have varied considerably during the last decade, even in times with low rates there are large numbers of people who lose their jobs and are forced into the search for new employment. The reasons for this phenomenon have varied. They include changes in national priorities, such as those in the early 1970s when there were layoffs in defense- and space-related industries. In the 1980s new automation technologies have closed or changed entire industries. There are also changes related to societal values, as illustrated by women re-entering the job market as well as entering the market in occupations that were previously closed to them. The latter point relates to job discrimination, which has been covered in an earlier section. However, variables related to second-career searches themselves involve a complex series of issues. There are a number of personal, societal, and work-system characteristics that have resulted in a search for second careers. They include the following (Haug & Sussman, 1970):

> 1. A major reason for job shifts is the incumbent's inability to continue in a chosen field. In some instances, this is a result of formal or informal age limits imposed by the occupation (for example, airline pilots or athletes), or of a variety of individual characteristics, such as physical handicaps.
> 2. Another reason is the recognition that the first career is at a dead end; that is, there can be no further advancement. Thus, members of the military

who recognize that future opportunities are limited retire at the first chance. Also, women who find that their child-rearing careers are finished explore new interests.

3. In many cases, rapid technological change, including automation in offices and factories, eliminates the employee's original job or occupation. This will continue to be a major issue for the decades of the '80s and '90s.

4. In other instances, the individual's desire for change stems from dissatisfaction with a career that is no longer perceived to be stimulating or adequate in pay, status, or security. While the causes are difficult to specify, representatives of state employment offices (Fait, 1970) describe experiences with lawyers, teachers, ministers, and managers who have discovered at the age of 40 that they are no longer interested in their first careers.

As might be expected, the characteristics of these individuals vary considerably from those of the HCU. In general, they tend to be older, with higher salary demands and considerable financial responsibility. However, it would be a mistake to suggest that second-career seekers have homogeneous characteristics. Persons who lost their jobs during defense-plant layoffs included workers with few basic technical skills as well as highly-skilled workers with graduate degrees. One interesting study (Haug & Sussman, 1970) that focused on these characteristics examined 326 students who graduated in the spring of 1965 from 38 training programs in rehabilitation counseling. Of these students, 112 represented a second-career group that had previously worked in such fields as nursing, teaching, and business. Basically, the second-career group was older (average age of 37 as compared to 27) and economically more affluent, as measured by funds available and home ownership. Most interesting is the fact that a third of the second-career group were disabled, with the most frequent afflictions being blindness and neuromuscular disorders. While it would be foolhardy to generalize from this study to other samples, it is important to recognize that second-career groups have their own set of descriptive characteristics that are likely to differentiate them from most other training populations. These issues have led to increased concern about professional obsolescence. This concept is defined as a reduction in professional competence as a result of not having acquired knowledge concerning new technologies that have emerged since the individual received his or her education (Dubin, 1972). The seriousness of this problem becomes apparent from the assertion that an engineer's education has a half-life of five years. That is, half of what has been learned in school is obsolete five years after graduation. Clearly, within 15 years after schooling is completed, an engineer is very dependent upon what is learned on the job or in training programs.

Regardless of the discipline or occupation, many persons (for all the reasons discussed above) find themselves searching for second careers at some point in their lifetimes. There is one common problem that affects a large part of this group—that is, age discrimination. The antidiscrimination laws have minimized overt forms of discrimination but have not necessarily provided increased opportunities. Most of this discrimination is based on the belief that older workers cannot perform as well on the job and cannot easily acquire new skills. A review (Rhodes, 1983) of 25 studies conducted over the last 30 years did not support such a pessimistic view. Basically, several studies found that relationships between age and performance disappeared when effects of experience were partialed out. In those instances where differences were found they tended to be related to performance where there were high demands for speed and accuracy of movement. However, for the most part, the demands of most jobs were not extreme enough for ability differences to show up. Also, of course, in many jobs which were extremely physically demanding the older workers who remained on the job were the persons who could perform it. The complexity of these performance issues is illustrated by questions concerning the age limit of 60 years for airline pilots. The major concern here is sudden death or acute incapacitation while working. An Institute of Medicine Report (1981) found that "usually no single age emerges as a point of sharp decline in function" (p. 128). It was also noted that there was reason to believe that well-practiced skills showed little if any age decline but about this the research was still scanty. Finally, they reported that more thorough testing might be a better system than using age 60 as an age limit because it made no sense to retire able pilots at age 60 while less able persons younger than age 60 continued to fly.

Of course, all of this becomes more complicated when measures other than performance are examined. For example, Rhodes's (1983) analysis of turnover data in 28 studies found strong evidence for a negative relationship—that is, the higher the age, the less the turnover. Similar studies have generally found that age is consistently and positively related to overall job satisfaction, job involvement, work motivation, and the like. Finally, it is important to note that much of the research still has a number of problems originally described by Sheppard (1970). They are:

1. It fails to differentiate various aspects of the work situation, including physical, psychomotor, sensory, and social characteristics.
2. Most of the emphasis is on average performance, with little, if any, attention to the substantial number of individual differences.
3. There is a blind faith in straight-line trend extrapolations. If 30- to 40-year-old workers have lower morale than 20- to 30-year-olds, it is simply assumed that 40- to 50-year-olds will have even lower morale.

These limitations point up the ignorance about the characteristics of our second-career population and about the relationship of particular methods to various required behaviors. As long as all behaviors, individuals, and jobs are treated as part of one large package, the picture will remain ambiguous. However, one point is emerging. The age-discrimination picture is not based simply on the ability of older workers. When skilled workers are displaced, the older among them are the ones who have difficulty finding re-employment. One study indicated that all the younger skilled workers of a displaced group obtained jobs, while 38% of the older workers stayed unemployed (Sheppard, 1970). In addition, the older workers who found jobs were usually paid less than they had previously earned. In this study, the older worker was defined as anyone over 38!

Besides contributing to bias, the lack of knowledge about appropriate training techniques and support variables makes it difficult to properly design training programs. However, there is some research that permits speculation on future developments of training programs.

Several studies in the learning literature indicate that methods stressing activity rather than conscious memorization or rote learning are especially helpful for older learners (Belbin, 1958). These types of studies have led to the development of a technique called the discovery method. It is described by Belbin (1970) as follows.

> The art of applying the Discovery Method lies in devising tasks which are not beyond the unaided accomplishments of the trainee at each stage in the learning process, even if he starts by knowing virtually nothing about a subject. The trainee may be helped to discover the right response by reducing the complexity of the task as it appears in the real situation; for example, by introducing cues such as the use of a colour to indicate which controls have to be operated on a complex machine and so leaving the trainee free to concentrate on other problems confronting him. . . . In other words, the physical changes are designed to increase the prospects that the trainee will be able to discover something for himself. (p. 57)

This method encourages the trainees to progress at their own pace, with a minimum of verbal instruction and physical demonstration. If mistakes occur, an instructor is available immediately to help the trainee onto the correct path. Essentially, the discovery method adapts shaping (the method of successive approximations) to older workers.

While the development of media appropriate to the characteristics of these trainees is an important step, experiences with the HCU and several developments in the study of second careers suggest that it is not good to emphasize only job skills and remedial education. Although the characteristics of the HCU and of those training for second careers are quite different, many of the attitudinal and motivational variables are remarkably similar. For example, there is evidence that the assurance of job placement and payments for training-program participation are important determinants of the individual's willingness to continue in a training program (Barkin, 1970). The needs for counseling are equally apparent. Many employees faced with losing their jobs refuse to enter training programs designed to create similar employment. One study (Rosen, Williams, & Foltman, 1965) found that older workers were not likely to volunteer for training programs because they had little confidence in their learning ability. The interaction between age and education was even more striking. Younger workers with a poor educational background were likely to volunteer for retraining, even though they were satisfied with the prospects for promotion and were unsure about their ability to learn. However, older workers with poor educational backgrounds were not willing to volunteer. Thus, it appears that older workers wait until they find themselves out in the street with what has now been termed "job-interview anxiety" (Sheppard, 1970), either afraid to enter programs or frozen by anxiety in those programs in which they are placed. In addition, many are unable to adjust to the thought of changing fields or lowering their salary demands to begin anew in another career, even though either activity might lead to re-training and a new job (Sobel & Folk, 1965).

Also, concerns about professional obsolescence are likely to in-crease with the continuing introduction of rapidly-changing technol-ogies. Some interesting research by Kaufman (1978) suggests that engineers who early in their career are given extremely challenging work tends to relate positively to professional competence in later years. This suggests the possibility that early learning challenges results in the individual being stimulated for later efforts. It may also suggest that these persons are continually being exposed to new learning chal-lenges that result in their being continually brought up to date. It is clear that there has not been much thought about how to apply needs assessment methodologies to determine what knowledge, skills, and abilities are necessary for persons to remain technically competent in their jobs. That seems to be an agenda item which is badly needed. Needs assessment methodologies to determine knowledge, skills, and abilities for jobs that do not exist but are on the planning board are also badly needed. Concerns about these types of issues are increasing. Thus, many states and professional associations have written continuing education stipulations into licensing laws so that persons must have a certain number of credits in order to maintain professional licenses in fields such as psychology and medicine. Obviously, issues concerning obsolescence, second careers, and aging are very complex. At this point, little is understood except that it will be necessary to deal with many attitudinal and motivational variables besides job skills and remedial training. Perhaps an editorial from the Washington Post re-printed in Table 9.1 says it best. The editorial combines most of the best thoughts available on the problems inherent in training both the hard-core unemployed and persons seeking second careers. Persons interested in training can learn at least as much from it as they can from a review of the literature in the field.

ORGANIZATIONAL ENTRY, TRAINING, AND SOCIALIZATION

It seems fitting to conclude this book on training by going back to the beginning. That is, the whole process of training often begins with a person entering the organization. Even when the person is already in

TABLE 9.1   How not to retrain workers

When General Motors laid off 3,800 assembly line workers in Southgate, Calif., a federal "trade-adjustment" grant enabled 30 of them to enroll in a specially created electronics training course. Washington Post reporter Jay Mathews spent eight months following the experience of the first enrollees. His observations—set forth in a four-part series in this newspaper last week—provide a handy guide for anyone who wants to run an unsuccessful training program.

The first requirement is to make sure the workers are unsuited to the training. You can administer a placement test just to make sure that you're on the wrong track, but be sure that the trainees are already enrolled and enthusiastic about their prospects so that there is no chance to replace them with a more suitable group. The Southgate program accomplished this mismatching so deftly that only two members of the class were able to pass a basic math test. Many couldn't use a simple calculator.

Run the class at breakneck speed. Many of the students will be highly motivated and will try to keep up by studying through the night even while holding evening jobs. But if you go fast enough—the Southgate course crammed a year of instruction into 20 weeks—you can quickly build up the frustration level so that even the best-prepared will fall behind. But don't flunk anyone. String the trainees along with inflated grades or they might drop out and cost you your training fee.

Of course, a little basic review could refresh the memories of the average trainee, who has, typically, been out of school for some years. And a few months of remedial education might help others to prepare for more suitable employment or training. But given the pace that you have set for the class, you won't have to worry that your trainees will be able to do any catch-up preparation.

You'll probably have to order some training equipment for appearance's sake. But make sure that it doesn't arrive on time and that certain key items are missing.

Create unrealistic expectations. You're dealing with longtime assembly line workers who have been earning as much as $12 an hour for what is basically unskilled work. They don't yet realize that most job openings for which they are qualified—including those in the electronics field—pay much less. Or that the higher-paying jobs in electronics—which are relatively few in number compared with the old-line manufacturing jobs—require substantially more training and experience than they are likely to get in your course. Tell them they are almost sure to find lucrative employment if they stick with the course so that they'll be especially embittered when they end up sweeping floors.

It's helpful to add to the stresses that the trainees and their families are already undergoing as a result of their prolonged—in this case more than six months—unemployment. That was accomplished by a two-month delay in paying continued unemployment benefits so that some of the trainees had to work at night in addition to their 12 hours of course work. (The administration's new job-training program has improved upon this technique by eliminating training stipends entirely.) General Motors also helped out in mid-course by ordering half the class to report to an assembly line in Oklahoma and terminating unemployment benefits for those who refused.

You can count on the fact that, once they have graduated, few of your trainees will have the foggiest idea how to find a job. Most of them went right from school to the assembly line, and they can't even write a resume much less sell themselves to an employer. Keep them away from "job clubs" and other successful placement programs. If you want to look as if you're doing something to help, offer employers special bonuses to hire and retrain your graduates—that's usually a sure-fire turn-off.

These lessons aren't new—ineffective training programs have flourished for years. But successful job programs keep cropping up, and their example poses a threat to training industry standards. That's why reporter Mathews' careful documentation of the necessary ingredients for failure is must reading for anyone concerned about the future of this country's training establishment.

the organization, entering training often occurs when a person is moving up to a new job or being given new responsibilities. It is even possible to say that persons being trained are often in an uncertain position. That is, they are moving from one organization to another; this often occurs when a person is seeking a new job in a new environment. Even when participating in a training program in the same organization, the trainee is being prepared for a new job and the uncertainties of that new position.

Wanous (1980) notes that one of the central themes in the entry process is the idea that persons become socialized by the organization. Van Maanan (1976) defines *organizational socialization* as a "process by which a person learns the values, norms and required behaviors which permit him to participate as a member of the organization" (p. 67). Wanous indicates that one of the first ways that persons become socialized is through the training program. He points out that you can consider a newcomer's effectiveness according to three factors:

1. having accurate knowledge of what is expected and clarity of the person's role in the organization;
2. having the knowledge, skills, and abilities necessary to perform the job;
3. being motivated to perform the job.

Most of the time, training programs are considered in relationship to point 2—the knowledge, skills, and abilities necessary to perform the job. Recently, however, the relationship between training and socialization issues has become a topic of interest. Table 9.2 illustrates Wanous's view of the stages in the socialization process. An examination of those stages makes it clear that many of the learning processes involved in stage one through three begin with a training program as a person enters the organization. The interactive themes and their relationship to the importance of early experiences is well expressed by Hughes (1958).

> The period of initiation into the role appears to be one wherein the two cultures (i.e. professional and organizational) interact within the individual. Such interaction undoubtedly goes on all through life, but it seems to be more lively, more exciting and uncomfortable, more self-conscious and yet perhaps more deeply unconscious—in the period of learning and initiation (pp. 119–120).

Research involving these questions is still not very extensive. However, there have been a number of interesting efforts. One such study was conducted by Buxton (1979). She examined the perceptions of experienced police officers and new trainees concerning various aspects of the organization, such as personnel practices effectiveness, reward orientation, status and image, and inflexibility. First, she discovered that in general the experienced officers had a more negative view concerning these variables than did new trainees. However, she also found that as the trainees moved through the 12-week academy training program and into on-the-job training, their perceptions become more negative, moving in the direction of the views of the experienced police officers. Buxton also predicted that the persons who had more realistic expectations after academy training would obtain higher performance ratings from their field training officers. She did not find such a relationship. However, a few other studies have found such effects.

TABLE 9.2   Stages in the socialization process

Stage 1: Confronting and accepting organizational reality
   a. Confirmation/disconfirmation of expectations
   b. Conflicts between personal values and needs, and the organizational climates
   c. Discovering which aspects of oneself that are reinforced, not reinforced, and which that are punished by the organization
Stage 2: Achieving role clarity
   a. Being initiated to the tasks in the new job
   b. Defining one's interpersonal roles
      (i) with respect to peers
      (ii) with respect to one's boss
   c. Learning to cope with resistance to change
   d. Congruence between one's own evaluation of performance and the organization's evaluation of performance
   e. Learning how to work within the given degree of structure and ambiguity
Stage 3: Locating oneself in the organizational context
   a. Learning which modes of one's own behavior are congruent with those of the organization
   b. Resolution of conflicts at work, and between outside interests and work
   c. Commitment to work and to the organization stimulated by first-year job challenge
   d. The establishment of an altered self-image, new interpersonal relationships, and the adoption of new values
Stage 4: Detecting signposts of successful socialization
   a. Achievement of organizational dependability and commitment
   b. High satisfaction in general
   c. Feelings of mutual acceptance
   d. Job involvement and internal work motivation
   e. The sending of "signals" between newcomers and the organization to indicate mutual acceptance

From J. P. Wanous, *Organizational Entry*, 1980, Addison-Wesley, Reading, Massachusetts. Pg. 180, Table 6.1. Reprinted with permission.

Research conducted by Hoiberg and Berry (1978) examined the effects of expectations and perceptions along ten dimensions of performance within navy environments of recruit training, six training schools, and subsequent fleet-duty assignment. Within the first 48 hours of attendance, subjects enrolled in recruit training and the six navy schools were administered questionnaires regarding their expectations of the recruit or school training. At the mid-point in the various training programs, a questionnaire on perceptions was given. Upon graduation, students were given expectation questionnaires about fleet duty, and at the end of one year all subjects still on active duty were given a perceptions questionnaire and asked to describe their present duty stations.

Performance effectiveness was measured in different ways. For recruit training, effectiveness was defined as graduation from training. For the other six training schools and for the two-year survival period, effectiveness was defined as persons who graduated from school and remained on active duty for at least two years.

The results indicated that, in recruit training, expectations were significantly related to graduation. Recruits with expectations for innovative training methods and minimal emphasis on efficiency and control were met with a situation incongruent to these expectations.

Ultimately, these unrealistic expectations were related to failure to graduate. The findings relative to the technical schools indicated that those schools which emphasized less pressure to complete work tasks and more opportunities for personal growth, support from instructors, and innovative teaching methods had greater percentages of effective students. These findings reemphasize the concept that the greater the congruency between actual and expected conditions the greater the performance effectiveness. Based on such results, a case can be made for attending to the context of training and organizational settings. As the authors (Hoiberg & Berry, 1978) point out in their discussion, "another recommendation would be to more accurately prepare and train individuals for the work that they will actually perform in the school and work setting. A coordinated effect to align recruiting and training materials with actual work environments and job requirements would be expected to reduce discrepancies between expectations and perceptions" (p. 15). A study by Lefkowitz (1970) supports this view. He studied turnover problems among sewing machine operators and found that an important determinant of turnover was encountering a job that was contradictory to the expectations developed through training.

Assuming that enrollment in training is a point of entry into an organization, then the organization has the opportunity at that point to provide the incoming trainee with a realistic view of what to expect from the organization. If the training program provides all of the necessary and accurate information required for the trainee to perform effectively in the new position, then it is possible that some of the later "reality shock" of entering the new organization may be eliminated. Many of these issues have become particularly pertinent for individuals entering occupations which were not "open" to them. A good example of this is women entering management careers. An analysis by White, Crino, and DeSanctis (1981) suggests that training for women should focus on a number of areas which clearly fall into the realistic expectations domain. These include programs designed to educate women in the perceptions, strategies, and skills needed in the corporate arena and the identification and removal of the in-place stereotyped behavior that results in blocks to the careers of women. Analyses and evaluations of such programs do not provide clear-cut conclusions but it is obvious from work with the HCU that the success of women will be as dependent upon organizations' willingness to change as it is on women's realistic expectations.

If the training program is designed to provide not only the necessary skills and knowledge, but also realistic expectations, then the probability of future job success may be enhanced. In addition, the use of training as a method for providing realistic expectations may help to obviate some of the negative consequences of unrealistic expectations of new job-holders. As Wanous (1977) pointed out, one of the most common consequences of job-holders with unrealistic expectations is turnover. An employee who has exaggerated beliefs about what the new job holds is likely to be disappointed and seek employment elsewhere. Unrealistic expectations may also result in poor transfer of training to the job, poor attitudes, and poor performance on the job.

In an early study, Gomersall and Myers (1966) investigated the effect of a realistic job preview given in the training program for technical operators who manufactured integrated circuits for Texas Instruments, Incorporated. They had determined that many of their turnover problems were related to the anxiety of new employees. Thus, they provided realistic expectations concerning the job and their supervisor. For example, one part of the training was related to disregarding "hall talk."

> Trainees were told of the hazing game that old employees played—scaring newcomers with exaggerated allegations about work rules, standards, disciplinary actions, and other job factors—to make the job as frightening to the newcomers as it had been for them. To prevent these distortions by peers, the trainees were given facts about both the good and the bad aspects of the job and exactly what was expected of them. (p. 167)

The preview resulted in improvements in a number of areas, including reduction in absenteeism and tardiness.

These views of organizational entry and the processes associated with it have considerably broadened the way researchers look at individuals and training programs. For example, Mobley and his colleagues (Mobley, Hand, Baker, & Meglino, 1979) have studied the trainee attrition process in military training programs. They considered such turnover from the perspective of the choice that a trainee makes in deciding to affiliate with an organization. Their study found a number of variables that predict whether a person will complete the military training program. For example, they discovered that dropouts, as compared to graduates, felt they had a significantly greater chance of being able to secure a civilian work role.

Before completing this chapter, it should be noted that the previous section on the use of training as a predictor and this section on realistic expectations suggest some interesting research interactions between the two approaches. For example, it is possible to consider miniature job training not only as providing prediction data to the organization, but also as providing realistic information to the potential job-holder. Thus, it provides the individual with the opportunity to see what abilities are required and what the new job situation will be like. In this way, the person may be enabled to make a more valid organizational choice. While these sections on prediction and realistic expectations are based on a limited number of research findings, it is clear that future support for such efforts may expand our conception of the usefulness of training programs. This conception again emphasizes the systems nature of training programs and the organizational environment in which they exist. If there is only one lesson to be learned from this book, it should be that training programs don't exist in isolation. They appear in organizations and interact with all of the other complex components in the work environment. An understanding of the technical nature of the design of training programs must also include an appreciation of the complex environments in which they exist in order to produce positive efforts for both the individual, the organization, and the training designer.

Epilog

TRAINING PROGRAMS: A RECAPITULATION

The training model presented in this book (see Figure 2.1) suggests that the success of instructional programs is dependent on an approach that considers a number of interacting components. It is necessary not only to attend to careful needs assessment and evaluation but also to understand that training programs are one element in a complex organizational system. In the previous edition of this book, I stated that the literature presented only a few programs that even bothered to worry about careful and thoughtful needs assessment and evaluation. I also noted that training programs could be characterized by a whirlpool of actions and reactions that utilized immediate testimonials in support of a favored approach. In my opinion, there has been significant improvement in the last ten years. I have detailed many of those thoughts in an *Annual Review of Psychology* (1980) chapter. As a conclusion to this book, I will discuss those ideas.

Research on training processes appears to be approaching an important stage. While the majority of writing in this area is still not empirical, theoretical, or thoughtful, there is a small but increasingly significant literature that focuses on important issues and raises expectations about future possibilities. It is to be hoped that continuing attention will be given to training issues which might include some of the following suggestions.

1. It should be possible, on the basis of needs assessment techniques, to determine what tasks are performed, what behaviors are essential to the performance of those tasks, what type of learning is necessary to acquire those behaviors, and what type of instructional content is best suited to accomplish that type of learning. Clearly, psychologists concerned with the instructional activity of children in school systems are moving more swiftly toward these goals. Training researchers should consider all aspects of the instructional process and begin the development of adult instructional theories. As a first step, attention should be given to the development of needs assessment techniques that emphasize the types of information needed as input to the training process. J. P. Campbell (1978) has noted that the field has ignored descriptive

studies. He suggests that understanding leadership might be enhanced by actually observing and recording what leaders do when they are leading. It is also likely that this type of information would provide very useful input for training.

2. In order to gain an appreciation for the degree to which training programs achieve their objectives, it is necessary to consider the creative development of evaluation models. These models should permit the extraction of the greatest amount of information within the constraints of the environment. Thus, it is important to continue to develop information about constraints that threaten the understanding of data collected in organizational environments. However, it is just as necessary to design models (for example, Komaki, 1977) that allow the collection of data with maximum confidence. Researchers cannot afford to be frozen into inactivity by the spectre of threats to validity. It would be helpful to have further information about alternative evaluation models, including the use of individual-difference methodology and content-validity strategies. These models should emphasize the relationship between training and on-the-job performance as well as the examination of selection and training performance. It is also important to recognize that all models are dependent upon the thoughtful collection of relevant criteria that reflect the dynamic processes of training programs.

3. Further understanding and recognition of the fact that training is a process within an organization must be reflected within the study of instructional systems. Thus, needs assessment should consider the possibility that relevant training programs might be consumed by organizational conflicts. Also, evaluation designs must recognize that the training program and the evaluation are interventions within the structure of the organization. Research on topics such as hard-core unemployed, the aged, fair-employment practices, career development, and realistic expectations continues to identify variables in addition to instructional quality that require examination. We must consider training as a system within work organizations rather than simply create instruction as a separate technology. It is also important to enhance knowledge by studying decisions that organizations make rather than trying to control all of the variables experimentally. Thus, researchers might ask what kinds of individuals in what types of organizations are threatened by being selected as members of a control group. Also, it is possible to explore what can be learned about organizations by the procedures their leaders employ to choose participants. It would also be interesting to examine what types of persons and training programs are selected by different organizations.

4. There is a desperate need for high-quality empirical investigations that examine the usefulness of training techniques. Latham and Saari's study (1979) of behavioral role-modeling in an organizational environment offers a fine model of what can be accomplished. It is sad that there are still few good illustrations to cite. It is also necessary to begin to explore the many boundary conditions for training studies. For example, most investigations of flight training, rater training, and business games employ undergraduate students as subjects. Even when studies are conducted in work organizations, the investigations usually are employed in a research-only design. It might be informative to explore the difference between these conditions and the use of procedures in an actual organizational system.

It is clear that there have been many contributions to the training literature since 1974. I hope that the earlier edition of this book stimulated a few of those and that this edition stimulates a few more. I look forward to the possibility of exploring those contributions in future editions.

References

Adams, J. A. (1961). Some considerations in the design and use of dynamic flight simulators. In Z. W. Sinaiko (Ed.), *Selected papers on human factors in the design and use of control systems.* New York: Dover.

Adams, J. S. (1965). Injustice in social exchange. In L. Berkowitz (Ed.), *Advances in experimental social psychology.* Vol. 2. New York: Academic Press.

Ammerman, H. L., & Pratzner, F. C. (1977). *Performance content for job training.* R & D Ser. 121-125. Vols. 1-5. Columbus, OH: Center for Vocational Education.

Andrasik, F. (1979). Organizational behavior modification in business settings: A methodological and content review. *Journal of Organizational Behavior Management, 2,* 85-102.

Argyris, C. (1964). T-groups for organizational effectiveness. *Harvard Business Review, 42,* 60-74.

Argyris, C. (1967). We must make work worthwhile. *Life, 62*(18), 56-68.

Argyris, C. (1968a). Issues in evaluating laboratory education. *Industrial Relations, 8,* 28-40, 45.

Argyris, C. (1968b). Some unintended consequences of rigorous research. *Psychological Bulletin, 70,* 185-197.

Argyris, C. (1980). Some limitations of the case method: Experiences in a management development program. *Academy of Management Review, 5,* 291-298.

Arvey, R. D. (1979). *Fairness in selecting employees.* Reading, MA: Addison-Wesley.

Atkinson, J. W., & Feather, N. T. (1966). *A theory of achievement motivation.* New York: Wiley.

Atkinson, R. C. (1968). Computerized instruction and the learning process. *American Psychologist, 23,* 225-239.

Atkinson, R. C. (1972). Ingredients for a theory of instruction. *American Psychologist, 27,* 921-931.

Ball, S., & Anderson, S. B. (1975). *Professional issues in the evaluation of education/training programs.* Arlington, VA: Office of Naval Research.

Ball, S., & Bogatz, G. A. (1970). *The first year of Sesame Street: An evaluation.* Princeton, NJ: Educational Testing Service.

Bandura, A. (1969). *Principles of behavior modification.* New York: Holt, Rinehart & Winston.

Bandura, A. (1977). *Social learning theory.* Englewood Cliffs, N.J.: Prentice-Hall.

Barbee, J. R., & Keil, E. C. (1973). Experimental techniques of job interview training for the disadvantaged: Videotape feedback, behavior modification, and microcounseling. *Journal of Applied Psychology, 58,* 209-213.

Barkin, S. (1970). Retraining and job redesign: Positive approaches to the continued employment of older persons. In H. L. Sheppard (Ed.), *Towards an industrial gerontology.* Cambridge, MA: Schenkman.

Bartlett, C. J. (1978). Equal employment opportunity issues in training. *Human Factors, 20,* 179-188.

Bartlett, C. J. (1982). Teaching scale developed for Division of Behavioral and Social Sciences. College Park, MD: University of Maryland.

Bartlett, C. J., & Goldstein, I. L. (1977). *Job analysis of police officers and sergeants.* Unpublished data, College Park, MD: University of Maryland.

Bartlett, C. J., & Goldstein, I. L. (1974). A validity analysis of employment tests for bus drivers. *Training Educational Resource Programs Technological Report.* College Park, MD: University of Maryland.

Bass, B. M., & Vaughan, J. A. (1966). *Training in industry: The management of learning.* Belmont, CA: Wadsworth.

Baumgartel, H., & Jeanpierre, F. (1972). Applying new knowledge in the back-home setting: A study of Indian managers' adaptive efforts. *Journal of Applied Behavioral Science, 8*(6), 674–694.

Becker, S. W. (1970). The parable of the pill. *Administrative Science Quarterly, 15,* 94–96.

Belbin, E. (1958). Methods for training older workers. *Ergonomics, 1,* 207–221.

Belbin, R. M. (1970). The discovery method in training older workers. In H. L. Sheppard (Ed.), *Towards an industrial gerontology.* Cambridge, MA: Schenkman.

Bellows, R. M. (1941). Procedures for evaluating vocational criteria. *Journal of Applied Psychology, 25,* 499–513.

Bernardin, H. J., & Beatty, R. W. (1984). *Performance appraisal: Assessing human behavior at work.* Boston: Kent.

Bernardin, H. J., & Villanova, P. J. (In press). Performance appraisal. In E. A. Locke (Ed.), *The generalizability of laboratory experiments: An inductive survey.* Lexington, MA: D. C. Heath.

Blaiwes, A. S., & Regan, J. J. (1970). *An integrated approach to the study of learning, retention, and transfer—a key issue in training device research and development.* (NAVTRADEVCEN-1H-178) Orlando, FL: Haval Training Device Center.

Blum, M. L., & Naylor, J. C. (1968). *Industrial psychology: Its theoretical and social foundations.* New York: Harper & Row.

Blumberg, A., & Golembiewski, R. (1976). *Learning and change in groups.* Clinton, MA: Colonial Press.

Bourne, L. E., & Ekstrand, B. R. (1973). *Psychology: Its principles and meanings.* Hinsdale, IL: Dryden.

Bove, R. (1984). Reach out and train someone. *Training and Development Journal, 38,* 26.

Bracht, G. H. (1970). Experimental factors related to aptitude-treatment interactions. *Review of Educational Research, 40,* 627–645.

Bray, D. W. (1976). The assessment center method. In R. F. Allen & S. Silverzweig, Group norms: Their influence on training effectiveness. In R. L. Craig (Ed.), *Training and development handbook.* New York: McGraw-Hill.

Briggs, L. J. (1968). *Sequencing of instruction in relation to hierarchies of competence.* Palo Alto, CA: American Institutes for Research.

Briggs, L. J., & Angell, D. (1964). Programmed instruction in science and mathematics. *Review of Educational Research, 34,* 354–373.

Briggs, L. J., Campeau, P. L., Gagné, R. M., & May, M. A. (1967). *Instructional media: A procedure for the design of multi-media instruction, a critical review of research, and suggestions for future research.* Palo Alto, CA: American Institutes for Research.

Bruner, J. S. (1963). Needed: A theory of instruction. *Educational Leadership, 20,* 523–532.

Buchanan, P. C. (1971). Sensitivity, or laboratory, training in industry. *Sociological Inquiry, 41,* 217–225.

Buchwald, A. (1970). Training on the train. Washington Post.

Bunker, K. A., & Cohen, S. L. (1977). The rigors of training evaluation: A discussion and field demonstration. *Personnel Psychology, 30*(4), 525–541.

Burke, H. L., & Bennis, W. G. (1961). Changes in perception of self and others during human relations training. *Human Relations, 14,* 165–182.

Buxton, V. M. (1979). *The evaluation of a police training program: Changes in learning, expectations and behavior.* Unpublished doctoral dissertation, University of Maryland.

Byham, W. C. (1975). The use of assessment centres in management development. In B. Taylor & G. L. Lipitt (Eds.), *Management development and training handbook.* London: McGraw-Hill.

Campbell, D. T. (1969). Reforms as experiments. *American Psychologist, 24,* 409–429.

Campbell, D. T., & Stanley, J. C. (1963). *Experimental and quasi-experimental designs for research.* Chicago: Rand McNally.

Campbell, J. P. (1971). Personnel training and development. In *Annual Review of Psychology.* Palo Alto, CA: Annual Reviews.

Campbell, J. P. (1978). *What we are about: An inquiry into the self concept of industrial and organizational psychology.* Presidential address to Division Industrial Organizational Psychology, 86th Annual Meeting of the American Psychological Association, Toronto.

Campbell, J. P., Dunnette, M. D., Lawler, E. E., III, & Weick, K. E., Jr. (1970). *Managerial behavior, performance, and effectiveness.* New York: McGraw-Hill.

Canter, R. R., Jr. (1951). A human relations training program. *Journal of Applied Psychology, 35,* 38–45.

Carmichael, L., Hogan, H. P., & Walter, A. A. (1932). An experimental study of the effect of language on the reproduction of visually perceived form. *Journal of Experimental Psychology, 15,* 73–86.

Caro, P. (1984). ISD-CAI technology applications to pilot training. *Training Technical Group Newsletter of the Human Factors Society, 10,* 3–4.

Carroll, S. J., Jr., Paine, F. T., & Ivancevich, J. J. (1972). The relative effectiveness of training methods—expert opinion and research. *Personnel Psychology, 25,* 495–510.

Cascio, W. F. (1982a). *Applied psychology in personnel management.* Reston, VA: Reston.

Cascio, W. F. (1982b). *Costing human resources: The financial impact of behavior in organizations.* Boston: Kent.

Catalanello, R. F., & Kirkpatrick, D. L. (1968). Evaluating training programs—The state of the art. *Training Development Journal, 22,* 2–9.

Chapanis, A., Garner, W. R., & Morgan, C. T. (1949). *Applied experimental psychology: Human factors in engineering design.* New York: Wiley.

Chu, G. C., & Schramm, W. (1967). *Learning from television: What the research says.* Washington, D.C.: National Association of Educational Broadcasters.

Cicero, J. P. (1973). Behavioral objectives for technical training systems. *Training and Development Journal, 28,* 14–17.

Clement, R. W., Walker, J. W., & Pinto, P. R. (1979). Changing demands on the training professionals. *Training and Development Journal, 29,* 3–7.

Cochran, N. (1978). Grandma Moses and the corruption of data. *Evaluation Quarterly, 2,* 363–375.

Cogan, E. A. (1971). Systems analysis and the introduction of educational technology in school. *HumRRO professional paper 14–17.* Alexandria, VA: Human Resources Research Organization.

Cohen, K. J., Cyert, R. M., Dill, W. R., Kuehn, A. A., Miller, M. H., Van Wormer, T. A., & Winters, P. R. (1962). The Carnegie Tech management game. In H. Guetzkow (Ed.), *Simulation in social science: Readings.* Englewood Cliffs, NJ: Prentice-Hall.

Collins, A. M. (1977). Processes in acquiring knowledge. In R. C. Anderson, R. J. Spiro, & W. E. Montague (Eds.), *Schooling and the acquisition of knowledge.* Hillsdale, NJ: Lawrence Erlbaum.

Collins, A., & Adams, M. J. (1977). Comparison of two teaching strategies in computer-assisted instruction. *Contemporary Educational Psychology, 2,* 133–148.

Collins, A., Adams, M. J., & Pew, R. W. (1978). Effectiveness of an interactive map display in tutoring geography. *Journal of Educational Psychology, 70,* 1–7.

Cook, T. D., & Campbell, D. T. (1976). The design and conduct of quasi-experiments and true experiments in field settings. In T. J. Bouchard, Jr., Field research methods: Interviewing, questionnaires, participant observation, systematic observation, unobtrusive measures. In M. D. Dunnette (Ed.), *Handbook of industrial and organizational psychology*. Chicago: Rand McNally.

Cook, T. D., & Campbell, D. T. (1979). *Quasi-experimentation: Design and analysis issues for field settings*. Chicago: Rand McNally.

Cooley, W. W., & Glaser, R. (1969). The computer and individualized instruction. *Science, 166,* 574-582.

Cooper, C. L. (1975). How psychologically dangerous are T-groups and encounter groups? *Human Relations, 28,* 249-260.

Cooper, C. L. (1977). Adverse and growthful effects of experiential learning groups: The role of trainer, participant, and group characteristics. *Human Relations, 3,* 1103-1129.

Craig, R. L. (1976). *Training and Development Handbook*. New York: McGraw-Hill.

Cram, D. (1961). *Explaining teaching machines and programming*. San Francisco: Fearon.

Cronbach, L. J. (1957). The two disciplines of scientific psychology. *American Psychologist, 12,* 671-684.

Cronbach, L. J. (1967). How can instruction be adapted to individual differences? In R. M. Gagné (Ed.), *Learning and individual differences*. Columbus, OH: Charles E. Merrill.

Cronbach, L. J., & Snow, R. E. (1969). *Individual differences in learning ability as a function of instructional variables*. Final report, School of Education, Stanford University (Contract No. OEC-4-6061269-1217), U.S. Office of Education.

Cronbach, L. J., & Snow, R. E. (1977). *Aptitudes and instructional methods*. New York: Irvington.

Crowder, N. A. (1960). Automatic tutoring by means of intrinsic programming. In A. A. Lumsdaine & R. Glaser (Eds.), *Teaching machines and programmed learning*. Washington, D.C.: National Education Association.

Cullen, J. G., Sawzin, S. A., Sisson, G. R., & Swanson, R. A. (1978). Cost effectiveness: A model for assessing the training investment. *Training and Development Journal, 32,* 24-29.

Dachler, H. P. Personal Communication, 1974.

Davis, J. D. (1977-1978). The Navy CMI system: A brief overview. *Journal of Educational Technology Systems, 6,* 143-160.

Decker, P. J. (1980). Effects of symbolic coding and rehearsal in behavior-modeling training. *Journal of Applied Psychology, 65,* 627-634.

DeCecco, J. P. (1968). *The psychology of learning and instruction: Educational psychology*. Englewood Cliffs, NJ: Prentice-Hall.

Denson, R. W. (1981). *Team training: Literature review and annotated bibliography*. (AFHRL-TR-80-40). Brooks Air Force Base, TX: Air Force Human Resources Laboratory.

DePhilips, F. A., Berliner, W. M., & Cribbin, J. J. (1960). *Management of training programs*. Homewood, IL: Irwin.

Digman, J. M. (1959). Growth of a motor skill as a function of distribution of practice. *Journal of Experimental Psychology, 57,* 310-316.

Dill, W. R., Jackson, J. R., & Sweeney, J. W. (Eds.) (1961). *Proceedings of the conference on business games as teaching devices*. School of Business Administration, Tulane University, April 26-28.

Division of Industrial-Organizational Psychology, American Psychological Association. (1980). *Principles for the validation and use of personnel selection procedures*. (2nd ed.). Berkeley, CA: Author.

Dorcus, R. M. (1940). Methods of evaluating the efficiency of door-to-door salesmen of bakery products. *Journal of Applied Psychology, 24,* 587-594.

Dossett, D. L., & Hulvershorn, P. (1983). Increasing technical training efficiency: Peer training via computer-assisted instruction. *Journal of Applied Psychology, 68,* 552-558.

Dubin, S. S. (1972). Obsolescence or lifelong education: A choice for the professional. *American Psychologist, 27,* 486-498.

Dunnette, M. D., & Campbell, J. P. (1968). Laboratory education: Impact on people and organizations. *Industrial Relations, 8,* 1-27, 41-44.

Eachus, H. T., & King, P. H. (1966). *Acquisition and retention of cross-cultural interaction skills through self-confrontation.* (AMRL-TR-66-8) Wright–Patterson Air Force Base, OH: Aerospace Medical Research Laboratories.

Eden, D., & Ravid, G. (1982). Pygmalion versus self-expectancy: Effects of instructor and self-expectancy on trainee performance. *Organizational Behavior and Human Performance, 30,* 351-364.

Eden, D., & Shani, A. B. (1982). Pygmalion goes to boot camp: Expectancy, leadership and trainee performance. *Journal of Applied Psychology, 67,* 194-199.

Edgerton, H. A. (1958). *The relationship of method of instruction to trainee aptitude pattern.* (Technical Report, Contract Nornr 1042 [00]). New York: Richardson, Bellows, Henry, & Co.

Ellis, H. C. (1965). *The transfer of learning.* New York: Macmillan.

Ellis, J. A., & Wulfeck, II, W. H. (1978). *The instructional quality inventory: IV. Job performance aid.* (NPRDC SR 79-5). San Diego, CA: Navy Personnel Research and Development Center.

Eurich, N. P. (1985). *Corporate classrooms.* Princeton, NJ: Carnegie Foundation.

Fait, E. (1970). Research needs in industrial gerontology from the viewpoint of a state employment service. In H. L. Sheppard (Ed.), *Towards an industrial gerontology.* Cambridge, MA: Schenkman.

Feeney, E. J. (1972). Performance audit, feedback, and positive reinforcement. *Training and Development Journal, 26,* 8-13.

Feifer, I. (1970). Training on the train: By Art Buchwald. *Training and Development Journal, 25,* 43.

Fiedler, F. E. (1964). A contingency model of leadership effectiveness. In L. Berkowitz (Ed.), *Advances in experimental social psychology.* New York: Academic Press.

Fiedler, F. E. (1967). *A theory of leadership effectiveness.* New York: McGraw-Hill.

Fiedler, F. E., Chemers, M. M., & Mahar, L. (1976). *Improving leadership effectiveness: The Leader Match Concept.* New York: John Wiley.

Fiedler, F. E., & Mahar, L. (1979). The effectiveness of contingency model training: A review of the validation of LEADER MATCH. *Personnel Psychology, 32,* 45-62.

Fiedler, F. E., Mitchell, R. T., & Triandis, H. C. (1971). The culture assimilator: An approach to cross-cultural training. *Journal of Applied Psychology, 55,* 95-102.

Fine, S. A. (1978). Contribution of the job element and functional job analysis approaches to content validity. Presented at the International Personnel Management Assessment Council Annual Conference, Atlanta, Georgia.

Fitts, P. M. (1965). Factors in complex skill training. In R. Glaser (Ed.), *Training research and education.* New York: Wiley.

Fleishman, E. A. (1972). On the relationship between abilities, learning, and human performance. *American Psychologist, 27,* 1017-1032.

Fleishman, E. A., Harris, E. F., & Burtt, H. E. (1955). Leadership and supervision in industry. *Bureau of Educational Research, Report No. 33.* The Ohio State University.

Ford, J. K., & Wroten, S. P. (1984). Introducing new methods for conducting training evaluation and for linking training evaluation to program redesign. *Personnel Psychology, 37,* 651-665.

Freeberg, N. E. (1976). Criterion measures for youth-work training programs: The development of relevant performance dimensions. *Journal of Applied Psychology, 61*(5), 537-545.

French, S. H. (1953). Measuring progress toward industrial relations objectives. *Personnel, 30,* 338-347.

Friedlander, F., & Greenberg, S. (1971). Effect of job attitudes, training and organizational climate on performance of the hard-core unemployed. *Journal of Applied Psychology, 55,* 287-295.

Fry, E. B. (1963). *Teaching machines and programmed instruction.* New York: McGraw-Hill.

Gagné, R. M. (1962). Military training and principles of learning. *American Psychologist, 17,* 83-91.

Gagné, R. M. (1970). *The conditions for learning* (2nd ed.). New York: Holt, Rinehart & Winston.

Gagné, R. M. (1984). Learning outcomes and their effects: Useful categories of human performance. *American Psychologist, 39,* 377-385.

Gagné, R. M. (1985). Instructional psychology. In *Annual Review of Psychology.* Palo Alto, CA: Annual Reviews.

Gagné, R. M., & Bolles, R. C. (1959). A review of factors in learning efficiency. In E. Galanter (Ed.), *Automatic teaching: The state of the art.* New York: Wiley.

Gagné, R. M., & Briggs, L. J. (1974). *Principles of instructional design.* New York: Holt, Rinehart & Winston.

Gagné, R. M., & Briggs, L. J. (1979). *Principles of instructional design.* New York: Holt, Rinehart & Winston.

Gagné, R. M., & Dick, W. (1983). Instructional psychology. In *Annual Review of Psychology.* Palo Alto, CA: Annual Reviews.

Galagan, P. (1984). The trainer in the machine. *Training and Development Journal, 38,* 4.

Ghiselli, E. E. (1956). The placement of workers: Concepts and problems. *Personnel Psychology, 9,* 1-16.

Gilbert, T. F. (1960). On the relevance of laboratory investigation of learning to self-instructional programming. In A. A. Lumsdaine & R. Glaser (Eds.), *Teaching machines and programmed instruction.* Washington, D.C.: National Education Association.

Gilbert, T. F. (1982). A question of performance—Part I—The probe model. *Training and Development Journal, 36,* 20-30.

Glanzer, M. (1965). Experimental study of team training and team functioning. In R. Glaser (Ed.), *Training research and education.* New York: Wiley.

Glaser, E. M., & Taylor, S. H. (1973). Factors influencing the success of applied research. *American Psychologist, 28*(2), 140-460.

Glaser, R. (1982). Instructional psychology: Past, present and future. *American Psychologist, 37,* 292-306.

Glaser, R. (1984). Education and thinking: The role of knowledge. *The American Psychologist, 39,* 93-104.

Goldstein, A. P., & Sorcher, M. (1974). *Changing supervisor behavior.* New York: Pergamon Press.

Goldstein, I. L. (1974). *Training: Program development and evaluation.* Monterey, CA: Brooks/Cole Publishing Co.

Goldstein, I. L. (1978a). The pursuit of validity in the evaluation of training programs. *Human Factors, 20,* 131-144.

Goldstein, I. L. (1978b). *Understanding research in organizational environments: Can process measures help?* Presented at Annual Meeting of the Eastern Psychological Association, Washington, D.C.

Goldstein, I. L. (1980). Training in work organizations. In *Annual Review of Psychology.* Palo Alto, CA: Annual Reviews.

Goldstein, I. L., & Bartlett, C. J. (1977). *Validation of a training program for police officers.* Unpublished data, College Park, MD: University of Maryland.

Goldstein, I. L., Macey, W. H., & Prien, E. P. (1981). Needs assessment approaches for training development. In H. Meltzer & W. R. Nord (Eds.), *Making organizations humane and productive.* New York: John Wiley.

Goldstein, I. L., & Musicante, G. R. (In press). From the laboratory to the field: An examination of training models. In E. A. Locke (Ed.), *The generalizability of laboratory experiments: An inductive survey.* Lexington, MA: D. C. Heath.

Goldstein, I. L., Tuttle, T. C., Wood, G. D., & Grether, C. B. (1975). *Behavioral action intervention strategies: Training.* Columbia, MD: Westinghouse Behavioral Sciences Center.

Golembiewski, R. T., & Carrigan, S. B. (1970). Planned change in organization style based on the laboratory approach. *Administrative Science Quarterly, 15,* 79-93.

Gomersall, E. R., & Myers, M. S. (1966). Breakthrough in on-the-job training. *Harvard Business Review, 44,* 66-72.

Goodacre, D. M. (1955). Experimental evaluation of training. *Journal of Personnel Administration and Industrial Relations, 2,* 143-149.

Goodman, P. S. (1969). Hiring and training the hard-core unemployed: A problem in system definition. *Human Organization, 28*, 259–269.

Goodman, P. S., Salipante, P., & Paransky, H. (1973). Hiring, training, and retraining the hard-core unemployed: A selected review. *Journal of Applied Psychology, 58*, 23–33.

Gordon, M. E., & Cohen, S. L. (1973). Training behavior as a predictor of trainability. *Personnel Psychology, 26*, 261–272.

Gordon, S. R. (1978). The impact of fair employment laws on training. *Training Developmental Journal, 32*, 29–44.

Gordon, M. E., & Isenberg, J. F. (1975). Validation of an experimental training criterion for machinists. *Journal of Industrial Teacher Education, 12*, 72–78.

Greenlaw, P. S., Herron, L. W., Rawdon, R. H. (1962). *Business simulation in industrial and university education.* Englewood Cliffs, NJ: Prentice-Hall.

Guba, E. G. (1969). The failure of educational evaluation. *Educational Technology, 9*, 29–38.

Guion, R. M. (1961). Criterion measurement and personnel judgments. *Personnel Psychology, 14*, 141–149.

Guion, R. M. (1977). Content validity—the source of my discontent. *Applied Psychological Measurement, 1*, 1–10.

Hagman, J. D., & Rose, A. M. (1983). Retention of military tasks: A review. *Human Factors, 25*, 199–214.

Haines, D. B., & Eachus, H. T. (1965). *A preliminary study of acquiring cross-cultural interaction skills through self-confrontation.* (AMRL-TR-65-137) Wright-Patterson Air Force Base, OH: Aerospace Medical Research Laboratories.

Hand, H. H., & Slocum Jr., J. W. (1972). A longitudinal study of the effects of a human relations training program on managerial effectiveness. *Journal of Applied Psychology, 56*, 412–417.

Harmon, P. (1968). A classification of performance objective behaviors in job training programs. *Educational Technology, 8*, 11–16.

Haug, M. R., & Sussman, M. B. (1970). The second-career variant of a sociological concept. In H. L. Sheppard (Ed.), *Towards an industrial gerontology.* Cambridge, MA: Schenkman.

Hendrickson, G., & Schroeder, W. (1941). Transfer of training in learning to hit a submerged target. *Journal of Educational Psychology, 32*, 206–213.

Herzberg, R., Mausner, B., & Snyderman, B. (1959). *The motivation to work.* (2nd ed.). New York: Wiley.

Hilgard, E. R., Atkinson, R. L., & Atkinson, R. C. (1979). *Introduction to psychology.* New York: Harcourt Brace Jovanovich.

Hilgard, E. R., & Bower, G. H. (1966). *Theories of learning.* (3rd ed.). New York: Appleton-Century-Crofts.

Hogan, J. C. (1978). Training of abilities: A review of nonspecific transfer issues relevant to ability training. *ARRO Technological Report 3010-TRI.* Washington, D.C.

Hoiberg, A., & Berry, N. W. (1978). Expectations and perceptions of navy life. *Organizations of Behavioral Human Performance, 21*, 130–145.

Holding, D. H. (1965). *Principles of training.* London: Pergamon Press.

Holt, H. O. (Spring, 1963). Programmed instruction. *Bell Telephone Magazine.*

House, R. J. (1967). T-group education and leadership effectiveness: A review of the empiric literature and a critical evaluation. *Personnel Psychology, 20*, 1–32.

Howard, A. (1971). Training for individuals and individual differences. Unpublished paper, University of Maryland.

Howell, W. C., & Goldstein, I. L. (1971). *Engineering psychology: Current perspectives in research.* New York: Appleton-Century-Crofts.

Hughes, E. C. (1958). *Men and their work.* Glencoe, IL: The Free Press.

Human Factors Society Bulletin. (1976). *19*, 1–5. Santa Monica, CA: Human Factors Society.

Hurlock, R. E., & Slough, D. A. (1976). Experimental evaluation of Plato IV technology: Final report. *NPRDC Technological Report 76TQ-44.* San Diego, CA.

Ingersoll, V. H. (1973). Role playing, attitude change, and behavior. *Organizational Behavior and Human Performance, 10*, 157-174.

Institute of Medicine. (1981). *Airline pilot age, health, and performance.* Washington, D.C.: National Academy Press.

Irwin, D. (1967). The Chrysler Corporation, Detroit. In *Research in apprenticeship training.* The University of Wisconsin, Center for Studies in Vocational and Technical Education.

Isaac, S., & Michael, W. B. (1971). *Handbook in research and evaluation.* San Diego: CA: Knapp.

Jaffe, S. L., & Scherl, D. J. (1969). Acute psychosis precipitated by T-group experiences. *Archives of General Psychiatry, 21*, 443-448.

Johnson, S. L. (1981). Effects of training devices on retention and transfer of a procedural task. *Human Factors, 23*, 257-272.

Kaplan, R. E., Lombardo, M. M., & Mazique, M. S. (1983). A mirror for managers: Using simulation to develop management teams. (Technical Report Number 13.) Greensboro, NC: Center for Creative Leadership.

Kaufman, H. G. (1978). Continuing education and job performance: A longitudinal study. *Journal of Applied Psychology, 63*, 248-251.

Kennedy, J. B. (1970). Use of audio-visual techniques in training the hard-core. *Training and Development Journal, 24*, 30-33.

King, P. H. (1966). *A summary of research in training for advisory roles in other cultures by the behavioral sciences laboratory.* (AMRL-TR-66-131) Wright-Patterson Air Force Base, OH: Aerospace Medical Research Laboratories.

Kirchner, W. K. (1965). Review of A. J. Marrow's "Behind the executive mask." *Personnel Psychology, 18*, 211-212.

Kirkpatrick, D. L. (1959, 1960). Techniques for evaluating training programs. *Journal of the American Society of Training Directors, 13*, 3-9, 21-26; *14*, 13-18, 28-32.

Klaw, S. (1965). Inside a T-group. *Think, 31*, 26-30.

Komaki, J. (1977). Alternative evaluation strategies in work settings. *Journal of Organizational Behavioral Management, 1*(1), 53-77.

Komaki, J., Heinzmann, A. T., & Lawson, L. (1980). Effect of training and feedback: Component analysis of a behavioral safety program. *Journal of Applied Psychology, 65*, 261-270.

Kozoll, C. E. (1971). The air left the "bag"—a training program that failed. *Training and Development Journal, 25*, 22-25.

Kraut, A. I. (1975). Prediction of managerial success by peer and training-staff ratings. *Journal of Applied Psychology, 60*, 14-19.

Kraut, A. I. (1976). Developing managerial skills via modeling techniques: Some positive research findings—a symposium. *Personnel Psychology, 29*, 325-328.

Kung, E. Y., & Rado, R. N. (1984). Teletraining applied. *Training and Development Journal, 38*, 27-28.

Latham, G. P., & Locke, E. A. (1979). Goal Setting: A motivational technique that works. *Organizational Dynamics, 8*, 68-80.

Latham, G. P., & Saari, L. M. (1979). The application of social learning theory to training supervisors through behavioral modeling. *Journal of Applied Psychology, 64*, 239-246.

Latham, G. P., & Wexley, K. N. (1981). *Increasing productivity through performance appraisal.* Reading, MA: Addison-Wesley.

Latham, G. P., Wexley, K. N., & Pursell, E. D. (1975). Training managers to minimize rating errors in the observation of behavior. *Journal of Applied Psychology, 60*, 550-555.

Lawrence, D. H. (1954). The evaluation of training and transfer programs in terms of efficiency measures. *Journal of Psychology, 38*, 367-382.

Lefkowitz, J. (1970). Effect of training on the productivity and tenure of sewing machine operators. *Journal of Applied Psychology, 54*, 81-86.

Lefkowitz, J. (1972). Evaluation of a supervisory training program for police sergeants. *Personnel Psychology, 25*, 95-106.

Leifer, M. S., & Newstrom, J. W. (1980). Solving the transfer of training problem. *Training and Development Journal, 34*, 42-46.

Levine, M. (1974). Scientific method and the adversary model: Some preliminary thoughts. *American Psychologist, 29,* 661-667.

Lindbom, T. R., & Osterberg, W. (1954). Evaluating the results of supervisory training. *Personnel, 31,* 224-228.

Liveright, A. A. (1951). Role playing in leadership training. *Personnel Journal, 29,* 412-416.

Locke, E. A., Shaw, K. N., Saari, L. M., & Latham, G. P. (1981). Goal setting and task performance. *Psychological Bulletin, 90,* 125-152.

Lorge, I. (1930). *Influence of regularly interpolated time intervals upon subsequent learning.* Teachers College Contributions to Education, No. 438. New York: Teachers College Press, Columbia University.

Lumsdaine, A. A., May, M. A., & Hadsell, R. S. (1958). Questions spliced into a film for motivation and pupil participation. In M. A. May & A. A. Lumsdaine (Eds.), *Learning from films.* New Haven, CT: Yale University Press.

Lynton, R. P., & Pareek, U. (1967). *Training for development.* Homewood, IL: Irwin.

Lysaught, J. P., & Williams, C. M. (1963). *A guide to programmed instruction.* New York: Wiley.

Macey, W. H. (1982). Linking training needs assessment to training program design. Presented at the 90th Convention of the American Psychological Association, Washington, D.C.

MacKinney, A. C. (1957). Progressive levels in the evaluation of training programs. *Personnel, 34,* 72-77.

Mager, R. F. (1962). *Preparing instructional objectives.* Belmont, CA: Fearon.

Mager, R. F., & Beach Jr., K. M. (1967). *Developing vocational instruction.* Belmont, CA: Fearon.

Maier, N. R. F., & Zerfoss, L. R. (1952). MRP: A technique for training large groups of supervisors and its potential use in social research. *Human Relations, 5,* 177-186.

Marx, R. D. (1982). Relapse prevention for managerial training: A model for maintenance of behavior change. *Academy of Management Review, 7,* 433-441.

Maslow, A. H. (1954). *Motivation and personality.* New York: Harper & Row.

Mayfield, E. C. (1972). Value of peer nominations in predicting life insurance sales performance. *Journal of Applied Psychology, 56,* 319-323.

Mayo, G. D., & DuBois, P. H. (1963). Measurement of gain in leadership training. *Educational and Psychological Measurement, 23,* 23-31.

McCall, Jr., M. W., & Lombardo, M. M. (1979). Looking Glass Inc.: The first three years (Vol. 8, Tech Report Number 13). Greensboro, NC: Center for Creative Leadership.

McCall, Jr., M. W., & Lombardo, M. M. (1982). Using simulation for leadership and management research: Through the Looking Glass. *Management Science, 28,* 533-549.

McCann, P. H. (1975). *Training mathematics skills with games* (Tech Rep. 75-28). San Diego, CA: Navy Personnel Research and Development Center.

McCauley, M. E. (Ed.) (1984). Research issues in simulator sickness: Proceedings of a workship. Washington, D.C.: National Academy Press.

McClelland, D. C. (1976). *The achieving society.* New York: John Wiley.

McClelland, D. C. (1978). Managing motivation to expand human freedom. *American Psychologist, 33,* 201-210.

McClelland, D. C., & Winter, D. G. (1969). *Motivating economic achievement.* New York: Free Press.

McGehee, W., & Thayer, P. W. (1961). *Training in business and industry.* New York: Wiley.

McGehee, W., & Tullar, W. L. (1978). A note on evaluating behavior modification and behavior modeling as industrial training techniques. *Personnel Psychology, 31,* 477-484.

McIntire, R. W. (1973). Behavior modification guidelines. In T. C. Tuttle, C. B. Grether, & W. T. Liggett (Eds.), *Psychological behavior strategy for accident control: Development of behavioral safety guidelines.* Final report for National

Institute for Occupational Safety and Health (Contract No. HSM-99-72-27) Columbia, MD: Westinghouse Behaviorial Safety Center.

Melching, W. H. (1969). Behavioral objectives and individualization of instruction. *HumRRO professional paper 18-69*. Alexandria, VA: Human Resources Research Organization.

Michalak, D. F. (1981). The neglected half of training. *Training and Development Journal, 35*, 22-28.

Miller, R. W., & Zeller, F. A. (1967). *Social psychological factors association with responses to retraining*. Final Report, Office of Research and Development, Appalachian Center, West Virginia University (Research Grant No. 91-52-66-56), U.S. Department of Labor.

Mindak, W. A., & Anderson, R. E. (1971). Can we quantify an act of faith? *Training and Development Journal, 25*, 2-10.

Miner, J. B. (1961). Management development and attitude change. *Personnel Administration, 24*, 21-26.

Miner, J. B. (1963). Evidence regarding the value of a management course based on behavioral science subject matter. *The Journal of Business of the University of Chicago, 36*, 325-335.

Mirabal, T. E. (1978). Forecasting future training costs. *Training Developmental Journal, 32*(7), 78-87.

Miron, D., & McClelland, D. C. (1979). The impact of achievement motivation training on small businesses. *California Management Review, 21*, 13-28.

Mobley, W. H., Hand, H. H., Baker, R. L., & Meglino, B. M. (1979). Conceptual and empirical analysis of military recruit training attrition. *Journal of Applied Psychology, 64*, 10-18.

Moore, L. F. (1967). Business games vs. cases as tools of learning. *Training and Development Journal, 21*, 13-23.

Mosel, J. L. (1957). Why training programs fail to carry over. *Personnel, 34*, 56-64.

Moses, J. L. (1978). Behavior modeling for managers. *Human Factors, 20*, 225-232.

Moses, J. L., & Ritchie, R. J. (1976). Supervisory relationships training: A behavioral evaluation of a behavior modeling program. *Personnel Psychology, 29*, 337-343.

Nagle, B. F. (1953). Criterion development. *Personnel Psychology, 6*, 271-288.

Nash, A. N., Muczyk, J. P., & Vettori, F. L. (1971). The relative practical effectiveness of programed instruction. *Personnel Psychology, 24*, 397-418.

National Center for Research in Vocational Education (1978). *Occupational adaptability and transferable skills*. Information Series No. 129. Columbus, OH: National Center for Research in Vocational Education.

Naylor, J. C. (February 1962). *Parameters affecting the relative efficiency of part and whole practice methods: A review of the literature*. United States Naval Training Devices Center (Technical Report No. 950-1).

Nester, O. W. (1971). Training the hard core: One experience. Pittsburgh Technical Institute Report. Undated. Review of work also appearing in *Training and Development Journal, 25*, 16-19.

Newman, D. (1985). The pursuit of validity in training: An application. Ph.D. dissertation, University of Maryland, College Park, MD.

Nord, W. (1970). Improving attendance through rewards. *Personnel Administration, 33*, 37-41.

O'Brien, G. E., & Plooij, D. (1977). Comparison of programmed and prose culture training upon attitudes and knowledge. *Journal of Applied Psychology, 62*, 499-505.

Odiorne, G. S. (1963). The trouble with sensitivity training. *Journal of the American Society of Training Directors, 17*, 9-20.

Ohmann, O. A. (1941). A report of research on the selection of salesmen at the Tremco Manufacturing Company. *Journal of Applied Psychology, 25*, 18-29.

O'Leary, V. E. (1972). The Hawthorne effect in reverse: Effects of training and practice on individual and group performance. *Journal of Applied Psychology, 56*, 491-494.

Olson, H. C., Fine, S. A., Myers, D. C., & Jennings, M. C. (1981). The use of functional job analysis in establishing performance standards for heavy equipment operators. *Personnel Psychology, 34*, 351-364.

O'Reilly, A. P. (1973). Skills requirements: Supervisor-subordinate conflict. *Personnel Psychology, 26,* 75–80.

Orlansky, J., & String, J. (1977). Cost-effectiveness of flight simulators for military training. Vol. 1: Use and effectiveness of flight simulators. *Inst. Def. Anal. Tech. Pap. P-1275.* Arlington, VA.

Panell, R. C., & Laabs, G. J. (1979). Construction of a criterion-referenced, diagnostic test for an individual instruction program. *Journal of Applied Psychology, 64,* 255–261.

Patten, Jr., T. H., & Stermer, E. P. (1969). Training foremen in work standards. *Training and Development Journal, 23,* 25–37.

Pearlman, K. (1980). Job families: A review and discussion of their implications for personnel selection. *Psychological Bulletin, 87,* 1–28.

Pedalino, E., & Gamboa, V. U. (1974). Behavior modification and absenteeism: Intervention in one industrial setting. *Journal of Applied Psychology, 59,* 694–698.

Pfister, G. (1975). Outcomes of laboratory training for police officers. *Journal of Social Issues, 31,* 115–121.

Pinto, P. R., & Walker, J. W. (July 1978). What do training and development professionals really do? *Training and Development Journal, 28,* 58–64.

Pratzner, F. C. (1978). *Occupational adaptability and transferable skills.* (Information Series No. 129). Columbus, OH: The National Center for Research in Vocational Education.

Pressey, S. L. (1950). Development and appraisal of devices providing immediate automatic scoring of objective tests and concomitant self-instruction. *Journal of Psychology, 29,* 417–447.

Prien, E. P. (1966). Dynamic character of criteria: Organizational change. *Journal of Applied Psychology, 50,* 501–504.

Prien, E. P. (1977). The function of job analysis in content validation. *Personnel Psychology, 30,* 167–174.

Prien, E. P., Goldstein, I. L., & Macey, W. H. (1985). *Multi-method job analysis: Methodology and applications.* Unpublished paper.

Prien, E. P., Goldstein, I. L., & Macey, W. H. (1985). *Needs assessment: Program and individual development.* Presented at the 89th Convention of the American Psychological Association, Los Angeles, CA.

Pritchard, R. D. (1969). Equity theory: A review and critique. *Organizational Behavior and Human Performance, 4,* 176–211.

Raia, A. P. (1966). A study of the educational value of management games. *The Journal of Business, 39,* 339–352.

Randall, J. S. (1978). You and effective training. *Training Development Journal* (Pts. 1–10) *32,* 10–19.

Randall, L. K. (1960). Evaluation: A training dilemma. *Journal of the American Society of Training Directors, 14,* 29–35.

Raser, J. R. (1969). *Simulation and society: An exploration of scientific gaming.* Boston: Allyn and Bacon.

Raynor, J. O. (1970). Relationships between achievement-related motives, future orientation, and academic performance. *Journal of Personality and Social Psychology, 15,* 28–33.

Raynor, J. O., & Rubin, I. S. (1971). Effects of achievement motivation and future orientation on level of performance. *Journal of Personality and Social Psychology, 17,* 36–41.

Reilly, R. R., & Manese, W. R. (1979). The validation of a minicourse for telephone company switching technicians. *Personnel Psychology, 32,* 83–90.

Report of the National Advisory Commission on Civil Disorders. (1968). New York: Bantam Books.

Reynolds, B., & Bilodeau, I. McD. (1952). Acquisition and retention of three psychomotor tests as a function of distribution of practice during acquisition. *Journal of Experimental Psychology, 44,* 19–26.

Rhodes, S. R. (1983). Age-related differences in work attitudes and behavior: A review and conceptual analysis. *Psychological Bulletin, 93,* 328–367.

Ritti, R. R. (1968). Work goals of scientists and engineers. *Industrial Relations, 7,* 118–131.

Robertson, I., & Downs, S. (1979). Learning and the prediction of performance: Development of trainability testing in the United Kingdom. *Journal of Applied Psychology, 64*, 42–50.

Rosen, N. A., Williams, L. K., & Foltman, F. F. (1965). Motivational constraints in an industrial retraining program. *Personnel Psychology, 18*, 65–79.

Rosenberg, B. D. (1972). An evaluation of computer-assisted instruction in the Anne Arundel County School System. Master's thesis, University of Maryland.

Rosenthal, R. (1978). How often are our numbers wrong? *American Psychologist, 33*, 1005–1008.

Rosenthal, R. (1966). *Experimenter effects in behavioral research.* New York: Appleton-Century-Crofts.

Ross, P. C. (1974). A relationship between training efficiency and employee selection. *Improving Human Performance, 3*, 108–117.

Rubinsky, S., & Smith, N. (1973). Safety training by accident simulation. *Journal of Applied Psychology, 57*, 68–73.

Russell, J. S. (1984). A review of fair employment cases in the field of training. *Personnel Psychology, 37*, 261–276.

Ryman, D. H., & Biersner, R. J. (1975). Attitudes predictive of diving training success. *Personnel Psychology, 28*, 181–188.

Salinger, R. D. (1973). Disincentives to effective employee training and development. Washington, D.C.: *U. S. Civil Service Commission, Bureau of Training.*

Salipante, Jr., P., & Goodman, P. (1976). Training, counseling, and retention of the hard-core unemployed. *Journal of Applied Psychology, 61*, 1–11.

Salvendy, G., & Pilitsis, J. (1980). The development and validation of an analytical training program for medical suturing. *Human Factors, 22*, 153–170.

Sanders, P., & Vanouzas, J. N. (1983). Socialization to learning. *Training and Development Journal, 37*, 14–21.

Saretsky, G. (1972). The OEO P.C. experiment and the John Henry effect. *Phi Delta Kappan, 53*, 579–581.

Sawyer, C. R., Pain, R. F., Van Cott, H., & Banks, W. W. (1982). Nuclear control room modifications and the role of transfer of training principles: A review of issues and research. (NUREG/CR - 2828, EGG-2211). Idaho Falls, ID: Idaho National Engineering Laboratory.

Schein, E. H. (1980). *Organizational psychology.* Englewood Cliffs, NJ: Prentice-Hall.

Schendel, J. D., & Hagman, J. D. (1982). On sustaining procedural skills over a prolonged retention interval. *Journal of Applied Psychology, 67*, 605–610.

Schneider, B., & Schmitt, N. W. (1986). *Staffing organizations.* Glenview, IL: Scott-Foresman.

Schramm, W. (1962). Learning from instructional television. *Review of Educational Research, 32*, 156–167.

Schramm, W. (1964). *The research on programmed instruction: An annotated bibliography.* U.S. Office of Education, Washington, D.C.: U.S. Government Printing Office.

Scriven, M. (1967). The methodology of evaluation. In *Perspectives of curriculum evaluation.* American Educational Research Association Monograph, No. 1, Chicago: Rand McNally.

Seashore, R. H., & Bavelas, A. (1941). The functioning of knowledge of results in Thorndike's line-drawing experiment. *Psychological Review, 48*, 155–164.

Seiler, J. (1969). Prevocational and vocational training programs. In *Breakthrough for disadvantaged youth.* U.S. Department of Labor, Washington, D.C.: U.S. Government Printing Office.

Seltzer, R. A. (1971). Computer-assisted instruction—what it can and cannot do. *American Psychology, 26*, 373–377.

Severin, D. (1952). The predictability of various kinds of criteria. *Personnel Psychology, 5*, 93–104.

Sharf, J. C. (1977). Fair employment implication for HRD: The case of Washington vs. Davis. *Training Development Journal, 31*, 16–21.

Sheppard, H. L. (1970). On age discrimination. In H. L. Sheppard (Ed.), *Toward* an industrial gerontology: An introduction to a new field of applied research and service. Cambridge, MA: Schenkman.

Sheridan, J. A. (1975). *Designing the work environment.* Presented at Annual Meeting of the American Psychological Association, Chicago.

Shoemaker, H. A., & Holt, H. O. (1965). The use of programmed instruction in industry. In R. Glaser (Ed.), *Teaching machines and programmed learning: Data and directions.* Washington, D.C.: National Education Association.

Siegel, A. I. (1983). The miniature job training and evaluation approach: Additional findings. *Personnel Psychology, 36,* 41–56.

Silverman, R. E. (1960). *Automated teaching: A review of theory and research.* (NAVTRADEVCEN Technical Report 507-2) Port Washington, NY: U.S. Naval Training Device Center.

Singer, I. (1968). CAI in the ghetto school. *CAI Newsletter of the Institute for Computer-Assisted Instruction, 1,* 3.

Sjogren, D. (1977). Occupationally-transferable skills and characteristics: Review of literature and research. Inf. Ser. 105, Cent. Vocat. Educ., Columbus, OH.

Skinner, B. F. (1954). Science of learning and the art of teaching. *Harvard Educational Review, 24,* 86–97.

Smith, B. D. (In press). *Psychology: An introduction.* New York: Wiley.

Smith, P. B. (1975). Controlled studies of the outcome of sensitivity training. *Psychological Bulletin, 82,* 597–622.

Sobel, I., & Folk, H. (1965). Labor market adjustments by unemployed older workers. In A. M. Ross (Ed.), *Employment policy and the labor market.* Berkeley: University of California Press.

Speroff, B. J. (1954). Rotational role playing used to develop managers. *Personnel Journal, 33,* 49–50.

Spool, M. D. (1978). Training programs for observers of behavior: A review. *Personnel Psychology, 31,* 853–888.

Stake, R. E. (1967). The countenance of educational evaluation. *Teachers College Record, 68,* 523–540.

Steadham, S. V. (January 1980). Learning to select a needs assessment strategy. *Training and Development Journal, 30,* 55–61.

Steers, R. M., & Porter, L. W. (1983). *Motivation and work behavior.* New York: McGraw-Hill.

Stewart, L. (1962). Management games today. In J. M. Kibbee, C. J. Craft, & B. Nanus (Eds.), *Management games.* New York: Reinhold.

Strauss, G. (1967). Related instruction: Basic problems and issues. In *Research in apprenticeship training.* The University of Wisconsin, Center for Vocational and Technical Education.

Strauss, G. (1972). Management by objectives: A critical view. *Training and Development Journal, 26,* 10–15.

String, J., & Orlansky, J. (1977). Cost-effectiveness of flight simulators for military training. Vol. II: Estimating costs of training in simulators and aircraft. *Inst. Def. Anal. Tech. Pap. P-1275.* Arlington, VA.

Suppes, P., & Jerman, M. (1970). Computer-assisted instruction. *National Association of Secondary School Principals Bulletin, 54,* 27–40.

Suppes, P., & Morningstar, M. (1969). Computer-assisted instruction: Two computer-assisted instruction programs are evaluated. *Science, 166,* 343–350.

Swezey, R. W. (1981). *Individual performance assessment: An approach to criterion-referenced test development.* Reston, VA: Reston Publishing Co.

Swezey, R. W. (1982–83). Application of a transfer of training model to training device assessment. *Journal of Educational Technology System, 11,* 225–238.

Teahan, J. E. (1976). Role playing and group experiences to facilitate attitude and value changes among black and white police officers. *Journal of Social Issues, 31,* 35–45.

Thayer, P. W., & McGehee, W. (1977). On the effectiveness of not holding a formal training course. *Personnel Psychology, 30,* 455–456.

Thorndike, E. L. (1927). The law of effect. *American Journal of Psychology, 39,* 212–222.

Thorndike, E. L., & Woodworth, R. S. (1901). (I) The influence of improvement in one mental function upon the efficiency of other functions. (II) The estimation of magnitudes. (III) Functions involving attention, observation, and discrimination. *Psychological Review, 8,* 247–261, 384–395, 553–564.

Thorndike, R. L. (1949). *Personnel selection.* New York: Wiley.

Training and Development Journal. (September 1980). For your information. *30,* 8–9.

Triandis, H. C., Feldman, J. M., Weldon, D. E., & Harvey, W. M. (1974). Designing preemployment training for the hard to employ: A cross-cultural psychological approach. *Journal of Applied Psychology, 59,* 687–693.

Triandis, H. C., Feldman, J. M., Weldon, D. E., & Harvey, W. M. (1975). Ecosystem distrust and the hard-to-employ. *Journal of Applied Psychology, 60,* 44–56.

Trowbridge, M. A., & Cason, H. (1932). An experimental study of Thorndike's theory of learning. *Journal of General Psychology, 7,* 245–260.

Uhlaner, J. E., & Drucker, A. J. (1980). Military research on performance criteria: A change of emphasis. *Human Factors, 22,* 131–139.

Underwood, B. J. (1964). The representativeness of rote verbal learning. In A. W. Melton (Ed.), *Categories of human learning.* New York: Academic Press.

Underwood, W. J. (1965). Evaluation of laboratory method training. *Journal of the American Society of Training Directors, 19,* 34–40.

U.S. Civil Service Commission. (1970). *Programmed instruction: A brief of its development and current status.* Washington, D.C.: U.S. Government Printing Office.

U.S. Civil Service Commission. (1971a). *Catalog of basic education systems.* Washington, D.C.: U.S. Government Printing Office.

U.S. Civil Service Commission. (1971b). *Computer-assisted instruction: A general discussion and case study.* Washington, D.C.: U.S. Government Printing Office.

U.S. Department of Education, National Center for Educational Statistics. (1982). *High school and beyond study.* Washington, D.C.: U.S. Government Printing Office.

U.S. Department of Labor, Manpower Administration. (1972). *Handbook for analyzing jobs.* Washington, D.C.: U.S. Government Printing Office.

U.S. Department of Labor. (1965). *Dictionary of occupational titles.* (3rd ed.) Washington, D.C.: U.S. Government Printing Office.

U.S. President's Commission on the Accident at Three-Mile Island (1979). *Report of the president's commission on the accident at three-mile island.* Washington, D.C.: U.S. Government Printing Office.

Van Brunt, R. E. (1971). Supervising employees from minority groups. *Education Exchange: Insurance Company Education Directors Society, 111,* 1–5.

Van Maanan, J. (1976). Breaking in: Socialization to work. In R. Dubin (Ed.), *Handbook of work, organization, and society.* Chicago: Rand McNally.

Vroom, V. H. (1964). *Work and motivation.* New York: Wiley.

Wallace, R. S. (1965). Criteria for what? *American Psychologist, 20,* 411–417.

Wallace, R. S., & Twichell, C. M. (1953). An evaluation of a training course for life insurance agents. *Personal Psychology, 6,* 25–43.

Wanous, J. P. (1977). Organizational entry: Newcomers moving from outside to inside. *Psychology Bulletin, 84,* 601–618.

Wanous, J. P. (1980). *Organizational entry: Recruitment, selection and socialization of newcomers.* Reading, MA: Addison-Wesley.

Warmke, D. L., & Billings, R. S. (1979). A comparison of training methods for altering the psychometric properties of experimental and administrative performance ratings. *Journal of Applied Psychology, 64,* 124–131.

Webb, E. J., Campbell, D. T., Schwartz, R. D., & Sechrest, L. (1966). *Unobtrusive measures: Nonreactive research in the social sciences.* Chicago: Rand McNally.

Weiss, E. C. (1975). Evaluation research in the political context. In E. L. Streuning & M. Guttentag (Eds.), *Handbook of evaluation research.* Beverly Hills, CA: Sage.

Wexley, K. N. (1984). *Personnel training.* In *Annual Review of Psychology.* Palo Alto, CA: Annual Reviews.

Wexley, K. N., & Latham, G. P. (1981). *Developing and training human resources in organizations.* Glenview, IL: Scott, Foresman.

Wheaton, G. R. (1976). *Evaluation of the effectiveness of training devices: Validation of the predictive model.* Alexandria, VA: U.S. Army Research Institute.

Wherry, R. J. (1957). The past and future of criterion evaluation. *Personnel Psychology, 10,* 1-5.

White, M. C., Crino, M. D., & DeSanctis, G. L. (1981). A critical review of female performance, performance training and organizational initiatives designed to aid women in the work-role environment. *Personnel Psychology, 34,* 227-248.

Williges, B. H., Roscoe, S. N., & Williges, R. C. (1972). *Synthetic flight training revisited.* (T. R. ARL-72-21/AFOSR-72-10) Savoy, IL: Aviation Research Laboratory.

Wulfeck, W. H. II, Ellis, J. A., Richards, R. E., Wood, N. D., & Merrill, M. D. (1978). The instructional quality inventory: I. Introduction and overview. *NPRDC Technology Report 79-3.* San Diego, CA.

Yukl, G. A., & Latham, G. P. (1975). Consequences of reinforcement schedules and incentive magnitudes for employee performance: Problems encountered in an industrial setting. *Journal of Applied Psychology, 60,* 294-298.

Author Index

Subject Index